The Conscious Brain

ABOUT THE AUTHOR

Steven Rose was born in London in 1938. A graduate of King's College, Cambridge, he received his Ph.D. from the Institute of Psychiatry at London in 1961. Since 1969, Rose has been Tate Professor of Biology at the Open University in England. He has previously published a book on the chemistry of life, has edited a book on chemical warfare (of which he is a committed opponent), and, with his wife, Hilary, a sociologist, has written a book on science and society.

Steven Rose

The Conscious Brain

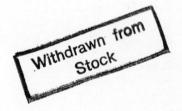

Weidenfeld and Nicolson   5 Winsley Street London W1

For Simon and Benjamin.
Because this book is about both environment and
genetics, plasticity and specificity.

Copyright © 1973 by Steven P.R. Rose

ISBN 0 297 76502 7
Filmset and Printed Offset Litho
in Great Britain by
Cox & Wyman Ltd,
London, Fakenham and Reading

Contents

List of Illustrations

Acknowledgements

figure 2 is from Descartes, *L'Homme* (1729), BRITISH MUSEUM

figure 3 is reproduced by gracious permission of Her Majesty the Queen

figure 4 is from G. Spurzheim, *Observations sur la Phrenologie* (1818)

figure 5 is from *The New Encyclopedia*, Vol. BIB–CHIC

figure 10 is courtesy of Dr. D. Tomsett, London, and THE SUNDAY TIMES

figure 13 is courtesy of Dr. T. Powell, Oxford

figure 14 is courtesy of Dr. A. Hamberger, Goteborg

figure 15, C. C. Thomas and the N. I. H., Bethesday, Maryland, from Cajal, *Studies on Vertebrate Neurogenesis*, Guth (Trans.)

figure 18 The Open University, *Biological Bases of Behaviour*, Unit 1

figure 22 courtesy of Dr. L. Iverson, Cambridge

figures 29 and 30 after Dr. W. Penfield, Montreal

figure 31 after Dr. M. Brazier, Los Angeles

figures 37 and 39 after Dr. T. Lentz, Yale

figure 38 after Dr. A. Horridge, St. Andrews

figures 40 and 51 after Professor J. Z. Young, London

figure 44 after Dr. R. F. Thompson, *Foundations of Physiological Psychology*

figure 53 after Dr. C. R. Noback. *The Human Nervous System*

figure 54 after Dr. M. Jouvet, Lyons

figure 60 after Dr. S. Blomfield and Dr. D. Marr.

The extract from *Fictions* by J. L. Borges is reproduced by courtesy of Calder and Boyars Ltd; the extract from *The Mind of a Mnemonist* is reproduced by courtesy of Jonathan Cape Ltd.

Preface

When, in my final undergraduate year of biochemistry, I had to come to terms with what I proposed to do next, assuming I was going on to do research, I had few doubts. If it was to be research, there was one biological problem above all else which concerned me—the workings of the brain and their relationship to mind and consciousness. There were, and still are, several reasons for this obsession. One, more personal than others, is simply the fascination of self-knowledge. A second is the challenge represented by the fact that the interpretation of brain mechanisms represents one of the last remaining biological mysteries, the last refuge of shadowy mysticism and dubious religious philosophy, the residue of all the "emergent properties" with which biology was once filled. Of more general significance is the fact that we live in a society in which the conditions of existence are such as to produce a continued mismatch between the potential of human performance for the vast majority of mankind and the actuality of their existence. Changing these conditions of existence demands action at the social and political level. But to an analysis of the appropriate direction of change, the study of the workings—and malfunctioning—of the human brain has something to contribute. If human history is the saga of man becoming, then at the individual level it is also the history of his brain becoming.

This leads to a concern not merely with the problems of what—misleadingly I believe—is known as mental illness, but even more to an examination of just what are the factors, in the individual and society, that determine both the differences and the similarities in performance of individual human brains. How do genetic, environmental and evolutionary factors influence the brain structure, beliefs and behaviour of the individual?

Such an examination is intimately bound up, too, with the analogous question concerning the "knowledge" to which a scientist professes. How is this knowledge itself affected by such factors? That is, to what extent is scientific "knowledge", particularly concerning brain mechanisms, itself genetically or ideologically based? This question has come to concern me increasingly during the genesis of this book, although it is often merely implicit in the text.

It was these undergraduate obsessions which drove me towards brain research, then unfashionable for the biochemist. My tutors attempted to dissuade me, indeed, on just these grounds. Far better to stick with molecular biology, simple viruses or bacteria. Or even classical metabolic biochemistry. The brain was too complex for mere biochemists. Of course, they were right. They still are, though the wheels of this particular bandwagon have turned, bringing the molecular biologists with them, seemingly in droves.

For what became clear to me very early on, was that to make an adequate study of brain mechanisms one needed the shared approaches of the anatomist, biochemist, physiologist, behaviorist and many other biological disciplines besides. No one discipline was adequate. The conditions for interdisciplinary research, which ought to be relatively easy to organize, have in fact not been simple to establish. What is needed is a coordinated institutional approach, the establishment for instance, of a Brain Research Institute. Instead piecemeal, *ad hoc* arrangements have been all that has so far been possible in Britain. This is quite different from the situation in either the United States or USSR, for example, where the need for such an interdisciplinary approach to brain mechanisms has long been formally recognized.

The last few years have, however, seen established a flourishing interdisciplinary Brain Research Association, which began as an informal discussion group over beer once a month in the Black Horse, a London pub – often continued to the accompaniment of kebab, taramasalata and retsina in a nearby restaurant. The atmosphere of these meetings was deliberately designed to break down the disciplinary and formal barriers of traditional scientific discourse (originally we excluded heads of departments from these meetings except by specific invitation . . . however times change and we grow no younger; gerontocracy will out). The BRA is now a flourishing national society with getting on for one thousand members and local meetings in many centers. A proportion of the material in this book reflects discussions started in the atmosphere of the Black Horse, and any list of acknowledgements should be extended to cover the participants in such discussions, but particularly perhaps John Dobbing, now at the Institute for Child Health, Manchester, and Pat Wall, at University College, London. More recently I have been involved in trying to establish an interdisciplinary neurobiology course for students at the Open University. It is too early yet to know how well it works, for the first eighteen hundred students only started in January 1972. But the experience of collaborating with the ethologists and psychologists in the team which has designed the course is also reflected in the organization of this book. In particular however its organization also reflects the direction of my own research.

I owe a particular debt of gratitude to my various research collaborators over the last few years – Pat Bateson and Gabriel and Ann Horn at Cambridge, Brian Cragg at University College, London, and Harry Bradford at Imperial College, London. Harry Bradford, Pat Bateson and Ann Hurry have all made pertinent comments on parts of the text, as indeed have Tony Godwin of Weidenfeld & Nicolson and Harold Strauss of Alfred A. Knopf. An earlier draft of the last chapter formed a discussion paper at a seminar on Ideology and Science organized by Pat Bateson and Bob Young at King's College, Cambridge. I am grateful to Ken Richardson and David Spears, of the Brain Research Group at the Open University, who made the Glossary and the Index, Clare Wight, of the Open University library, who chased a number of – often obscure – references and Dr Herman Bachelard who read the proofs. All the original drawings were done by A. M. Greenwood.

The strongest and most pertinent critique, however, which has materially and continuously affected my ideas and the thrust of the arguments advanced in the book, often in ways which neither of us could clearly specify, has come from Hilary Rose; without her active participation it would have been a very different – and worse – book.

There is also a special debt of gratitude to the rest of my family, which has endured the creation of this book over the past two and a half years. No one but me, of course, is responsible for any errors of fact or interpretation that remain, or for the general theses.

I should say a final word about style and intention. This book is neither a textbook nor anything like a comprehensive account of "where brain science is now". It is an argued case for particular interpretations of brain and mind phenomena and it is addressed to a wider audience than my fellow neurobiologists – who will doubtless find enough to disagree with or to anger them. This has left me with a problem over references and footnotes. I have decided, perhaps incautiously, to keep all such ancillary material to a minimum, providing the signposts only to the most significant of the primary source material to which I have referred, and to further basic reading for the individual topics discussed. I do not know if this was unwise. It is, perhaps, not wholly academically respectable. But it seemed the only alternative to having a text totally cluttered with references, like one of those indigestible reviews of the literature which appear annually in so many of the basic biological sciences. It will be for the reader to assess how well this model achieves its purpose.

STEVEN ROSE *August* 1972

1 The Development of the Brain Sciences

The brain is biology's greatest challenge. Perhaps in a sense it is the greatest challenge for science as a whole, beyond moon landings, the ultimate particles of the physicist and the depths of astronomical space. The engineering of a space shot or of a giant particle accelerator or radio telescope, the mathematics to analyze the results, the vision to design or to ask the questions in the first instance, are all the products of man's brain—or the collectivity and assembled experience of 3,000,000,000 such brains and their more or less immediate genetic precursors. Within each of these brains, two fistfuls of pink-gray tissue, wrinkled like a walnut and something of the consistency of porridge, store more information than all the computers and the libraries of the world can hold. The task of this book is to attempt an explanation of the functioning of the brain, in terms which relate its unique properties—particularly that of being in some sense the organ of "mind"—to the ground rules that are known to operate in the rest of biology.

But explaining and understanding the brain is more than merely interesting. It presents problems which relate both to philosophy and to power. The scientific work that is done, the questions asked of nature, the methodology and terminology that is proposed, reflect not merely the internal logic of the subject, but also the purposes and preconceptions of the scientist himself. These purposes and preconceptions are imposed by the social constraints within which the scientist operates; sometimes they are apparent, for research costs money, and funds are available for some projects and not others; sometimes they are less so, for they are internalized by the scientist and affect his thinking about his work at a much more basic level—in a word, they are ideological constraints. These types of constraints characterize the external logic of scientific development.[1]

For many areas of science, the fact that it is far from the abstract pursuit of truth that much of the standard Anglo-Saxon tradition of teaching it suggests, may be of relatively little moment. Not so with the brain; it will be part of the case made in this book that, as well as the core of knowledge about the workings of the brain, much of the interpretation and many of the experiments done reflect quite closely the views of the experimenter concerning brains—and hence, in a very direct way, concerning humans. Some of these views have received a good deal of popular attention recently, by expositors whom I shall characterize variously, in summary of their differing views on human behaviour, as *irrationalists*, *chimpomorphs* and *machinomorphs*. They are concerned respectively with claiming:

1. that the uniqueness of brains (and humans) is irreducible and inexplicable in terms of the traditional methods of science, thus introducing a more or less sophisticated version of "the god of the gaps";[2]

2. that human behavior is best understood by studying that of chimpanzees, rats or other species, in cages or the wild, and that much of it is innate, genetically determined and unmodifiable;[3]

3. that human behavior can now be, or soon will be mimicked or improved upon by computers and other machines, which in the mid-term future will be given the vote and in the longer term will rule the world.[4]

Each of these views leads to, or supports, particular types of philosophical and political conclusions concerning the nature and fate of humanity; each, if widely influential, could—and I believe in some cases already does—both reflect and help induce a feeling of despair concerning the fate and direction both of humanity and its science.

It is amongst the purposes of this book to challenge some of these myths. To make this challenge, I look first, in this chapter, at some of the history of the development of ideas on mind and brain. For most of the chapters that follow, I am concerned with describing the properties of the brain considered as a neuronal system; the units of which it is composed and their working, the assemblage of the units into a structure, the evolution and development of that structure and how the model proposed can account for memory, emotion, consciousness. In the final chapter, I attempt to synthesize this material into a coherent picture which specifically reflects my own views concerning the nature of man and hence his brain.

The Relationships Between the Brain and the Outside World

It has been a constant concern of philosophers as to how it is possible for man to know or to predict aspects of the world outside himself. After all, the information upon which such predictions are based depends on the arrival of data at the body surface in terms of light and sound of varying wavelengths and intensities, fluctuations in temperature, pressure on particular points of the skin, concentrations of certain chemical substances which are detected by nose or tongue. Within the body this data is transformed into a series of electrical signals passing along particular nerves to the central brain regions where the signals interact with one another producing certain types of response. If these responses are thoughts, if the totality of electrical signals represents in some other frame of reference the "mind", then what is the nature of the links between mind and the world outside? In other words, if the eyes are the windows of the soul, how does that soul distinguish between real events in the external world and reflections in its own window? Is the window – can the window be – anything more than a mirror? If we know the world only in terms of the workings of our own brain, in studying the world and interpreting it are we not in some way merely imposing an order upon it, an order which only exists by virtue of the fact that it reflects an internal logic of our own brain mechanisms, not one external to our brains and intrinsic to the universe?

As the eighteenth century philosopher and cleric[5] Berkeley once put it:

> That neither our thoughts, nor passions, nor ideas formed by the imagination, exist without the mind, is what everybody will allow. And it seems no less evident that the various sensations or ideas imprinted on the sense, however blended or combined together (that is what objects they compose), cannot exist otherwise than in a mind perceiving them. . . . The table I write on I say exists – that is I see and feel it; and if I were out of my study I would say it existed – meaning thereby if I was in my study I might perceive it, or that some other spirit actually does perceive it . . . for as to what it says of the absolute existence of unthinking things without any relation to their being perceived, that seems perfectly unintelligible. Their "*esse*" is "*percipi*", nor is it possible that they should have any existence out of the minds of thinking things which perceive them. . . . "But," say you, "surely there is nothing easier than for me to imagine trees, for instance, in a park, or books existing in a closet, and nobody by to perceive them." I answer "You may say so, there is no difficulty in it; but what is all this, I beseech you, more than framing in your mind into certain ideas which you call *books* and *trees* and at the same time omitting to frame the idea of any one that may perceive them? But do not you yourself see or think of them all the while? This, therefore, is nothing to the purpose; it only shows you have the power of imagining or forming ideas in your mind: but it doth not show that you can conceive it possible the objects of your thought may exist without the mind. . . ."

In other words

> *There once was a man who said God*
> *must find it exceedingly odd*
> *if he finds that this tree*
> *continues to be*
> *when there's no-one about in the quad.*

This limerick by Ronald Knox found an anonymous answer.

> *Dear Sir, your astonishment's odd*
> *I am always about in the quad*
> *and that's why the tree*
> *will continue to be*
> *since observed by, yours faithfully, God.*

Berkeley's preoccupations find a modern echo, too, in the work of such contemporary figures as the social anthropologist Claude Lévi-Strauss[6] and the linguistic analyst Noam Chomsky.[7] Both argue that there are "built-in" features to the mind—and hence, in Lévi-Strauss's case, human society—which are both *consequences* of its mode of action and at the same time *determinants* of the way we view and classify the world.

Generally, despite philosophical doubts, we operate on the assumption that what our eyes tell our brains about the external world is real. Nonetheless in some sense we are all solipsists; the external world is seen and reinterpreted through our mind's eye, and our vision of it is the one that matters when dealing with it. To some extent we all believe that the world goes to bed when we do, and our daytime visions are replaced by night imaginings. And when dealing with objects as significant for us as those we interpret as "fellow men" we view their actions in particular from a point that owes much to a solipsist perspective. For many purposes this solipsism doesn't matter, because, in viewing the rest of the world, our neighbor's solipsist perspective is very little different from our own, possibly because, as both Chomsky and the neurobiologist would agree, our neighbor's brain is very similar to our own. If this were not the case, Berkeley would have written only for himself and a dream audience of his own imagining. Science, with its rational pursuit of universal laws, helps to unify these perspectives, to externalize them and to give them a validity which is beyond short-term changes in point of view and perspective. And scientists, being practical people, have operated on the assumption that this procedure is valid because it works—by virtue of the fact that it enables one to make predictions about the way the world works—that on the tenth day of next month there will be a partial eclipse of the moon, or that such and such a mass of uranium 235 will explode with an energy release equivalent to ten million tons of TNT—and on the whole such predictions are accurate.

It is only when the philosophers ask them how it is done that scientists come to a standstill; until then, like the man who learned to his amazement that all his life he had been speaking prose, they had done it without knowing any better. Asked to justify this procedure, or to explain it, they are in the same difficulty as the bicyclist asked to describe how to ride a bike.

The effort of description is so great that it is more likely that he falls off than that his listener will immediately and without further practice be able to get up on a bike of his own and ride off.

But on the whole the philosophers don't disturb the scientist unduly; he is prepared to let them speculate on how he goes about his business, while at the same time going about it in his own way irrespective, unconcerned about the relationship of the observations he makes to abstracts like "truth" or the "objective world" because he takes these for granted. They only cease to be taken for granted at times of conflict, either within a scientific area, or about the nature and rôle of science itself. The present time is such a period; there are conflicts of view within biology and powerful challenges to the whole myth of scientific objectivity which, dominant over a long period, has closely moulded the views of scientists. Threats to this world-view seems almost incomprehensible to many scientists. To revert to the bicycle analogy, those who utter them are regarded as if, instead of riding their bicycles in the normal way, they are doing so upside down or backwards, for they appear to insist that the logic of the world is quite different from that which most scientists take for granted.

Those who challenge the scientists' view of the world may start with different logical premises, like the schizophrenic who insists that he is not what other people recognize him to be, and whose world is thus ordered according to the same laws as everyone else's but around a different basic position–he rides his bicycle with dignity and grace, but pedals resolutely backwards. More disturbing are those many mystics, both ancient and modern, who deny that the bicycle is there for riding at all and insist it has quite different functions–it is to be adored, or to experience communion with, or maybe to be used as a spade for digging the ground. It is these encounters rather than those with the philosopher which may cause scientists to re-examine their working assumptions about the rôle of the bicycle.[8] And nowhere do these encounters come more frequently, and generate more heat, than in the exploration of brain function.

Much of the heat arises, however, not because of problems integral to the subject itself, but because of a continuous confusion of terms amongst the protagonists. This is seen very clearly in a contemporary conflict between two groups of biologists. One group, predominantly molecular biologists, claim that it is possible to specify the workings of the cell–and hence the organism–by analyzing the structure of its component parts, for instance to understand heredity in terms of DNA or RNA sequences. The second group argues that this is not the case, that there is in some mysterious way "more" to the cell than the sum of its interacting parts, that analysis can never provide a complete specification of the cell as a whole. The position of the first group may be termed *reductionism*, that of the second *holism*.[9] This conflict is particularly important in terms of the understanding of brain mechanisms. Is the brain to be understood by dissecting it, or by examining its workings intact? In several of the chapters that follow, we shall find this conflict of approach expressing itself experimentally and in terms of the interpretation of results.

Latent in the conflict, of course, is the belief or hope of the holists that biological systems will show "emergent" properties which the traditional laws of physics or chemistry cannot explain, and the equally dogmatic—and so far mostly valid—claim of the reductionists that there are no such emergent properties which cannot be encompassed within an existing scientific framework. "Mind" is seen as one of these emergent properties, a viewpoint this book will challenge.[10]

But there is a more important aspect of the controversy yet. Behind the holists' very proper concern with the need to consider the system as a whole, lies also a fear that reductionism attempts not just to explain but to explain away; that by reducing man to an assemblage of working parts, his humanity has been in some measure also reduced.[11] This is an important fear, and one which should be treated with respect. Some of the more arrogant pronouncements of the molecular biologists may indeed lend credence to the concern that they really do see humans merely as a large number of close-packed cells with particular relationships, while a similar explanatory naïveté among ethologists had led to complaints that they regard the human as nothing but a "naked ape", or larger rat.

Mind, Brain and Hierarchy

This is not the point at which to enter into the substance of this controversy. The point I wish to make here is that much of it rests simply on confusion of terminology. There are many levels at which one can describe the behavior of the brain. One can describe the quantum structure of the atoms, or the molecular properties of the chemicals which compose it; the electron-micrographic appearance of the individual cells within it; the behavior of its neurons as an interacting system; the evolutionary or developmental history of these neurons as a changing pattern in time; the behavioral response of the individual human whose brain is under discussion; the familial or social environment of that human, and so on. Each of these descriptions may be complete in its own terms, yet which one is relevant must depend on the circumstances. A statement about a particular human being, "He is in love", could be provided with a description at any one of these varying levels. It could be in terms of the social interactions of the particular human; of an analysis of his own "state of mind"; of a specification of the changes in hormonal level in his circulating bloodstream and variations in sensory input; the altered firing patterns of the cells of the hypothalamus and cortex; new synapses in particular brain regions; changes in the rates of synthesis of proteins or other macromolecules; changes in the quantum state of the atoms composing his body.

Within its own frame of reference, none of these descriptions would be invalid; however not all are equally useful. Which is the most useful depends on whether the purpose for which the description is intended is related to the writing of a novel, sociological analysis, chemical description or experimentation on cellular phenomena. The group (set) of possible descriptions of what is meant by the phrase "He is in love" can be seen as a vertically parallel array of horizontal lines. Points on each line correspond to points on all lines below and above. These therefore represent equivalent statements in different universes of discourse, and can be translated one into the other. There is a general consensus, at least amongst physical scientists, that the statements represented by the lower lines are more fundamental or general because they can be made over a broader range (it is no good saying of a stone "He is in love" but one can specify its molecular structure or quantum state). For many purposes, statements on the lower lines have broader explanatory powers. But just because they have broader explanatory powers, they may also lose something in depth or compactness. "He is in love" may not be so specific a statement as a list of quantum numbers or molecular orbits, but it is a shorthand way of conveying a great deal of information with the degree of precision which may be all that is necessary.

The arrangement of explanations at a series of levels of this sort is said to constitute a *hierarchy*, and we can represent it by a simple diagram (figure 1). But it must be emphasized that in establishing this hierarchy we are not suggesting that the boundaries between levels are in any sense absolute. Far from it. They are defined *operationally*, in terms of how we handle questions and problems at any level, and why we are asking of our subject matter the particular questions which interest us.

Confusion may arise either if one regards these hierarchical levels as absolute–made by nature rather than by man–or if attempts are made to cross the levels of the hierarchies of explanation. If, for instance, one says "being in love" is "caused by changes such-and-such in molecular structure in the brain" one is attributing a causal relationship between the point-set on one level and that on another, where it is not always legitimate to

1 Hierarchies in
biological explanation.

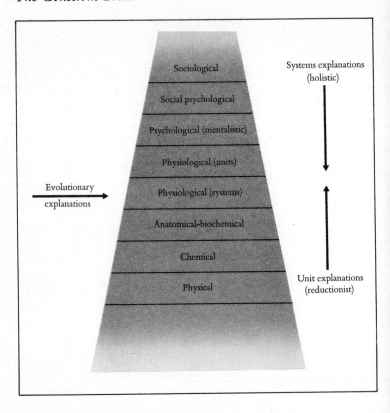

Sociological

Social psychological

Psychological (mentalistic)

Physiological (units)

Physiological (systems)

Anatomical-biochemical

Chemical

Physical

Systems explanations
(holistic)

Evolutionary
explanations

Unit explanations
(reductionist)

attribute more than a correlative relationship. A causal explanation means that we are saying, for instance, that "being in love"
is *a result* of such and such changes in molecular structure. But
we could also say such and such changes in molecular structure
are a *result of* "being in love". Such causal statements imply both
a temporal sequence – one event always precedes the other – and
a non-reversibility: *Either A causes B or B causes A*. A correlative
relationship, on the other hand, does not imply that one event is
the result of the other, merely that when one event occurs, the
second also invariably takes place: When the state "being in
love" occurs, then such-and-such changes in molecular structure
also always occur.

Describing the properties of the brain in molecular terms is
not the same – as seems sometimes feared – as explaining away
these properties, reducing their significance at higher hierarchical levels. In my view, much of the confusion over the
relationship of mind to brain has arisen because of attempts to
cross hierarchical levels of discourse. For the purposes of this
book, the "mind" will be defined as "the sum total of brain
activity" at a hierarchical level above that of the physiological
description of the interaction of cells and below that of social
analysis.[12]

In advancing such a definition, I am, I know, treading with rather large boots over a philosophical minefield of great extent and antiquity. Indeed some aspects of how this minefield was laid are discussed later in this chapter. In claiming that mind is the description of brain activity at a particular hierarchical level, I am adopting a version of what is known as the *identity hypothesis*.

Having made this definition, I am then able to provide a biological "explanation" for the evolution of mind, its appearance as an attribute of a particular living form, the human, in terms of the evolution of brains. Particular aspects of the activity of mind, such as consciousness, memory, creativity and will are described, using the language system appropriate to the brain, in subsequent chapters. In particular, consciousness and mind are seen, in chapter 6, as being an inevitable consequence of the evolution of particular brain structures which developed in a series of evolutionary changes in the pathway of man's own emergence. The hypothesis is advanced that consciousness is a consequence of the evolution of a particular level of complexity and degree of interaction among the nerve cells (neurons) of the cerebral cortex, while the form it takes is profoundly modified for each individual brain by its development in relationship with the environment (chapters 7 and 8). Memories are interpreted as being coded in the brain in terms of particular changes in the pattern of the connections between cells (chapter 9), will and emotion as representing aspects of the cellular properties of a particular brain region – the hypothalamus – and its interactions both with the cerebral cortex and with the rest of the body (chapter 10), while arousal, attention and alertness are seen as related to yet another brain region, the reticular formation (chapter 11). Finally the failures of the mind, leading to neuroses and psychoses, are also related to the behavior – or malfunctioning – of particular brain cells and regions (chapter 12). None of these explanations, however, which correlate brain activities and mental activities, should ever be seen as reducing the value – in their own terms, and when used for appropriate purposes – of description or explanations of these mental events in terms appropriate to their own hierarchical level. Nor do brain explanations, any more than mentalistic explanations, diminish the immense importance of explanations at a higher hierarchical level still – that of the interaction of humans, with other humans and with their environment. Which hierarchical level of explanation is chosen must depend on circumstances and intention. There should be no dispute between rival explanations of schizophrenia, for instance, based on biochemical abnormalities in the brain, on the mental history of the individual and on the social and environmental pressures upon him deriving from his family and social class. For some types of purpose one level of explanation and for other purposes another level is appropriate. The heat which is generated in debates between whether schizophrenia, for instance, is a biochemical or a social illness (chapter 12) is largely based on these confused attempts to confound several levels of explanation, to assert the primacy of one level at the expense of the others.

My personal view, which will be expressed most coherently in the last chapter, is that there is a need for the development of a new neurobiology which comprehends and embraces the interactions at all these levels of the hierarchy, one which is concerned with stressing the value and uniqueness of the whole human being rather than of his components. Thus I see many of what I regard as aberrations, systematic philosophical distortions of the image of man and the science that is performed in the name of that image, as arising out of the use of monocausal, single-level explanations of human activity. In the last chapter, too, I attempt the task of relating these philosophical distortions to the social structure which generates them, in accord with my contention that the social form has a profound effect on man's images of himself and his fellow men, and hence on the conduct of his science.

For the present, though, it is relevant to see that the definition of the relations of mind and brain that has been proposed still leaves unanswered two questions on which the reductionist/holist dichotomy, in so far as it is real and not purely semantic, impinges closely. The first is the internal equivalent of the solipsist standpoint, the relationship of thinking to the brain in which the thinking occurs. Not only can one think, but one can be conscious of oneself thinking. One can think about oneself thinking about oneself thinking about . . . . The infinite regress of the hall of mirrors that this makes possible seems closely related to the search for the meaning of an individual's identity which permeates much of contemporary cinema and literature.[13] What is the "I" which does the thinking? How is it possible for one's mind to be *in* one's brain if, at the same time, it can think *about* one's brain?

As the discussion which follows in this chapter, and to which we return in chapter 13, makes clear, I believe this paradox to rest on a semantic confusion, based on a habit of dualistic speaking, deriving from Descartes, which seems curiously hard to slough off. While it is true that the "I thinking about me", the process of self-consciousness, may be a uniquely human characteristic, it is not an inexplicable characteristic, provided one does not fall into semantic traps. One of these traps is latent in the term *consciousness*, which is a portmanteau word of many meanings. Thus it may simply imply a state different from that of being asleep or in a coma; that is, the reverse of being "un-conscious". Or it may be used to relate to the private world of the mind in contrast with a presumed "public" world of ob-served behavior. In this book my use of the word perhaps owes more to the Marxist than the Freudian tradition. I relate it specifically to the sum total of brain activity, the brain state, as affected by both the internal development of the individual and the external events impinging upon him. I am not at all con-cerned with consciousness in the sense of the reverse of being asleep, except insofar as this affects brain state, of course, nor with the Freudian sense in which conscious actions or motives are contrasted with unconscious or subconscious ones. If, following our definition of mind, we define the "I" as the sum total of the brain activity of an individual from birth (or some other suitable start-point) to the present time, then the "I thinking about me" and "I thinking about me thinking about me . . ." regress is seen as a pattern of events ordered on a time-based sequence. They do not ride on top of one another hier-archically but stretch out in time. Each (and it is questionable that the regress is real, or just linguistic, a pattern of words, after a certain point) description represents a particular brain state at a particular time in relationship to other brain states at times just before or just after. The terminology one uses to describe these brain states depends purely on the hierarchical level at which one is talking. It is important to appreciate how to avoid the particular linguistic trap of this paradox, particularly when, as later in this book, there will be occasion to consider the effects of interferences with the brain, by drugs or electrical stimula-tion, upon the properties of "I".

The second, interlocked question, refers to the extent to which it is possible to "know" the brain of another. Could it ever be possible, even theoretically, to specify the brain of an individual to the extent that every thought, emotion or sensa-tion he has is predictable? It is obvious, of course, that one can-not know one's own brain (in so far as the concept is meaningful) in this way, for the act of knowing, and hence of making a prediction about one's future action, itself becomes part of that action, thus changing it. For one's own brain, the very act of predicting changes the prediction—a statement, in terms of the biological and behavioral sciences, which is the parallel of Heisenberg's Uncertainty Principle in physics. Heisenberg's principle states that one can never know simultaneously the position and velocity of an electron, because the act of measur-ing one changes the other. The most one can give is a proba-bilistic statement, in which one computes the chances that an electron mass so-and-so has a velocity such-and-such. The same is clearly the case so far as "knowing one's own brain" in this sense is concerned. But how about "knowing" someone else's brain?

If we mean by this "at any moment holding in one's own brain the sum total of information relevant to the brain activity of another individual from birth to the present time", leaving quite aside the question of how one could have obtained this information, it is obvious that the only way it could be fitted into one's own brain would be, essentially, by replacing the existing information—that is, substituting the other individual's brain for one's own—clearly not a possibility. There is unlikely to be the storage capacity in one's own brain to "know" another person's brain in this sense.*

There remains the possibility, however, albeit theoretical, of building a computer with a storage capacity big enough to hold the total information concerning brain activity that is required. Suppose that one could do this, and then in some way as yet unimaginable wire up an individual's brain to the computer, to record all aspects of his "brain state". The question is then whether this information would be adequate for the computer to specify the individual's brain and predict his future actions. It will be apparent that this is the nub of questions which in an earlier generation were discussed under the terms "free will" and "determinism". The answer that this book will make to these questions is ambiguous. It will be argued that, in the sense used here, the brain is a deterministic system, so that if the brain state at any one time is specified, its subsequent states can also be predicted—within a certain degree of error. Thus I will maintain that any prediction that can be made about the brain is limited in the same way that the Uncertainty Principle limits prediction in physics: that is, the predictions are of a probabilistic and not an absolute nature. This uncertainty arises from the properties of the nervous system itself. It is in this sense, it will be argued, that the brain is determinate. But it will not be until considerably later in the book that it will be possible to take up again the points made here. By then, on the basis of the discussion of the hardware and mechanism of the brain that the intervening chapters provide, it will be possible to set the argument into a social framework.

The inflexions of a word tabulated as an example.

The Paradigms of Mind and Brain

The "solution" I adopt to the problem of the relation of "mind" and "brain" must however be seen in some sort of historical

---

*In this context I am always reminded of Michael Polanyi's haunting phrase, in exploring the limits of science and man's power of communication, "We know more than we can tell."

perspective.[14] One may well wonder why it is assumed to be a problem at all. To understand this it is necessary to see that all attempts at scientific explanation of a particular matter operate within a context, a general statement of the way in which the problem should be approached, a view of what should be included and what excluded from such an explanation. In general terms, the context in which the scientific explanation is attempted is referred to as a paradigm, and it is instructive to consider the ways in which the paradigms of mind and brain have changed in the three hundred years of serious attention to the problem since the time of Descartes, whose separation of "mind" and "body" was to provide the impetus towards libraries of philosophical confusion.

The literature of philosophy and medicine is filled with attempts to describe the relationships of brain and mind, appropriate to the age and level of scientific understanding in which they were made. Science's way of thinking about the brain has, historically, been profoundly colored by the prevailing view of the universe; as God's house, or clockwork machine, or improbable sum of probabilistic events. Medieval men were full of insubstantial humors, shadowy characteristics of the soul which permeated all portions of the body. Because neither brain nor body, mind nor matter, were distinguishable one from another, there were no problems as to the separation between brain and mind. There was no mind/body dualism in the sense that came to plague a more apparently rational eighteenth- and nineteenth-century world in which the mind and soul as insubstantial entities in a determinist mechanical world ("ghosts in the machine") became major intellectual problems.

Before the seventeenth century, and particularly before Newton and Descartes, the physical and biological worlds alike were populated with spirits, driven by heavenly forces co-substantial with the physical bodies they inhabited. In a world in which the stars and planets were fixed to revolving glass spheres drawn by angel-power, the body was the natural home of the soul and there was no incompatibility between them. The one housed the other, but the points of coupling between them were irrelevant – a meaningless question to ask for one who was not a mechanist.

When first Copernicus, then Galileo and finally Newton demystified the universe, banishing the crystalline spheres forever, and angels to their proper place in church choirs, and more or less at the same time Descartes "reduced" the body to a machine driven by a hydraulic system of vital liquids coursing down the nerves, there was no place left for the soul. Yet it could not be discarded, so Descartes provided for it a convenient residual home in the brain's pineal gland, that tiny

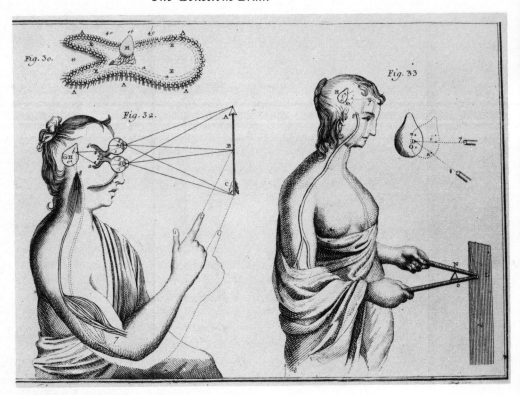

2 Descartes' view of the relationship of external world, brain, soul and body.

organ which forms a sort of "third eye" apparently left over from some earlier phase of the brain's evolution (figure 2). Here the soul resided, driving the body through the brain and nerves, yet separate from both. Thus emerged the fatal dualism which survived the careful anatomy of Leonardo da Vinci (figure 3).

Descartes, of course, was driven by the need to reconcile the problem of a mechanistic universe with a world view which embraced both the pre-eminence of mind ("*Cogito, ergo sum.*") and the dictates of Catholic ideology. Later eighteenth- and nineteenth-century irreligious or empirical philosophers had no such need, yet they took over the dualism, lock, stock and barrel, as part of the intellectual baggage of a previous century. Mind may have replaced soul, but still it was present, expanded now from its cramped pineal home to fill the entire brain cavity – or sometimes incorporeally located at a site just above the head – but still irrevocably there, testing the wit of man to invent ever more elaborate couplings to link the mind inside the brain inside the head, that ever receding infinite regress of "I"s, of egos, with observable bodily behavior. To quote Berkeley again: "The brain, therefore, you speak of, being a sensible thing, exists only in the mind. . . ."

For Descartes the brain and nerves were a sort of hydraulic system, an elaborate arrangement of canals, pistons and pumps through which vital spirits infused, invigorating muscles and tissues with their energizing content. The mechanically-minded eighteenth century preferred a clockwork model full of cogs and pulleys, by which the mind twitched the body's limbs like a master puppeteer. By the nineteenth century the discoveries of electricity, and particularly of "animal electricity", which led to detached frogs' legs twitching when galvanized with a voltaic cell, gave rise to descriptions based on electrical attractions and repulsions and current flow, while the incomparable Dr. Mesmer explained his fabulous displays of "mesmerism" (hypnosis) with still more fabulous theories of "animal magnetism". Such vagaries were uneasy to the late nineteenth-century rationalists,[15] men who were convinced that the triumphant march of Victorian progress was unstoppable, who lived in an ordered world of well-understood Newtonian mechanics, whose ultimate atomic particles were small, solid and perfectly elastic billiard balls, whose biology was being ordered by Darwinian evolution and whose chemistry, from a monstrous pile of disoriented facts, had been shaken into rationality and coherence by the formulation of the "periodic table" of the elements by the Russian Dmitri Mendeleev. The untidiness of current views on brain mechanisms remained a constant flow in this tidy universe. To mend the flow, it was necessary that the brain be analyzed into its constituent parts and each be given an appropriate function. But to subject the brain to analysis was to banish – or at least restrict – the role of mind and soul still further. Nor did the pretensions of the brain analysts automatically carry conviction. The first part of the 19th century saw a bitter dispute between those who maintained that different mental functions could be associated with different brain regions, and those more classically minded philosophers, doctors and anatomists, who disputed that such incorporeal functions could possibly be localized.

The cause of the "localizers" was brought into disrepute by the absurdities to which it was carried in the phrenology of F. J. Gall and J. C. Spurzheim, who claimed to be able to distinguish, through the skull, separate brain regions for each of a large number of human faculties (e.g. mathematics, love of children, and so on; figure 4). Although phrenology retained its believers (and still does) it was rejected by the orthodox academic community, and it was not until the second half of the 19th century, with the work of such men as David Ferrier in Britain and Paul Broca in France that a more rational basis for localization of function was eventually to be accepted. Different parts of the brain were now seen as controlling or analyzing different body functions, though "higher mental activities" were still without a clear-cut home. By the end of the century brain would be accommodated at last into that certain Victorial universe of Lord Kelvin, archetypal technologist and physicist, who refused to accept any scientific theory or datum for which he could not design a mechanical model or analogy. To T. H. Huxley, the great champion of Darwinism, the relationship of mind and brain could be summed up in the most classic of Victorian analogies, as the whistle to the steam train.

But by that time there had emerged a new physical device from which to draw the appropriate brain analogy. The coming of the electric telegraph, and later the wireless telegraph and the telephone, provided the model. Here was surely a system that was like the brain; it converted sense data into symbols—in the hands of Morse and his successors into specific codes for given individual letters—which could be passed over large distances and be decoded at the other end, revealing once again the information which had been fed in previously. Perhaps the telephone was even more analogous, for speech was here converted into patterns of electrical flow along a wire, to be translated once more later. Hence the familiar model of the brain as telephone exchange, messages coming in and going out, signals from eyes connected to muscular contractions in legs and so on.

Such analogies were made even more popular by the discovery during the 1920s that the brain was indeed in a state of constant electrical flux, that if electrodes were placed upon the scalp they would record a ceaseless rhythm of electrical activity, regular rhythmic bursts that were almost predictable enough to set a watch by. This continuous electrical flux, which changed in pattern depending on whether the brain was active or asleep, was instantly interpreted as a record of the workings of the "central telephone exchange" of the brain.

These telephone-exchange models, of subscribers dialling in and being connected to their required addresses by a "central operator", was equally in accord with another physiological model that became popular in the years following the turn of the century, so well in accord with the principles of economics dictated by factory management in Victorian and Edwardian England, to be effectively taken up and expanded by Henry Ford and his successors in the United States. In this model the whole human body was a factory with inputs and outputs, control centers, distribution points and so forth. The brain was the management of the factory, the administrator, receiving information about the state of progress and rapidly and efficiently taking the appropriate actions. Such a model will be familiar to many readers.

Those raised on a diet of popular-science magazines and

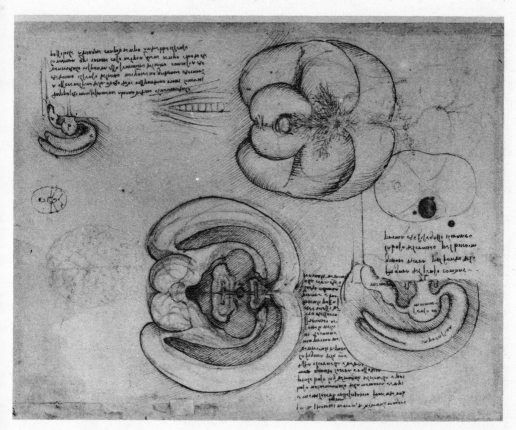

3 (*above*) Anatomical drawing of the ventricles of the brain by Leonardo da Vinci, made by pouring wax into the cavities, fluid filled in life.

4 (*right*) Brain regions associated with a variety of functions and human faculties by Spurzheim.

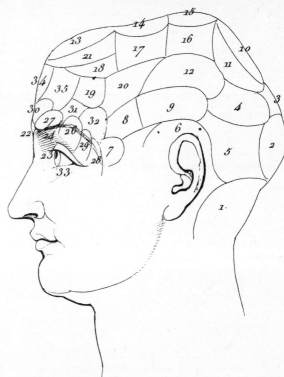

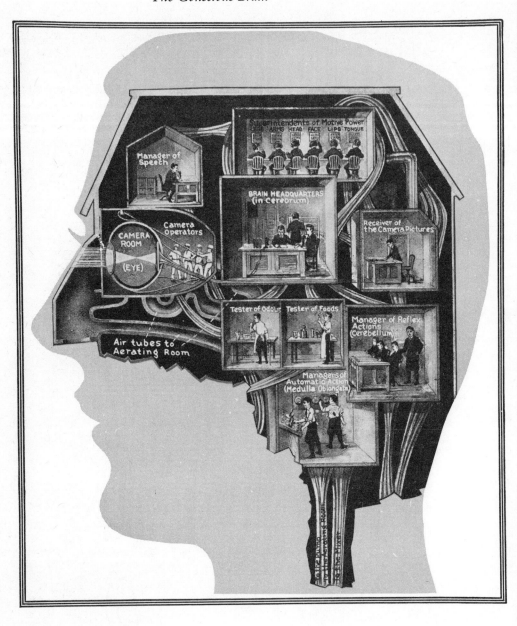

5 'The Control Station
of Your Body'–a 1930s
metaphor of brain
function.

children's encyclopedias, both pre- and post-Second World War (so substantial is the time lag between the development of prevailing scientific models and their permeation into popular culture), will recall one of the many variants on this theme of the sort of figure 5. The caption to this one, from a just pre-war children's encyclopedia, is particularly revealing.

> Imagine your brain as the executive branch of a big business. It is divided, as you see here, into many departments. Seated at the big desk in the headquarters office is the General Manager – your Conscious Self – with telephone lines running to all departments. Around you are your chief assistants – the Superintendents of Incoming Messages, such as Vision, Taste, Smell, Hearing, and Feeling (the last two hidden behind the central offices). Nearby also are the Superintendents of Outgoing Messages which control Speech and the movement of Arms, Legs, and all other parts of the body. Of course, only the most important messages ever reach your office. Routine tasks such as running the heart, lungs, and stomach, or supervising the minor details of muscular work are carried on by the Managers of Automatic Actions in the Medulla Oblongata and the Manager of Reflex Actions in the Cerebellum. All other departments form what the scientists call the Cerebrum. Suppose that you are walking absentmindedly in the street and meet your friend Johnny Jones. He calls your name, you stop, say "Hullo!" and shake hands. It all seems very simple, but let's see what happened during that time in your brain. The instant Johnny Jones called your name, your Hearing Manager reported the sound, and your Camera Man flashed a picture of him to the camera room. "Watch out!" – came the signal to your desk, and at the same instant both messages were laid in front of you. As quick as lightning your little office boy, Memory, ran to his filing case and pulled out a card. The card told you that that voice and that face belonged to a person named Johnny Jones and that he was your friend. Instantly you began issuing orders: "Tell the Speech Manager to say 'Hullo Johnny' for me! Tell the Leg Superintendent to stop walking at once! Tell the Arm Superintendent to stick out my hand right away and take Jones's hand! Tell the Face and Lips Superintendent to give this man a good big smile!" In less than half a second all your orders were faithfully carried out. Think how much work is done in your brain office every 24 hours!

The implications of such a model are, of course, of some interest from the point of view of the model-makers' vision of the human world, one in which the management always knows best and is right, one in which big and little executives and factory operatives know their place. If the big toe doesn't tell the brain what to do, what right has a worker to tell his employer? It is really a contemporary version of "All things bright and beautiful", with the "rich man in his castle and the poor man at his gate", only in this case the rich man is the central manager in the brain, the poor man the big toe, or the less poor man is perhaps the Hearing Manager or Manager of Automatic Operations. This is a universe ordered, if not by God, then a post-Victorian rationalist economic and physiological imperative.

Such crudely mechanistic analogies, though, were not to survive indefinitely. The first decade of the twentieth century took the rigid, ordered and mechanical post-Newtonian physical universe and shook it with a vigor from which it has never recovered. Quantum mechanics, relativity, sub-nuclear complexity and finally, by the 1930s, the overthrow of classical causality by a statistical picture of the atom and the events within it, were all parts of this shaking. The far-reaching statement of the Uncertainty Principle by Heisenberg, reduced cause, at least at the level of the electron, to a situation in which all one could ever give was a *probable* statement of its position and velocity. If probabilistic statements were the order of the day so far as the physics of such fundamental objects as elementary particles was concerned, how much more should this be the case when dealing with the vast complexities of the brain? At the same time the economic certainties of the Victorians and Edwardians were shaken by the increasing violence of boom and slump, culminating in the Depression and salvation through war and Keynesian economics, which suggested a more sophisticated and interlocking set of analogies for economic behavior than that of the manager and his office boy and operatives.[16]

The developments of theories of control processes and of information, embraced under the name of cybernetics by the mathematician Norbert Weiner in the United States in the 1940s, provided a mathematical underpinning both for the new economics and for the behavior of a new class of machinery whose power and sophistication far outstripped that of a telephone exchange or telegraph: the computer. It is not surprising, therefore, to find many of today's brain analogies based on a language system which derives both from the premises of statistical and probabilistic mechanics (a recent book by one leading neurophysiologist, Ben Delisle Burns,[17] is entitled *The Uncertain Nervous System*-enough to make Kelvin rotate in his grave), and from the experience of two decades of computer engineering. Thus we can compute probabilities of neuronal firing and the coupling of random nerve nets, and talk of control, feedback, holographic models of information storage and the systems-analysis approach to the brain. The difference, it has been suggested, between this and the earlier telephone-exchange model was that it was now as if, when a subscriber dialled into the exchange, he could never be sure whom he would be connected to, but that all the other subscribers to the exchange would certainly be able to receive at least a portion of the message.

All this goes to show that the habit of scientists in arguing about one system in terms of analogies with another is a fairly fundamental part of scientific activity. Is there any reason to believe that the contemporary analogies are better than those that have gone before? The answer is almost certainly Yes, provided it is recognized that they are *only* analogies and "better" in this context means "more productive scientifically". It was useful to talk about the brain in terms of telephone exchanges just as it was useful for the physicist to pretend that atoms were perfectly elastic billiard balls. The latter pretense made possible the derivation of physical predictions, such as the laws of behavior of gases, for instance, the former led to the possibility of regarding nerve axons as "wires" along which coded messages passed. Today's analogies have deeper explanatory power, are closer to describing the observed phenomena and are more capable of being used for predictive purposes concerning brain activity, than ever before. Thus, I will argue, we are closer to "explaining" the brain than ever before.

None the less, it must always be noted that in some measure the analogies help determine the experiments that are being made and the way the scientist views the material of his study. In this way they tend to be self-fulfilling. And the analogies are "set" not so much by the internal development of the science itself, but the external shape of the society in which the science is being done—hence the eighteenth century's clockwork and today's computer analogies. These are the paradigmatic frameworks within which today's neurobiology, like yesterday's, is being conducted. But although the sorts of experiment that a scientist can make are heavily determined by the prevailing paradigm, that is the questions that it seems relevant to ask of his material at a given time, the approach that he has to his material in terms of the analogies and the model systems in which he is working are not entirely external to the science itself. To a major extent the advances and the models are suggested by internal developments in the direction of research, the application of new techniques to the subject and the analysis and interpretation of experimental results. Some of the delay in proceeding from the analogies of Descartes to the analogies of Weiner in our understanding of brain mechanisms has depended on an equal delay in the development of the experimental and analytical tools with which to approach the problem. The brain sciences have lagged behind the developments of physics, of chemistry and of other areas of biology in handling the intractable material of the brain and applying to it techniques which have been developed successfully elsewhere. This time-lag was in part due to the complexities of the material itself, and in part to not knowing what sort of questions one could legitimately ask of this material. Only recently have the tools become available to approach the problem of the brain in a way which makes it possible to ask meaningful questions.

In this period of changing analogies, it may be asked whether any space is to be found for today's Cartesians, those who still separate mind and brain. Indeed there are a few distinguished neurobiologists who are still unashamed dualists. However, more dualists are probably to be found among the ranks of the philosophers than among the scientists. Among scientists, most of the concern over the "abolition" of mind has come from those who are convinced—often because they are physicists rather than biologists—that there are still to be found in biology new laws, forces and properties of matter which cannot be subsumed under the classical laws of physics and chemistry. Mind to them is just such an emergent property. It will be the task of the final chapter of this book to analyze these views further. The intervening chapters are an attempt to provide an integrative statement of "where we are now" in neurobiology.

There are three reasons for trying to do this. One is to show how far we are justified in our belief that this particular biological frontier is within marching distance. The second is to show the extent to which, in attaining the frontier, it has been and will be increasingly necessary for many branches and disciplines of science which have hitherto been fairly stand-offish about one another, each regarding the others' results as perhaps arcane and irrelevant, perhaps too complex or too trivial for consideration, to come together in a collaborative effort of research. The last few years have seen the formalization of this coming together in that usual scientific accolade of arrival, the coining of a new name for the research area. We are all neurobiologists now, and regard ourselves as operating in a scientific community of the sort that those who study scientists rather than science describe as an "invisible college". And the third and most important reason for describing these aspects of the brain system is to try to evaluate the potential social and intellectual significance of the apparent successes of this latest scientific endeavor.

It is against the background of the arguments of this chapter that the material of chapters 2–12 must be evaluated. But before advancing from description to analysis, a word of caution is necessary. In order to make the case for my version of the identity hypothesis convincing, and in order to provide the scientific facts and observations on which to base any theory of brain action, it is necessary first to describe the brain as interpreted by the neuroanatomist, neurochemist, neurophysiologist and experimental psychologist. Chapters 2–4 provide that description in the depth necessary for understanding what follows. There is no mention of mind and consciousness in those three chapters, but instead a description of "how the brain is" at the biological levels of explanation. Only after the description of the brain system is completed in chapter 4 can we turn, in chapters 5 and 6 to consider how the human brain and consciousness evolved, in chapters 7 and 8 how the brain develops in interaction with its environment, in chapter 9 the mechanisms of memory, in chapter 10 the brain correlates of emotion, and in chapter 11 of sleep and wakefulness. The questions of failures of brain, of madness and mysticism occupy chapter 12. Finally, in chapter 13, I attempt the task of synthesis.

2 The Human Brain

The Form of the Brain

The brain is a machine for communicating, receiving information, storing it, issuing instructions based on it. The most elaborate and elegant theoretical descriptions of the way the machine works must in due course come to terms with the real brain rather than model ones. So in this chapter we describe the brain, what it looks like to the naked eye and to the microscope, what its components are. The brain is a complex structure and the terminology of those who have studied it is equally, if not more, complex. What is more, each of the different brain disciplines has contributed not only its own mite of wisdom but its own baggage train of words, descriptions, definitions, jargon, with at least a proportion of which it is necessary to come to terms. "Coming to terms" may not be easy for anyone who is not scientifically initiated, and it would be wrong to pretend that this and the next chapter will be easy to read. But there is no option but to define and describe before interpretation becomes possible.

The plan of this chapter is to begin with a visual inspection of the brain, what can be seen by the naked eye or be separated by scissors and scalpel and forceps. Having toured the brain on this macro-scale we then return to the start once more and look at it again, this time with the additional tools of the light microscope, the electron microscope and some of the formidable machinery of contemporary biochemistry. Only then is it possible to consider how the whole apparatus is wired up. But note that throughout this chapter we are considering the brain as an object, a static, dead thing to be cut up and observed, analyzed by whatever appear to be the most relevant tools. In this analysis there is no room for questioning of *process*, for a consideration of the brain as even a working machine, still less the seat of thought, emotion or consciousness. But to understand the brain at work and in operation it must first be seen as a static, three-dimensional fixed and stained object. Only then will it be clear what are the operating units which must be assembled in order to make a working brain.[1]

The Cerebrum

Removed from its skull and weighed, a human brain tops the scale at some fifteen hundred grams, heavier than most organs in the body. Its appearance, dominated by the massive CEREBRUM,* is roughly walnut like; its colour is pinkish gray on the outside, yellowish white within. Even the crudest inspection reveals that the cerebrum is like a walnut in another way than just its wrinkles: It divides neatly in half down its mid-line. To visual inspection (and to microscopic inspection as well) each half is the mirror image of the other. The brain is a twin structure; such a shape is known as BILATERALLY SYMMETRICAL (figures 6 and 7).[2] In addition, it soon became clear to early anatomists, from the ease with which the mass of tissues could be divided, that the brain was composed of a number of readily separable parts, mini-organs so to say.

The existence of many of these sub-structures is apparent from figure 6. First, there is the division between "gray" and "white" matter. (In these less medieval days we ought to abandon the term "matter" but do not. In fact the entire subject of the brain's anatomy is sprinkled with terms deriving from earlier attempts to comprehend, describe and define it, so much so that it is almost difficult to proceed without becoming submerged under a sea of Latin–or rather dog-Latin–terms for bits of the brain which the old anatomists fancied resembled more familiar materials–almonds, olives or bridges for instance.) The gray matter lies largely on the surface of the brain, the white below, in the interior. This surface is known as the CORTEX. Three to four millimeters thick, it wraps, wrinkled and fissured, around the entire external surface of the most prominent feature of the human brain the two massive infolded *cerebral hemispheres*.

It is the relative size of the cerebrum, and its cortex in particular, which distinguishes humans from most other organisms. It is not that the cerebral cortex is crucial for survival. Many lower organisms can perform quite complex brain functions without a cerebrum at all. Some, like birds, do not have a cerebral cortex, and even in mammals, which have one, it is possible to make experimental preparations of creatures whose cerebral hemispheres have been removed or cerebral cortex stripped off. Such animals will survive indefinitely under slightly special protected conditions and will exhibit a broad range of behavior. In the absence of the cortex though, it is as if the behavior of the mammal were in a sense *automatic*–unmodified, stereotyped

---

*Terms which appear in small capital letters like this are all defined in the glossary.

responses out of proportion to the stimuli which cause them.

The curves and wrinkles, folds and grooves of the cortex are characteristic. The same wrinkles appear almost in the same place in any human brain examined. They represent a series of landmarks whereby particular cortical regions can be demarcated, enabling the cerebrum to be divided into a number of major separate regions or lobes: that at the rear is the OCCIPITAL LOBE; at the side, above the ear when the brain is in its skull, is

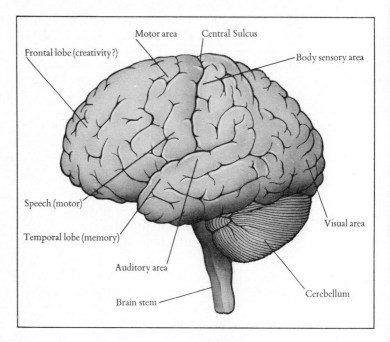

6 The human brain from the side.

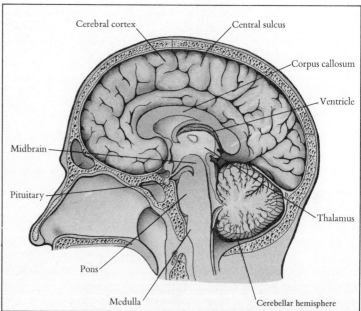

7 The human brain in section.

the TEMPORAL LOBE; at the front behind the forehead is the FRONTAL LOBE; the region running over the top under the hair is the PARIETAL region. The anatomical divisions also correspond approximately to a set of regions with particular functions in the control of bodily activity and in the processing of sensory information (figure 6). In general terms the parietal cortex contains those areas which are responsible for the coordination and control of sensory input and motor output, while the frontal and temporal lobes have much more diffuse and less understood functions relating to speech, learning, memory, intelligence and performance, and other, even more hard to define–but nonetheless real–human attributes. Around the primary areas concerned with the direct processing of sensory information or the organization of motor output are diffuse zones which, we shall see in chapter 6, are concerned with more sophisticated treatment and analysis of sensory input or motor output. These are the so-called association areas of the cortex. In chapter 4 we will see how the stimulation of particular cortical regions evoke appropriate responses: stimulation of the motor area produces movement, of the visual area the sensation of light, the auditory area of sound and so on. Yet despite these effects, large areas of cortex can be removed without apparent deficit in performance in experimental animals. In humans, some areas are occasionally destroyed by disease, and large regions of some of the lobes can be removed in operations without easy-to-see deficits in performance. In particular, the role of the association areas is not revealed by studying the consequences of such removals. On the other hand, animals whose primary visual cortex region has been removed behave as if they are virtually blind; they cannot analyze shapes or patterns, although some relearning is possible.

The cerebrum, as we mentioned above, is a bilaterally symmetrical structure. That is, it consists of two halves, each the mirror image of the other. The input from half of the body, and output to it, goes to and comes from one half of the cerebrum. However, rather surprisingly, the left half of the brain is concerned with the right half of the body, and the right half of the brain with the left half. Thus damage to the right visual cortex results in functional blindness in the left eye, while stimulation of the left motor cortex results in movement of the right side of the body. The evolutionary and functional significance of this crossing over of inputs and outputs is not certain. It does however represent the pattern on which brains are built, in all vertebrates. However, there are exceptions to the statement that every function in one half of the cerebrum is mirrored in the other. For a number of brain functions it does seem as if there is only one cortical site of control. This is particularly true for speech. The speech centers of the brain, which are considered further in chapters 4 and 6, are, in adults, confined to one hemisphere, the so-called dominant hemisphere, while the equivalent regions in the other hemisphere, which are anatomically identical so far as can be observed, are functionally silent. In humans, it is generally the left hemisphere, which is connected to the right side of the body, which contains the speech center and is said to be dominant. It is possible that this dominance has something to do with handedness as well. In left-handed people the dominant hemisphere, containing the speech center, is often, though not always, found to be the right one.

Both the symmetry and asymmetry are important. How does information present in one cerebral hemisphere become transferred to the other—that is, how does the right-hand side of the body know what the left-hand side is doing? There is one major connection between left and right hemispheres, visible in figure 7, a broad squiggle made entirely of white matter. This squiggle is the CORPUS CALLOSUM. To split the brain down the middle so as to make the drawing of figure 7, it is necessary to cut the callosum, and such cuts, when they occur in the living organism, produce a SPLIT BRAIN, a brain which is double, in which the left-hand side does not know what the right-hand side is doing.[3] Both halves of the body and brain then operate with a fair degree of autonomy. This autonomy is not obvious under normal circumstances, partly because a lot of bodily activities are controlled, as we shall see, from lower in the brain than the cerebral hemispheres, and partly because under normal circumstances a split-brain individual can, for instance, see with his left eye what the right half of his body is doing, and so compensate for the lack of transfer of information in his brain.

Some bizarre situations do arise, however, which have been explored in a famous set of experiments and observations by Roger Sperry in Stanford, California, both with experimental animals and in human patients whose corpus callosum has had to be cut for medical reasons. In humans, the most intriguing observations relate to the speech asymmetry. If the patient has his speech center in the left hemisphere, connected with his right eye, and this eye is covered, the left half of the brain does not see the objects presented to the right half. Suppose the patient is now shown a familiar object, a spoon say, and asked to name it, it turns out that he cannot—although he is perfectly capable of describing it and explaining what it is used for. If he is given it to hold, however, so that information can travel to the left side of the brain by non-visual sensory pathways, he can instantly name it. We return to the importance of these observations from the point of view of understanding certain key brain functions in chapter 9. For now we merely note them as an example of the localization of particular functions in particular cortical regions.

The demonstration of cortical functions which are localized, and yet of some cortical regions which apparently have no discernable function, is important for a number of other key themes to which we will have need to return again and again. In adults, if particular brain regions are destroyed, unlike the situation with say, skin or liver, they will not regrow. The function of the region is permanently lost. This is an example of what we shall describe, in later chapters, as the SPECIFICITY of the brain. None the less, as time goes by, it is often found that an individual who has been damaged can regain some of his lost capacities, and relearn lost skills. This is not because new brain tissue has regrown to replace the old, but because other parts of the brain have taken over the functions lost with the destroyed tissue. We will come back again and again to this feature of the brain, which is so important yet so puzzling; an index of what seems to be its considerable spare capacity, so that it is as if the result of damage to one part is to make other parts of the brain system work overtime. The fact of the REDUNDANCY OF FUNC-TION in the brain, so that at a pinch many different regions can fulfill a particular task, is another important unifying principle to which we shall have occasion to return.

This redundancy, while important in the adult, is even more important in the young child. Even if damage or loss of brain tissue occurs in the young child the brain region cannot regrow, but often, provided the lesion is not too severe, and only occurs in one half of the brain, considerable recovery of function is possible. Other bits of the brain – perhaps the equivalent region to the destroyed one, but in the opposite hemisphere – are called into play to fulfill the function of the destroyed area. This is notably the case with damage which affects the speech areas, where if the left hemisphere has been dominant and is damaged, then almost complete takeover of the function can be made by the equivalent region in the right hemisphere. Thus PLASTICITY of function, achieved by virtue of the tremendous redundancy of structure in the brain, can triumph over specificity of pathways. The three themes which this account of cortical function has revealed, of specificity, of plasticity and redundancy, will run like guidelines through much of the discussion of brain mechanisms in chapters 5–12.

The Cerebellum

Behind the cerebral hemispheres, and practically covered by them above, lies a smaller, fist-sized structure which is even more convoluted than the cerebrum, the CEREBELLUM. A third of the cerebral surface is exposed to the outside of the brain, but only one sixth of the cerebellar surface is. The rest lies buried deep in the convoluted folds. Like the cerebrum, the cerebellum is covered with its own cortex and is bilaterally symmetrical. Obvious in figure 7 is the relationship between the cerebellar gray and the cerebellar white, which runs up inside the cerebellar cortex like the veins of a leaf. The cerebellum is one of the few brain regions which can be ascribed a precise and specific function and whose structure can in a sense be related to that function. If the cerebellum is removed, or the nerve tracts linking it to the rest of the brain are severed, then there is a loss of control of fine movement, that degree of muscular coordination which makes it possible, for example, to reach out and pick up a distant object accurately, not to overshoot it or for the hand to shake so violently as to upset it. The cerebellum appears to monitor all of these tiny muscular movements that are made in purposeful action and to ensure that they are adapted to the intention; that they are not too wild, too gentle, too far or too near for the purpose. It is disorders of this function of fine control of muscular coordination that occur particularly in elderly people and lead to characteristic shaking and hand tremors.

The Brain Stem

Cerebrum and cerebellum can be plucked off the rest of the brain like apples, large and small. And indeed when they are plucked like apples they leave a stalk behind them, a thick white tube which runs up the centre of the brain and from which the other structures branch. This tube or BRAIN STEM, largely white matter, is in fact the continuation of the spinal cord which runs from the brain right through the spine to its end at an animal's tail or the residual human equivalent. In humans, the cord is about 40–45 cm in length and, in cross-section, the shape of a butterfly. The butterfly's body is made of gray matter, its wings of white (figure 8). The white carries the nerve fibers running to and from the brain, while along the cord at varying points branch the nerves which run to the periphery of the body, bringing every distant point in communication with the cord and, through the cord, the brain. It is the spinal cord and the brain which together constitute the CENTRAL NERVOUS SYSTEM of the human, and of all other vertebrates. Indeed it is from the cord that the other structures so much more prominent in the human brain originally evolved.

The brain stem itself begins to thicken as it emerges from the spine into the skull cavity which contains the brain. It broadens out, first into a region which in section is rather like a slice of cake, the MEDULLA, and then beyond the medulla into an arched region a little like a humpbacked bridge—at least so must have

8 Cross-section of the
spinal cord.

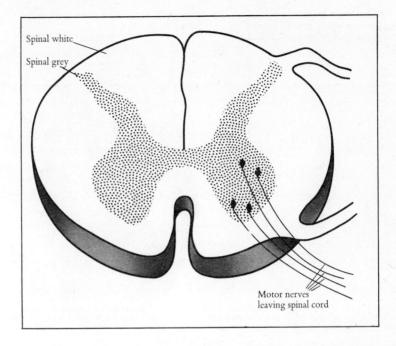

Spinal white

Spinal grey

Motor nerves
leaving spinal cord

thought the old anatomist who called it the PONS, which is Latin
for bridge. Beyond this bridge it is difficult to trace the brain
stem easily because it merges into a number of structures which
are attached to it by subsidiary stems: little spheres or spheroids
which have complex Latin names which we will not list here,
but some of whose functions will become apparent in due
course. Some of them are labeled in figure 7. Two might be
noticed at this point. One, above the pons, is the PINEAL body or
GLAND (*body* is another of those hang-over anatomical terms)
which is where Descartes located the seat of the soul. A second,
the PITUITARY, hangs down like a plum below the brain stem,
and is known to be the organ which produces a large number of
different hormones controlling a wide range of body activities,
including growth and sexual development.

   There are two more important things to note about the brain
at this point, which can be discovered by naked-eye observation.
One becomes apparent if the brain shown in figures 6 and 7 is
upended and looked at from the bottom (figure 9). A number of
thick branches can be seen running into the stem at the level of
the medulla and the pons. These are nerves other than those
which run down the spinal cord; those of the face and of the
major sense organs of the head, the eyes (OPTIC NERVE), the
mouth and the nose, providing the input into the brain for the
senses of vision, taste and smell.

9 The brain from below.
Note the entry of the
various cranial nerves.

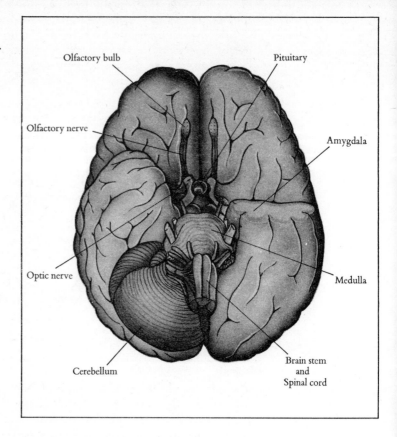

Olfactory bulb

Pituitary

Olfactory nerve

Amygdala

Optic nerve

Medulla

Cerebellum

Brain stem
and
Spinal cord

Cerebrospinal Fluid and Blood

The second important feature is revealed by considering what
separates the various structures of the brain – the corpus callosum,
the cerebrum and so on. Each is distinct, joined only in defined
places by stems or stalks. The spaces between these structures are
themselves a set of intercommunicating cavities, like a chain of
caves. They form a continuation of the central canal which runs
right through the spinal cord. These spaces are known as
VENTRICLES and, in the living brain, are filled with a particular
liquid, the CEREBROSPINAL FLUID, whose composition is not
dissimilar to that of blood from which red and white blood cells
have been filtered off. It is this cerebrospinal fluid which the
early theorists of brain action considered as the reservoir of the
vital spirits of the nerves. In fact it is an internal circulatory system
for the brain, helping bring nutrients to regions distant from a
blood supply and in turn washing out waste products.

Not that the brain is without a blood supply of course. Over
its surface and within its interior runs an arterial system which
carries a large portion of the total blood supply of the body
(figure 10). The brain is indeed urgently dependent upon two of
the vital substances carried within the blood – oxygen and

10 (*opposite*) The blood
supply of the brain (from
a cast made of a still-born
child).

44

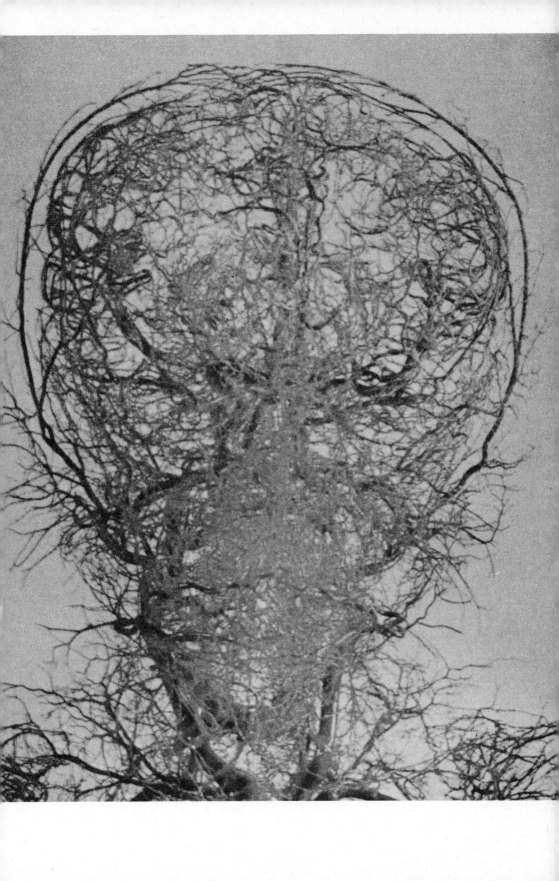

glucose. Although the adult brain makes up only 2 percent of the body weight, its oxygen consumption is 20 percent of the total—and as much as 50 percent in the young infant. Twenty per cent of the body's glucose consumption occurs in the brain. Fully one-fifth of the blood pumped by the heart passes through the brain—eight hundred milliliters a minute. If the brain is deprived of its oxygen or glucose for more than a few seconds, fainting results. If the period is more prolonged the results can be disastrous. Unlike the liver or muscle tissue, for example, the brain maintains almost no reservoirs of stored glucose on which it can draw; it is absolutely dependent on that supplied by the circulating blood supply. In the absence of glucose or of oxygen, fainting, followed by coma and death, occur. Fainting in itself could be regarded as a righting mechanism by the body. By lowering the head it helps ensure that blood can arrive at the brain without being pumped up-hill. The sequence of fainting, coma and death will also follow an overdose of insulin (the hormone missing in diabetics), for it causes a rapid uptake of glucose from the circulating blood into liver and muscle, to the detriment of the brain.

The Brain under the Microscope

The naked eye of the anatomist will reveal a good deal more about the brain. But possibly too much more, for the eye, scissors and scalpels, fancied comparison with other structures, and the checking of the human brain against that of animals was all the anatomists had for so long, while the fascination of the brain was so great, that to continue listing the results of their labors now would risk becoming really lost. Not only do the separate mini-organs have names, but also the anatomists have not resisted the temptation, common to all sciences in their descriptive, natural history phase, of classifying, grouping together different sets of brain regions as RHOMBENCEPHALON, DIENCEPHALON, TELENCEPHALON, MESENCEPHALON . . . the list is long, the groupings often self-contradictory. Just as the human brain has evolved by a process of accretion, of the accumulation of structures developed in lower organisms, discarding almost nothing, so too with these Latin and Greek categories. It is all accumulation, rarely are outmoded terms discarded. As long ago as the early nineteenth century, Gall, the founder of phrenology, inveighed against the tendency of the classical anatomists to this pseudoclassification,[4] and in some ways the situation has not improved since then. So at this point it is necessary to leave the gross structure of the brain to apply a finer resolution to it.

The Neuron

The finer resolution is of course the microscope. If one just takes a microscope and looks at the surface, cut or natural, of the brain, one can see very little. It is necessary to bathe the surface in a dye which is selectively taken up by some parts of the brain and not others, or to cut and prepare thin sections and stain them. Then the cellular structure of the brain is revealed. The difference between gray and white matter becomes obvious. The gray regions are seen to be packed with cells, the *nerve cells* (known as NEURONS); the white regions are bundles of NERVE FIBERS, nerve tracts running from one part of the brain to another. The most obvious cells to be seen in the gray matter are frequently quite large–from ten to one hundred microns* in diameter–which is big by the standard of many cells in the human body. The red blood cell, for instance, has a diameter of only seven microns.

The body of the neuron often appears to take quite a distinct geometric form, like a pyramid, a star, a rhombus or a pear, but more striking even than the form of the cell body (the central region of the cell, containing, as we shall see, most of its "conventional" biochemical apparatus) are the numerous projections, or processes, like fingers which can be seen running off from the cell in all directions. At the end of the nineteenth century a remarkable new microscopic stain, which involved treating a thin section of tissue with a variety of silver salts under very precise conditions, was invented by Camillo Golgi. This treatment seems, for reasons that are still wholly obscure, to select out for staining only a selection of brain cells, but to stain these almost in their entirety: cell body, major processes branching off, and minor processes off these, right to the end of the last delicate piece of tracery (figures 11 and 12).

I do not believe that anyone who has ever looked at a Golgi-stained preparation of nerve cells will ever forget it. They form one of the truly magically beautiful sights of science. To Golgi and his followers it must have been as great a revelation as that when Galileo first turned his telescope on the stars. The delicate tangle of each individual cell stands out clear and sharp, and in a strange way the pictures give a three-dimensional appearance; cells behind those which are seen clearly, appear more faintly or are only hinted at. Figures 11 and 12 show what can be seen with the Golgi technique. It is estimated that there are some ten thousand million (10^{10}) such neurons in the human cerebral cortex (though figures which put the numbers at up to a hundred times higher have also been quoted).[5] The neurons

* A micron is 10^{-4} cm.

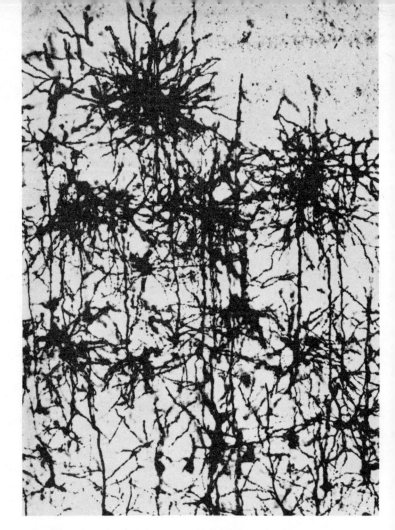

11 Brain cells stained by
the Golgi method
(Xabout 200).

12 Brain cells stained by
the Golgi method
(Xabout 300).

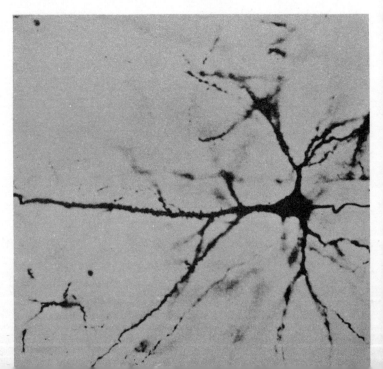

pack together in layers in the cortex of the cerebrum and of the cerebellum, and in clusters, each containing perhaps 10^7–10^8 cells, in the mini-organs attached to the brain stem below the cerebral hemispheres. Diffuse sets of neurons also occur in some regions which are largely white matter, like the medulla.

Even in the hands of the best of observers and with the most ingenious staining techniques, the light microscope can reveal only a limited amount about the internal structure of the individual neurons. To see more clearly into the cells one needs, not the light microscope with its maximum magnification of about fifteen hundred times, but the electron microscope, an invention of the 1940s and 1950s which makes possible magnifications of up to half a million. The latest electron microscopes can make individual molecules and even certain atoms visible. One does not need this high a magnification here though; a mere thirty thousand or so will reveal as much as necessary of the inside of the neuron.

Figure 13 shows a single neuron (all of the surrounding material has been blanked off in this picture to make its interpretation easier). The cell body is seen to contain a large NUC-LEUS, carrying the cellular DNA, the genetic material ultimately responsible for directing the synthesis of the PROTEIN on which the day-to-day running of the cellular economy depends. Packed into the CYTOPLASM which surrounds the nucleus are numerous oval-shaped structures; the MITOCHONDRIA, which are responsible for providing the bulk of the cell's energy requirements by oxidizing substances derived from glucose to carbon dioxide and water, and the granular RIBOSOMES, con-

13 Electron micrograph of a single neuron. See text for description. (X about 5000).

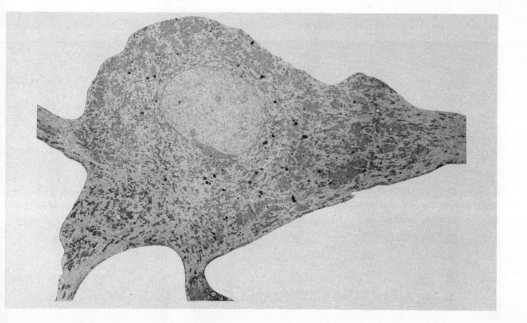

taining the RIBONUCLEIC ACID (RNA) on which the cell proteins are continuously fabricated. The cell is surrounded by a MEMBRANE, which under the electron microscope, has a characteristic sandwichlike appearance, of two parallel dark lines with a lighter space between them. It is across this membrane that much of the cell's business with the outside world is conducted. Except in the large size of its nucleus and the very large number of ribosomes, indicating an active protein-synthesizing capacity, a typical neuron under the electron microscope does not differ too much from any other cell of the body. Even its characteristic shape is harder to see in the vanishingly thin section it is necessary to cut in order to observe it with the electron microscope.

One may feel that the beauty and order revealed by the light microscope diminish into unnecessary complexity at this degree of magnification. Certainly it is harder to become as aesthetically excited by these pictures as one can be by Golgi-stained preparations, but it is important to add this knowledge of the internal structure of the cell to the synthesis of brain function.

It is always difficult for the nonmicroscopist to interpret the pictures the microscope presents. They may seem a mass of unrelated darks and lights. A prominant object seen under the microscope may turn out to be an artifact—an air bubble, or a piece of dust, or even eye-lashes, which are all many of us can see for a long time after beginning microscope work. Above all it is difficult to relate the flat, two-dimensional forms to anything approaching a three-dimensional structure. Yet the shapes so neatly laid out in section do have a three-dimensional structure. Slices through them may reveal only the corners, or even two views of the same object if it is bent back on itself and the cutting blade which makes the sections goes through it twice. What is true of the light microscope is still more true for the electron

14 Micrograph of a single neuron taken with the scanning electron microscope, a device which reveals the three-dimensional surface structure. The cell has been dissected clear of surrounding material (X about 3000).

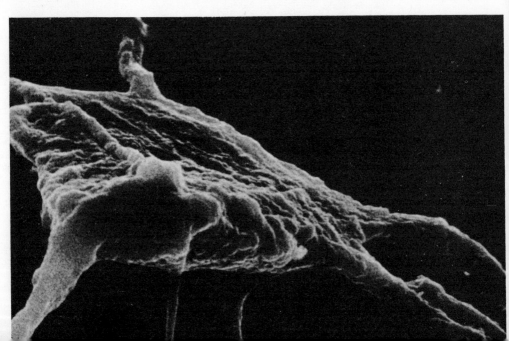

microscope. So it is perhaps helpful to show here also a picture of a single neuron made with another type of microscope, the scanning electron microscope–to help recall that not all within the brain is paper-flat and paper-thin (figure 14).

It is at this point that the technique of the biochemist[6] can be added to that of the anatomist, for biochemical methods now exist which enable a piece of the brain cortex (from a rat, for example) to be disrupted so gently as to leave a large portion of the neurons relatively undamaged, but separated from each other and the surrounding tissue.[7] These neurons can then be studied in isolation. A slightly more vigorous disruption technique breaks the external cell membrane and shakes the internal contents of the cell loose into suspension: a porridge of nuclei, mitochondria, ribosomes, bits of membrane, etc. This mixture can then be separated into its individual components by taking advantage of their different physical properties–the nuclei are the heaviest, followed by the mitochondria and so on. A technique known as CENTRIFUGATION, which subjects the porridge of subcellular particles to high gravitational fields by whirling them in an ultracentrifuge–the biochemical equivalent of a spin-drier–enables the individual classes of particles to be separated.

Cell Processes

What of the cell processes? Even within the brain they may be many millimeters long. Those running along the spinal cord or from the cord outwards into the periphery of the body, forming the nerve fibers, may be many centimeters long, though only a few microns in diameter. As a percentage of the total cell volume, the processes may indeed contribute the majority. In one type of neuron in the cerebellum, for instance, the volume of the cell processes is up to 95 percent, the cell bodies only 5 percent, of the total.

One of the great debates among neuroanatomists at the end of the nineteenth century related to these processes, or DENDRITES as they are called (i.e. "little fingers"). One school of thought, founded by Gerlach in 1871 and later led by Golgi, maintained that they were continuous within the brain, so that every neuron was connected by dendrites to all others to form a complete tissue web. Another, originated by Hiss in 1886 and championed by the Spaniard Santiago Ramon y Cajal, claimed otherwise. This second school maintained that each cell and its processes were separate. At points the processes touched, but there was not continuity of tissue. One cell stopped, with its border close to that of the next cell. These border points, or junctions, were called SYNAPSES by Charles Sherrington in 1897 (from the

Greek word meaning "to clasp"). Cajal took the concept of the synapses and the non-continuity of brain cells and combined them into the *neuronal theory*. It was in fact to prove correct, and Cajal used Golgi's own staining techniques to demonstrate it to be so. Golgi never conceded though, and neither scientist would speak to the other when they finally met to receive the joint award of the Nobel Prize for Medicine and Physiology in 1906.[8]

Santiago Ramon y Cajal was undoubtedly one of the greatest microscopists ever, and his drawings of the cells he saw are still regarded as so accurate that they are used to illustrate standard

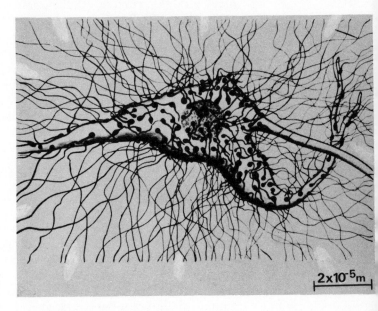

2x10⁻⁵m

15 Drawing of a single neuron and synapses upon in by Ramon y Cajal.

neuroanatomy texts even today. Figure 15 shows one of his drawings of neurons and their processes. Each neuron is composed of a cell body, branching processes, or dendrites, and one generally longer process which can branch in its turn called an AXON (figure 16). It is down this axon that, as will become clear in the next chapter, the nerve impulses are propagated. Higher power magnification of the dendrites (figure 12) shows that many of them branch into innumerable little twiglets, known as DENDRITIC SPINES. The axon branches at its ends to make synaptic contacts with the dendritic spines or cell bodies of other neurons, and it is across these synapses that one neuron signals to another. The message travels in turn down the dendrites and through the cell body to the second neuron, resulting, under the appropriate circumstances, in an impulse traveling down the axon of the second neuron. The synapses between the cells can be seen under high-power magnification as swellings at the end of

16 Schematic drawing of a single motor neuron, showing its functional components: cell body, axon, dendrites and synapses onto the muscle.

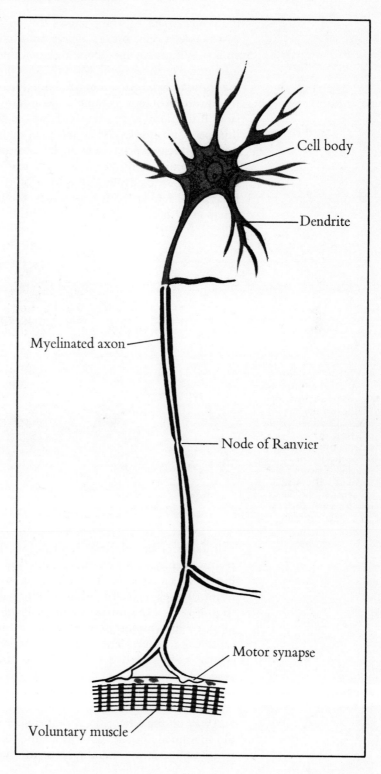

Cell body

Dendrite

Myelinated axon

Node of Ranvier

Motor synapse

Voluntary muscle

the axonal branches. The synapses are the points at which signals pass between cells, providing the brain with the possibility of coding, classifying and operating upon information arriving at it from the outside world. Most theories of brain action, including those to be presented in this book, depend upon the idea of the operation of these synapses as devices for processing information. If the number of nerve cells within the brain is large, the number of synapses is astronomical. In some brain regions in the monkey each neuron may make upwards of ten thousand synaptic connections with its neighbours.[9] With 10^{10} neurons, this would be equivalent to a total of 10^{14} synaptic contacts in a single human cortex, or thirty thousand times as many synapses as there are people in the world.

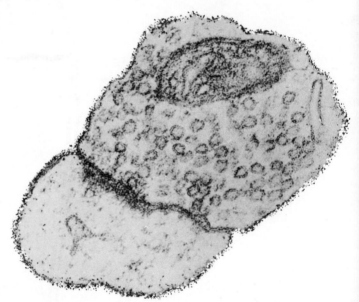

17 A single synapse under the electron microscope. All the surrounding material has been blanked off. Note the characteristic thickening of the membrane at the junction between pre- and post synaptic sides of the synapse, and the vesicles which pack the pre-synaptic swelling.

It requires the electron microscope though, to show the reality of Cajal's vision of synaptic junctions between cells. Figure 17 shows what he could never see, the actual synaptic terminal itself revealed in all its internal structure. Beside it (figure 18) is a reconstruction of what this shape may look like in three dimensions. The axon swells at its terminal into a capsulelike shape. The capsule contains mitochondria, the cellular energy providers, and a mass of small almost circular objects known as SYNAPTIC VESICLES, which are believed to be related to the process of transmission between cells across the synaptic junction.

Away on the other side of the synapse, the *post-synaptic* side, the membrane of the dendrite of the second cell can be seen lying alongside the membrane of the synapse itself. The gap

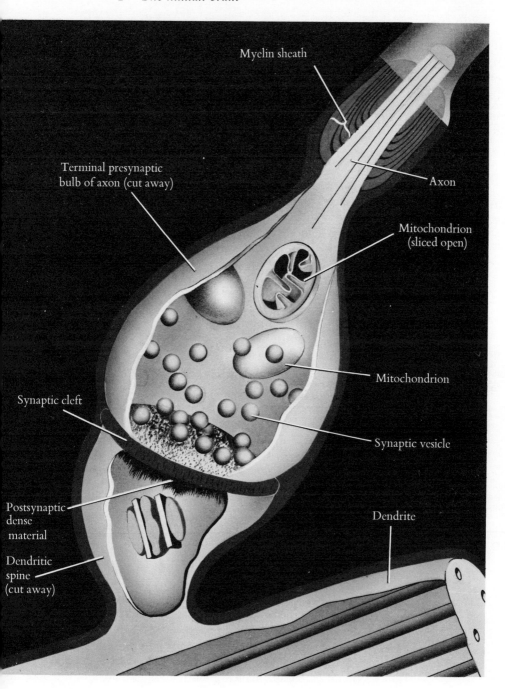

Myelin sheath

Terminal presynaptic
bulb of axon (cut away)

Axon

Mitochondrion
(sliced open)

Mitochondrion

Synaptic cleft

Synaptic vesicle

Postsynaptic
dense
material

Dendrite

Dendritic
spine
(cut away)

18 Reconstruction of
what a synapse may look
like in three dimensions.

between them, the synaptic cleft, only two-millionths of a centimeter across, is that which the message, running down the axon of the first cell, must jump to arrive at the second cell. This picture is the vindication of Cajal as a microscopist, who could just distinguish structures the interpretation of which demanded a degree of magnification his instruments could not achieve, but which he could intuit must indeed be so.

Once again, at the hierarchical level below that of the electron microscope, the biochemist takes over. Just as methods exist for the separation of individual neurons and their subcellular components, so too they exist for the separation of synaptic terminals. A surprisingly large proportion of the brain cortex is composed of synapses—perhaps 10 percent of the total volume. Gentle mincing of the cortex in an appropriate solution results in a "pinching off" of the synaptic terminals from their axons. The membranes apparently reseal at the point of breakage, launching a separated synapse, like a space capsule, into suspension. Variations of the centrifugation technique discussed on page 51 enable a preparation of almost pure synapses to be made available for biochemical and physiological analysis.[10] The results of such analyses will become apparent in the next chapter.

Axons

Each nerve cell then consists of four major parts, the dendrites on which other cells synapse, the cell body, the axon down which the messages accumulated at the cell-body pass, and the synapses at which the cell communicates with others. We need to say a little more about the axon and its relationship to those structures that have so far been referred to rather loosely as "nerves" running up through the spinal cord, from cord to periphery and from region to region of the brain in the white matter. These too are axons, but outside the gray regions of the brain each axon is surrounded by a sheath which provides a thick outer tube around it, like the plastic or rubber insulation of an electric cable. These sheaths are composed of a fatty material known as MYELIN and are much thicker than the axon itself. One of the functions of these sheaths is precisely that suggested by the comparison with the rubber tube, to insulate each axon from its neighbors, thus preventing confusing the message passing down each. It is the great mass of myelin surrounding the axons running between the brain regions which gives the white matter of the brain its characteristic appearance, by contrast with the gray, and also helps account for the large amount of fatty substances like cholesterol which are found as so striking a feature of any chemical analysis of the brain.

Outside the gray region of the brain axons travel together in organized bundles, or NERVE TRACTS, connecting a group of neurons in one region with those in another. Nerves running into the brain, like the optic nerves, or to and from the spinal cord, are bundles of such myelin-sheathed axons, each connected to individual cells. A single bundle, such as the optic nerve, passing from the eye to the brain, may contain as many as 10^6 such individual axons.

The Structure of the Cortex: Glia

One of the features of the cortex which was noted by Cajal and later microscopists, was that it shows a measure of internal structure. It does not require much imagination (and a lot of microscopy depends on the use of this sort of visual imagination) to see, in the Golgi-stained section of figure 11, the cortex as consisting of a series of layers of cells bearing a definite relationship to each other, and running like geological strata, parallel to the surface of the cortex. Thus some layers consist predominantly of pyramidally-shaped neurons, some of stellate (star-shaped) cells, while others are mainly dendritic regions, etc. The eye of faith can distinguish at least six of these layers in the cerebral cortex, while in the cerebellar cortex an even sharper stratification into layers of fibers, large and small neurons can be seen. This stratification enhances the impression that the cortex is not just a random collection of cells making chance connections with their neighbors, but rather that there is a regular and precise wiring diagram involved, by which the connections between individual cells are specified.

The neurons, however, are not the only cells present in the cortex. In fact, in large regions it is difficult to see neurons at all. Although some entire layers are almost filled with cell bodies and others with their twisting dendritic and axonal processes, embedded within them or closely adjacent to the neurons themselves lie quite different cells, smaller than the neuron, either unbranched or surrounded with an aura of short stubby processes like a sea urchin.

These cells are known as GLIA (from the Latin for "glue") for they appear to stick and seal up all the available space in the cortex, outnumbering the neurons by about ten to one. Their real function in the brain system is far from clear. It has been proposed that, curling around the neuron and its processes as they do, they provide it with essential nutrients which it cannot synthesize itself, or that they serve to regulate the immediate micro-environment of the neuron, mopping up unwanted substances and keeping it cushioned and insulated from the outside world. One audacious physiologist even went so far as to propose that it was the glia, and not the neurons, which were the seat of the brain's memory.[11] One of the few functions that can with certainty be ascribed to them is that of fabricating the myelin sheaths in which the long-distance axons are wrapped. Fortunately, biochemical methods now also exist to separate out the glial cells from the rest of the brain tissues and study them separately. These techniques may yet provide the elusive clue to the function of these cells.

With neurons and their processes, glia and blood capillaries, the brain's gray matter is a fairly crowded place. More crowded with cells indeed than any other tissue in the body. Take a typical tissue, like the liver, say, and from electron microscopic and biochemical studies it would seem that some 20 percent or more of the total volume of the tissue is outside the cells; an EXTRACELLULAR SPACE which surrounds individual cells with a bathing fluid which resembles filtered blood or cerebrospinal fluid in composition. It is through this extracellular space that nutrients diffuse to the cell from the circulating blood, and waste products or chemicals synthesized for export, hormones for instance, leave the cell and enter the circulation.

By contrast, the brain's extracellular space is very small. Estimates vary, but a consensus would put it at around 7 to 12 percent

19 An electron micrograph of a section through the cerebral cortex, including neuronal cell bodies, glia, dendritic and axonal processes and synapses. The synapse of Fig. 17 is an centre. (X about 10,000).

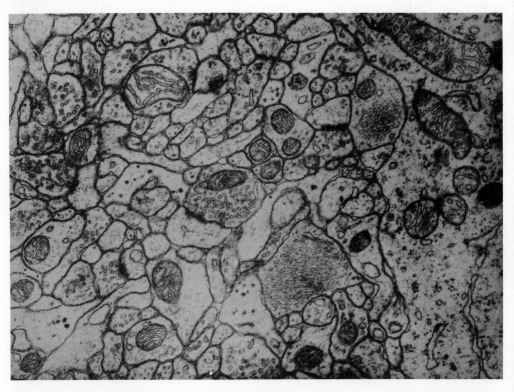

of the total volume (about the theoretical minimum possible for the packing together of more or less spherical objects). This means that the processes, cell bodies and synapses are extremely close-packed and intertwined, leaving almost no room for material to enter or leave the tissue by way of the extracellular space. This presents the brain a considerable problem in obtaining nutrients or removing waste matter. It is almost as if a barrier existed between brain and blood (some workers have indeed referred to a BLOOD-BRAIN BARRIER).[12] One effect of this barrier is to make the brain more resistant than it might otherwise be to assault by toxic or unpleasant substances in the circulating bloodstream, which find it harder to enter the brain than, say, the liver. The close-packing has even led some to propose, improbably in my view, that for any substance to enter a neuron from the blood it must pass into the glial cells, and then out again. I think otherwise: there is space enough between the cells–but only just. Be that dispute as it may, the close-packing of the brain contributes to its almost frightening complexity when looked at under the electron microscope. We can end this chapter with an electron micrograph of a typical piece of cortex–not one blanked off just to show the neuron or the synapse (figure 19). The mass of processes, structures and interactions possible within this web beggars both description and mathematicization. The fascination is almost akin to terror, of such complexity, multiplied so many times, within every individual human's head. If consciousness is possible anywhere as a result of the interactions of cells and biological systems, then it is surely here.

3 The Electrical Maze

In the last chapter the brain was considered as a static, frozen system, a pickled three-dimensional model of itself. Its cells and connections were frozen at an instant of time so that regions could be plucked apart anatomically, like fruit from the brain stem, examined microscopically in their most intimate details, their composition identified chemically. Now, having established this pattern of connections, we can unfreeze again, to put back the life and motion into the system once more. To do this the techniques not so much of the anatomist but of the physiologist and biochemist are required.

Nerves transmit information electrically. This was suspected for many years, but only given reasonable certainty following the famous eighteenth-century observation by Luigi Galvani, who noted the twitches of a frog's legs when connected to a fortuitous battery made of different metals—though he never really understood the phenomenon he had discovered. This did no more at first, perhaps, than give a new meaning to those "vital spirits" which the nerves carried and which had for so long before been the working models of brain theorists, although it did turn out to be a highly fashionable meaning so far as the nineteenth century was concerned, with its overtones of animal magnetism and hypnosis. By the mid-nineteenth century it was known that not only was the nerve-muscle mechanism electrical in nature, but that when a signal passed down a nerve it did so as a wave of electricity, a pulse which passed from the cell body to the end of the nerve fiber. This pulse is the ACTION POTENTIAL (the reason for the name will become apparent shortly). In today's terms, the language of the brain, in which the neurons transmit information is electric.

To be turned to practical use the demonstration of the electrical properties of the nervous system needed to be made the subject of experiments. Devices had to be developed, first for electrically stimulating particular nerves and for recording the twitch from the muscles, later for recording the electrical events that occurred in the same nerve that was being stimulated, or one connected to it by way of a synapse. The development and exploitation of these techniques was above all the achievement of the Cambridge school of neurophysiology of Sherrington and his followers in the late nineteenth and early twentieth centuries.[1] We shall not pursue here the sequence of questions asked historically of these preparations. Historically, the study of the electrical properties of the brain system as a whole has gone on simultaneously with the exploration of the single cell; studies at one hierarchical level have informed and illuminated those at another. However, it is easiest to begin with a consideration of the electrical properties of the single neuron, and the way these electrical properties relate to its function. Only then, in the next chapter, will the linkage of neurons into groups, networks and assemblages be considered.

Membrane Potentials

Chapter 1, in discussing models and analogies for the brain, was rather disparaging of that analog which regarded the brain as a telephone exchange. The single axon is, in fact, the one part of the system for which that analogy may be appropriate, for its function may indeed be compared to that of a telephone wire, and the bundle of myelinated axons making up a nerve fiber to a telephone cable. How to study the mechanism of this message-conducting tube?

If the signal is passed down the tube as an electrical pulse, to study its propagation effectively it is necessary to place one fine electrically-conducting wire (an ELECTRODE) inside the tube, another outside, and measure the voltage across a particular region of the tube's surface.* One problem in doing this is that most myelinated axons are very thin, and it is difficult to put an electrode inside them, however fine it is made, without damaging them irretrievably. The technical solution to this problem was suggested in the 1930s by J. Z. Young, who was investigating the anatomy of the sea squid. He noted that one of the non-myelinated axons of the squid was particularly large – it could go up in diameter to almost a millimeter. In 1939, Alan Hodgkin and Andrew Huxley were able to develop an electrode with a fine enough tip to put inside the axon without damaging it and the squid giant axon became the key preparation with which to study axon mechanisms.

If an electrode with a fine tip (a MICROELECTRODE perhaps no more than a micron in diameter) is gently pushed through the

---

* We shall have frequent need to mention ELECTRODES in what follows, and it should therefore be emphasized that they come in two general classes. Those, like the ones discussed here, which are used to *record* the electrical state of the cells, are essentially measuring devices. Another class of electrode can be used to administer a small electric shock to the cell. This stimulates the cell and may cause it to respond by transmitting a signal, the effects of which can then be analyzed. These electrodes, which are very similar in construction to recording electrodes, are called *stimulating* electrodes.

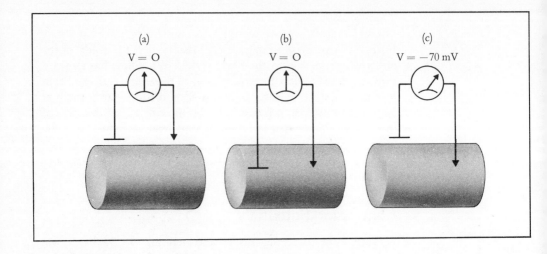

(a) V = O

(b) V = O

(c) V = −70 mV

20 Measurement of the resting membrane potential. (a): two electrodes at any location outside the resting nerve membrane always record a zero potential difference. (b): two electrodes at any location within the nerve fiber always record a zero potential difference. (c): one electrode outside and one inside the fiber in any location always record the full resting membrane potential of approximately −70mV.

external cell membrane into any living cell, from the amoeba to the human red blood cell or neuron, while a second electrode is placed on the external surface of the cell or in the surrounding fluid, and the two are connected up through a voltmeter, the voltmeter will record a potential difference (a voltage) between the inside and the outside of the cell. For most cells, this voltage across the external membrane is of the order of seventy to one hundred millivolts (thousandths of a volt) with the inside of the cell negative, and the outside positive (figure 20).

This potential difference does not sound very large. None the less, it is the key to the electrically excitable properties of nerve and muscle. The chemical reasons why the membrane potential exists are now well understood, and are discussed in more detail in Appendix 1; for readers not interested in the detailed mechanism it is enough to know that it exists, and is known as the cell's RESTING MEMBRANE POTENTIAL.[2]

In summary, the potential is caused by the uneven distribution of the positively charged IONS of sodium (Na^+) and potassium (K^+) across the cell membrane and the large negatively charged protein molecules present in solution inside the cells. The potential sounds less tiny if it is recalled that the cell membrane is only one-millionth of a centimeter across. Expressed as a voltage across a distance of a centimeter, the resting potential turns out to be one hundred thousand volts per centimeter–quite a tidy charge!

The Action Potential: The Axon

All the regions of the neuron–dendrites, cell body, axon, synapses–as well as the glial cells, maintain a resting potential of this sort, as do almost all other living cells. What distinguishes the neuronal cell membrane from that of other cells is the property illustrated by the axon in the following experiment.

Suppose there is an electrode recording from the axon at a particular spot along its length and registering a steady 70 millivolts negative. Now suppose that, some distance away from the recording electrode, the axon is stimulated–by an electric shock, or mechanically, or even with certain chemicals. Within a very brief space of time after the stimulation, the reading of the voltmeter attached to the recording electrode will alter; it will change rapidly from 70 millivolts negative toward zero. Then the polarity of the membrane will briefly reverse, so that the needle of the voltmeter swings from negative to read up to as much as 40 millivolts positive. Almost at once, the voltage will decline to zero again, and back to, or beyond, the original level of − 70 millivolts. The entire process

21 The passage of an action potential in a squid giant axon.

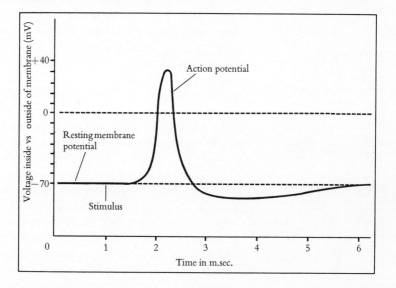

is completed in less than a thousandth of a second (a millisecond). The recording electrode has registered the passage of an action potential down the axon. Graphically the process is shown in figure 21.

If the events at several different points along the length of the axon were to be recorded, it would be seen that the action potential started at the point of shock or stimulation of the axon and passed along it in both directions from the origin, like a wave. The speed at which the action potential traversed the axon depends on a number of factors–particularly the axon diameter; in a typical axon the wave may travel at about twenty-five meters per second. This then is at last the unique property of the neuronal cell membrane: its capacity to conduct an action potential. The neuronal membrane is EXCITABLE.

There are a number of features to note about the conduction

of the action potential along the axon. First, the wave can travel in either direction along the axon from the site of the initial disturbance–the axon is indifferent to the direction in which it conducts. Second, whatever the magnitude of the initial excitation, provided it is above a certain THRESHOLD size, the size of the action potential does not alter. The shape and size of the wave drawn in figure 21 would be identical *whatever* the magnitude of the stimulus that has caused it. This phenomenon of constancy of wave form and size is known as the ALL-OR-NONE LAW of axon transmission.

These rules make clear in what sense it is accurate to use a telephone-cable analogy in relation to the axon. The axon carries one type of signal, and one only, faithfully and at some speed, from one end to the other. It cannot even have the luxury of the variety of a morse-code operator, who can at least vary dots and dashes. The axon's language is entirely one of dots. How then can more than the crudest sort of yes/no information be transferred along the axon? The one aspect of the axonal signal which is modifiable, despite these constraints, is the FREQUENCY of response. The axon could transmit no action potential, or one a minute, or one a second, or a hundred a second, or a fluctuating number, all depending on the nature of the incoming message. It is the frequency of signal which functions as the basis of the axonal information transfer system.

There is however a limit to the number of impulses that can be conducted in a given time. For a certain period after an impulse has passed, a second stimulation will not result in a signal; the axon is temporarily incapable of conducting. This incapacity lasts for a period of about a millisecond following the initiation of the impulse, a period known as the ABSOLUTE REFRACTORY PERIOD, during which no further impulse can be transmitted. This refractory period provides an absolute upper limit to the frequency at which signals can be transmitted down the axon. There is no lower limit provided within the axon. The lower limit is to all intents and purposes set not by the axon but by the synapse. Below a certain frequency the post-synaptic cell will not respond to the message.

As with the resting potential, so with the action potential; it is possible to provide a detailed molecular mechanism for the way it works. The model depends on the squid axon experiments of Hodgkin and Huxley, and it provides a scheme whereby a local breakdown of the membrane potential at any point along the axon (a DEPOLARIZATION) produced by some stimulus above a certain threshold, results in a wave of activity spreading along the axon. During this wave the charged ions of sodium (Na^+) and potassium (K^+), whose asymmetric distribution across the membrane maintain the resting potential, move across the membrane. Sodium enters and potassium leaves the axon. The reversal of polarity shown in figure 21 reflects this changed distribution. Once the wave has passed, the cell expends energy, derived from the oxidation of glucose, on restoring the original distribution of sodium and potassium. Again, it is not necessary to explore the mechanism in greater detail here. Appendix 2 goes rather further for those who are interested.

Synapse

Messages arrive at the synapse from the axon in the form of action potentials. They arrive with that degree of certainty and invariance which reminds one of the leaden tones of that Victorian poet on the sickness of a great man:

> *Across the wires the electric message came*
> *He is no better, he is much the same.*

The variations permitted to the action potentials are neither in magnitude nor form, but only frequency. Not much plasticity about the axon; it either does or doesn't fire. It is to the synapse that we must look to begin to introduce that element of variance which must be the key to the nervous system, which must distinguish it from an inevitable system in which, for a given input, there is an invariant output response. For it is at the synapse that it will be decided whether or not the next cell will fire in its turn. The synapse is a type of valve or gate. If the post-synaptic cell fired invariantly whenever an action potential arrived down the axon from the propagating cell, there would be no point in having a synapse. The axon might as well continue unbroken to the end of the axon of the second cell. No modification could ever occur. The axon has no choice but to fire. At the synapse between cells lies the choice point which converts the nervous system from a certain, predictable and dull one into an uncertain, probabilistic and hence interesting system.[3] Consciousness, learning and intelligence are all synapse-dependent. It is not too strong to say that the evolution of humanity followed the evolution of the synapse.

For a long time it was thought both that there was actual continuity of internal cell cytoplasm at the synapse, and that synapses were made wherever two nerve processes were adjacent. As is the case with nearly all scientific theories, it was not discarded as a result of some Pauline—or even logical and evidence-based—conversion on the part of the nerve-net theorists. It was merely that the adherents to the nerve-net theory grew old and died, protesting their belief to the last—as late as 1940 in some instances. To the generation which replaced them there was no room for doubt: neurons and not nets were the way the system worked. Like old soldiers, old scientific ideas do not die, they merely fade away. The universality of this phenomenon in science has been remarked upon by scientific historians and social philosophers like Thomas Kuhn in relation to physics and some aspects of nineteenth-century biology. We lack as yet an adequate history of neurobiology which is more than hagiographic, an account of the contributions of great men to the onward march of science, but in such a history the erroneous ideas of nerve nets and the misunderstanding of the rôle of the synapse which followed them must play as full a part as ideas we regard today as valid. For it is the interplay of hypothesis and experiment, the controversy, which is important about such interpretations, providing the forward dynamic of the subject.

The dispute over nerve nets and neurons, resolved but not conceded before 1910, gave way to a new one concerning the synapse. What was the relationship of the pre- and post-synaptic cells at this point, and what was the mode of conduction between them? By analogy with the axon, the simplest hypothesis was that of electrical conduction by ion discharge. And perhaps the electrical conduction would be facilitated if, not only did the two cells come close together at this point, but also that their membranes actually fused into a single dividing membrane. The case for such electrical synapses and the single membrane was argued through the 1930s and 1940s. John Eccles, who is more than most individuals responsible for our contemporary interpretation of synapse function, has described the controversy, though without appreciating its neat illustrative value from the point of view of the philosophy of science, in his book *Physiology of Synapses*.[4] He himself began as a protagonist of the electrical model of synapse function, but later abandoned this view in favor of that of chemical transmission. Without further elaborating this controversy here, the clear relationship to the working model of the brain the experimenters were testing is worth noting. A certain, determinate cortex is served best by certain, electrically operating synapses. Introduce a gap between synapses, a junction with room for uncertainty, and the determinate brain becomes less certain, more probabilistic, more dependent upon events external to the neuron which can affect transmission at the synapse in that critical gap between pre- and post-synaptic cells.

Like many disputes, that over the synapse had to depend for its final resolution on new technology, in this case the electron microscope, which could provide pictures at sufficiently high magnification to make clear the demarcation between pre- and post-synaptic sides of the system and the cleft between them (figure 17). Studying the synapse was made easier by the use, not of a brain or spinal cord synapse – or even a neuron/neuron synapse at all – but the synapse between nerve and muscle, the ultimate point of the nerve effector system, at which signals coming along the nerve are converted into commands for the muscle to contract. The use of the NEUROMUSCULAR JUNCTION and its properties as a model synapse – its microscopic structure is different from that of the synapses of the central nervous system but its functioning does not appear to be too dissimilar – owes much to another London group, led by Bernhard Katz, who shared the Nobel Prize in 1970 for his rôle in elucidating synapse mechanisms.[5] But here we shall talk mainly about the workings of the central synapses, only bearing in mind that many of their properties have been described by analogy with the peripheral neuromuscular junction.

Although in some parts of some nervous systems – that of the crustacean, for example – electrical synapses with very close contact between the membranes of the pre- and post-synaptic cells exist, the typical synapse of the brain is that of figure 17. The key to the understanding of synaptic mechanisms comes from the recognition that the axonal signals arriving at the synapse in the form of action potentials of particular frequencies are translated by the synapse into signals for the triggering of a chemical mechanism. The release of particular chemical substances which diffuse across the gap between the pre- and post-synaptic membranes and interact at the post-synaptic side with particular receptors, thereby triggers a sequence of post-synaptic events which may result in due course in the firing of the post-synaptic neuron.

The chemicals whose release is the rationale of the workings of the synapse are known collectively as TRANSMITTER SUBSTANCES (EXCITATORY and INHIBITORY). Once again, their discovery was first made in the PERIPHERAL NERVOUS SYSTEM and only later extrapolated back to the central brain. As far back as the beginning of this century it had been noted that certain parts of the peripheral nervous system (the AUTONOMIC SYSTEM, so-called because believed to be outside conscious control, although it is now known that this is not strictly true) when stimulated, produced effects remarkably similar to those of some hormones which had then only recently been discovered. There are two such parts of the autonomic nervous system operating within the body, whose activities are more or less in opposition to each other: the so-called SYMPATHETIC and PARASYMPATHETIC NERVOUS SYSTEMS. For example, the effect of stimulating the sympathetic nerve which travels to the heart is to speed up the heart rate, while the effect of stimulating the parasympathetic is to slow it; the effect of the hormone ADRENALIN (secreted by the adrenal gland which lies just above the kidneys) is also to speed up the heart in the same way as the sympathetic system. Other properties of the sympathetic system throughout the body, on muscular contraction, etc., are all mimicked by the hormone adrenalin, and the analogy was early remarked upon. It remained however merely an analogy, until in a series of classic experiments in the 1920s Otto Loewi in Germany was able to show that the parasympathetic and sympathetic nervous systems actually worked by secreting chemical transmitters. Although that of the parasympathetic was the substance ACETYLCHOLINE, which has no direct hormonal equivalent, the sympathetic secreted NORADRENALIN, a substance very similar to that produced by the hormone-generating adrenal gland. This striking relationship between nervous and hormonal effects is something we shall return to when considering the evolution of the nervous system, for it is a coincidence too strong to ignore.

The rôle of the nervous transmitters in the peripheral nervous system was known for many decades before it could be shown that a similar mechanism operated in the brain itself, although this had been proposed by Sherrington's pupil E. D. Adrian in Cambridge as early as 1924. It could be established in the peripheral system because the effects of stimulating or inhibiting the heartbeat for example, were large and easily measurable. Direct application of acetylcholine or adrenalin to the heart could mimic the effect of nerve stimulation, and other control experiments were relatively easy to perform. To show the same effect centrally, though, more complex experimental devices were needed – in particular the development of elaborate recording techniques and electrodes.

Present-day recording electrodes for studying transmitter substances in the brain are not made of metal, but are glass tubes filled with a conducting solution and with tips no more than half a micron in diameter, which can be inserted into the post-synaptic cell. A series of additional fine-tipped glass tubes are welded to the recording electrode. Five- or seven-barreled electrodes are now common. The electrodes which are not being used for recording are filled with solutions of substances like noradrenalin or acetylcholine which are suspected of being transmitters. Alone or in combination, minute quantities of these are expelled from the external barrels of the electrode while the changes in potential in the post-synaptic cell are measured through the recording electrode.[6] The technique is called IONTOPHORESIS and has proved of considerable value, not only in identifying possible transmitters, but also in investigating the effects of drugs upon these transmitters. For the chemical synapse with its transmitters is the site of action of very many agents which affect the functioning of the nervous system.

But unequivocally identifying transmitters within the central nervous system has not proved an easy task. One of the few known to play a part is acetylcholine. Adrenalin may not be a central transmitter at all, but certain substances chemically related to it, noradrenalin, SEROTONIN and DOPAMINE, are, or at least are suggested to be. There may be very many others. It seems probable that any one neuron contains only a single type of transmitter operative at all of its synaptic terminals, and that for at least some multisynaptic pathways the same transmitter is implicated in each synapse in turn along the path. This possibility has led to some ingenious and rather beautiful studies of systems involving certain transmitters which take advantage of the fact that the substances concerned have the properties of fluorescing brilliantly when exposed to light of certain wavelengths. Photomicrographs show the neurons containing fluorescent transmitters standing out beautifully but eerily against a dark background (figure 22).

On the basis of what has so far been described in this chapter, it is now possible to ascribe a rôle to those round, dark-staining vesicles which electron microscopy revealed as packed within the synapse (figure 17). They appear to contain high concentrations of transmitter substances. During the 1950s, Katz and his colleagues, in a series of experiments using the neuromuscular synapse model system, showed that transmitter release across the gap between pre- and post-synaptic membranes occurs at a low rate all the time, but that it increases in response to action potentials arriving down the axon. Katz was able to show that the amount of transmitter released in response to stimulation is not smoothly variable, but that it is released in tiny packets, or QUANTA (by analogy with quantum theory in physics). The post-synaptic membrane is not just flooded with transmitter only in response to an axonal signal. Instead, it is being continuously bombarded with packages, each containing a prescribed amount of transmitter.

This quantal transmitter release, which has been amply confirmed, together with the existence of vesicles apparently packed with transmitter within the synapse itself, led to the seemingly obvious proposition that each quantum of transmitter was equivalent to one vesicle as seen under the electron microscope; that during transmission the vesicles move from the inside of the synapse to its membrane, where they expel their charge of transmitter into the synaptic cleft, to diffuse across to the post-synaptic side.[7]

This would have been such a neat relationship of electron microscopic structure to cell function (and the structure/function relationship in biology is one of the most powerful of unifying concepts, which pervades biological thinking and experimenta-

tion) that it is sad to record that nearly a decade of experimentation, both with synapses *in situ* in the nervous system and with
synapse preparations isolated biochemically has failed to confirm
that it actually occurs.[8]

Even if the rôle of the vesicles is annoyingly unclear and un-
proven, arrival of the action potential must trigger the release
of the transmitter from its stored form within the synapse and
into the synaptic cleft. Perhaps the change in the ionic environment of the synapse as a result of the changing potassium and
sodium levels associated with the action potential can function
as the trigger for increasing transmitter release, or perhaps there
are other intervening steps—and certainly the way in which
mitochondria are packed into the synapse, as the electron microscope pictures show, suggests that a substantial expenditure of
energy is required in synaptic function. This energy must be
involved both in the chemical synthesis and the subsequent
release of the transmitter substance. Thus in synapses which
utilize the transmitter acetylcholine it can be shown that the
enzyme systems required to fabricate the substance from the
two simpler molecules acetate and choline, at the expense of
cellular energy, are present. The synapse is thus more vulnerable
than the axon, which is capable of conducting up to a hundred
thousand impulses before fading away, even after poisoning. In
the synapse, in the absence of glucose or oxygen, or in the
presence of poisons, the slack is less by several orders of magnitude. In this, as in other respects, the synapse is the weak link in
the chain of nervous events.

The Post-synaptic Events

Once released into the gap, the transmitter diffuses across to the
post-synaptic side. The time taken to do so, the delay in transmission, is in neuronal terms quite substantial. From 0·3 to 1·0
milliseconds may be involved. The cleft, although almost
unimaginably narrow by nonmicroscopic standards, still represents a journey many times the length of a transmitter molecule.
While on this journey, the transmitter is vulnerable, as we shall
see later, to chemical attack.

Waiting to receive the transmitter at the post-synaptic side
are a set of precisely tailored receptor molecules. Recent evidence, based on studies with molecules which closely resemble
acetylcholine in structure, suggests that the receptors clasp hold
of the transmitter molecule. As they bind it, their own shape
becomes modified.[9] The receptors are embedded in the cell
membrane, whose structure, it will be recalled from what was
said about membrane permeability and axonal transmission, is
crucial to the maintenance of the resting potential. A change in

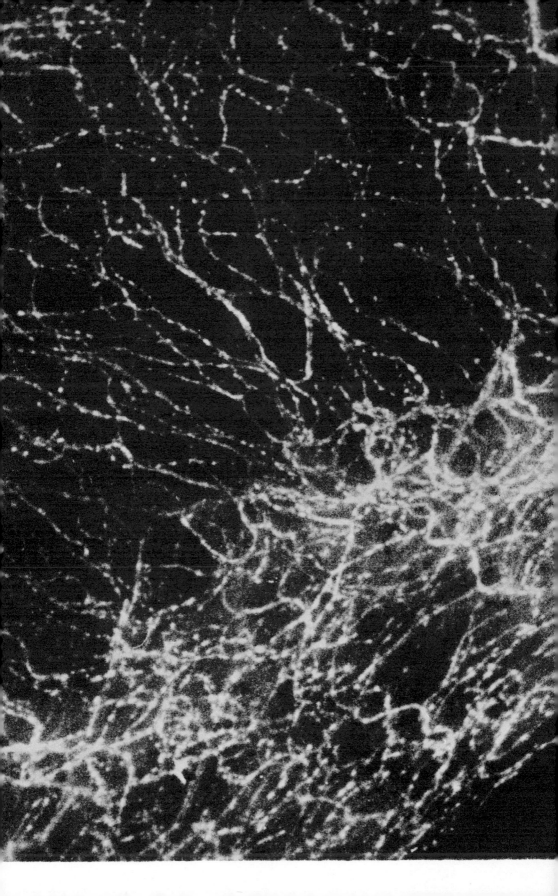

the membrane structure results in a change in permeability to the entry and exit of ions, and hence results in a change of polarization.

In the case of an excitatory transmitter the change in polarization is a decrease of the resting potential towards zero—a depolarization. If this depolarization goes beyond a certain threshold, as will be clear from what was said earlier about the propagation of an action potential, a wave of depolarization will be triggered; the post-synaptic neuron will fire. It has, however, to reach that threshold. How can this be achieved? The action potential is an all-or-none phenomenon. The axon either transmits or it does not, and if it does not, the initial stimulus merely dies away. At the post-synaptic membrane though, this need not be the case. The arrival of a small amount of transmitter —a quantum say—will cause a small depolarization, not enough to trigger an action potential which will spread, but enough to be measured as a miniature EXCITATORY POST-SYNAPTIC POTENTIAL (EPSP).

If more transmitter arrives, before the first EPSP has had time to decline, either a short distance away in space at an adjacent synapse, or a short period away in time at the same synapse, the effect of the second quantum of transmitter will be added to that of the first; they will SUMMATE. If enough quanta of transmitter arrive within a circumscribed area or time the summation will build up until the threshold for the action potential is reached. The trigger will be pulled; the cell will fire an impulse down its own axon. The receptors allow the post-synaptic neuron to compute the strength of the signal arriving at it; if it is merely the continuous random release of a few quanta of transmitter, the EPSPs will rarely be of sufficient magnitude for the cell to fire. If the quanta of transmitter arrive fast enough, firing will occur.

However, the transmitter cannot be allowed to accumulate at the post-synaptic site, or a state of permanent depolarization would occur. The post-synaptic neuron would not get a measure of how frequently the pre-synaptic neuron was firing, or how many adjacent synapses were operating in conjunction. Instead, transmitter would build up indefinitely, and the cell would enter a state of steady maximal excitation. To prevent this happening the post-synaptic cell must have a mechanism for destroying the transmitter almost as soon as it arrives. This indeed it has. It has enzyme systems which break down the transmitter molecules into inactive substances; in the case of acetylcholine the enzyme is CHOLINESTERASE, which reconverts it to acetate and choline, just as on the pre-synaptic side acetylcholine had to be fabricated from acetate and choline in the first instance.

We are now in a position to appreciate the range of vulnerability of the synapse. If the transmitter is destroyed in the cleft, and cannot reach the receptors, the synaptic mechanism will not function. If a chemical analogous to the transmitter is introduced which becomes trapped by the receptor sites but cannot be removed by the destroying enzyme, the synaptic mechanism will not function. If the enzyme which destroys the transmitter is inactivated or poisoned, the synaptic mechanism will not function. Examples of all these types of malfunctions are known. CURARE (the poison once used by South American Indians on their arrow tips) produces a muscular paralysis by blocking receptor sites for acetylcholine such as the neuromuscular junction. Messages instructing the muscle to contract simply cannot get through, and paralysis follows (death from curare results from paralysis of the respiratory muscles, preventing breathing).

An even more effective type of poison has been developed by contemporary military technology, first in Germany during the Second World War and later in Britain's chemical warfare plant at Porton Down. Organic phosphorus-containing compounds which inhibit the enzyme cholinesterase have been synthesized. The result of their activity is that acetylcholine cannot be destroyed at the receptor sites; its concentration builds up, and the muscles go into a state of continuous excitation and contraction. The agents are effective at very low concentrations, and the death which results is said to be exceedingly unpleasant.[10] These substances are known as NERVE GASES, such as the so-called G AGENTS and the newer V AGENTS which are now being mass produced and stockpiled in the United States—one of those aspects of the development of neurobiology which gives perhaps most cause for concern as to the uses and significance of this new knowledge. It is at best only mildly encouraging to note that they were originally developed prior to the present understanding of synaptology by the industrial firms Bayer in Germany and ICI in Britain in the search for insecticides. Indeed a close relative to the nerve gases is an organophosphorus compound which affects insect cholinesterases but not those of mammals such as humans. It therefore makes an effective and relatively non-toxic insecticide, though the potential health hazards of some of these substances, like Shell's Vapona, have given cause for alarm in the last few years.[11] It is distinctly discouraging to see how many NATO-sponsored conferences and defense research contracts with universities in the United States have been concerned with the properties of transmitter substances in recent years.

The vulnerability of the synapse has led to an intensive search for other agents which affect its performance less drastically than the nerve gases; in chemical warfare laboratories, in the pharmacology industry, and, on a sort of "cottage-laboratory" scale, in the kitchens and bathrooms of the more ambitious among drug experimenters who permit themselves to move off the well-explored routes of drug experience such as nicotine, alcohol, marijuana or LSD. One site of action of many such drugs may be at the synaptic level. The effects of nicotine, and the more interesting ones of marijuana when inhaled and LSD taken orally, have all been attributed to a subtle interference with synaptic transmitter properties. Such a possibility is supported—we return to this theme in chapter 12—by the fact that the chemical structure of some of the hallucinogens and "mind expanding agents" is related to that of substances which are known to be transmitters at central synapses. Hence, of course, the extreme interest of pharmacologists in university, industrial and military laboratories in the results of experiments involving iontophoresis as a technique for the micro-application of such agents.

So far the synapse and transmission across it have been discussed as if all transmission was excitatory. But this is only a half-truth. Synapses can say No as well as Yes. They can inhibit as well as excite the post-synaptic neuron. We have already discussed the analogous situation of the antagonistic effects of the sympathetic nerves on heartbeat: The sympathetic noradrenalin speeds heartbeat; the parasympathetic acetylcholine slows it. Acetylcholine inhibits the heartbeat. Centrally, inhibition means that a neuron in receipt of inhibitory commands from one synapse is less likely to fire when it receives what would otherwise be an adequate excitatory stimulus from another synapse. The inhibitory synapse is virtually identical in appearance and mode of action to the excitatory one; the difference lies in the effect that the inhibitory transmitter has on the post-synaptic cell. Just as the excitatory transmitter exerts its effect by causing a membrane depolarization, an excitatory post-synaptic potential, so the inhibitory transmitter functions by increasing the polarization (negativity) of the post-synaptic cell. This is called HYPERPOLARIZATION, and is measured as a miniature INHIBITORY POST-SYNAPTIC POTENTIAL (IPSP).

There has been an intensive search for the inhibitory transmitter substances of the central nervous system in the last decade, and one has now been identified with a fair degree of certainty. It is the relatively simple GAMMA-AMINO-BUTYRIC ACID (GABA). GABA is a compound virtually unique to the nervous system—it was originally identified as a transmitter substance in some crustacean nerves and seems to have a particularly marked inhibitory rôle in the cerebellum. A substance chemically very similar to GABA, the AMINO ACID GLUTA-

MATE may well be an excitatory transmitter, and the relationships between them as transmitters may explain one of the stranger aspects of the way in which the biochemistry of the brain differs from that of the rest of the body, that is, the particularly high concentration of these amino acids to be found within the neuron and the degree to which the metabolism of the brain's main (almost sole) energy source, glucose, is specialized to assist in the synthesis of such amino acids. One possible rôle for the glial cells, it is being increasingly suggested, is in fabricating these amino acids from glucose, and then transferring them to the neuron where they will play a rôle in transmission and the synthesis of protein.[12]

The Post-synaptic Cell: Dendrites

We have referred to the synapse as the decision point of the nervous system. And this is indeed so. But the decisions, if they are made anywhere, are made at the post-synaptic side of that system. On the myriad branching dendrites and the cell body of a single neuron there may be up to ten thousand synapses. Each of these synapses is passing information to the post-synaptic neuron – some by signalling with excitatory post-synaptic potentials, some with inhibitory post-synaptic potentials; for some the signal is one of silence – the absence of an IPSP for instance. Each incoming EPSP or IPSP will carry its message to the post-synaptic cell in a wave of depolarization or hyperpolarization. How far the wave will spread down the dendrite and the membrane of the cell body will depend upon the sum of all the incoming signals at that given time.

Messages flow from the dendrites and cell body towards the axon like water from the tributaries of a river. Although the axon in isolation can conduct in either direction, in real life it is a one-way system; the action potential begins at a point where in a typical neuron (the sort of figure 13) the cell body narrows down towards the axon. Whether the axon fires or not depends on the sum of all the events arriving at this point at a given time. To these events, computed as a result of signals which may be arriving at far distant dendrites, the axon will respond by firing only if the depolarization climbs over the threshold.

This is a certain, deterministic response: the uncertainty of the system arises from the computation of the events within and along the dendrites and cell body; the certainty of the arrival of particular EPSPs and IPSPs from some synapses, and the uncertainty of the chance bombardment by spontaneous transmitter release from others. Nor has each synapse or each cell equal weight in such interactions. Detailed analysis of some synaptic interactions shows that in the arrangement of synapses in some parts of the brain, the axon from one cell lies closely intertwined along the dendrite of a second cell, making not just one, but thousands of synaptic connections with it along its length. The two, axon and dendrite, twist around each other like bindweed around brambles, with synapses at each of the thorns of the bramble–the dendritic spines.[13] Signals from such an axon should "matter more" to the recipient dendrite than those from an axon which makes but a few contacts.

The number of synapses between an individual cell and its post-synaptic neighbor is but one factor though. Another is indicated if we recall that the dendrites are long; their ends may be far distant from the cell body and the axon. Is a synapse on the end of a dendrite distant from the cell to be given the same weight as one close to or on the cell body? One can detect at least three classes of synapses: those which the axon makes with post-synaptic dendrites (axo-dendritic); those it makes with the post-synaptic cell body (axo-somatic); and finally another class of synapses which one axon makes with another just before the second axon itself synapses (axo-axonic).[14] There have been many attempts to classify synapses, according to their different positions in relation to the post-synaptic cell, as inhibitory or excitatory. Axo-somatic synapses have on occasion been regarded as inhibitory and axo-dendritic as excitatory. There have similarly been attempts–dependent more on the microscopist's eye of love and faith than on judgment perhaps–to see different-shaped vesicles within the synapses, round or oval, for instance, as reflecting excitatory or inhibitory properties, but such interpretations remain speculative. There is one exception to this negative statement, though, that of the cells of the cerebellum, where a rather clear model of function, and hence of which cells are inhibitory and which excitatory, has been developed–it will be discussed in the next chapter.

The Neuronal Cell Body

If the computational function of the cell is the sum of dendritic activity reflected in the threshold of potential at the axon, the axon an all-or-none conducting system, and the synapse the gate into the next unit of the conducting pathway, what function is left for the neuronal cell body itself? If one reflects on those cells in which it represents only 5 percent of the total cell volume, not much one might guess. But for most neurons it is a far greater percentage of total cell volume than that, and it is the neuronal cell body which contains most of the conventional biochemical apparatus of the cell, nucleus, mitochondria and ribosomes, although there are mitochondria in the synaptic terminal as well.

The cell body can best be regarded as a chemical factory, actively performing the major chemical transformations necessary for the functioning of the neuron as a cell system; the generation of usable cellular energy by the oxidation of glucose to carbon dioxide and water, and the synthesis of transmitter substances. No part of the neuron except the cell body can synthesize protein in any quantity, for it is there that the protein-making machinery–the nucleus for blueprints and the ribosomes for fabrication–is present. Cut off from the cell body, axons and dendrites soon wither and die; the cell body will grow new ones. The substances which are necessary for the synthesis and maintenance of the axon, synapses and dendrites, must all be produced within the cell body itself. Indeed, there is a continuous flow of materials fabricated in the cell body down the axon to the synapse. Proteins synthesized on the ribosomes in the cell body flow down the axon at a rate of up to 200 mm per day.[15] The continuing production of all this material makes the neuron one of the fastest protein-synthesizing systems of the body.[16] Yet just what it is all for no one really quite knows as yet. Some of it–perhaps most–is certainly replacement material; enzymes for transmitter manufacture at the synapse, lipid and protein for the replacement and modification of membranes and receptor sites. These are indicators, as we shall see, of the plasticity of the brain, its capacity to modify its structure and performance in response to changing external circumstances. But much of this is speculation, as are views on the relationship between the vast protein-synthesizing capacity of the neuron and the low rate in the surrounding glia, which can make protein only one-half to one-third as fast. There is evidence that, for instance, it is the glia which fabricate the amino acids which the neuron may then store or use as building blocks from which to synthesize protein. These are merely hints, suggestions. At present we can only guess at the value to the cell of this ceaseless production of protein. But it continues to stand as an index of the rôle which differentiates the cell body from the rest of the parts of the neuron: its *trophic* function, nurturing and supplying dendrites, axons and synapses with vital materials.

The Structural Analysis of the Brain

The arguments of this chapter suggest that the workings of the single neuron can be analyzed into the operation of four partially interconnecting components: cell body, dendrites, axon and synapses, each cell having one cell body and many of all the other components. Their functions are reasonably well defined at the level of biochemistry and cell physiology. The axon has conducting properties of a cablelike character. It carries impulses, as a result of stimuli above a certain threshold, which are invariant as to magnitude or velocity. The biochemistry and biophysics of the passage of these impulses is well understood. The synapses represent the junction points of the system. Impulses arriving down the axons are converted into the quantal release of chemical transmitters which may either excite or inhibit the post-synaptic cell. The point of major vulnerability of the nervous system to exogenous drugs or other agents is the cleft between the pre- and post-synaptic cells. The dendrites and the membrane of the cell body are concerned with computing the information arriving at them, in terms of transmitter, from all the synapses. Depending on the sum of this activity at any given time, the stimulus at the axon will climb above the threshold necessary for it to fire.

The uncertain, probabilistic nature of the nervous system depends on this computing function of the dendrites and cell body. Information in the form of excitatory or inhibitory transmitter arrives at them as a result of three types of event: (a) firing in a nerve which synapses upon the dendrites or cell body in question in response to events external to it in the rest of the nervous system or in the environment; (b) the spontaneous firing of the pre-synaptic nerve in response to events internal to it; and (c) the quantal release of small amounts of transmitter without axonal impulses to trigger them. Of these three types of stimulus which the dendrites and cell body must compute, only the first is always certain and predictable at the hierarchical level of the system. The second may be determinate, but it may also occur as a result of events which, at the present level of our knowledge, appear random, indeterminate and probabilistic. The third appears, in so far as present knowledge goes, to be a random, probabilistic event. Thus it would seem that the synaptic structure of the nervous system is such as to make its functioning only partially predictable. Even if the mode of computation of the dendrites and cell body is itself deterministic, albeit complex, in terms of the "weighting" given to particular synapses, they are none the less computing on the basis of information which appears to have a measure of indeterminacy built into it. It is this feature which accounts in part for the considerable spontaneous activity of the brain and which, as we shall see, is of importance when we come to consider the predictability of the responses of the brain.

But it is time to turn from this model of the working of the individual neuron, to that of the brain as an integrated system— a task which should properly be accorded a chapter of its own.

4 The Brain as a System

We are now in a position to build up from the picture of the neuron as the unit of the brain system, to show how these units, with their structural and physiological properties, can be assembled to produce the working brain which results from their interactions.[1] But is a nervous system anything other than simply a collection of the individual units we have described? Thomas Bullock and Adrian Horridge, in their monumental study of invertebrate nervous systems, describe a nervous system as "an organised constellation of cells (neurons) specialised for the repeated conduction of an excited state from receptor cells or from other neurons to effectors or to other neurons".[2]

How adequate is such a definition? Can we in fact account for the properties of the nervous system as a whole from the study of the operation of its several parts? That is: if the position, conductivity and connectivity of each of the individual neurons of the system is known, could we specify how the system as a whole would operate?

The direct answer to this is that we do not know, because such a specified system does not yet exist—even in theory. The nearest that can be got to it at present is certain mathematical models of "neuronlike" networks, and even the properties of the quite simple networks which are all that can presently be handled are not always readily predictable. It does not seem that there is any inherent reason, apart from the complexity of actually doing it in practice, rather than in a "thought experiment", why the nervous system should not be ultimately specifiable, that is, capable of a total description, at least in theory. I believe that this is a position which would be accepted by most, but not all, neurobiologists. There is however an articulate group, including both philosophers and neurobiologists, who would not accept this, claiming rather that the brain cannot be specified in this way from the study of the assemblage of its parts, because the examination of the properties of the system as a whole is properly made at a hierarchical level above that of its parts. This school of thought argues that parts can never be used—at least in biology—to specify wholes, because wholes take on a set of properties *as* wholes which are more than merely the sum of their parts. For example, if one were to attempt a complete description of a motor car simply in terms of the composition and relations of its components, one would fail to understand the *function* of the car conceived as a whole–a means of transportation. There are other ways of avoiding the problem of what Donald MacKay has called the "bankruptcy of determinism", to which we return. The purpose of this chapter is to show how far can be got in the assembly of the brain from its components.

Some Possible Pathways

The axon→synapse→dendrite→cell body arrangement of neurons allows pathways of connected cells to be assembled. Thus if several neurons are connected synaptically, one with the other, they make a *linear* pathway, as in figure 23.

The neurons are drawn in stylized form, with the axons as lines, the synapses as v's, and the dendrites are ignored in this type of schematization. Other branch points can be inserted into a multi-synaptic pathway as in figure 24, and other feeder pathways can enter the system, providing additional information which will help decide the outcome of what is to be transmitted down the pathways emerging from the assembly at the right (figure 25). Finally the pathway, or part of it, can bend backwards on itself to form a net (figure 26). Nets can be made with three, or even two neurons (figure 27). If we assume just four neurons, each making but one synapse, the number of possible nets available is eleven. If it is recalled that each synapse can either be inhibitory or excitatory, then the number of interactions of even this simple network becomes quite large.

23 (*below*) A linear neuronal pathway.

24 (*bottom*) A branched neuronal pathway.

If we were to include even a fraction of the real number of synapses which may be involved it is clear that the number of interactions between four neurons becomes so large as to be almost impossible to compute. Obviously, as the number of cells increases, so does the complexity of the system.

From what has already been said in the previous two chapters, though, it would be expected that the pathways of the nervous

25 *(below)* New inputs into the system.

26 *(bottom)* The pathway becomes a network.

27 Two simple neuronal
nets.

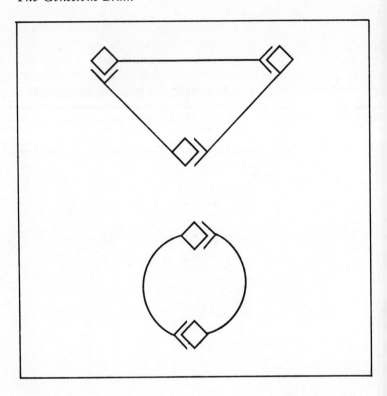

system are not randomly connected, but linked with a degree
of precision and specificity. Pathways go from somewhere to
somewhere else, serving, as in Bullock and Horridge's definition, to gather information, in the form of an AFFERENT (incoming) signal, from a sense receptor and to transmit it as an
EFFERENT (outgoing) signal by a nerve which is connected to a
muscle or gland, so that the effector organ can be instructed as
to how to do its job – to contract more or less, or to secrete more
or less.

What goes on in between, in that mass of neurons of the central nervous system which are not connected directly to sense
organs or effectors but merely to one another, is a system for
refining and modifying those instructions. These INTER-
NEURONS (those connected only to each other and not to sense
organs or effectors) are of value because of what they add to
the information on which the instruction is based, by virtue of
their capacity to compare it with past information, and draw
conclusions. But in all probability, the system is not as complex
as might appear from simply computing the possible connectivity, that is the total number of possible connections. For
instance, practically all of the synapses that one interneuron may
make might be on no more than one or two other cells, as is
true in the case of the cerebellum, considered later in this chapter.

Studying the Brain as a System

Models and statements of theory can only go so far. To turn to
reality demands experimental techniques, methods for unpick-
ing the tangled pathways of the brain. Neither light or electron
microscopy, nor the isolated squid axon, neuromuscular junction or separated synapse, will go far to show how the actual
components of a real brain are wired together. For this task,
more complex than those yet described, new techniques are
needed. The two approaches open to an experimenter in a study
of the pathways and functions of the brain system may, for the
sake of argument, be classified as either reductionist or holistic
in their orientation – although this classification begs a number
of questions. In the reductionist approach, the specification of
the whole brain is attempted by the analysis of each of its individual pathways. Eventually it should be possible, it is argued,
to clip the entire system together, like one of those plastic
assemblable men which are now offered for sale as a contemporary version of Rembrandt's anatomy lesson. Hopefully, a
full size, fully functioning brain – or at least the model of one –
will be produced. The second approach abandons this piecemeal
attempt for a study of the system in its entirety. The whole brain
is taken as it is, and its properties are studied as a system; pieces
of the system may indeed be removed, but this is done in order
to show the effect of their *absence* upon the rest, rather than to
study the individual piece. It is bold, such an approach: admir-
able in its self-confidence; and it may be spectacular in its
results. Or, more often than not, it may lead into a morass of
disappointment.

The reductionist approach is almost Baconian in its dependence on the steady accretion of individual chunks of information from which, hopefully, the full story will in due course
emerge. The holistic approach has been propounded with great
vigor by today's "systems theorists" who maintain that how
the *units* of which the system is composed function doesn't
really matter; what matters are the properties of the *system*.
Understanding the system, they believe, will allow one to
predict the behavior of the units.

I do not believe it is possible to understand and evaluate the
conclusions which experiments draw from their data without
looking hard at the experimental methods and philosophical
assumptions which underpin them – a statement of my own
philosophy which I shall justify, or try to justify, in chapter 13.
So before looking at the results which studies of the brain-as-a-
system have yielded, we therefore spend some time describing
the techniques involved, their theoretical underpinning and
their limitations. Readers interested only in the main line of

results, without caring too much how they are got, could turn directly to page 95 where that story is taken up again.

Reductionist Techniques

We start with the slow and piecemeal building up of pathways and the interactions of individual cells and small sub-sets of the overall system. The goals are modest, but the successes are measurable. One simple method of tracking a nervous pathway, known to anatomists for many years, is to cut an axon, in an experimental animal, relatively close to the cell body from which it leads. Characteristic changes take place on the sides of the cut both toward and away from the cell body. Those on the cell-body side are concerned with the synthesis of new material for rebuilding the axon, but it is those on the side of the cut farthest from the cell body which are more interesting in the present context. We have already referred to the fact that the maintenance of an axon and its synapses depends on a flow of material, including protein, from the cell body. If this flow is stopped because of the cut—tying the nerve or crushing it will achieve the same effect—the axon and its synapses begin to disintegrate and die. Eventually, under favorable circumstances, the cell body may put out a new axon which replaces the old. This process is known as regeneration, and is a dramatic demonstration of the vital function played by the neuronal cell body.

Meanwhile the route followed by the dead or dying axon can be followed like the track of a bullet wound in flesh. In rare cases the cells on which the severed axon synapsed will themselves show characteristic changes and even disintegrate in their turn. The neuronal pathway can then be tracked beyond its first synapse as well. This technique, referred to as degeneration, is of most use in tracking the pathways of spinal-cord nerves and the large tracts of white matter which link up the great areas of gray within the brain. It can obviously help less within the cortex itself, where the pathways are more confused and the axons too short to cut in this crude way.[3]

A physiological parallel to this anatomical tracking system is that of cellular recording. If an electrode is placed in, or adjacent to, a given cell, and a cell or axon which is distant but connected to it is stimulated, then a changed potential can be recorded as the second neuron responds to the signal arriving from the first. Such a recording will indicate that cells x and y are connected by way of a functional pathway, so that if one fires the other then responds. But more information than this can be obtained. If both the velocity of conduction down an axon of given diameter, and the delay at the synapse are known, then by measuring the time delay between the stimulation at one cell and the changed potential at another, it is possible to calculate how many synapses there are in the pathway between the cells.

Recording techniques of this sort allow pathways to be traced step by step, synapse by synapse, through the nervous system. For example, the afferent nerves of the visual system arise from neurons in the retina of the eye. These neurons can be stimulated, either electrically or more "naturally" by appropriate light flashes on to the eye. The axonal response can be monitored in the optic nerve. The first synapse beyond the retina in the pathway of the visual system en route to the cortex is within a region of gray matter known as the LATERAL GENICULATE BODY (figure 28). Particular cells in the lateral geniculate will show electrical responses when particular retinal neurons are stimulated. From the lateral geniculate the visual pathway ascends to a major region of the cerebral cortex, the VISUAL CORTEX. Particular neurons in the visual cortex will give an electrical response when *either* the lateral geniculate *or* the retinal neurons are stimulated. But the time taken for the cells to respond after

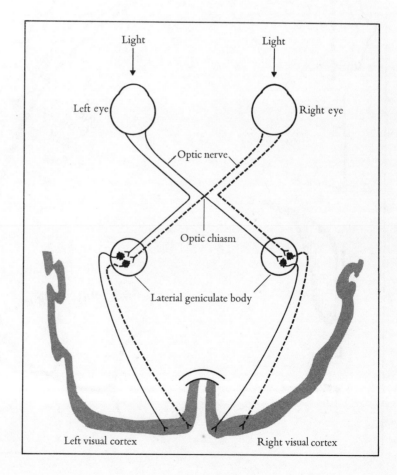

28 The visual system of the human.

29 The "motor homunculus". Cross-section of the cerebral hemisphere, showing regions controlling the motor activity of particular regions. Note the disproportionate amount of cortex concerned with fingers, lips and tongue.

stimulating the geniculate neurons will be relatively less than after stimulating the retinal neurons. The impulses from the retinal neurons have two synapses to cross to get to the cortex, and the message is therefore delayed.

This is an example of recording from afferent systems. Efferent ones can be treated similarly. The motor pathways to a particular muscle or group of muscles can be traced, and just as the retinal neuron can be triggered by a "natural" stimulus, such as a light flash, so the motor response to the stimulation of an efferent nerve can be a grouped and coordinated set of muscular contractions.

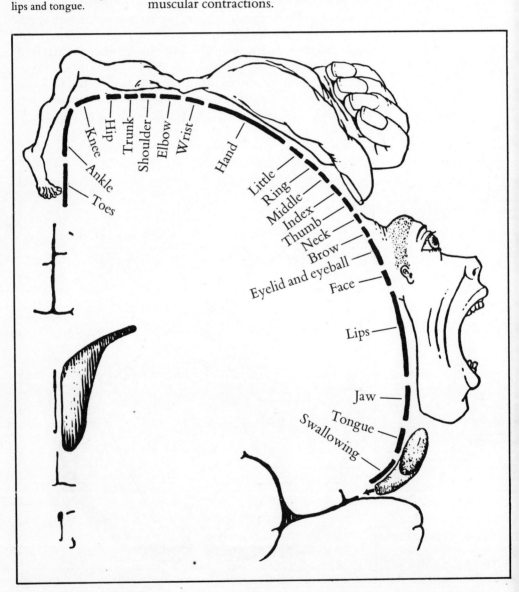

Such techniques allow the mapping of regions of the cortex to be carried out with a fair degree of precision, both in animals and in human patients. The regions of cortex associated with the processing of sensory input on the one hand and of motor output on the other, have been extensively studied in this way. For example, stimulation studies on the MOTOR CORTEX region allow the identification of cortical areas associated with fairly precise sets of muscular responses—as suggested by the "motor homunculus" of figure 29. Similarly, experiments on the electrical stimulation of brain regions in human patients whose brains have been exposed for surgery, generally for the treatment of epilepsy, enabled the Montreal neurosurgeon Wilder Penfield to identify a group of cortex regions associated with the control of speech, conceptualization and naming (figure 30).[4] But always it is found that the activity of the cortex is concerned not so much with a particular muscle or word but a particular action. If one muscle is damaged and the action cannot be achieved by its use, stimulation of the area of cortex which originally caused it to respond may now call into play a different set of muscles which none the less achieve the same effect.

A word should perhaps be said about the *reliability* of this sort of recording. A physicist or a chemist may be expected to repeat an experiment under identical conditions several dozens of times, and to get a result which is absolutely repeatable and

30 Speech mechanisms in the dominant hemisphere. derived from stimulation studies.

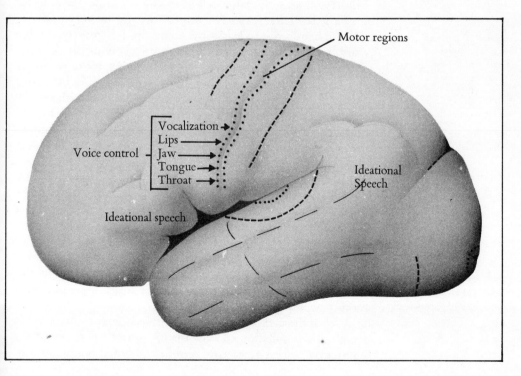

Motor regions

Vocalization →
Lips ——→
Voice control — Jaw ——→
Tongue →
Throat →

Ideational Speech

Ideational speech

reliable, provided the conditions under which it is conducted can be regulated (high-energy physics is for various reasons something of an exception to this rule). Even a biochemist, if he is purifying a substance from a biological source or conducting a study of the metabolism of a particular compound in a slice of tissue, will expect to perform a set of repeat experiments, as identical as he can make them, and would be unhappy if the scatter on his results – their range around their average – was more than 15 percent or so. But how identically can a neurophysiologist repeat an experiment? It is true that the existence of elaborate machinery will allow him to place his electrodes into the brain in the same region, to within less than half a millimeter, with considerable reliability. He must then penetrate the brain with the electrode until he hits a "good" cell; that is, one which responds. Many may not respond, because the electrode tip strikes them only a glancing blow, or because the slight movement of the anaesthetized animal is enough to throw the delicate electrode out of the cell again, or because the electrode, in passing through the cell, does excessive damage to it. Perhaps in a good preparation the neurophysiologist may be able to record for several hours and get good data from quite a few different cells. But when he goes to another animal, how can he possibly find the same cells again? Do they indeed exist in the vast complex brain structures? Is it indeed likely that any two brains will have *exactly* the same cell in *exactly* the same place, wired in *exactly* the same way? The improbabilities are very high.

So high indeed as to lead some neurophysiologists to abandon work with the mammalian brain on the grounds that it is too complex. They have turned instead to rather more primitive organisms, such as snails, insects or crustaceans, which may have central brains containing only a few hundreds or thousands of neurons, many of which are easily distinguishable from each other, using a low-power dissecting microscope, on grounds of size and position.[5] In such preparations it is possible to be sure of placing an electrode in the same cell in different animals time and again. Highly reproducible results can be obtained. But then, what is the relationship between an observation in the brain of a snail and the workings of the human cerebral cortex? Is the difference too great for studies on one to tell us anything about the other? The relative universality of biological principles across creatures so diverse as snails and men has proved to be an immensely profitable working hypothesis for biologists so far – but doubtless they should beware stretching their luck.

So with these exceptions the neurophysiologist must rely on sampling a population of cells for his recordings rather as the pollster or market researcher samples a human population for his. Except that in the neurophysiologist's case, he does not know how many "don't knows" he fails to record as his electrode plunges deep through the internal regions of the brain. Were the cells really not responding, or simply silent because the electrode did not introduce itself properly to them? Is a "good" cell the same thing as a "typical" cell–or not? Such considerations pose great problems for scientific method, which I sometimes have the impression that the neurophysiologists underrate. What they tend to do is score up instead "positive" instances. "In seven cats, we found, in all the thirteen cells which we sampled, such and such a response to such and such a stimulus" is the type of data frequently presented in the neurophysiological literature. Is this science or stamp collecting? Despite all these difficulties some profoundly exciting results have come out of this type of study. David Hubel and Torsten Wiesel's visual cortex cells and Olga Vinogradova's novelty registering and counting cells in the hippocampus are among those we shall shortly discuss. They are, as we shall see, beautiful and fascinating results. But the need for caution remains. If one cell in a population of 10^5, observed less than a dozen times in less than a dozen cats, shows particular properties, one should certainly be permitted to build theories of thought and consciousness upon them, but only with proper recognition for the shakiness of the experimental data upon which such theories must depend.

Holistic Techniques

This examination of reductionist techniques for the analysis of brain systems leaves one cautious. But do the holistic alternatives fare any better? Certainly what was once considered as likely to be the most promising has, in a sense, proved the most disappointing. It was H. Berger, in Switzerland in the 1920s, who first taped a set of recording electrodes to the scalp and reproducibly recorded the continuous passionate bursts of electrical activity which rippled through the brain.[6] The ELECTROENCEPHALOGRAM (EEG), that complex recording of wave on wave, the pale shadow through the skull of the electrical beat of the brain itself, was the result. It achieved almost instant notoriety. Could one "read" the brain through the EEG; interpret thoughts through analyses of wave trains?

There was a time when all was thought possible. The EEG of a sleeper differs from that of an awake person; the pattern often changes when an individual is set complex mathematical tasks, being jerkier, more erratic, "desynchronized". Certain characteristic rhythms (figure 31) appear under well-defined circumstances–the "slow wave" (ALPHA WAVES), in the resting,

31 Human EEG
patterns. Typical traces
from individuals in
various states. Alpha
waves (8–12 per second)
are seen in awake, resting
and drowsy states (b) and
(c). The trace in (e) shows
"paradoxical" sleep,
referred to in Chapter 11

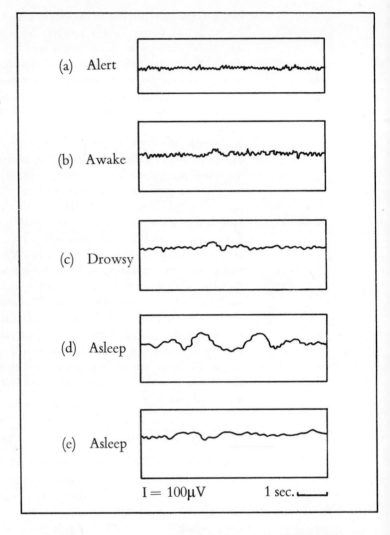

(a) Alert

(b) Awake

(c) Drowsy

(d) Asleep

(e) Asleep

I = 100μV   1 sec.

"thought-free" state for instance, where the EEG pattern is clean and synchronized. Wave forms were found to be different in the very young, the very old, in certain cases of gross mental disorder or neurological disease – indeed it was even suggested they were different in individuals of different personality types or different social records such as criminality, ambition and so on. Within a short time the EEG-mongers had become the contemporary descendants of the nineteenth-century phrenologists.

But what has been the result of the subsequent fifty years of research into EEG effects? The physiological basis of the characteristic waves, alpha, theta and so on, is little more understood today than it was then, despite their utility from the behavioral point of view. Indeed one suggestion is that the most striking of all, alpha, is not even a record of the brain at all, but of a tremor in the muscles of the eye. At least one neurophysiologist proved able to record characteristic alpha waves from his own scalp by simply applying a party trick of rolling his eyes up and back.[7]

If the major rhythms are unclear in interpretation, what does the continuous jitter of the recording needle which underlies them mean? Until recently, it could not be analyzed; it seemed random, disorganized and unrelated. The computer has brought some order to this chaos. It can be set to analyze the sum of all the jitters occurring at a given time, and all the mini-peaks above a certain size and below another. Out of the idiot tracing, some order then begins to appear. But despite the optimism and enthusiasm of such protagonists of the EEG as Grey Walter, whose book *The Living Brain*[8] makes the case for it so persuasively, it is hard not to be disillusioned.

Better recordings can be made in experimental animals by tapping a hole in the skull and placing the recording electrode on the surface of the cortex. Information is cleaner, signals less diffuse. More information still can be obtained using specially prepared brain systems. For instance, if the nervous connections to particular parts of the brain, such as the cerebrum, are severed but the blood supply is left intact, the brain region may be kept functional, in terms of electrical activity, for some hours. In such preparations, certain classes of signals in the external environment—light flashed to the eyes, changes of tune to the ear—result in an overall change in the pattern of the potential in the cortex as measured by the recording electrode. These changes are EVOKED POTENTIALS triggered by external events—they can also be obtained in intact brains, but are more complex to interpret. Their analysis, by such workers as E. Roy John and Frank Morrell in the United States for example, has raised hopes again that these modified descendants of the old EEG-type records can prove of analytical value in interpreting the brain system.[9]

An even more simplified preparation has been developed by Ben Delisle Burns working in Montreal. In this undercut cortex preparation, made in an anaesthetized or "isolated brain" animal, a neat piece of surgery will cut away all the nervous connections to a piece of cortex a few millimeters square, leaving only the blood supply intact.[10] Stimuli can be applied to this cortical slab and the resulting potential changes studied. This preparation is coming very close to the biochemists' isolated tissue slice—a thin slice of cerebral cortex, perhaps no more than a third of a millimeter thick by a centimeter square, which, when cut quickly from the brain and maintained in a warm, oxygenated, glucose-containing medium mimicking the composition of the brain's extracellular fluid, will retain many of the vital functions of the nervous system for periods of hours on end. The slice will oxidize glucose and manufacture transmitter substances, amino acids and protein, and respond by an increased energy utilization to electrical stimulation, and individual cells within it will retain both resting and action potentials.[11]

These techniques help to bring the complex properties of the whole system down to a more simplified level where they are amenable to analysis. But still, complexities in the analysis of all such systems, stimulated by gross inputs, recorded from electrodes which measure changes in the state of the system, rather than in the individual behavior of units, has so far proved to be of only limited value, despite the input of technical ingenuity and experimental devotion by many workers over several research lifetimes. It is many years now since Sherrington compared the functioning of the brain to that of–in his famous analogy–an "enchanted loom". He imagined each nerve impulse traveling an axon within the brain as represented by a flash of light. Open the brain, and one could see a myriad of such flashes traveling in groups, intercrossing in a continuously changing pattern, a pattern woven upon the enchanted loom.[12] Such an image remains a thing of beauty–but a thing unanalyzable despite all. The analysis of the brain as a system has only, therefore, given tantalizing glimpses of function, a fleeting shimmer behind a veil of obscurity.

Although this group of approaches may be regarded as holistic, in that they attack the problem of the brain as a system, one might be justified in pointing out that the size of the system may be quite small, as in the case of the Burns preparation, for example–small enough to satisfy the reductionists as to its possibilities and perhaps to discourage the holist. Any grouping of techniques is bound to be arbitrary, though it does reflect different approaches to the brain, which in their turn result in disagreements about function.

Such a disagreement can be seen very clearly, if we turn to what is the neuroanatomist's contribution to the examination of the brain as a holistic system. For the reductionist approach, an appropriate neuroanatomical technique is that of degeneration. The equivalent for the whole brain have been methods practiced by neuroanatomists for many years of ABLATION, the removal of a large area of brain tissue, or LESIONING, the severing of particular tracts, followed by an examination of the performance of the remainder. The rationale for this approach, which derived originally from the neurological study of patients with particular brain disorders, is clear and superficially compelling. For example, in the mid-nineteenth century, the French neurologist Paul Broca carried out an autopsy on a patient who had suffered from APHASIA, a speech disability which prevents the sufferer from recalling particular words or formulating particular sentences. Broca found that the patient's brain showed massive damage to a particular region at the base of one of the frontal convolutions of the cerebral cortex. This region, Broca affirmed (although in fact more extended regions of the cortex were also damaged in this particular case), was a region whose damage *caused* the patient's aphasia: it was the brain's speech center, now known as the area of Broca, and only one of several areas now known to be associated with speech (figure 30). The logic of Broca's argument–and it proved a reasonable one in this case–was clear: given a failure in brain function, and a damaged area of the brain, the former is 'caused' by the latter.[13] If as an experimental neuroanatomist or psychologist, one wishes to study the region of the brain responsible for a particular function–or the function associated with the particular brain region–what could be more logical than to remove it in an experimental animal, and to examine the effects on the animal when it has been removed?

Such ablation studies have been made more popular and easier because of their relationship with human clinical neurology. It may seem difficult to devise methods which will allow one accurately to cut or destroy a region of a few cubic millimeters in volume, and maybe buried centimeters deep within the brain, without affecting the surrounding structures. Yet the instruments devised by brain surgeons to deal with such needs in patients are of great ingenuity, enabling one to achieve operations ranging from such minute and precise deletions to the removal of huge areas, as in the case of the deplorable operations fashionable even now among certain psychiatrists, the cutting of the pathways to all or part of the prefrontal lobe of the cortex of those they could not otherwise cure.

It is more doubtful what one can discover from such removals of brain tissue, even of vast ingenuity. The interpretations are not as unequivocal as the experience of Broca would lead one to believe. Functions do not appear to be so sharply localized in the brain as all this. True, a distinguished line of neurologists has followed Broca in ascribing particular functions to particular brain regions, as in the Penfield stimulation experiments, which resulted in the generation of such maps of the speech centers of the brain as in figure 30.

But there have equally been those to argue that there is little to be learnt from such techniques. One such was Karl Lashley, of the University of Minnesota, who devoted many years of patient experimentation, which culminated in the 1940s, to the effects of the removal of different cortical regions on the capacity of rats to remember their way round a maze. To Lashley's surprise he could find no region of cortex whose ablation *specifically* removed the animal's capacity to find its way round. Instead it was as if the memory system were distributed throughout the cortex; the more cortex that was removed, the less good the animal's performance, whichever part of the cortex had been taken out. He was forced to conclude that no specific brain region contained any specific memory-storage function. The functions were distributed so that each part of the cortex appeared to be equivalent, or *equipotential* in this respect. It is not necessary to accept Lashley's conclusions to share his puzzlement at the failure of his experiments; the tool of ablation studies had turned in his hands.[14]

Such failures have not diminished the popularity of the technique, but we are more aware today of its limitations. In particular, the specificity of effect produced by lesion or ablation tends to diminish the higher the damage occurs in the central nervous system. The effect of severing a single efferent nerve is straightforward; a lesion in the spinal cord produces paralysis of motor function or loss of sensory input, or both, over a defined area of the body; lesions in the brain stem or midbrain regions such as the hypothalamus may produce, as we shall see in chapters 10 and 11, specific effects, albeit not on simple motor responses, but on such activities as sleeping, eating or sex. Lesions or ablations in the cortex—even the removal of whole areas or lobes—may be much harder to relate to any specific performance deficits at all.

The general fallacy of interpretation which may hinder the interpretation of the effects of lesions high in the nervous system, has perhaps been most effectively summed up by the psychologist and inventor Richard Gregory:[15]

> The removal of any of several resistances in a radio set may cause the emission of strange sounds, but it cannot therefore be concluded that the function of the resistances is to inhibit howling. . . .
> The southern region of British railways is a complex system of railway lines, signal boxes, stations and control systems. A breakdown of a section of the line, a power failure or a slip in the central control room at Waterloo may disrupt traffic over a wide area. But we cannot therefore say that the function of the system is localised in the permanent way, the power station, the central control room . . . all are essential. . . .

Gregory's analogy is apt, although some brain functions are certainly localized, as in the motor homunculus (figure 29). It would be wrong to maintain that the holistic approach to the brain, exemplified by the type of studies described in this section, has failed intellectually or in the generation of experiments and results. We shall use material derived from the approach in much of what follows. It is simply that so much was expected, from Berger to Grey Walter, from phrenology via Karl Lashley, to the current exponents of ablation, such as Karl Pribram at Stanford and Larry Weiskrantz at Oxford.

The real point is that to draw valid conclusions one needs to consider evidence derived from all available techniques, both holistic and reductionist. If data from lesions and ablations, electrical recording and stimulation, all give concordant results, then it becomes possible to make reasonably positive statements; if the techniques give conflicting results, one must be more cautious.[16] Which circumspect statement allows us to turn back to the main line of argument; when results from all these techniques are assembled, what types of conclusion can be drawn as to the way the brain system works?

Sense Receptors and Information Transmission

The simplest type of neural pathway imaginable is a monosynaptic one; i.e. one with a single synapse. In it, an incoming afferent nerve synapses with an outgoing efferent one; an incoming message from a sense receptor produces an invariant response in an effector organ. It is hard to find a real situation as simple as this model in the brain. Within the spinal cord, however, this type of simple monosynaptic pathway does occur. Scattered through the periphery of the body are an immense variety of sense organs, not the grand organs of vision, sight, smell or taste, but those registering "unconscious sensations" which find their expression in bodily responses such as breathing, muscular coordination, digestion and conscious registration of pressure, temperature, pain. In general such receptors consist of neurons more or less modified in structure. The modification is such that they will fire in response not merely to electrical stimulation of the sort which triggers all other neurons of the body (although their axons can, of course, be induced to fire by artificial electrical depolarization of the sort already discussed), but they respond in addition to other types of stimulation: mechanical, as pressure or touch, or temperature, as in registration of heat or cold.

The receptors may be embedded near the surface of the body, in or just below, the skin, in which case they monitor information arriving from the external world to the organism (they are sometimes known as EXTEROCEPTORS). Alternatively, they may be located deep in the interior of the organism, in internal organs or muscles. They respond to changes in the internal bodily economy and state; they tell the organism how it is in itself – stomach full or empty, food eaten good or bad, bladder empty or distended, muscles cramped or relaxed. Such receptors are sometimes known as PROPRIOCEPTORS and the stimuli they monitor are called kinaesthetic by experimental psychologists. In either event, the rôle of the sense receptors is to translate information arriving at them into the language of the nervous system. To show what this means, take the following analogy.

Consider my front door with a bell-push. I am inside my house and someone arrives at the door. How is he to inform me of his presence? He presses the bell. Inside I cannot respond to the pressure on the bell: I cannot sense it. Nor yet can I respond to the fact that pressure on the bell results in the closing of an electrical circuit and the flow of current. I cannot, sitting in my study, sense this current. However, if the passage of the current results in a bell ringing, I can hear this and interpret the ringing of the bell as meaning "someone is at the front door, wanting to come in". Thus the information concerning a person's presence at the front door has been converted twice, first into the completion of an electrical circuit, second into the ringing of the bell. The ringing of the bell has transformed the completion of the circuit—and the pressure of the finger on the front doorbell—into a language I can register and interpret. The information has not changed its content, but it has changed its form: pressure on the bell-push to the ringing of the bell. Each time information changes its form in this way it is said to go through the process of translation. It is the job of the sense receptors to convert different forms of information arriving at them into the language of the nervous system, the firing of an axon.

Receptors are specialized as to what information they will translate in this way—it is no good shining a light into the ear and expecting the receptors there to respond, any more than it would be possible to see a television picture through a radio set. Within the nervous system itself though, a common language operates: there is only one type of signal that any receptor can provide the system—the all-or-none firing of an axon. The only modification available is how frequently this event occurs. *Frequency*, the number of events occurring within any given time, is the key to the interpretation of a receptor signal within the system. A single short ring on my front door bell is likely to be a polite visitor, a long imperious one, the milkman—particularly if it is Saturday and he needs to be paid—and a series of short sharp erratic bursts, my younger son who has as usual forgotten to put the door on the latch and has also left his key at home. The signal varies, though its elements are constant, and will be interpreted as meaning a variety of different things. In the case of nervous system receptors, the different types of information may be interpreted as "something is sticking into my foot" or "I can smell roast meat" or "I can see a blue motorcar", depending on which cells in the spinal cord or the brain the impulses arrive at. All might, in principle, be signaled by pulses of the same frequency. A common language operates throughout the nervous system, and the interpretation of a message depends on the address to which it is dispatched.

Spinal Cord Reflexes

But to return to the monosynaptic pathway. There is, in the muscles, a set of receptors known as neuromuscular spindles. They register the degree of stretch of a muscle. Consider sitting with one's knees crossed loosely; the muscle which extends the knee joint (the *quadriceps femoris*) is relaxed. Within it are neuromuscular spindles whose afferent axons run to the spinal cord. There they synapse on to motor neurons whose efferents run back to the same muscle. If the tendon of the knee is then tapped sharply with a hammer, the muscle suddenly stretches, the neuromuscular spindles discharge down the afferent, the afferent excites the efferent neuron which fires, instructing the muscle to contract; the contraction of this extensor muscle results in a swift jerk of the knee. This is the knee-jerk reflex. Nothing could be simpler, more automatic—indeed this automatic response is precisely what one means by a reflex. It is not surprising to find it so frequently used by doctors as a sign of spinal and nervous integrity. But its sheer simplicity and automatism—a real telephone-wire function—is both primitive and unsubtle compared to what is possible within the nervous system—and indeed as has already been suggested, this simple, invariant response is so rare as to be hard to find. Even among reflexes there are few as simple as the monosynaptic knee jerk.

In the knee-jerk reflex the afferent could synapse directly on to the efferent because they both arose at the same spinal region; they related to the same muscle. Consider a slightly more complex event: one puts one's finger on to a hot stove; one withdraws it. The muscles involved in the withdrawal are not those of the finger however, but of the arm. A minimum of three neurons and two synapses must be involved here. For the afferents from the skin receptors signaling "I am burning" will arrive at one level in the spinal cord, while the efferent motor neurons which must signal the muscles of the arm to contract arise not in the same spinal region but higher up the cord. An interneuron is needed to link the afferent with the efferent; an interneuron which travels between the two regions of the spinal cord. By means of this interneuron the REFLEX ARC is completed and the finger lifted.

But this is not all. One has not performed an act of which one is unconscious or whose reasons escape one. The message

"finger burning" gets to the brain as well, and into consciousness. There are great sweeps of ascending tracts in the spinal
cord carrying the information from the myriad sense receptors
of the body up to the brain as well. Many do not reach conscious
attention, or do so only when some changing situation develops.
Thus, when one sits down the pressure receptors tell one that he
is sitting; pressure is registered in the buttocks and the small of
the back. Within a short while however this information will
no longer appear at the conscious level. It may be "switched off"
at a lower level, and only re-register when changing position
(we come to the full significance of this "switching off" in
chapter 9). As for the message from the burnt finger, because of
the time delay involved in getting a message up through the
synaptic stages to the cerebral cortex, it may even arrive at the
brain and consciousness some time after the reflex arc has been
completed and the finger has already been removed from the
source of the pain. Somewhere in that disynaptic pathway an
axon must branch to allow its signal to go right up to the brain
as well. (Fig 32)

But the moment we allow such a disynaptic reflex pathway
we allow the prospect of complexities. One touches a hot stove
with one's finger; reflex action will withdraw it automatically
by the disynaptic pathway of figure 32. Suppose, however,
that someone is holding a revolver at one's head—move the
finger and he shoots. The odds are that the finger will stay there
rather longer at least than with no such constraint. How could
such a modification to the reflex occur? Because within the
spinal cord there are not only interneurons involved in ascending pathways, carrying information to the brain, but also great
descending tracts running down the cord from the varying
brain regions. Over a million nerves, for example, leave the
region of the motor cortex, their axons springing from the large
PYRAMIDAL CELLS to be found there. They run down the brain
stem and along the cord, ensuring the possibility of higher
cortical control over many aspects of motor activity. It is such
nerves as these which are called into play in countermanding
the simple reflex instruction "remove the finger". "No. Leave
it there," they say, "or worse will befall." To construct such a
negative pathway with its possibilities of countermand it is
enough to insert additional interneurons into the same system
which can be excited by the stimulus from the center. If such a
neuron is inhibitory in its effect upon the efferent motor neuron,
it will block its action. And indeed the spinal cord gray matter
appears to be dense with such inhibitory interneurons.

There are many other reflexes involving spinal cord neurons
which could be analyzed in a comparable manner. Those
involved in walking for example, which demand the reciprocal

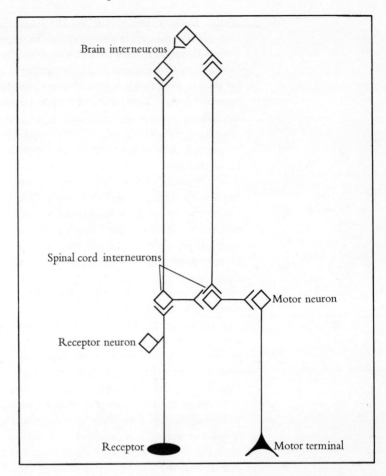

32 Spinal cord reflex arc, mediated by interneurons and modulated by information descending from the brain.

Brain interneurons

Spinal cord interneurons

Motor neuron

Receptor neuron

Receptor

Motor terminal

action of groups of muscles to either side of the body, some contracting while others relax, are among the more complex; other reflex actions whose control lies higher in the nervous system in the brain stem include breathing. But the general principles, which should be apparent from even this partial analysis, are that while we can in theory define a simple reflex monosynaptic system, even with the relatively "unconscious" nervous functions organized within the spinal cord, the actual degree of interplay and modification of each other's actions by the interneurons is vast.

The range of activity, of choice, open to the individual afferent or efferent neuron is limited, as we saw in the last chapter in the case of the limitations of the individual axon: to fire or not to fire. Choices are made as a consequence of the sum of all the information impinging upon each such neuron. And when considering this final stage in the process, it must not be forgotten that, far from the single synapse on an individual motor neuron responsible for the knee-jerk reflex, or even the two of the modified flexor reflex incorporating an inhibitory interneuron, in reality some two to ten thousand synapses occur on each motor neuron, some inhibitory, some excitatory. Nor of course is a single neuron alone involved even in a mono-synaptic reflex. Thousands of motor neurons are involved in any coordinated piece of muscular action. Anything more subtle involves millions–though even a million, it must be recalled, represents only some 0·01 percent of the total available neurons of the cortex.

It is because of the convenient capacity of the spinal cord and the lower brain regions such as the brain stem to carry out the relatively automatic responses of maintenance of posture, walking, the removal of a limb from a noxious stimulus, and so forth, that it is possible for animals whose spinal cord has been severed at any point–even high into the brain itself–to continue to carry out a repertoire of activity which is striking in its extent. Humans who suffer from PARAPLEGIA, where by accident or disease a severing of the spinal cord has occurred, although they lose all sensations for the regions below the break, because the ascending tracts to the brains are lost, none the less retain, or gradually recover as the time after the accident extends, quite elaborate sets of spinal reflexes which enable some control over bodily functions to be exerted. At the same time though, released from the inhibitory influences from above, which say "caution" when the reflex says "act", which say "remember" when the reflex has no memory, such activities in the spinal animals seem somehow exaggerated, automatic, unmodifiable, out of key with the overall context in which the animal finds itself.

The spinal cord, in both its capacities and limitations, thus serves as a simple model for the more complex processes and functions which occur higher in the organism. But before we can proceed further to look at these, it is necessary to say a little more about the nature of the input message that the sense receptors dispatch. It has so far been adequate simply to assert that frequency of firing is the code used by the nervous system in the translation and transmission of information. It is now becoming important to test more closely the validity of this statement.

Some Coding Mechanisms for Sensory Inputs

The discussion of this point which follows is derived from an analysis provided by Vernon Mountcastle, of Johns Hopkins, who asks: what are the problems faced by the nervous system in receiving input from a sense receptor? What does the system "need to know"? He distinguishes the following sets of questions:[17]

(1) "Has anything happened?" or "Is anything there?", basically the problem of detecting a change in input against the background of continuous activity and "noise" of the nervous system. The issues here are those of the threshold of the response of the receptor, which can be monitored by recording from the afferent nerve, and of the behavioral threshold of the organism: What is the least pressure on the fingertip or the quietest sound or the dimmest light which a person can perceive? How is this threshold related to the threshold of nervous response?

(2) There follows from this the question "What is it?" Identification clearly depends on noting just which inputs to the brain, which receptors or their afferents are stimulated.

(3) The question "How much of it is there?" This is the problem of quantification, which can again be analyzed both in terms of neural and behavioral responses.

(4) The comparative question, "Is this stimulus stronger than some other occurring at the same time or just previously?" which is obviously derived from the previous question, "How small a difference can in fact be detected?"

(5) Given that a stimulus has been registered, "Where is it?" Such a question cannot be answered in terms of the response of a particular nerve, but only by noting the summed responses of many nerves and their representation in the central nervous system. Between them these can define the location and the bounds of the stimulus in space, that is its place and shape.

(6) And finally: "Is the stimulus changing in space or time?" – moving, increasing or diminishing in magnitude? This analysis depends not only on the responses of populations of afferent nerves and their central connections, but on the relations of this present analysis to past events.

The system of receptors and their analyzers within the brain can indeed perform all of these analyses so effectively as to make it almost insultingly obvious to discuss them in these terms. But how? What coding possibilities are available to the system, once it has been wired up in an appropriate form? The study of reflex pathways showed how a wiring diagram could be produced which generates both invariant and variant responses. These new questions take such wiring for granted and are concerned instead with the methods of conveying information along such wires. Mountcastle has suggested a set of types of code that could be used:

(a) The simplest is one that has already been suggested: the frequency of firing of a single axon. If an axon signaled a change in intensity of the stimulus in terms of a changed frequency of

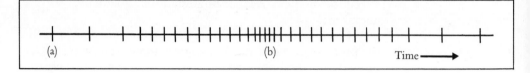

(a)   (b)   Time ⟶

33 Coding by the frequency of firing of a single neuron. Each spike represents the passage of an action potential; intensity of stimulus and frequency of firing are both low at (a), higher at (b).

firing, questions (1), (2) and (3) could be answered (figure 33). But other codes are possible. Another would be:

(b) The frequency profile in a population. This implies the extension to a large number of axons of the signaling device suggested for one axon. The profile of the differences in frequencies in a number of axons from adjacent receptors could map in space the contours of the stimulus. An example would be squeeze pressure applied to the fingertip. The "focus" of the squeeze would be represented by fast firing axons, the periphery by slower firing ones. The dimensions of the stimulus would thus be mapped. Note, though, that this ducks, for the moment, the question of just how the mapping is interpreted, it only tells us that a map of a particular type could be put into the brain. None the less, it is a way of coding information which is adequate to answer question (5) and part of question (6).

(c) The rate of change with time of the firing of a single axon, or of the frequency profile over a population. For instance, an axon may fire for ten seconds at a rate of fifty firings per second, for the next ten at forty per second and the next ten at thirty per second. Such a change can provide a device enabling the answers to the question "Is this stronger than that?" and the question "Is the stimulus changing in time?"

Such forms of information coding do not exhaust the possibilities available to the system. Other considerations make possible further codes. Rhythmic oscillations superimposed on a basic firing rate, or the interactions between several sets of such oscillations, which might all have to coincide at a particular point in time or space to make a particular interneuron respond are just two examples of the sorts of hyper-code or meta-code which might operate–but it is only the principle which is important here, not the details.

Note that the answers to all of the more sophisticated questions demand the existence, not merely of the set of inputs and their codes, but also at least one set of "comparator" cells deeper within the nervous system, which can actually read and interpret the codes. For a time-derivative code like that of (c) above to be meaningful, there has to be a set of cells which can not only read the information that "the rate of firing now is thirty per second" but that "twenty seconds ago it was fifty per second". This is the essence of a memory system, the key feature of the operation of the brain. Just how such a mechanism could

34 A simple neuronal comparator memory mechanism using synaptic delays. Neuron E receives two inputs deriving from A: one direct, the other by way of interneurons B, C and D. Because synaptic delays are much greater than axonal transmission times, the input via B, C and D takes longer to arrive at E than input direct from A. Thus, two synapses on E present the neuron with information about the state of A one arriving direct, and one arriving via B, C and D, giving the state of A a few milliseconds earlier. Changes in the state of A can thus be monitored.

operate is something we discuss in chapter 9, but for the sake of the completeness of the account here, the diagram in figure 34 is one possible method of achieving a short-term comparator memory. This model shows how the introduction of a "time delay" into the branching interneuron of an input circuit could result in a situation such that at any time a comparator cell has two inputs being fired into it. One originates "now" from the receptor and the other carries the record of the behavior of the receptor at some brief previous time. The comparator can then match the two inputs appropriately.

Do afferents in fact operate in ways which could be predicted by such a model? In an ingenious set of experiments, Mountcastle has shown that some indeed do. Two parallel experiments were made. In the first a recording electrode was attached to the nerve running from the pressure receptors of the skin in a monkey's hand. The pressure on the skin above the receptors was varied and the frequency of axonal firing was measured. Pressure was exerted by prodding the skin with a blunt rod. The degree of pressure was estimated by measuring the skin indentation produced. There turned out to be a direct relationship between the pressure and the firing rate – the deeper the indentation, the faster the firing. The neural code for pressure intensity is thus a linear one. In a parallel experiment, volunteer human subjects had the same receptors stimulated in the same way, and they were asked to estimate subjectively the amount of pressure on the skin. Once again there was a linear relationship between skin indentation and subjective estimate of the intensity of the stimulus – the harder the prod, the greater the rapidity of firing. The linear code of the afferent axon had obviously preserved its form through all the transformations which must take place in the brain, between the arrival of the impulses, their analysis, comparison and finally the behavioral response of the human, in recording his estimate of the pressure. The physiological events within the nervous system parallel in form the behavioral output. Similar parallelisms have been shown for the spatial mapping of a tactile stimulus of this sort as well. For at least one sort of receptor and its afferents a linear coding method seems to operate.

The Visual System

Certainly not all receptors are as straightforward as these. In other cases the increase in firing rate may fall off with increasing stimulus intensity to reach a behavioral and physiological maximum above which further increases in intensity of stimulus cannot be detected. Perhaps Mountcastle was fortunate to choose so relatively simple a system to work with, and in particular one in which he was dealing with a relatively straightforward type of information–changes in intensity of stimulus. In the processing of information from the vastly more complex visual or auditory systems, a different type of result becomes apparent. The most spectacular is certainly the visual system. In humans and other mammals the types of data to be conveyed and processed by this system are more complex than any other–not only does the human visual system recognize light and dark, it analyzes objects and patterns, movements and color; it retains its discriminatory capacity over a range of inputs which may vary over many orders of magnitude in light intensity. Such a wealth of information far surpasses that provided by the simple touch receptors–indeed it has been argued by Richard Gregory, in his book *The Intelligent Eye*, that the evolution of the brain followed that of the eye, in that only with the development of the visual system did the problem of analysis and interpretation demand so complex a structure for handling it.[18] Whatever the validity of this hypothesis–and not everyone agrees with it by any means–it is a token of the complexity of a system which here receives only a partial and primitive analysis, which is however hopefully adequate for the present purpose.

The primary receptors of the mammalian visual system are the neurons of the RETINA, a thin sheet of cells at the back of the eye.[19] These receptors are broadly divided into two categories, the RODS and CONES (so-called from the shape of the cells). It is the rods which are primarily responsible for light/dark discrimination, the cones for color discrimination. There are generally stated to be three classes of cones, sensitive to different wavelengths–in the monkey the three are maximally stimulated at 445, 535 and 570 nm* (i.e. blue, yellow/green and red respectively). The receptors are connected to a set of secondary neurons in a complex manner, such that each receptor makes synapses with many secondary neurons, while each secondary

---

*The abbreviation "nm" stands for "nanometers", or 10^{-9} m, and is a measure of the wavelength of light.

neuron makes synapses with many receptors. The secondary neurons, in their turn, connect with a further set of neurons (ganglion cells) whose axons form the optic nerve which runs from the back of the eye to the brain. The whole set-up is shown in figure 35. Thus the receptors do not have "private lines" to the brain at all, but the input from many is collated in the information which passes up the optic nerve. What is more, there is a reduction in the number of lines (axons) compared to the number of receptors, for in man there are some 10^8 rods and 5×10^6 cones to each eye, while only 10^6 ganglion cells send their axons up each optic nerve. It is only when the pathway from the eye reaches the visual cortex of the brain (by way of the lateral geniculate body) that the cell number approaches that of the retina once more. In the cortex, the axons of the optic nerve reach out to some 5×10^8 neurons, or nearly five times as many as the original number of receptors.

A clue to the operation of the system is provided by an.

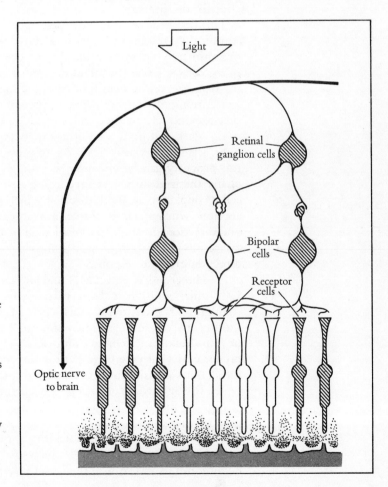

35 The structure of the retina. Images fall on the receptor cells, of which there are about 130 million in each retina. Some analysis of an image occurs as the receptors transmit messages to the retinal ganglion neurons via the bipolar cells. A group of receptors funnels into a particular ganglion cell's receptive field. In as much as the fields of several ganglion cells overlap, one receptor may send messages to several ganglion cells and thence along the optic nerve to the brain.

examination of visual acuity—one can actually see and distinguish objects whose image on the retina is narrower than a single cell across. A telegraph wire is visible against a bright sky at a distance of a quarter of a mile. Its image may cover no more than one twenty-fifth of the receptor, yet it is seen sharply. It is the reduction in number between the receptors and the retinal ganglion cells which is responsible for this: what is transmitted up the optic nerve depends on the overlap in fields (a field in this sense is the area in contact with the dendrites of a particular cell) between the secondary neurons and ganglion cells. If the fields of the ganglion cells are mapped by shining a bright spot of light on to selected regions of the retina, it is found that the field of each cell has a "center" within which it responds with a lower threshold, and a "periphery" of a higher threshold. If the spot of light excites in the center, it will inhibit in the periphery; if as in other cases, it inhibits in the center, it will excite in the periphery. This provides the basic "on-off" code for the system.

This does not complete the description of the cells, but the stimuli they respond to over and above this differ in different organisms. In higher mammals more seems to be left as the job of the cortex, less as the job of the retinal ganglion cell, while in the frog, the retina does more and the higher brain centers do less. Among the types of detectors present in the retina are those that respond selectively to lines or edges, that is to contrast between dark and light, and others that respond to motion of a light across the visual field. An impressive demonstration of this property can be given by recording from the brain of an unanæsthetized animal. If a recording electrode in the ganglion cell is coupled to an audible output which chatters, like a geiger counter, when a cell fires, then movement—of a finger say—in one direction through the visual field in front of the animal's eye results in a cascade of signals; moving it back in the opposite direction gives no response.

It is Hubel and Wiesel at MIT and Horace Barlow at Berkeley, California, who have been particularly responsible for designing and interpreting this type of experiment.[20] Such motion analyzers can respond either to "left-right" movements or "up-down" movements, and clearly signpost, not only the presence of a moving edge but the direction of its movement. Other units are "nothing" detectors—recognizers of uniformity, which fire only when no change is occurring in the system. Any change in the field results in an inhibition of firing, which gradually returns once the change is complete and a new pattern is present in the visual field. In the frog, though not in mammals, there are also "newness units" which fire only in response to a novel stimulus and cease as the novelty wears off.

The next staging post en route to the visual cortex occurs in the collection of neurons known as the lateral geniculate body (figure 28). Before the optic nerves arrive at the geniculate they have already undergone the characteristic crossing over which occurs to all inputs to the brain, so that information from the right side of the body arrives at the left hemisphere and from the left side to the right hemisphere. Thus the left lateral geniculate receives axons predominantly from the right eye and vice versa (figure 28). The most striking feature of the geniculate though, is that the arrangement of neurons within it is such to produce a "map" of the retina. Although the neurons are arranged in a compact three-dimensional block of tissue not obviously resembling the layout of cells in the retina, they combine to maintain a point-for-point representation of the thin skin of cells that forms the retina. The geniculate neurons are arranged in layers, and stimulation of two adjacent ganglion cells will result in a response in two adjacent geniculate cells. It is not clear if the geniculate is merely a staging post en route for the cortex, or how much, if any, processing of the visual information occurs there, but in monkeys it does seem to have a particular rôle in the processing of color information. Thus some geniculate cells respond to green and not to red, or blue and not to yellow, etc. Although its function is uncertain, the retinal map contained in the geniculate is one of the most striking and best studied examples of the specific topographic relation of cells that occurs within the brain, and there will be reason to return to the question of how this specificity is achieved in due course.

It is at the visual cortex that the major processing of retinal information must occur, and our understanding of the coding of the cortex is largely due to the work of Hubel and Wiesel (figure 36). Once again, as in the lateral geniculate, a mapping of the retina occurs in the cortex, but one which, by virtue of the greater number of cells involved, is vastly richer. The basic on/off units still occur, but now receive inputs not just from one, but from both eyes; each half of the cortex has a map of both visual inputs. It is this map which presumably makes possible the binocular three-dimensional vision of human sight rather than the flat two-dimensional pictures that a camera takes.

As with the lateral geniculate, the cortical map of the retinal world is contained in a block of neurons, arranged anatomically into connecting columns that run the depth of the cortex from the outer surface to the white beneath. Within the columns there are cells of a variety of types. For the "simple" or on/off cells, firing can be triggered by a light spot on the retina, and indeed can be accurately predicted from the position of the spot. The "complex" cells are activated instead by a light slit in a dark

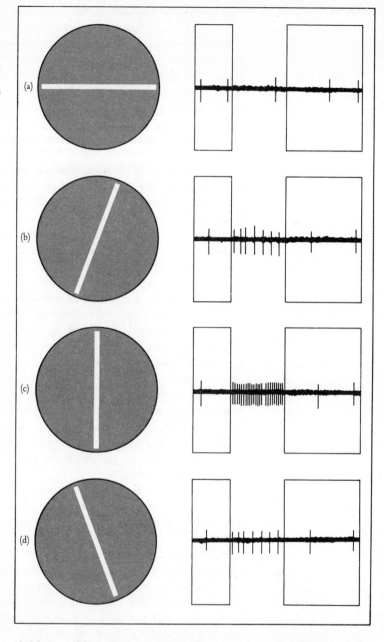

36 A single complex cell in the cortex shows varying responses to a slit projected onto the cell's visual field in the retina in an experiment by Hubel and Wiesel. The cell only responds to the image of the slit when it is in a particular orientation (vertical) with respect to the retina. Various positions of the slit are shown at left: at right the responses of the cell.

field, or a black bar in a bright one, or an edge between light and dark. For either type of cell, it is necessary for the stimulating light or edge to move if the cell is to fire and to be oriented at a particular angle with respect to the retina. Thus the cell may respond only to a light slit moving vertically upwards but not moving downwards or horizontally or diagonally.

A third type of cell is described as "hypercomplex". These are mainly not located in the same columns as the other two types discussed, but instead are grouped in an adjacent area of cortex. They may respond selectively only to a line with a defined beginning and end, in a particular orientation, or to an edge or a particular angle. In addition, all the other ranges of selectivity suggested earlier as occurring among the retinal ganglion cells in lower organisms like the frog, are found in the cortex in higher mammals such as the cat.

The process of increasing selectivity, as to whether to respond or not to respond, which seems from this description to characterize the various cortical cells, provides a mechanism whereby information relevant to the organism can be identified and abstracted from the mass of crude data arriving at the retina. Different cells in the cortex respond to different questions concerning the retinal image. What shape is it? If moving, in which direction? Is it getting brighter or darker? As with the simpler case of the touch receptors though, this is still not enough; a higher order of cells must always be involved in comparator functions, which identify the abstracted image as like or unlike something in the organism's past experience. Obviously certain inputs can be learned—the letter "A" for example—and one of the most striking features of such inputs is that subsequently they are recognized provided the context is right irrespective of the orientation—A or V or ⪦ or ⪧, for instance—or whether the figure is a partial one, obscured or broken—A or Ꭺ.

This is not the point at which to enter into the complex perceptual, psychological and philosophical arguments about what constitutes the "A-ness" of such an object, nor the debate as to why we recognize it whatever its orientation, and whatever the angle its image subtends on the retina (how large it is). But it seems reasonable to assume that there are present in the visual cortex classificatory cells, which are responsible both for the learning of a particular input—that of "A" for example—and later for its recognition in a variety of guises.

Yet in some sense the capacity to recognize, for example, the letter "A", is distributed over the whole region of the visual cortex. There does not appear to be a single (or even a number of such) specific cell which fires in response to "A" and only to "A". On the other hand, specific lesions in the visual cortex region of both hemispheres can result in blind spots in particular retinal regions which would normally ultimately connect to the regions which have been removed. Visual analysis thus seems in part to be the specific function of particular cells, but in an important and not clearly defined manner also to be an aspect of the total activity of all the cells. Thus the phrase "I am seeing such and such" may, at the hierarchical level appropriate to physiology, be rendered as "state so-and-so of all the cells of the visual cortex at that time". This is an example of the phenomenon of cortical equipotentiality and its limitations.

Nor for that matter is the activity of "seeing" totally obliterated by removal of the visual cortex. In animals in which this operation has been performed, some visual responses (discrimination between light and dark for instance) still appear to remain possible, and relearning of sorts can occur. This is an example of another general principle of the organization of the brain, its *redundancy*, whereby functions are apparently duplicated in several regions, perhaps as a result of evolutionary modifications and duplications of structures, but in any event resulting in a situation such that if one structure or region is injured, partial or total replacement of the function by another structure or region can occur.

But at this point I am concerned only to make the point that the coding and classification mechanisms of the brain can be analyzed, so that it is feasible at least in principle to account for these aspects of behavior in terms of neuronal responses.

The Brain as a System

In this chapter we have considered the workings of the brain as an integrated system. In order to do so, we first defined the brain as an assemblage of excitable cells (neurons) arranged in definite functional relationships to one another, such that excitation of particular cells can result in a defined spread of excitation to certain other cells. The function of the cells, it was argued, can only be considered in terms of the existence of a nervous *system* of which the cells are units.

But as we move from a consideration of the individual components to that of the system as a whole, the clash of paradigms becomes sharper, and is more clearly reflected in disputes between techniques for study, as between attempts either to specify the system as the sum of its pathways, or to manipulate the system as a whole and draw conclusions about its functioning. A consideration of the information-processing function of the system shows how information of considerable complexity can be coded in terms of components which, like the axon, can only signal with units of constant magnitude. The key to this capacity is that the nervous system operates in terms both of a position code (which axon is firing, from which cell, and connected to which, determines the interpretation of the information, for instance, between sensory modalities) and in terms of a frequency code (how frequently the axon is firing now in relationship to the rate of firing of its neighbors now and to its own frequency a short time interval ago). Relatively simple neuronal circuitry can provide at least model mechanisms for a variety of brain functions, from the simple reflex, through to the reception and analysis of visual information.

We have so far said nothing about the output from the brain, in terms of motor activity, and how far this can be interpreted in neuronal terms. In fact, some aspects of the control of motor output can be subject to even more rigorous analysis than is possible with the visual system – particularly the cerebellum, which in some senses represents the furthest neurobiology has yet got to providing a complete specification of the properties of a massive chunk of nervous tissue over a whole change of hierarchical levels ranging from the cellular to the behavioral.

Knowledge of coding within the cerebellum is rather more detailed than the flashes of insight coupled with illuminating experiment which have so far been all that has been possible when dealing with brain regions such as the visual cortex. So rigorous indeed can the specification of cerebellar properties be, that John Eccles has gone so far as to describe it as a "neuronal machine",[21] while a remarkable piece of analysis by David Marr has provided something very close to a full theoretical description of its possible functioning.[22] For the interested reader, discussion of Marr's analysis can be found in Appendix 3 (p. 311). All the examples of this chapter have been intended to demonstrate both the specificity and precision of neuronal pathways. It is not claimed that all neuronal pathways and their connections are mapped; this would manifestly be untrue. No single pathway in a mammalian system is known in detail even in the spinal cord, and even the broad outlines are understood for only a small percentage of the total cell mass of the brain. Even for such major systems of receptors, effectors and their afferents and efferents, the outlines of whose operation have been sketched here, the level of detailed knowledge is scarcely enough to make anything but the broadest type of generalization and to hint at the mechanisms involved. But the point, as is the case in so much of this book, is not to catalog the specific, but to provide a draft sufficient to justify the claim for a particular principle. In this case, that the mechanisms of input to and output from the nervous system and its behavioral and perceptual correlates, lie within the range of specification even now experimentally available. In outline, it is possible to demonstrate the existence of pathways within the brain, and of mechanisms for the transmission of information along such pathways, which can account for the behavior of the brain system at this level. Such pathways do not yet allow an approach to the major brain functions of learning and memory, drive, motivation or consciousness. But before these can be considered, it is necessary to look further at how the brain system has evolved and how it develops.

5 The Origins of Nervous Systems

Why and how, have brains evolved?[1] The evolutionary history of living forms can be traced back with reasonable certainty to those apparently simplest of creatures, one-celled, living in sea, river or pond, early variants, some three hundred million years ago, of the tumultuous world of living creatures first revealed to the painstaking van Leeuenhoek when, in the late seventeenth century, he became the first man ever to look down a microscope and observe life smaller than the naked eye could see. Behind those one-celled ancestral forms, lies a region of uncertainty and speculation. But it is now possible to describe with a fair degree of probability the sequence of events which led from the primitive earth and its prebiotic atmosphere, by way of the synthesis, powered by the sun's radiation and the earth's internal heat, of increasingly more complex organic chemicals. In certain areas, perhaps drying ponds or sea edges, the concentration of these substances must have passed a critical value, forming a chemical broth, a "primordial soup" in which increasingly elaborate chemical interactions could occur. Eventually the whole chemical brew, including perhaps proteins and nucleic acids, coalesced into primitive cells. Many of these early phases of life's origin can be mimicked today in artificial experimental situations such as one in which particular mixtures of simple, nonliving gases such as carbon dioxide, ammonia, water vapor and methane ("marsh gas") are placed together in a closed chamber and heated for several days, while an electric discharge, to simulate the energy source present on the primitive earth, is passed through the mixture.[2] Quite complex organic chemicals, similar to those found in all today's living organisms, can be synthesized in this way. Such a development of basic cellular mechanisms must have occurred before any specialization of organisms or differentiation of plants, animals, bacteria or fungi.

The world of the preliving is a shadowy one. Were these primordial cells alive or not? The decision is arbitrary; it depends upon what one means by living. Simple organic chemicals are clearly not alive; men, oak trees, yeast cells and bacteria clearly are. Between lies a gradation in which only the end points are clear. At what point in the cooking procedure does a fresh egg become hard boiled?

We may however, without undue fear of inaccuracy, postulate the world of these creatures as not too dissimilar from that of a present-day drop of water viewed on a microscope slide. Such a drop contains photosynthetic organisms, the simplest plants, which, with the help of the pigment chlorophyll and a complex series of enzymes, utilize the sun's energy to convert carbon dioxide, from the atmosphere or dissolved in water, into sugar. These two, the sun and carbon dioxide, and in addition a source of nitrogen, perhaps ammonia or nitrate, from which proteins and nucleic acids could be fabricated, represent the total of such an organism's requirements for survival.

Other primitive organisms, which did not possess the photosynthetic mechanism, could not synthesize their own foodstuffs, such as glucose, and instead were committed to rely on preformed sources of such food substances. Their need was to find, capture and digest either isolated molecules of such substances, or, more frequently, other living organisms containing them. Such activities of consuming, rather than producing, has demands for survival more complex than those of the plant.

Behavior in Single-Celled Organisms

None the less, both plant ancestor and animal ancestor must have developed a considerable range of "behavioral properties" in order to survive. Evolutionary success must have gone to those photosynthetic organisms which tended to seek the light and shun the dark, to those consumers which moved towards sources of preformed foodstuffs. And when one examines the behavior of present-day unicellular organisms, they can in fact be shown to demonstrate such attributes.

The tiny whiplike projections, or cilia, with which many of the unicellular organisms, such as PARAMOECIUM are equipped, beat regularly in coordination with one another, a coordination probably achieved by a system of fine threads which run longitudinally, connecting the bases of all the cilia together. This coordination–a forerunner of neuromuscular control perhaps– results in organized behavior on the part of the creature. Thus, except when it is actually feeding (on bacteria), paramoecium is in constant peregrination, frequently bumping into obstacles in its path, like a clockwork motorcar. Like the more sophisticated of such toys, after a collision it goes into reverse, by reversing the beat of the cilia on one side, repeating this sequence whenever it makes a collision until a free path is found. This sort of movement is called an *avoiding reaction*, and as well as fixed obstacles, heat or cold or the presence of irritating chemicals (such as sulphuric acid), can all result in the same response.

Another sort of behavior shown by paramoecium occurs if, for instance, the organism moves into a region rich in its food material, bacteria. If it should by chance then move out of the region again, it will tend to reverse back into it, so that it stays where the food supply is richest. Thus it behaves as if it is avoiding the food-poor area and seeking the food-rich area. The pattern of movement that results can be described as trial-and-error, or *goal-seeking* behavior.

Thus, even paramoecium can exhibit quite a complex behavioral pattern. This behavioral repertoire is shared by other one-celled organisms too. The photosynthetic plant prototype EUGLENA has, in addition to the activities described for paramoecium, the property, when placed in an unevenly lit environment, of moving towards the light, so that a group of euglena tend to aggregate on that side of a glass vessel which is nearest the light, thus maximizing the efficiency with which their photosynthetic systems can utilize light. This movement towards the light is associated with the presence in euglena of a large red granule which appears to contain light-sensitive chemicals.

All this behavior occurs in cells which have no nervous system at all. Yet obviously there must be some system of communication operating within such cells, so that one part can know what the other is doing. Indeed, such behavioral properties can be seen in living forms even simpler than paramoecium or euglena, such as bacteria, which may be one hundred or more times smaller. As long ago as the 1880s W. Pfeiffer, in Germany, dipped a thin capillary tube containing glucose into a drop of liquid containing bacteria, and observed that the bacteria tended to collect at the mouth of the capillary. How do the bacteria "know" that the nutrient is there? What must happen is that the glucose slowly diffuses out of the capillary into the surrounding solution. At the edge of the capillary, the concentration of glucose is high; as the distance from the capillary increases so the concentration of the glucose drops. There is thus a gradient of glucose, with its highest point at the capillary mouth. The bacteria, in reaching the concentrated glucose at the center, are running uphill along this gradient until they reach the summit.[3]

One of the useful things about bacteria is their relative amenability to experimental manipulation compared to more complex organisms, and in recent years this phenomenon of CHEMOTAXIS (movement in response to chemical stimuli) has been studied in some detail. Quite a number of chemicals will attract the bacteria, even those which, although chemically similar to glucose, cannot serve as foodstuffs for the organisms. Other substances that the bacteria can use as food will none the less not attract them. Most interestingly, it is possible to produce mutant bacteria (by exposing them, for instance, to x-rays) which can still use glucose as food, but seem not to be attracted to it. These experiments suggest that the mechanism of attraction is separate from the mechanism of digestion of the nutrient.

Probably there are present on the surface of the bacterial cells particular molecular structures which are tailored to fit the individual glucose molecules. These structures, CHEMORECEP-TORS, must in some way respond to the gradient of nutrient and in turn cause a change in the mechanism that directs the bacterial movement. Possibly this link is mediated by way of a change in the electrical potential of the cells.

These molecular mechanisms may seem remote from the neurobiology discussed up to now in this book, for what have bacteria or paramoecium to do with brains? Yet the point is that even these minute one-celled organisms show a range of properties which can be regarded as "behavior"; a range which is at first sight surprising in its extent. The evolutionary advantage provided to the ancestors of these one-celled organisms when they first developed the capacity to move toward the light or nutrient, and away from obstacles or noxious substances, is obvious. The diversity and relative complexity of the behavioral patterns that have emerged even in these primitive organisms suggests that such developments must have taken place fairly early in evolutionary history. This is not to say that such organisms possess anything resembling the properties of thought or conscious experience we recognize in ourselves as humans. But none the less, the links between paramoecium avoiding obstacles and the activities of writing, or reading, this chapter, are evolutionary and capable of being mapped step by step.

Multicellular Systems

The next obvious evolutionary step was the emergence of multicellular organisms, first as colonies of one-celled creatures, living together to mutual advantage (sponges are rather close to this form of organism), later as true multicellular organisms. At this point a rather sharp divergence took place between plants and animals. In the evolutionary development of photo-synthesizing creatures, like plants, the solution to the problem of obtaining light energy that was found was not that of moving to where the light was, but of staying in one place and growing up-ward, exposing a large surface area, in the form of leaves, toward the light. Plants thus became essentially stationary organisms dependent on the daily and yearly cycle of sunshine for their existence, and content to wait upon this cycle, with their leaves spread to receive its life-giving energy. Such an evolutionary choice was clearly very successful, as witness the immense variety of plant forms and their total biomass.* This choice did

* That is, the mass of the total number of organisms of this form alive in the world–a measure sometimes adopted to indicate evolutionary success.

not however require the development of elaborate behavioral patterns, communication and signaling devices.

Many green plants show the same positive PHOTOTROPISM as euglena, growing towards the light. A comparable behavioral response is that of the sunflower, which turns toward the sun, thus changing position during the course of the day. But together with similar types of directed movements of the roots during growth, and one or two more, these represent the limit of the behavioral responses of the plant world.

Internal signaling devices like hormones, which are one means of communication between the cells of a multicellular organism, and devices which enable the plant to communicate (in the most general sense of that word) with the insects which carry pollen, may be included to complete the catalog. But the conclusion follows that the plant world has turned away from the evolution of nerves and brains.

The reverse is true in the evolutionary sequence within the animal kingdom. Here a static life is not permissible: prey and be preyed upon is the order of the day. Always excluding such oddities as the sea anemone, standing quietly with one's arms out waiting for food to fall into one's mouth is not a recipe for long survival in the animal world. Hence the need for the development of very rapid means of communication between cells in different parts of the body, so that the head very quickly knows what is happening at the tail. Information arriving at the surface of the animal therefore needs to be interpreted by sense organs, while action based upon that information demands the emergence of muscle systems.

Granted these needs, what possibilities of signaling and information gathering and processing are open to the multicellular animal? Above all the development of multicellular organisms makes possible the achievement of a degree of cellular specialization. For a one-celled organism, self-sufficiency is imperative. Within that cell the entire apparatus of existence must be packed, not merely for the cell but for the organism and the species. Multicellularity permits the development of specialism. Some cells can be concerned primarily with the digestion of foodstuffs taken in, some with providing a protective layer for the organism against the external environment, some with producing a skeleton framework, some with a circulation system, some with the contractile musculature, some with the signaling system.

The simplest form of signaling system is one analogous to the bacterial chemoreceptor systems discussed above. Granted that the cellular biochemistry is sensitive enough for chemicals arriving at the cell surface to modify the behavior of the cell in some appropriate manner—like the bacterial response to the glucose molecule—then one type of signaling system would be that in which the cells at one end of the animal communicate with those at the other by means of the fabrication of a specific chemical which, passing through the circulation system, arrives at its target cells and modifies their behavior—for instance, if the target cell were a muscle, the chemical might signal it to contract. This would demand specialism at the communicating end of the system as well as the end being communicated with, the development of cells with a particular property, that of synthesizing and secreting the chemical "messenger" concerned.

Such chemical messenger systems (or hormones) are a familiar part of animal life. In humans several hormones have just that rôle of signaling to the muscles—notably adrenalin, produced by the adrenal glands which lie above the kidneys. Other hormones have more subtle effects on their target organs, causing cells to divide or grow, metabolize faster or slower, with consequent effects on the organism at the physiological level. Such hormone systems exist even in the most primitive of multicellular organisms, and even at these primitive levels, specialized cells can be found which appear, by analogy with similar ones in higher organisms, to be concerned with the secretion of such hormones.

But there are limitations to the way in which hormones can signal. They have to diffuse out of one cell and into another a relatively long distance away, so they can work only slowly, and because they reach very many cells the message they carry cannot be a precise one. The analogy is with the tone or volume on the radio set. Rapid and specific action, the equivalent of the radio's tuning control, is the prerogative of a nervous system in the sense that this phrase has been used so far.

Individual neurons are part of this system. Nerves speed up the job of carrying a message from the signaling to the receiving cell by providing a direct cellular link, the nerve, between the two cells, and by conveying information along this nerve in the form of an electrically propagated wave.

Note that the unit nerve cell, specialized as it is for the reception of stimuli, conduction of excitation and transmission of signals, is only the individual member of this complex. For nervous transmission of information to be of value to the organism, it is not the individual nerve cell but the *system* which is important.[4]

There are a number of possible ways in which such a system could emerge. One model would be that in which the first development was the appearance of special classes of cells modified to produce hormones or hormonelike substances; secretory cells, that is. These secretory cells might then have developed so that instead of discharging their contents into a circulation which randomly brought them to the target organ, the cells themselves grow into a shape which would bring them into direct physical contact with the target. The secretion need then only be passed across the "synaptic" gap between the two.

A second model would be one in which the membrane potential of the surface of all cells, which occurs because of the differences in chemical composition between the inside of the cell and the surrounding extracellular fluid (see Appendix 1), was exploited. Perhaps at points of close contact between adjacent cells, an event in one cell which caused a membrane depolarization would trigger a comparable phenomenon in the adjacent cell. Thus a wave of depolarization through a chain of cells would be established. Such a phenomenon is known to occur even in some plants, although its function within them is quite obscure. The distinction between these two types of hypothesis for the origin of a nervous system is that the first accounts for the development of a system in terms of the emergence of its unit components, the neurons; and the second in terms of a transmitting system carried by a depolarizing wave which could subsequently be specialized into a nervous network.

The available evidence does not enable one to distinguish between these two alternatives. Indeed it is possible that both developments may have occurred simultaneously and that the system that has evolved may be a product of the interaction of two different types of mechanism.

The First Nervous System

The first step toward a nervous system can be seen among the large group of primitive organisms known as COELENTERATES (meaning "hollow gut") which are among the earliest-known multicellular animals. These creatures, of which the best-known example is the tiny pond-living HYDRA, show a variety of specialities.[5] The hydra sits at the bottom of a pond or stream attached to rocks or water plants and waving its tentacles above its mouth. Like a sea anemone, it closes these down and contracts to a blob of tissue if touched. It feeds, too, like its relative the sea anemone. When a small organism, like a crustacean, brushes past the tentacles, the hydra shoots out poisonous threads, made in special "thread cells". The paralyzed victim is then collected by the tentacles, thrust into the mouth and swallowed. Such complex behavior demands coordinated activity of quite a high order. Sensory mechanisms must exist to indicate the presence of prey or danger and the response of emission of poison or contraction into a blob must be made appropriately, the mouth must open at the right time and the gut muscles must be controlled – if the coordination goes wrong, the hydra will swallow its own tentacles, or even its own base.

(Fortunately for its survival, it cannot digest its own cells.)

Depending on its internal state, that is, whether it is well fed or starved, the hydra will be quiescent or will wave its tentacles about in a more or less agitated manner. The hydra moves in a series of somersaults, turning repeatedly head over heels.

This movement is not random. Like the one-celled organisms already described, the hydra moves toward food- and oxygen-rich regions and away from less attractive ones. But now, because a multicellular organism and not just a single cell is involved, the degree to which all these movements can be made efficiently depends on the operation of the organism's communication system, to coordinate, control, receive sensory information and carry out the appropriate responses to it. This set of properties demands a set of specialized cells. A large proportion of the hydra's tissue is composed of sheets of rather similar adjacent cells, the forerunners of those surface cells in higher organisms which are generally described as EPITHELIAL. But in addition a number of specialized cells occur. There are muscular cells, secretory cells of various sorts, sense receptors and primitive nerve cells (figure 37).

Hydra's pattern of responses is already clearly the forerunner of the behavioral repertoire of much higher and more complex animals. What does the hydra's nervous system look like? Certainly individual neurons can be seen within the hydra's body, while specialized sensory cells, which can respond to touch or pressure or chemicals, lie embedded in the surface layer of tissue, with their sensory regions exposed to the outside environment. For the system to operate, however, the existence of the individual receptors and other neurons is not enough. What matters is the pattern of the pathways which connect them. Some indication of the nature of these patterns and pathways can be obtained by placing recording electrodes on the surface of the hydra. Two types of record appear. There is a burst of electrical activity when the body of the hydra contracts spontaneously. This electrical activity arises at the base of the tentacle and spreads across the body at a rate of about fifteen centimeters per second. In addition there is another type of potential, a steady, slow beat which arises from various points on the body and which can quickly be changed in frequency, when, for example, a hydra which has been in the dark is exposed to light. Such potentials very likely represent waves of electrical activity over the entire surface epithelium of the organism rather than the firing of specific nerve cells. This then represents the forerunner of a nervous *system* in operation rather than of individual neurons. A conducting epithelium of this sort is almost like a continuous two-dimensional extended nerve axon across the outside of the organism. But such a system of conduction is not truly nervous, because there are no neurons as such. Although the wave of excitation starts at a particular point ("pacemaker") on the surface, all the cells in the epithelium are involved. By contrast, in a proper nervous system, only particular cells are involved in any given response. In the case of the hydra, it is as if all the cells of the brain were to be involved in the knee-jerk reflex. However, we may perhaps regard the situation in the hydra as the precursor of nervous systems proper.

This leaves undefined the rôle of the individual neurons which are clearly visible within the hydra's epithelium. Such cells may have originally been isolated neurosecretory ones within epithelial sheets which themselves show conducting properties. The way in which this type of cell could have evolved into a nervous system is shown in figure 38 which suggests a hypothetical scheme in which there were initially conducting epithelia leading to muscle cells which contracted when the signal arrived, with the muscle cells themselves being connected to each other by their tails. In the next stage of develop-

37 The nervous system of the hydra. The neurons, which are of different shapes, form a nerve net.

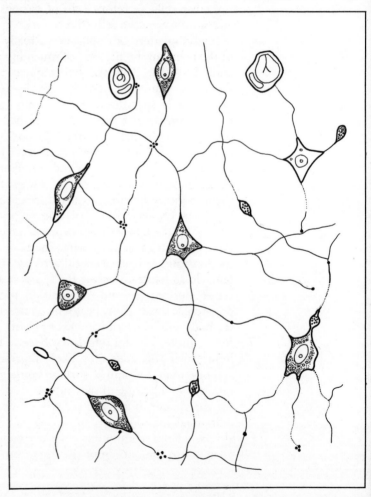

ment some of the epithelial cells have become specialized (neurons) so as to connect with each other and the muscle cells, but to bridge over the rest of the epithelial cells. Thus a specific conducting system linking neurons and muscles developed. The final stages of the process would have been the linking up of the specialized sensory cells which responded to external changes, to the rest of the system by way of the epithelial neurons, and hence to the muscles. This at last provides the classical full sequence – sense organ → nervous system → effector organ – necessary to complete the system. Notice that this type of model implies that the internal neurons (interneurons) connecting sense receptors and effector system arose to some extent independently of both muscles and sense organs.

There is another key property of the nervous system that had to emerge before its development could be taken much further, however, and that is the specificity of nervous communication and conduction. In the hydra or the sea anemone or jelly-fish, interneurons exist in large numbers and processes run

38 Hypothetical evolution of the nervous system, according to Adrian Horridge. In (a), a conducting epithelium leads to a muscle cell; in (b), the same epithelial cells are specialized to form conducting lines which bypass other cells; in (c), connections to muscle, and in (d), to sensory cells, have emerged.

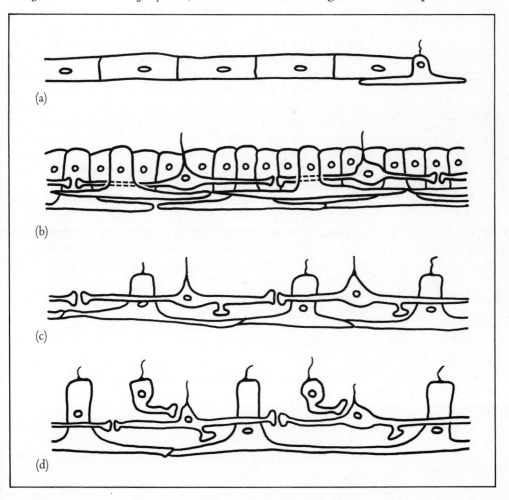

(a)

(b)

(c)

(d)

from one nerve cell to the next, connecting the whole group up into a NERVE NET. This net differs from the fully developed nervous system in that, if one of the cells in the net is stimulated, the wave of excitation passes from that cell so as eventually to involve all others. Such a wave of excitation is obviously capable of producing the symmetrical, rhythmic movements of these organisms. Transmission occurs in all directions. The neurons in the net frequently have axons running off in two directions, so that impulses can pass either way along them. The same is also true at the junctions of one neuron with another. This is of course quite different from the situation described in the previous chapters, in which, in the fully developed nervous system of higher organisms the synapse is essentially a one-way junction between cells, a valve, and the system is therefore direction-specific so far as conduction is concerned.

The properties which distinguish a nerve net from a direction-specific system can be seen quite clearly with the jelly-fish, which swims with a rhythmic beating of its bell, or the sea anemone which, when disturbed, closes down its processes on to itself. G. H. Parker, in a series of experiments beginning in 1912, made cuts in different directions through the jelly-fish bell and the sea anemone and showed that these cuts did not interfere with the coordinated action of the beat or the closure. Even though some pathways of the nerve net were cut, other pathways remained intact and the message could get through. The nerve net was not like a maze with only one correct path through, but like a forest in which many tracks converge and diverge but all lead eventually to the other side. In slightly more sophisticated organisms of the same general type, it is possible to show, by careful selection of the direction of the cuts, that not all the nerve cells belong to the same net. Instead there are two or more overlapping systems, one for instance concerned with coordinated movements in feeding, one in swimming. Such systems are already beginning to show the specificity of the fully-developed nervous system. But to see clearly the presence of a nervous system in which one-way specific connections and well-defined nervous wiring occurs, one must move up from the coelenterates to a rather more complex group of organisms, the worms.[6]

Flatworms: The Development of Ganglia and Brains

The simplest of these are the flatworms. Put a piece of raw meat into a stream, and within a few hours it will be covered with little, flat black worms feeding upon it. These worms, about a centimeter long, are called PLANARIA, and are a good deal more sophisticated than the hydra. Most obviously, they have a well-defined head and tail end, exhibit a more complex motion and have a more elaborate behavioral repertoire. Above all, they have a specific set of connections between their neurons, so that if a cut is made in a set of nerves leading to a muscle, that specific muscle becomes paralyzed, because the neurons which served it were specific to it and were not part of a generalized nerve net.

The flatworms have another important innovation so far as their nervous system is concerned. The jelly-fish nerve net is dispersed throughout the organism, so that the number of nerve cells per unit tissue volume is more or less the same everywhere. This is obviously not the case in humans—most of the neurons are in the brain. It is with the flatworms that this fundamental change in the distribution of neurons first appears. The interneurons, instead of being dispersed, are clustered together into relatively close-packed groups, with short interconnecting processes between the cells of the group, and rather well-defined nerve tracts leading out. Such a cluster of close-packed nerve cells is called a GANGLION. Nerves arrive at the ganglion from sense organs or other ganglia (afferent nerves) and leave it for muscles or other ganglia (efferent nerves). Each nerve tract leaving or entering the ganglion is a bundle containing many hundreds or thousands of individual axons, either arriving from the grouped cells of a sense receptor or leaving from the ganglion neurons towards the muscle. Within the ganglion there are three types of nerve cell, those on which the afferent fibers synapse directly, those whose processes reach out of the ganglion and run to a muscle (motor neurons) and those whose activity is confined to receiving and putting out synapses to and from other cells within the ganglion itself (interneurons). The ganglion is thus the link between the evolution of nerves and the evolution of brains, possessing as it does, in miniature, all the essential constituent parts of a central nervous system.

It is not clear just how many nerve cells need to be brought together to constitute a ganglion in this way, because the term tends to be used a trifle loosely, but tiny clumps of nerve cells which can be regarded as ganglia occur in insects, crustaceans and molluscs such as octopus. There are quite small ganglia involved in the control of the crab heart and the octopus arm. Adrian Horridge, in his book on *Interneurons*, has described a group of as few as nine motor neurons which interact amongst themselves and are involved in the control of the beating crab heart. Of these, four are pacemakers, starting the burst of activity and hence the contraction of the heart. The remainder join in subsequently, stimulated by the first set. The nine neurons receive inputs from three axons, two of which are excitatory and hence accelerate the firing of the pacemaker motor neurons and therefore the heart's rhythm, and one of which is inhibitory and thus slows the rhythm.

Ganglia are an adequate way of organizing the nervous systems of animals which do not have a clearly defined head and tail, a going forward and a going backward direction, like jelly-fish, anemone, or hydra. In addition the distinction between the cell types within these organisms is not well maintained. Cells appear frequently to de-differentiate and revert from their special rôle into a more general type, and subsequently to DIFFERENTIATE into other special cell types again. This means that a chunk of hydra, say, can be cut out and will grow into a complete new hydra. Indeed hydra can reproduce by budding in this way.

Worms however are directional. Although they can travel forward or backward, they have a clear head end and a tail end (figure 39). It is obviously advantageous for the animal to receive more detailed information about where it is going to than about where it has come from, and therefore not only is the mouth at the head end of the organism, but also sense receptors such as the light-sensitive eye pits are congregated there. It is in conformity with this arrangement that a group of ganglia are clustered in the head end of the flatworm. These head ganglia form its brain. With a flatworm, brains arrive on the scene for the first time. Not that the flatworm's brain is yet very dominant. Like other more complex worms (the earth-worm for example), if the flatworm is cut in half, both head and tail ends survive: The head grows a new tail, the tail a new head. Some of the de-differentiation shown by hydra is thus still present even in the directional worm.

None the less, despite its primitive form and its relatively small number of nerve cells, the flatworm brain is a real brain. From the brain, two strandlike bundles of nerves run backward through the organism toward its tail. From these major nerve tracts numerous side branches are given off to the margins of the body and the two cords are connected with each other by many cross-strands like the rungs of a ladder. Indeed this type of system has been called the "ladder type" of nervous system, a kind of main highway for nervous impulses going from one end of the body to the other. The result of this structure is that although the different portions of planaria are capable of a certain amount of independent activity, as in the case of the hydra, the overall effect is of a much more closely knit and coordinated behavior than is possible with the diffuse nervous system of more primitive organisms.

The existence of this central nervous system and of specialized

39 The ladder-like nervous system of the flatworm. Note the concentration of nerve cells at the head end, forming a brain.

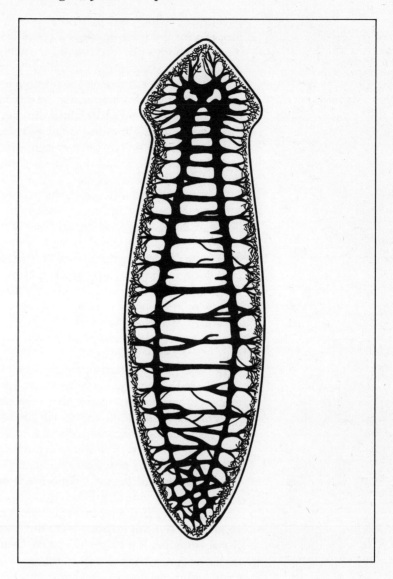

sense organs such as eyes means that planaria show a more varied behavior and much more rapid responses than do hydra. In general, planaria avoid light and are to be found in dark places, under stones or the leaves of water plants. If placed in a dish exposed to the light they immediately turn and move toward the darkest part of the dish. They are highly sensitive to touch and tend to keep the under-surface of their body in contact with other objects. They respond to chemical substances in the water and quickly react to the presence of food by turning and moving toward it. They can react to water currents, moving regularly upstream against the current. They also exhibit phenomena which are in a way closely related to that key property of the fully-developed brain, learning. If a planarian is touched with a glass rod it will curl itself into a ball. This is the response to a danger stimulus. Slowly and cautiously it will uncurl again. If it is touched again with a glass rod it will curl up once more and subsequently extend again. If the touching procedure is repeated a substantial number of times, eventually the response of curling into a ball will diminish and disappear and the planarian will no longer respond. It is as if it had become accustomed to the stimulus of the glass rod touching it and no longer regards it as dangerous.[7]

This phenomenon, in which the nervous system responds to a repeated piece of information arriving at it by eventually disregarding it, can be described as HABITUATION. It is a common property of higher animals. One analogous situation, referred to earlier, is that in which, when one first puts one's clothes on in the morning, one is very aware of the feel of the fabric of the clothes on one's body. However, after a fairly short period of time one ceases to be aware of the sensation. The nervous system has become habituated to this particular set of stimuli, which are no longer of relevance to an assessment of the immediate sensory situation.

Because of the capacity of planaria to habituate in this way there have been many experiments attempting to show that they can do more than habituate; that they can also learn. Show a flatworm a bright light and it will tend to elongate. Shock it electrically and it will roll itself into a ball. Pair light and electric shock enough times—so it has been claimed—and the worm will eventually learn to respond to the light alone by curling into a ball—an analog of Pavlov's famous conditioned-reflex experiments in which dogs could be taught to salivate in response to the ringing of a bell which had in the past signified the arrival of food. And as if this learning were not complex enough for the flatworm, more elaborate claims have been made. The tendency of flatworms to move from light into dark regions has been exploited in attempts to teach the animals by placing them in a water-filled trough in the form of a "Y" in which one arm of the "Y" leads to a dark pool and the other to a lighted one. Eventually, it is claimed, they learn to choose the arm leading to the dark pool. In addition, planaria have been the subject of some of the more sensational experiments involving the transfer of learning by injection of material from the brain of one planarian into the body of another, or by cannibalism of one planarian by another—a topic to come back to later.[8] It is however, worth making clear even at this point, that the evidence on which planaria can be shown to learn even these simple responses, still less the evidence on which it has been claimed that learning can be transferred from one organism to another, is far from convincing to many researchers. However, whatever the validity of the specific claims, it does not seem altogether surprising that, from the point of view of evolutionary development, the capacity to learn should begin about here.

Ganglionic Brains, Arthropods and Molluscs

The concentration of groups of neurons into ganglia – even the concentration of ganglia toward the head end of an organism – were important steps forward, but still far from the specific emergence of a real brain. The head ganglion may be dominant, but it is not exclusively so, as the experiments on the regeneration of planaria show. One line of evolution continued from this point towards the development of more complex relationships between groups of ganglia dispersed around the body. Arthropods (insects, crustaceans and related organisms) and molluscs, groups which have been phenomenally successful both in terms of numbers of living organisms and separate species existing today, and in terms of the length of time they have remained in existence since they first evolved, fall into this category.

Ganglia controlling particular forms of activity are widely separated from each other and capable of continued and autonomous existence – nowhere more graphically demonstrated, perhaps, than in the capacity of the male praying mantis to continue copulating with the female while she steadily devours him from the head end downwards. The ganglia controlling the copulatory sequence are apparently quite independent of what is happening to the rest of the body. Cut off the abdomen of a wasp, and the head end continues feeding irrespective of the fact that food is no longer relevant and cannot be digested. Even the octopus, the mollusc which has the largest number of nerve cells of any – almost as great a number as in the brain of a rat – shows this property. Each of its eight individual tentacles has its own controlling ganglion. Octopus behavior may be coordinated from its central brain, but sever a tentacle from an octopus' body and it will go on threshing around in organized movements for as long as an hour or more.

It is not simply the diffuse nature of the ganglionic nervous system which limits the capacity of arthropods or molluscs – there is a fundamental design problem for both of them. This lies in the fact that both the central ganglion (the nearest they get to having a brain) and the principal connecting pathways between it and other ganglia lie arranged in a ring around the gut. This is an evolutionary device which first emerges clearly in the earthworms and their relatives – one rung higher up the evolutionary ladder than the flatworms. The limitation that this imposes is primarily one of size—as the number of nerve cells increases, so the nerve ring around the gut must thicken. This tends to reduce the diameter of the gut itself—a limitation sharply revealed in the spider, whose gut is so narrowed by its nerve ring that it can digest its prey only as a thin trickle of liquid. Retention of this type of structure implies limitations even at its most developed stage, in the octopus for example (figure 40).

The consequence of this limitation is that the size of the brain, and hence the number of cells within it and their possible interactions, cannot increase indefinitely. This limit is met even more obviously for another reason in the arthropods, which have no internal bony skeleton but instead a tough outer shell, which serves as an external skeleton. There are strict limits to the dimensions of this type of structure. If it grows too large it will break under its own weight from mechanical failure. So there

40 The brain of the octopus. Nerves enter a variety of lobes, each of which is anatomically distinct and involved in different behavioural functions. The central lobes surround the gut.

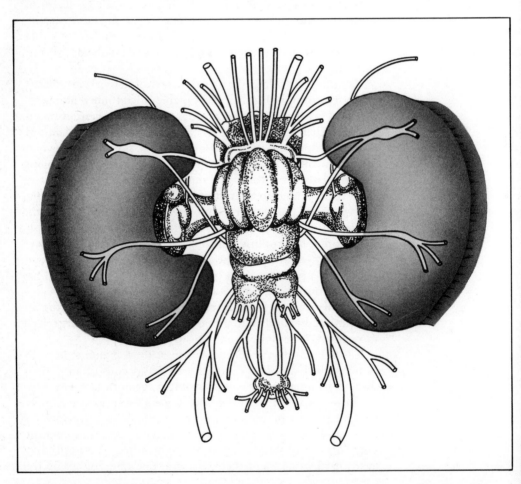

are limits to the physical size of the organism, just as there are limits to the size of a single cell within it. Insects, for instance, apparently cannot grow more than a few centimeters in length. This imposes an additional limit on the size of the insect's brain.

It is this fundamental limit which has prevented fuller evolution of insects and their kin in the direction of larger brains. It has not prevented them from being spectacularly successful in other directions, in terms of biomass, for example. But in terms of the evolution of brains it is a limitation. Hence the behavior of these organisms is limited to only a relatively small repertoire. One is sufficiently impressed by the behavioral capacity of, say, bees or ants to sometimes overlook this limitation. Ant or bee communities have remarkably well developed social forms. Individuals can signal to one another in complex and meaningful communication. Ants from different ant hills cross one another's paths without becoming confused as to where they belong, possibly because of their well developed chemical sense (or sense of smell). Each community is characterized by a slightly different type or concentration of particular chemical signaling agents, called *pheromone*, emphasizing their relationship with the internal chemical signaling devices, the hormones. An ant can signal to its colleagues the presence of food or enemies.[9] One species of ant has developed such a signaling capacity to the point where it can use it to subdue and capture another species by producing a "propaganda" pheromone which has the effect of disorienting and apparently "terrorizing" its prey.

The signaling capacity of bees, both by way of pheromones and the performance of elaborate ritual dances, is even more complex. A bee can make and retain internal "maps" of the position of its hive relative to the compass and appropriate landmarks. And it can signal to the rest of the hive the compass direction of food relative to the sun.[10]

But despite this impressive signaling and storage capacity, the limitations are clear. There is very little that can be taught to an individual ant or bee—one has only to watch a bee trapped in a room, attempting to get out by a resolute display of positive phototropism until it batters itself to death or exhaustion on the window pane, to become convinced of this. Show it an escape route, then bring it back into the room again, and the same positive phototropism will occur—it cannot learn the right way out, however many times it is shown it. Its cell connections appear to be prewired into a degree of specificity that prevents the plasticity shown by the learning brain of the mammal. The three hundred thousand cells of the bee's brain allow it to show much behavior but relatively little learning.

Molluscs are at least free of the size constraint imposed by an external skeleton. The shells of snails do impose limits, but the naked octopus or squid can grow many meters in length and many kilograms in weight. Yet the limitations on brain size imposed by the design which wraps it around the gut remains. The largest squid or octopus may be a hundred times bigger than the rat. Making all the allowances for its peripheral ganglia, its brain may just match the rat's in size. Already however, this is enough for a behavioral repertoire a great deal more plastic than that of the insect.

Octopuses are individual, not social, creatures. They live at the sea bottom in nooks and crevices, ready to lurch forward or reach out a tentacle to grab in the unwary passing crab. They must learn to interpret and anticipate the activity of such a moving prey. In experimental tanks within the laboratory, the learning skills of the octopus can be more rigorously tested. They can be taught to seize a crab as prey *only* if a white card is shown at the same time, for instance–they learn that if a black card is shown instead of the white, then if they seize the crab they will receive a mild electric shock. A use of similar training techniques will show that the octopus can discriminate between particular shapes and patterns of cards shown to it, or between different textures of objects given to it to feel with its tentacles.

Some researchers on aspects of learning and memory– notably J. Z. Young (also the developer of the squid giant axon preparation referred to in chapter 3)–feel that the octopus is an ideal animal in which to examine the brain mechanisms involved in learning. However different the ganglionic brain is from the mammalian brain, they argue, the basic neurophysiological, neuroanatomical and neurochemical changes involved in the learning activity are likely to be identical, while the ganglionic brain has the advantage that different brain functions controlling different aspects of the organism's behavior are neatly separated into individual lobes which can be teased apart.[11] Certainly Young's approach has proved experimentally very fertile, and some of its tangible results will become apparent in considering learning and memory mechanisms in chapter 9. But the path which led to larger brains, greater learning capacity–and man–was not this.

6 The Evolution of Brains and Consciousness

The development of large brains required two major changes in the construction of the nervous system – the separation of the nerves themselves from the gut, and the central concentration of nervous power. It also required the first step towards the development of a bony skeleton. Both these developments can be seen in a small sea-floor fish, the AMPHIOXUS, which is much less behaviorally advanced than the octopus or the bee. Down its back runs a solid, flexible rod made of cartilage, which is the forerunner of the spinal column of the vertebrates. This NOTO-CHORD provides a number of advantages, among them being that it serves as a bracing device against which the muscles can pull, enabling their actions to be more effectively coordinated than in a spineless organism. In addition though, amphioxus' evolutionary ancestors were the forerunners of the major group (phylum Chordata) which includes all the vertebrate organisms and of which man is but one representative.[1]

Amphioxus is an organism which has disentangled its gut from its brain. The major nervous pathways and the central ganglion are present not in a ring around the gut but in a separate continuous tube, the NEURAL TUBE, which, bedded deep in the interior, runs the length of the organism's body. To this neural tube run the afferent nerves from the sense receptors, and away from it run the efferents to the musculature. This system of afferents and efferents is virtually free of external size constraints; it is the evolutionary advance, away from ganglionic nervous sytems, which provides the model for the subsequent development of the spinal cord and brain.

And, as bony organisms developed from cartilagenous ones, grow the neural tube did. One step was to encase the tube itself within the spinal column, thus serving to protect it. This limits the growth in diameter of the tube along a large portion of its length but leaves the head end free to expand. And for the reasons already discussed in relation to planaria, the logical place for the growth of the neural tube is at the head end, and in association with the development of the special senses. It is probable that even in the earliest of vertebrate brains there were a series of swellings at the head end of the neural tube itself. There are likely to have been three such swellings initially, constituting a forebrain, a midbrain and a hindbrain, each of which was associated with one of the special senses (figure 41):

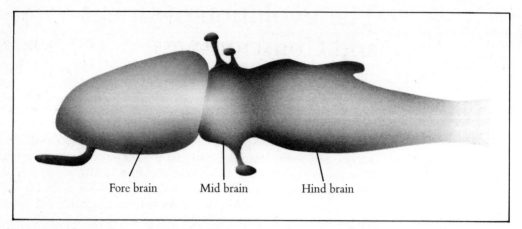

Fore brain Mid brain Hind brain

41 The primitive vertebrate brain, showing the three swellings of forebrain (cerebral hemispheres), midbrain (diencephalon) and hindbrain. The cerebellum appears as a tiny projection above the hindbrain, the pituitary as a projection below the midbrain.

the forebrain with smell, the midbrain with vision and the hindbrain with equilibrium, vibration and balance.

These three structures form the brain stem of primitive CHORDATE animals. All the subsequent structures which were to evolve in higher organisms developed by additions to the numbers of these neural swellings and increases in their size. As evolution proceeded, the swelling of the forebrain became the cerebrum, of the midbrain the *optic tectum*, and of the hindbrain the cerebellum. In early vertebrates, such as, for example, the bony fish, it is the optic tectum which is the most important. This is probably because the sense of sight developed significantly before the other special senses. The last chapter described how, in as primitive an organism as planaria, there are light-sensitive eye spots capable of distinguishing light from dark. Even among the primitive fishes, the eyes are already present. The complexity of the information that can be received by the central nervous system is thus vastly increased. As it increases, the number of cells required to analyze and interpret the visual information also increases. Where amphioxus is virtually blind, slightly more complex fishes whose fossils have been examined show quite clearly developed eye sockets.

We may speculate that, along the evolutionary pathway that has been discussed,* eye spots in planaria or amphioxus developed into eye pits, with light sensitive cells at the bottom, surrounded by pigmented cells which could increase the contrast of light and dark. In more advanced organisms the pit was deeper, serving to increase the contrast of shadows in the light sensitive regions still further and, indeed, because of this contrast, introducing the possibility of analysis of directionality as well. Perhaps the lens of the eye began as a transparent window protecting the eye pit from floating particles. Only later may it have thickened at the center until it developed focusing proper-

*Insect eyes operate on quite different principles.

ties as a lens. An image-forming eye could thus have developed which could present optical patterns to the nervous system.[2]

The retinal surface of this image-forming eye is an outgrowth of the neural tube and remains connected to it by the thick stalk of the optic nerves along which the visual signals run. It is to process these signals that the thickening of the neural tube in the region of the optic tectum must have developed. This can be seen quite conspicuously in, for example, today's bony fishes. In the fish the two lobes of the optic tectum are among the largest of the structures of the brain, and it is at them that the signals traversing the fibers of the optic nerves eventually terminate (figure 42).

In the fish, the two optic lobes are not only composed of

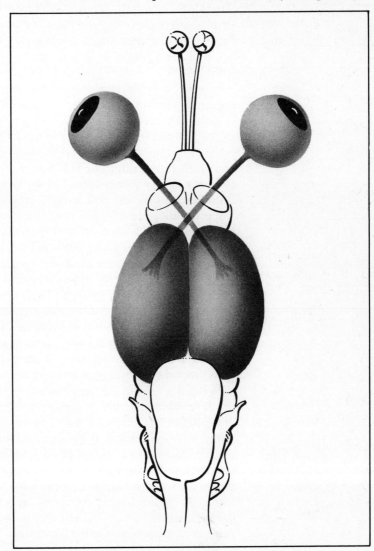

42 Brain of a typical bony fish. Visual analysis is conducted by the well developed optic lobes of the midbrain. The cerebral hemispheres, in front of the optic lobes, connected to the olfactory nerves, are still primitive. Behind the optic lobes, the cerebellum is well developed.

large masses of cells, necessary to handle the complex visual input that the eyes receive, but their arrangement also shows for the first time a pattern which is to become of supreme importance in the mammals and man—the optic lobes of the fish have a central mass of white myelinated connecting axons which is overlaid by a thin skin of cell bodies—the cortex. This is a quite new arrangement of cells and processes. In the neural tube of more primitive organisms, as in the spinal cord of man and the lower centers of the brain, there is a central mass of gray tissue overlaid with white. As with the structure of the nerve ring surrounding the gut, this too imposes a design limitation on the number of neurons which can be packed into any individual cluster. By contrast, if the neurons are arranged as a skin or cortex overlaying the internal white matter their number, and their interconnections, can be very much greater: A small increase in surface area will make a very large difference to the cell number without greatly increasing the overall size of the brain.

It is this which makes possible the expansion in cell number required to process the new information which the development of the eye presents to the brain. But it is not only from the eyes of the fish that information arrives at its brain. The other sense organs are also tolerably well developed. The chemical sense receptors, representing the fish's sense of smell, are arranged in the OLFACTORY BULBS in the nose. From the olfactory bulbs impulses traverse the olfactory nerves to arrive at the brain. Their ultimate processing occurs in the cerebrum, which in the fish is much less well developed than the optic lobes. It can be seen in figure 42, a small wrinkled mass lying in front of the optic lobes, forming the forebrain swelling of the neural tube, still primitive in the fish and overshadowed by the optic lobes, but in the long run to prove an even more crucial structure in organisms which evolved subsequently.

And finally the fish brain also contains, behind the optic lobes, a cerebellum whose function, of muscular coordination and regulation of equilibrium has remained unchanged throughout its subsequent evolutionary transformations.

What does change in subsequent development is the size of the cerebellum relative to other brain regions. Thus the bird brain (figure 43) shows a much better developed cerebellum, which may be related to the considerable logistical problems the bird must face in terms of coordination and control of its activities and balance in flight. By comparison with the fish brain, the optic lobes of the bird have shrunk relative to the forebrain region. Indeed the forebrain is now the most prominent feature. When one recalls that it arose as the brain region primarily responsible for the processing of olfactory informa-

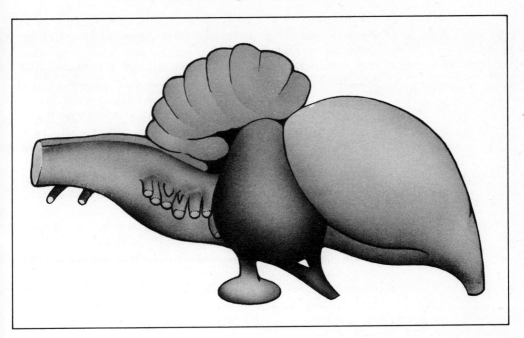

43 Brain of a typical bird. The cerebellum is well developed. Visual inputs are still largely (but far from exclusively) monitored in the midbrain. The forebrain is well developed but lacks a cortex. The pituitary lies below the midbrain.

tion, this is something of a surprise, for the bird's sense of smell is fairly rudimentary.

It is probable that even in the bird this forebrain region has already begun to take on some of the central and higher processing functions that are associated with the cerebrum in the mammals. It is indeed with the first land-based animals, the amphibia and reptiles, that the great development of the forebrain region begins. Perhaps this may be associated with the fact that a sense of smell is a good deal more important for a land-based than a marine animal. Whatever may be the reason, in the reptiles the forebrain is enlarged at the expense of the optic lobes, and by the time the mammals are reached the once highly-developed optic tectum is reduced to a very small shadow of its earlier self. There are now merely four small swellings of the midbrain roof, sometimes known as the two superior and inferior colliculi. And while some visual and auditory inputs are still mediated by way of these midbrain regions, the major processing of both visual and auditory stimuli has now moved to the cerebral cortex itself, with which it is to remain from hence right up to the development of man himself.

Thus the evolutionary pattern of forward movement of the major brain functions continues; where in the fish the midbrain region with its optic lobes is of prime controlling importance, even with the amphibian the move forward to the forebrain has begun. In fact, even the primitive forebrain is already divided into two regions, the furthest forward (TELENCE-PHALON) and that just behind it (THALAMENCEPHALON), containing the thalamus.

It is the THALAMUS which is dominant in amphibia. Its rôle becomes clear when we consider the several already highly-developed senses of the frog: sight, smell, hearing. How are the inputs from all of these to be coordinated, matched against one another and analyzed? The problem is not critical where, as in the fish, one sense is predominant. But the frog's emergence on to dry land has changed all this, giving importance to olfactory as well as visual input. So the thalamus developed as a principal coordinator, and the other brain regions relatively diminished in size.

In evolutionary terms, the thalamus was not to remain dominant for long–just enough for the regions of the thalamencephalon to sprout the pineal gland, the hypothalamus and the pituitary, seat of the "third eye" and controllers of hormones respectively, as described in chapter 2. The evolutionary development from the amphibians through the reptiles to mammals was to result in the dominance of the furthest forward part of the brain, the telencephalon, which in mammals developed from the olfactory lobes so as to swell outwards, enlarging and folding over all other brain regions to form the cerebral hemispheres.

With the mammals the cerebrum takes over the task of coordination and control from the thalamus. Some of the thalamic regions become mere staging posts, relay stations en route for the cerebral cortex. We have already seen, in chapter 4, such thalamic centers as the lateral geniculate fulfilling this rôle in the processing of visual information from the retina. Some regions, however, such as the hypothalamus and pituitary, remain of vital significance in control of mood, emotion and complex behavioral patterns. The hypothalamus contains centers concerned with the regulation of appetite, sexual drive, sleep and pleasure (chapter 10), the pituitary regulates the production of many key hormones and forms the link between nervous and hormonal control systems. Those who would stress man's relationship with other animal species always point out how critical these drives and behavioral states are for humans, how much they dominate the totality of man's behavior and what a large proportion of total human existence is taken up with activities associated with or driven by them. Man has in the core of his brain, such popularizing behavioral determinists have maintained, a "fish brain" and a "frog brain" which are in many ways more important, if less suspected of being so, than the much-vaunted cerebral cortex.[3] It is true that in the evolutionary development of the brain, few structures have ever been totally discarded. Rather, as new ones have developed the old ones have become reduced in importance and relative size. But many of the connections and pathways remain. It is also true that the hypothalamus is of considerable importance in mood and behavior determination, in mammals and even humans.

But to extrapolate from these facts towards the claim that because similar brain structures exist in men and frogs, man's behaviour is inevitably froglike, is nonsense whatever some ethologists might maintain. It is like arguing that we think by smelling because the cerebral hemispheres developed from the olfactory lobes. In brain development structures remain through evolution, their functions are transformed. The pineal gland might conceivably be the seat of the soul; it is certainly not in any meaningful sense a third eye in humans, whatever the situation in some reptiles, and to argue otherwise is to attempt a sort of trivial linguistic mystification.

Even amongst the mammals themselves, the series of developmental changes which the cerebral hemispheres undergo is considerable. Primitive monotremes or marsupials like the Australian duck-billed platypus or the North American opposum, are well developed by comparison with the reptiles, whose cerebral hemispheres have a cortex not more than a single layer of cells thick. By contrast even the early mammals have a cortex with many layers of cells. But in the primitive mammals the cortex is probably almost entirely olfactory in function – the PALAEOCORTEX. Among the first new regions of the cortex to emerge is the so-called ARCHICORTEX, largely concerned with the integration of information from different sensory modalities – the first sign of a dominance of cortical over thalamic control. Finally the great expansion of the region between the two begins, forming the NEOCORTEX itself.[4] As the neocortex increases in area, so the archicortex and palaeocortex are forced deeper into the brain structure; the archicortex becomes curved in the process to form the region known in mammals as the hippocampus, primarily concerned with the storage of short-term memory processes. An index of this development is the fact that where in primitive mammals like the hedgehog the ratio of the volume of the neocortex to hippocampus is 3:2, in monkeys, it has increased to about 30:1.

All the cerebral regions except the neocortex have some sort of rudimentary equivalent in reptiles; it is the neocortex which is unique to mammals, and the way in which it has taken over the thalamic functions can be shown by mapping the connections between neocortex and thalamus; each thalamic region is found to match an appropriate neocortical area – the lateral geniculate with the visual cortex, for instance. In the earliest

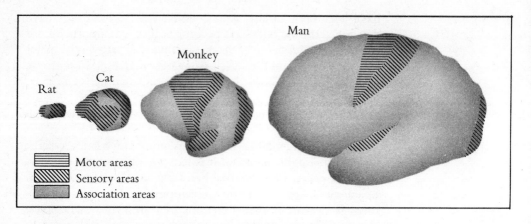

Man

Monkey

Cat

Rat

Motor areas
Sensory areas
Association areas

44 The emergence of the association cortex. Approximate scale drawings of the cerebral hemispheres of four mammals. Note both the absolute and relative increase in size of the area of association cortex.

mammals, as in today's marsupials, practically all of the neocortex is occupied by the motor area and the cortical targets of the thalamic centers. Functionally, then, it must be largely concerned with the more sophisticated analysis of information which in the amphibia is handled by the thalamus alone.

The major development in the higher mammals is the expansion of the area of neocortex between the sensory and motor regions. These are the so-called *association areas*–areas of cortex which do not have direct projections outside the cortex (figure 44). Neurons of the association areas talk only to one another and to other cortical neurons; they relate to the outside world only after several stages of neuronal mediation. In man, these areas include the prefrontal lobe and regions of the occipital, temporal and parietal lobes (figure 6). Functionally, the association areas are clearly *acting upon* information which has already received quite sophisticated processing. The primary cortical area for each sensory modality is surrounded with a more diffuse region of cells which communicate with the primary cells. This diffuse region is concerned with higher order analyses, such as those hyper-complex functions discussed in chapter 4, with respect to visual coding. But the association areas spread beyond these secondary sensory regions, and these further areas must be integrative, combining data from different sensory modalities, perhaps in a comparative way, relating it to past events. In experimental animals whose association areas have been stripped off, there seems to be a learning deficit, although not always a straightforward one, but basic analysis of sensory input seems unimpaired. It is tempting to propose that the rôle of these association areas of cortex must be associated with typically human-like brain functions–for example what the psychologists call perception as opposed to sensation.

It may be argued that the intellectual capacity of a species depends upon the extent of its association cortex. But this assumption, while at first sight superficially attractive, will not stand up to examination by the sort of techniques of ablation analysis discussed in chapter 4. Attempts to trace a simple evolutionary correspondence between cortex size and intellectual capacity among the mammals have so far been doomed to failure. Possibly different mammals develop different types of cortical function–carnivores for example, have highly developed olfactory capacities, and they need them, for they hunt their prey primarily by smell. By contrast, the primates have a diminished sense of smell but need highly-developed eyesight to survive in their arboreal environment, where they must be able to climb, swing and jump. Man, descended from the primate, has a similarly well-developed visual cortex. The basic tool for each of these types of specialization is the cerebral cortex; which particular areas developed predominantly has depended on the evolutionary niche of the particular organism.

However, it does seem to be the case that for each family of vertebrates, there has been a steady increase in size and complexity of cerebral cortex from the most primitive, first-evolving members of the family to the most advanced. Primitive carnivores had less well-developed cortices than advanced ones, and early primates than more recently evolved ones, including man.

One consequence of this is that the more recently evolved the organism the greater the volume of the cerebral cortex, and in order to pack in this volume, not only do the cerebral hemispheres increase in size but their area is increased by twisting and convoluting their surface. As a result the number of neurons in the cortex increases. In order to put this increase on some sort of scale, and bearing in mind that mammals differ very much in size, it is more meaningful to speak of the brain weight or cell number not as an absolute, but instead to evaluate it as a ratio of brain weight to body weight. When this is done, it turns out that humans have among the highest brain/body weight ratios of cell organisms examined, and in addition, among the highest number of cortical neurons/body weight. Actually this type of calculation is also important for another reason. Human brain weights differ quite markedly; for instance, females generally have lighter brains than males. But when expressed on a brain weight/body weight ratio this difference disappears, and as will become clear later in considering the effects of malnutrition on the developing brain, there are good reasons for regarding the ratio as a more meaningful measure than the absolute value.[5]

Another striking observation is that among Homo sapiens there is no sign of further brain development–today's humans have the same cranial capacity, and hence presumably the same brain weight, as the earliest Homo sapiens found in the fossil record. It may be that further brain evolution has taken place, although the few hundred thousand years since Homo sapiens emerged is a very short time in evolution. But clearly if changes have occurred they have been very small. The changes in human society have been brought about by the utilization of the brain capacity developed in Homo sapiens those many years ago, and of that evolution, it may also be argued, such has been its destructive potential, that the end is now in sight. We will come back to the implications of this question of the future of the brain, if indeed it has one, later in the book.

Learning and Consciousness

One capacity that all mammals seem to have developed to a high degree along with their cortices is that of learning. Fish can perform a large repertoire of varied behavior; so too can amphibia, reptiles and birds. Much of this behavior is stereotyped, as wired in as the bee's. Baby thrushes will open their mouths when they see their mother's head—or any silhouette which at all resembles it. Baby ducks or chicks will respond to the first prominent moving object they see within a few hours of emerging from their shells as "mother" and can be IMPRINTED with it, following it thereafter whether it is their natural mother, or the ethologist making the experiment or a flashing light.[6] Such a recognition procedure is wired in as part of the animal's developmental repertoire, though the object on which the infant imprints may be varied. So for that matter are large elements of the song of many species of birds. Although some learning on variants on the song certainly take place, much of the basic pattern of chaffinch's song, for example, is wired in from birth.

Although the range of learning capacity shown by birds is large—pigeons, for instance, can be taught to count, by pecking a button a given number of times for food, and to form quite complex concepts and generalizations during learning—there is no doubt that learning capacity increases substantially with the higher mammals. The amount of behavior which is *not* wired in, specified from birth, is enormous. The learning capacity of pets like dogs, or even dolphins, the ingenuity of predator carnivores like foxes, and the humanlike behavior of chimpanzees, are all proverbial. All these can be ascribed to the possession of larger and larger areas of uncommitted cortex, which is available for precisely this function of learning by experience, as opposed to the deep species memories of wired-in organisms whose behavior is specified even though it may only emerge developmentally.

This is not to say that there is no wired-in behavior in mammals—even humans of course. Watch a new-born pig walk laboriously around its mother's legs to arrive safely at the nipples, or the human baby seek and suckle from its mother's breast, and you will have no doubt of that. It is the *ratio* between wired-in and unwired-in neurons which must be significant, and there is as yet no experimental way of distinguishing one from the other, although the significance of each will be further explored in the next chapters.

What then distinguishes human from nonhuman brains? Is it only a matter of size and cell number? If so it is fair to say that, although man comes out satisfactorily near the top on these scores there is certainly no great difference between him and some of the great apes, or even the dolphin. What then is the difference in quantity which must result in such a profound difference in quality? I believe that a combination of factors, rather than one single "humanifying" transformation, are involved. Homo sapiens has a number of distinct advantages over his nearest evolutionary relatives alive today; a somewhat larger brain size in proportion to body weight, a hand structure which makes the operation and manipulation of tools vastly easier for him than for even a chimpanzee, vocal cords which, unlike those of the apes, permit clear articulation of sounds and his capacity to live in social groups. The literary critic and philosopher George Steiner has argued[7] that the uniquely human feature is foreknowledge, the capacity to anticipate the future. Yet that this will not suffice as a "unique" transforming factor should be apparent to anyone who has ever trained a rat to run a maze "in anticipation" of avoiding electric shock or finding food. It is undoubtedly the social character of human relationships which has enabled man to exploit his other—perhaps initially only marginal—evolutionary advantages. For social existence demands the capacity not merely to be able to learn individually, but to signal meaningfully between members of the group; that is, to communicate. And the ability to communicate, first face to face in speech, later at a distance by writing, made possible the decisive evolutionary breakthrough in human history. Learned information could now be transferred between individuals and, by means of oral and later written communications, between generations as well. It became unnecessary for each generation to learn afresh everything its ancestors had painfully and slowly accumulated.

Yet if it is asked what it is about the human brain that makes speech possible, where for other organisms it is not possible, a convincing answer cannot as yet be provided. Speech is intrinsically human. Babies begin to attempt to make and imitate sounds and to communicate from an early age, though these capacities need encouragement if they are to develop normally. Even in the tiny number of children who have been reported to have been reared in total isolation without speech, words and their utilization are relatively rapidly learned when they enter a normal environment.

Yet is it true that only humans speak? How about animal communication? Dismissing the parrot's capacity to imitate sounds, most mammals and birds have a signaling system by which they can communicate to each other, by odors, visual display or auditory signals. The combination of these makes possible announcements of territory, anger or fear, sexual receptiveness, dominance and submission or filial relationships. Such primitive levels of communication are clearly the forerunners to human capacities – but how remote they seem.

Recently a number of developments in sciences at first sight very distant from neurobiology, have refocused attention on this problem. Most conspicuous has been the work of the psycholinguists, especially Noam Chomsky at the Massachusetts Institute of Technology and his followers, in demonstrating certain characteristics of human speech. Essentially, Chomsky claims to have shown that it is possible to analyze the superficial surface structure of different human languages and show that they all contain a deep structure which is basically identical, and which can be transformed into the surface structure by means of what Chomsky refers to as a generative grammar.[8] This contention has certainly revolutionized linguistics. From our point of view, however, what is important is the structural implication for neurobiology. If all languages have a similar deep structure, the implication must be that aspects of this structure are therefore in some sense wired-in to the brain, that within the cortex certain connections are programed in such a way as to make the emergence of language inevitable and part of the essence of being human. We are committed to speaking *because* we are human. One of the most remarkable verifications of such a hypothesis is that the Chomsky analysis of linguistic deep structure seems to apply not merely to normal human language but to the sign language developed by the deaf and dumb as well.[9] That is, whatever the signaling modality used, the structure of use is the same: the logic of the expression is precast, like solid-state electronics, into the brain.

These theories of Chomsky (with which, as will become apparent in the next chapter, I do not find myself fully in agreement) do have important neurobiological corollaries. In chapter 4, mention was made of the remarkable experiments by Wilder Penfield on cortical stimulation, which, coupled with observations on speech defects in people suffering from a variety of cortical lesions or malfunctions, have enabled a number of cortical regions to be located which are primarily concerned with conceptualization, naming, the motor activities of lip and tongue movement in speech, etc. Perhaps some of these areas may in fact be not so much concerned with speech but with problems of general communication, associated with the wiring of Chomsky's "deep structures", while others may be concerned with the generation of surface structures from deep structures. Roger Sperry's observations on split-brain individuals, where the corpus callosum connecting the two cerebral hemispheres had been cut, were mentioned in chapter 2. In most individuals, where the left hemisphere is dominant, the speech centers are located in the left hemisphere. As discussed there, in the case of a person with a split brain whose right eye but not left is shown an object, he can name it properly, because the right eye connects with the left side of the brain. When an object is shown to his left but not his right eye, however, so that the information concerning it is received only by the right hemisphere, he is generally able neither to *say* nor to *write* the name of the object, though he knows how to use it correctly when holding it.[10] Only one half of the brain has the "naming" center.

But intriguing as these observations are, they still do not answer the question why can humans speak where their relatives cannot? A few years ago such a question might have seemed unanswerable, if only because no one questioned that it was true. Many workers have tried and failed to teach apes to use language. But very recently, at least two American laboratories have in fact had some success in doing just this with chimpanzees.[11] They recognized that one major problem the chimp faced was that its vocal cords were not structurally suited to the modulations which make human speech possible, nor, it seems is their auditory system capable of analyzing complex sounds. Instead, an alternative form of symbolic language was used. R. A. and B. T. Gardner taught their chimp, Washoe, who had lived with them since its infancy, a sign language based on symbols used by the deaf and dumb. David Premack and his co-workers taught their chimp, Sarah, the use of colored symbols which the animal could pick up and place in appropriate combinations to make sentences. In both cases the chimps have learned to construct simple sentences by manipulating signs and symbols to express new thoughts. It is true that their linguistic capacity, even after years of intensive training, is still below that of a two-year-old human child. But the significance of these studies cannot be overrated. Perhaps chimpanzees, too, have "naming centers"? The human capacity for speech is certainly unique. But the gulf between it and the behavior of animals no longer seems unbridgeable.

The evolution of human speech must therefore have depended upon the development of the vocal cords. The human brain is capable of making abstractions and generalizations beyond that of the chimpanzee. But it may no longer be necessary to look for some absolute difference between humans and chimpanzees in order to account for this specific human characteristic and capability.

What does this leave us with, then, which is characteristically human? The more determined ethologists, such as Desmond Morris, seem to imply that there is very little. Among neuro-biologists, some who have attempted to rationalize their religious beliefs, such as the neurophysiologist John Eccles or the communication scientist Donald MacKay, claim that the gulf remains unbridgeable, and resides in the human capacity for consciousness and self-consciousness.[12] When, during evolution, does consciousness emerge? There is, as was argued in chapter 1, an element of nineteenth-century dualism about the question. It implies a certainty that there *is* a quality which is definable and is entitled "consciousness", and that one can say specifically of humans that they possess it, and of other organisms that they do not. Humans, it is agreed, possess a quality called consciousness, which was defined in chapter 1 as a capacity for thought and self-awareness, so that I can say that I know that I am thinking . . . etc.[13] Let us assume that stones, for example, or viruses or bacteria or amoeba or trees, do not possess consciousness. But how about sea anemones or flatworms or octopus or frogs or dogs or chimpanzees?

Objectively, learning capacity and the possibilities of behavioral complexity increase in organisms which are evolutionarily the closest neighbors to man, while the size of the neocortex and its association areas, and the number of its cells and hence their possible interconnections, increase in the same direction. I suggest that all these observations are related, and that the phenomenon which is described at its appropriate hierarchical level as "consciousness" (in the sense limited by the description given in Chapter 1) is related to factors of neocortex size and cell number. There is almost certainly not a linear relationship between them, but in some form or another it should be possible to write some equation of the form $C = f_1(n) \, f_2(s)$ where consciousness (C) is a function of neuronal cell number (n)–perhaps of the uncommitted neurons of the association cortex–and of connectivity (s).[14] This was one of the theses advanced in chapter 1.

Granted that this is the case, we may ascribe consciousness to organisms in relationship to some function of the number of appropriate neurons and the connections they possess, in such a way that Homo sapiens appears at the top of this particular league chart, the primates rather lower, and so on. Such a function would be of necessity one which, when plotted graphically, would show an enormous discontinuity between humans and the rest of living organisms; almost a threshold phenomenon, like the all-or-none of axonal firing, compared with which the level of consciousness even of man's nearest evolutionary neighbors is no more than a very tiny excitatory post-synaptic potential. But mathematical functions of this sort are of course not uncommon.

I am not saying that I know what it is like to have the degree of consciousness of a dog or a bee or even a chimpanzee. One should not confuse empathy, which one may feel when watching the monkeys at the zoo or even a litter of playing pups, with the basis for even partially rational speculation. Still less is this an invitation to unbridled anthropomorphism. What I am arguing is that humans possess a characteristic, "consciousness" as we have defined it here, to a much greater extent than other species. This consciousness has emerged as an *inevitable* consequence of one particular evolutionary strategy which has so far proved remarkably successful, that of the development of increasingly flexible and modifiable behavioral performance, achieved by increasing the size of the brain and the complexity of the possible interactions of its components.

With the emergence of consciousness a qualitative evolutionary leap forward has occurred, making for the critical distinction between humans and other species, so that humans have become vastly more varied and more subject to complex interactions than is possible in other organisms. The emergence of consciousness has qualitatively changed the mode of human existence; with it, a new order of complexity, a higher order of hierarchical organization, becomes apparent.

This qualitative change in the properties of the subject matter of science—from animals to humans—also demands a change in scientific approach, in the questions asked, and the answers desired. In two important senses neurobiology and the study of individual behavior become both more and less relevant to the human condition than to that of the animal. In the discussion of the human condition, biological explanations must be seen as hierarchically subordinate to sociological ones. It is this which makes irrelevant most of the rather trivial speculations of the ethologists as to the relationships between human and animal behavior (that chimpomorphia referred to in chapter 1, and to which we return in the final chapter). The increase in the quantity of the function $C = f_1(n) f_2(s)$ between man and the primates is great enough to produce a transformation of quality. But it is *not* so great that we must deny a scientific explanation for it, postulate the emergence of a god of the synapses and the intrusion of a quality of "soul" which is the obverse proposition to that of the followers of Descartes, of which the argument advanced by Eccles in his book *Facing Reality* is but the latest example.

We may summarize the argument of the last two chapters in four brief paragraphs. Goal-seeking behavior is a function of all organisms, including bacteria and plants, but the evolution of mobile multicellular organisms made the development of rapid means of communication between different body regions essential. There are two possible evolutionary origins for the nervous system: In one the neurons evolved individually as hormone-secreting cells and later became functionally linked, in the other a network of electrically conducting cells developed which gradually became specific, separate pathways with one-way synapses. Neither model necessarily excludes the other; both evolutionary routes to nervous systems could have occurred simultaneously in different or perhaps even the same organism.

Brains, together with a major system of neurons running the length of the organism, first emerge with the development of directionality in organisms with a defined head and tail end. The head or central ganglion remains at most as the first among equals in molluscs and insects, whose central nervous systems are also subject to severe size limitations. These limitations are matched by a similar limitation in the behavioral potential of these organisms, despite the remarkably varied and sophisticated behavioral pattern (largely specified and wired-in) of insects like the bee or the ant, and the plastic capacity of a large mollusc like the octopus.

The evolutionary path which led to larger brains, greater plastic capacity and man was that which followed the development of the vertebrates and the spinal cord. This development resulted in the eclipse of all other minor ganglia by the head ganglion or brain and a steady increase in brain size (expressed as a ratio of brain weight to body weight) through fish, amphibia and mammals. A series of evolutionary transformations of the brain has resulted in a dominance of the forebrain region above all others. The development of a cell-plan by which the neurons, instead of being embedded in the center of the white matter of the nerve tracts, are arranged in layers on the surface or cortex, makes possible vastly increased neuronal cell numbers.

Among the higher mammals the great development of neo-cortex occurs. In each group of mammals there is a steady increase in the area of the association cortex from the most primitive to the evolutionarily most recent type; there is an increase in the number of neurons and of their connections. The degree of consciousness of an organism is some function of neuronal cell number and connectivity, perhaps of neurons of a particular type in association cortex regions. This function is of a threshold type such that there is a significant quantitative break with the emergence of man. Although the importance of language and the argument that it is genetically specified and unique to man must be reconsidered in the light of the recent evidence as to the possibility of teaching chimpanzees if not to speak, then to manipulate symbolic words and phrases, there are a number of unique human features which combine to make the transition to man not merely quantitative, but also qualitative. In particular these include the social nature of human existence, and the range and extent of the human capacity to communicate. These features have made human history not so much one of biological but of social evolution, of continuous cultural transformation. Insofar as man can only be comprehended in terms of his history and this history is one of societies of men, new modes of explanation are needed; social description becomes superimposed at a hierarchical level above those of neurobiology or individual behavior.

But with these hypotheses, we have moved further into the broader argument than is proper at this stage. The next chapter retraces the argument to look at the status of the adult brain, not this time from the point of view of its evolutionary, phylogenetic development, but from the somewhat related one of its embryonic and childhood development, the viewpoint of *ontogeny*.

7 The Child's Brain, and the Adult's

Ontogeny and Phylogeny

The examination of the evolutionary relationships of species is known as PHYLOGENY; the study of the developmental path from embryo to adult is ONTOGENY, and the two are strangely linked. It is often said that ontogeny recapitulates phylogeny; that at stages during its development in the womb, the human child resembles a fish, an amphibian, a furry mammal, in the bizarre retreading of the evolutionary pathway which has led to the embryo's parents and to the embryo itself. But, like all simplifications, the "recapitulation" description of human embryonic development is both attractive and fallacious. Certainly, there are resemblances which link this development with the evolutionary sequence of the last chapter. But these are only resemblances: they may be like the images of a distorting mirror; one must never regard them as photocopies.

The previous chapters have traced how the human brain, a mass of interconnecting cells and pathways, emerged following three hundred million years of evolution, the product of endless genetic experiments, the inevitable result of the interplay of chance and necessity, of the interactions of organisms with their environment and the selection of those organisms which are best fitted to that environment. But what is meant by "the human brain" in this context—that within the head in one's mirror, or of members of one's family, of the man or woman who is sitting opposite in the bus or train, or the millions of the inhabitants of ones country, or, rather more remotely, of the 3,500 million humans on the planet?

All these humans are alike in very many respects, all are different in some. No two, not even identical twins, are identical in all respects. How about their brains then? Chemically and anatomically and physiologically there is astonishingly little variation, except for those whose brains have been genetically, chemically or anatomically mutilated. The same structures and substances repeat in every human brain. When a correction is made for body size, then the brains of all humans are closely matched in weight and structure, Einstein's or Lenin's with that of the writer or reader of this book, and that of a "simple-minded" or retarded person.[1] The apparent similarity is what finally broke Gall's naïve phrenology: the brain does not have an anatomically distinguishable "organ of philoprogenitiveness", for example, which is more developed in a loving father of four than in a misanthropic old bachelor.

Yet the two theses of this book are that for all humans, the quality of being human is that of possessing brains which are capable of interacting in a magnificently adaptable way with the environment, and that the differences in performance and behavior between individual humans reflect differences in their brains. That is, their brains demonstrate at the same time the essential unity of humans and their essential individuality. If we are to accept these theses, then two questions follow, which it is the purpose of this chapter to attempt to answer. These are, first, what accounts for the invariance of the human brain, which develops from egg to embryo to adult with such fantastic precision; and second, what accounts for the differences between brains which have so developed? This chapter begins with an account of the specificity of development of the brain, making possible the subsequent consideration of the possible plastic influences upon it.

The Brain in Embryo

One of the features which distinguishes the brain from that of any other organ of the body is that the neurons will not regenerate, either in the child or the adult. If a portion of liver or skin is removed, fresh liver or skin will grow to replace it; the cells of the remaining tissue will divide, grow, and divide again until the space occasioned by the removal is filled up once more. But this is not the case for the brain; the neurons are essentially a non-dividing cell population. If a neuron dies, it is not replaced by another. Instead, the space is filled up by glial cells, for the glia, unlike the neurons, can divide. Each of us is born with very nearly his full complement of neurons–a very few more may be formed in the first few months of life, but after that, no more. The glial complement, on the other hand, is very far from complete at birth. There is a rapid increase of glial number after birth. The postnatal importance of these changes we shall come back to; for the moment the significance of these observations is that, in the period of prenatal development, an average of over twenty thousand neurons must be formed each minute during the entire period from conception to birth–though the production does not occur evenly over this period, of course. From birth to death, it has been claimed, some 10^4 neurons die and are not replaced each day–a fantastic number, if true, but only adding to about 3×10^8 in an average lifetime–3 percent of the total.

The growth and differentiation of the nervous system takes a complex but determined pathway.[2] The first observable development occurs when the embryo is no more than eighteen days old, 1·5 mm in length. Before this time, the fertilized ovum develops into two hollow balls of cells. Where they touch, a thickening develops, which, by eighteen days, changes shape to become the *neural groove*, precursor of the neural tube. The forward end of the groove thickens and enlarges–it will later develop into the brain–while, also at the head end of the embryo, other surface regions swell and begin the path of differentiation which will lead to eyes, ears, and nose. Even at 1·5 mm in length, the embryo is gathering itself together for its spurt towards sentience.

As development proceeds, the neural groove deepens, like the channel of a fast-flowing river. Its walls rise higher. Then they move towards one another, touch, and seal over: The channel has become a tunnel. The neural groove is now the neural tube. By twenty-five days, when the embryo is about 5 mm long, the process is complete. The tube is buried along its entire length, and begins to sink beneath the surface of the embryo until it is embedded deep inside. Buried along the 5 mm length of the embryo, the neural tube is indeed, and will remain, a tube. The central cavity will become, in due course, the central canal of the spinal cord, and, at the head end, the ventricular system, washing the inside surface of the brain with a continual soothing flow of cerebrospinal fluid. It is at the head end that the important developments now occur. Three swellings appear in the neural tube to become the forebrain (*prosencephalon*) midbrain (*mesencephalon*) and hindbrain (*rhombencephalon*).

The basic structure is now laid for the rapid development of the central nervous system. From the cells of the neural tube all the neurons and glia of the central nervous system will develop in the subsequent few months. The rate of cell division and differentiation now becomes very rapid. In the first stage the cells of the neural tube become specialized into two broad types, precursors of neurons and glia respectively–*neuroblasts* and *glioblasts*. Cells in this stage of differentiation can be extracted from the embryos of experimental animals–chick embryo is a favorite source– and maintained alive, dividing and differentiating *in vitro* through many thousands of generations, for at this stage the neuronal precursors, neuroblast cells, have not yet lost their capacity for division. This comes later in their development when they turn into full-grown neurons.

This burst of cell growth allows the various regions of the central nervous system to begin to organize themselves into something approximating their ultimate cellular architecture. Below the level of the brain the neural tube begins to turn into the spinal cord; the neurons and glia migrate towards the positions that they will eventually take up and the characteristic segmented structure of the cord emerges at the same time as the embryonic muscles. The links between the spinal cord and the emergent musculature – the peripheral nervous system – develop early, often before the muscle cells have themselves migrated to their final position. The muscles arise fairly closely adjacent to the neural tube, and, once the nerve connections are formed, the muscles move outwards, pulling their nerves behind them like divers their oxygen lines. Once some nerves have formed primary links in this way, others may join them as well, following the path traced by the original nerve and finally spreading to adjacent tissue.

But it is the changes in the brain itself which concern us most. By the time the embryo is 13 mm in length, the early three-vesicle brain has differentiated into a five-vesicle brain, with the

45 The development of the human brain. (a) 3-week embryo, (b) 7-week embryo, (c) 4-month foetus; (d) new-born infant.

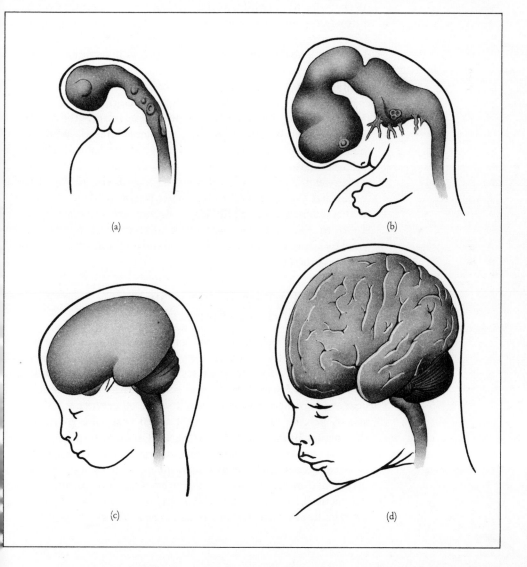

(a)

(b)

(c)

(d)

forebrain separating into the *diencephalon* (the thalamic region referred to in the amphibian brain, page 136) and the telencephalon, the region eventually to become the cerebral hemispheres, which are already apparent as two bulges on either side of the tube.

These structures are already becoming too large to accommodate as part of a straight tube and the tube begins to bend back on itself with two distinct kinks, one toward the base, the other at the midbrain region (figure 45). Althpugh these curves change in orientation as development proceeds, they are already beginning to locate the brain in a characteristic position with respect to the spinal cord, with a ninety-degree bend in the axis of the brain between the medulla and the cerebrum.

Beyond the hindbrain, the tube thickens to become the cerebellum. Meanwhile, at the level of the forebrain, two little outgrowths appear on either side, which grow toward the surface into gobletlike shapes connected by stalks to the rest of the brain. They are the optic cups, which in due course develop retinae. The stalks form the optic nerves, and the eyes, developmentally parts of the brain, have emerged.

From now on the appearance of recognizably brainlike features is rapid. By the end of the third fœtal month, the cerebral and cerebellar hemispheres can be plainly traced, while the thalamus, hypothalamus and other vital nuclei can also be differentiated. In the following months the cerebral hemispheres swell and extend. By the fifth month the characteristic "wrinkled" appearance of the cortex begins to develop. Most of the main features of the convolutions are apparent by the eighth month, although the frontal and temporal lobes are still small by comparison to the adult, and the total surface area of the cortex is much below its eventual size.

Postnatal Growth of the Brain: Anatomy and Biochemistry

Even at nine months there is still a long way to go in this respect, for the brain of the newborn baby weighs only about 350 grams compared with the 1,300 to 1,500 grams of the adult. It will be 50 percent of its adult weight at six months, 60 percent at one year, 75 percent at two-and-a-half years, 90 percent at six years and 95 percent of its adult weight at ten years old. At puberty the average brain weight is 1,250 grams in girls and 1,375 grams in boys, though the relationship between growth rates in the two sexes is complex. Meanwhile, the rapid growth of the brain is reflected in the growth of the head. Everyone knows that a baby's head is large for its body compared to an adult's. In fact, average head circumference is 24 cm at birth, 46 cm at the end of the first year, 52 cm at ten years and not much more in the adult. What all this means is that in the newborn the brain is closer than any other organ to its adult state of development. At birth the brain is 10 percent of the entire body weight compared to only 2 percent in the adult.

As the number of neurons in the brain does not significantly change after birth, one may well ask of what the postnatal quadrupling of the size and weight of the brain consists? Partly it represents a measure of the increase in number of glial cells, which are still relatively infrequent at birth but whose numbers increase rapidly over the first eighteen months of infancy, toward the final adult glial/neuronal ratio of 10:1.[3] Recent work by John Dobbing in Manchester has shown that cell formation in the human brain occurs in two bursts.[4] The first, which is completed after the first six months of fœtal life, is the burst of neuronal cell growth. Then there is a pause, and only around and subsequent to birth is there a second burst of cell growth representing the development of the glial cells. Partly though, the growth in brain size represents a change in the relationships between the cells over this period. At birth the human brain is relatively low in myelin. Most of the pathways that have been formed are unmyelinated, and the gray matter of the cortex is rather hard to distinguish from the white matter of the subcortical tissue. The major increase in the laying down of the myelin lipid sheaths of the axons occurs during the first two years of life, a process closely coupled with the development of the glia, one at least of whose functions is to conduct this myelination.[5]

Not only the development of myelinated axons but the vast ramification of pathways and interactions between cortical cells also occurs postnatally. As the dendritic and axonal complexes spread, so the distances between the cells of the cortex increase and the surface area of the cortex enlarges, forcing the development of more and more convolutions. The increase in dendritic processes must bring with it as well an enlargement in the number of synaptic contacts between cells, which also greatly increase over this period. In addition the cells themselves change in appearance. The neurons become noticeably larger, their cytoplasm and ribosomal content—a sign of active protein synthesis (figure 13)—increasing. Within the cytoplasm a number of small fiberlike structures develop, known as *neurofibrils*. These are probably closely related to the transmitter function of the cell, but their exact mode of action is still uncertain.

Most of the evidence concerning the biochemical development of the brain comes of course from animal rather than human studies, and, while neuronal multiplication has virtually ceased in all mammals at or around birth, the general developmental state of the brain at birth varies markedly from species to species. The young of the rat are born blind, naked and helpless; those of the guinea pig are born with their eyes open, they are covered in fur and able to run, following their mother. Compared with the rat, the guinea pig is clearly practically senile at birth. Yet the rat and the guinea pig are fairly closely related organisms. These differences in developmental age at birth can be mapped against the degree of brain development at birth for a number of indices, the presence of certain biochemical enzyme systems, and so forth, and when this is done one can obtain graphs of the sort of figure 46, taken from Dobbing's work. From this diagram it seems that in terms of brain development at birth the human falls between the pig and the rat: About 10 percent of the spurt in brain growth is postnatal in the guinea pig, 50 percent in the pig, 85 percent in the human, and 100 percent in the rat.

Because the rat's brain development at birth is limited, it is easy to follow the development of postnatal changes in its brain biochemistry. Over the first three weeks postnatally—that is, until weaning—a series of dramatic changes occur. The activity of the enzymes responsible for the synthesis of lipids such as myelin increases markedly for a fortnight or so, and then levels off and declines, while the rate of protein and ribonucleic acid synthesis, extremely high at birth, declines dramatically to about a third of its original level before leveling off between fourteen and twenty-one days, at a rate which does not subsequently change. The levels of the free amino acids in the brain

46 Human brain growth compared with other species. Plotted on the same graph are the rates of increase of brain weight in humans (scale in months), guinea pig (scale in days), pig (scale in weeks) and rat (dotted and dashed line, scale in days). Note that the curve for the human and pig show a maximum growth rate around birth; the guinea pig by contrast is advanced and the rat slightly retarded.

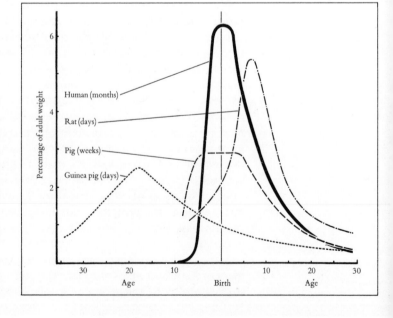

associated with transmitter function, and of the enzyme acetyl-cholinesterase itself, a key marker for certain sorts of transmitter systems at the synapse, also increase substantially over the period of the first twenty-one days of the rat's postnatal life, until reaching an adult level at around the end of this period. These first few days are clearly seeing a massive growth spurt in brain development and may be regarded as a critical period, during which a variety of intervening environmental factors can have far-reaching effects on brain structure and performance. For the pig and the human these critical growth periods are both pre- and postnatal, and, according to Dobbing, may last for the first eighteen months of a young human child's life.

The Development of the Electroencephalogram

The physiological signs of brain development show a similar pattern to the biochemical changes. Electrical activity can be detected in the brain even before birth by the harmless proced-ure of placing electrodes on the outside of the mother's abdomen. From the third month of fœtal life, very slow waves of electro-encephalogram activity can be detected at the surface of the brain, and continuous electrical activity in the brain stem seems to occur from the fourth month onward. The making of such recordings is of course a complex procedure, though it is possible to record the EEG pattern directly from prematurely born babies who are maintained in incubators. But the question is always open as to whether the EEG of the prematurely born baby is different from that occurring in the normal course of development of the baby in the uterus.

The earliest patterns that have been recorded in this way have been from twenty-four- to twenty-eight-week-old prematurely born babies, and it is found that a striking change takes place over this period of time. Before twenty-eight weeks the patterns are very simple and lacking in any of the characteristic forms which go to make up the adult EEG pattern. At twenty-eight weeks the pattern changes, and bursts of regular waves, similar in frequency to the theta waves of the adult (page 90) occur. By thirty weeks the slower delta waves appear and at about the same time the alpha waves begin to be detectable. All this activity is still only periodic, occurring in brief spasmodic bursts, but after thirty-two weeks the pattern of waves becomes more continuous, and characteristic differences begin to appear in the EEG pattern of the waking and sleeping infant. By the time of normal birth the pattern is well developed, although certain characteristic and specific differences between children appear, partly depending upon the condition of the individual child at birth. From then on the EEG pattern gradually approaches that of the adult. The final emergence of the adult pattern appears between the eleventh and fourteenth years.

A great deal of effort has been put into the analysis of the properties of the EEG in children—as indeed it has in adults as well—and attempts have been made to correlate EEG pattern with the behavioral development and individual personality characteristics of the child, but most of these studies are subject to the same sorts of criticisms as attempts to interpret the adult EEG pattern. Certain changes do occur, in association, perhaps, with certain stages in the behavioral development of the child, but the analysis is uncertain. While it would be convenient from the point of view of the thesis which has been advanced in this book concerning the relationships between brain structure, function and behavior, to be able to demonstrate specific changes in EEG pattern in association with particular develop-mental stages, the difficulties which lie in the way of this sort of analysis cannot be burked. Nor for that matter is such successful analysis strictly necessary for my purposes; that the EEG does change with development is enough at this point.

Prenatal Brain Performance

How far can changes in the brain structure parallel changes in performance? Starting from the assumption that performance must be supported by an appropriate brain structure, how far can one analyze the development of behavior against the emergent structure of the brain?

Some simple aspects of the functioning of the central nervous system appear very early indeed. Indeed the blood circulation system and the nervous system are the first to function in embryonic life, with heartbeat commencing in the third week following conception. By the second month, an avoidance reaction—the withdrawal of the hand region by contraction of the neck muscles—occurs if an unpleasant stimulus is applied to the embryonic upper lip. These developments imply that simple reflex arcs are already differentiated at this stage with appropriate synaptic connections and interneuronal activity being brought into play in order to coordinate muscular movements.

The area of sensitivity which will evoke reflex activity also gradually expands, until, by the fourteenth week, touching the embryonic face will evoke not only rotation of the head, but also grimacing, stretching the body, extension of the arms at the shoulders and rotation of the pelvis so as to turn away from the side of the stimulus. At eleven weeks the foetus will make swallowing movements if the lip regions are touched, at twenty-two weeks it will stretch out its lips and purse them, and at twenty-nine weeks it will make sucking movements and sounds. By twelve weeks it will "kick", by thirteen the diaphragm muscles will produce the breathing sequence. The whole gamut of simple and more complex reflex systems is brought into operation as birth nears.[6]

The drama of birth itself is simply an episode in this sequential production of reflexes, albeit a major one in which a whole new set begins to develop, while those which have so far been unexploited in the protected environment of the womb now show their utility – the sucking reflex for example. Respiratory and digestive reflexes, urination and sweating are now all fully in play. None of these reflexes is cortex-dependent. They relate to the lower brain regions, the medulla, pons and midbrain. Babies tragically born without a cerebral cortex show them, for example. The suggestion is that the activities of the newborn infant are controlled mainly by the spinal cord and the lower part of the brainstem. The thalamus may also be involved, but the cerebral cortex at any rate plays little part in the life of the newborn child.

Nor is the cortex itself evenly developed at birth. Thus the motor cortex is more highly developed than the temporal and occipital cortex. Of the motor cortex, the most mature part is the region which will later control movements of the upper part of the body. This is the only area in which, by birth, the large pyramidal neurons have their neurofibrils and are already well organized.[7] Very shortly afterwards, the main sensory area of the cortex develops, and subsequent to that, the visual area itself. In functional terms, this suggests that the most important functions for the newborn infant are those of motor coordination of the top part of his body. Sensory input is less important and it is quite likely that, although the child can see at birth, he will be unable to interpret what he sees.

Postnatal Developments

But for the normal infant, there is something else which is new about the emergence from the womb – the arrival in a public world in which he is constantly in contact not merely with the dark womb and its background sounds of maternal heartbeat and bowels, but with a continuous battering of new stimuli from the environment. Signals assail every one of his senses. New information floods in at a vast rate. It is perhaps in response to this that the cortex begins to grow, neuronal connections sprout, synapses are made, consciousness emerges.

By the first month after birth, an increase in the thickness of most parts of the cerebral cortex has occurred, particularly in the motor region and the primary sensory regions. But it is not clear whether any of these neurons are yet capable of transmitting nerve impulses. For example, the axons of some of the large neurons from the motor cortex can be seen to extend as far as the spinal cord, but it is doubtful if the link is functioning yet. The myelin sheaths which have begun to develop on the upper part of the axons do not extend as far as the spinal cord, while it is far from certain if there is any communication between one area of cortex and another. The one-month-old baby is plainly still a subcortical organism.

The three-month-old child shows a different picture. The neurons have been separated by the continuous growth of their processes and of glial cells, while this expansion has forced the convolutions of the cortex to begin. The cells of the motor region are well developed, particularly those controlling the hand, followed in turn by the trunk, arm, forearm, head and leg. All of them begin to show signs of myelination, most advanced in the region of the trunk, arm and forearm. The cells which will eventually be concerned with the control and regulation of the movements of speech, have not yet developed significantly.

A similar pattern can be seen in the sensory region, where the cells responsible for the receipt of sensory information from the top part of the body and the hands are relatively well developed, while the head and leg regions are less advanced. The auditory cortex has developed significantly, followed by the visual cortex. The axonal pathways between different brain regions, and the nerves entering the cortex from lower parts of the brain have begun to develop as well. This is particularly true for the pathways arriving at the cortex from the top part of the body, and in conformity with this, the myelination of these nerves is most advanced, with the auditory and visual-area fibers coming next.

The implications of these changes should be that the motor activity of the three-month-old child is in advance of its sensory processing ability, while of the variety of motor actions available to the adult, those associated with the hand and the upper part of the body should be those which have developed most. And so indeed it proves to be. By the third month after birth, conscious motor movements are possible, the child can control the position of his body, head and legs. He can begin to grasp things with his hands; soon his fingers will be capable of making those precise and coordinated movements which are so supremely human. There is evidence of the increasing control by the cortex over the activities of lower-brain regions, as the more primitive reflexes, such as the grasp reflex, which characterize the one-month-old child, begin to disappear, presumably as a result of inhibition of the functioning of lower motor centers by the developing cortex.

So far as sensory information is concerned, the three-month-old child can focus his eyes on an object and move his hands toward it, so it would seem likely that he is capable of coordinating to a certain extent the visual and motor responses associated with the visual and motor areas of his cortex. The development of his auditory cortex is indicated by the fact that, at about this age, a crying child will become quiet at the sound of his mother's voice. The auditory area is therefore capable of processing information associated with sound arriving at the ears from the outside world and the association areas to control the appropriate action in response to this sound, for example, the inhibition of the movements of crying and kicking.

The subsequent development of both brain and behavior run in parallel. The dendrites and axons of cells in all parts of the cortex continue to increase in length, in thickness, in degree of myelination. Glial cell development continues.[8] The sequences of all these changes continue to be such that the motor cortex and the primary sensory cortex are more advanced than other cortical regions, but by six months some of the regions more backward at three months have begun to catch up. More and more bodily activities come under cortical control. By six months the average European or American child can spread out his fingers or touch his fingertips with his thumbs, although these movements are not yet fully developed. He can roll his body over, and sit up without support. By the seventh month he can crawl, by the eighth he can pick up small objects, by the ninth, stand, by the tenth month walk with help, and by the twelfth, walk without support.

Meanwhile, as well as acting on the outside world, the child responds to it. He begins by smiling or laughing, focusing on an object and following it with his eyes, responding to sounds, beginning to vocalize and make communicative noises, all within the first few months after birth. All these sequences are well mapped out and the normal behavioral range of children well understood. But once one has begun to move out of the area of simple sensori-motor responses in order to map more complex subsequent developments, it becomes harder to analyze these developments in terms of the "typical" response. Even the pattern described so far varies with the individual child and its circumstances, which may make speech advanced in some, walking retarded in others, and so forth. Considerable deviations outside this range can occur without any apparent later performance deficits.

In assessing all of these sequences of skill organization, it must be remembered that they are in some measure culture-bound: the development of particular skills at particular times is expected in our, and every, culture; *which* skills are expected *when* will vary. At different historical periods and in different cultures, children may be expected to walk at different developmental stages. Their performance, within limits, will conform to these expectations. An example of the variation in performance between different groups is the fact, pointed out some fifteen years ago by M. Geber and R. F. A. Dean, that the newborn African black baby is from four to eight weeks more "mature", judged on the sort of scales of performance suggested above, than is the Caucasian European child.[9] The extent to which this difference is environmental and how far genetic factors are involved, cannot be determined, and indeed it will be argued below that the question is a strictly meaningless one.

Thus even the simplest of generalizations may be open to qualifications. The further we advance beyond this, the further the area of doubt begins to expand. How far subsequent developments of behavior patterns and their modification can be associated with changes in brain structure, is a question almost impossible to answer except as part of a general premise that there are brain events associated with all such changes in behavior. What is more, although a good deal is known about the gross alterations in brain structure that occur during the major sequence of events in prenatal and just-postnatal life, if only by extrapolation from the studies with animals, virtually nothing is known about the details of the more subtle changes that occur later in childhood up to puberty or adulthood as the brain continues to respond to environmental changes.

Inevitably, the experience of the individual is superimposed upon generalizations covering a population of individuals—a feature of the plasticity, rather than the specificity of the brain. It is neither possible nor desirable to make the sort of experiments which might help identify such changes in humans—nor indeed is it quite clear what sort of changes one should look for if a procedure could be developed which would enable the examination to be made in an experimental animal. Thus about the development of the brain substrates of behavior there is little to be said beyond this point except in terms of generalizations.

Genetic Epistemology

About the behavioral situation though, there is a good deal more. Child psychologists have attempted for many years now to classify behavioral changes that occur developmentally in children as part of the process of learning and growing. Despite the uncertainty about what they actually measure, intelligence tests do provide one way of calculating an aspect of behavior which increases with age over the period of childhood and adolescence and that is in some way clearly associated with one feature of brain performance. Such tests have enabled norms to be set within a community, and an individual's performance matched against these norms. There are many possible conclusions about what such tests may indicate concerning any individual compared with another, which are not relevant at this point. Clearly though, the tests do say something about the *process* of development within a given individual, for his score changes with time as he develops.

Perhaps the most comprehensive attempt to define the changes in behavioral performance with development that has been made in the last decade has been the work of the Swiss child psychologist and zoologist, Jean Piaget, and his school. The aspects of Piaget's work which are of relevance here are based on the very detailed examination of the speech modes and activities of a very limited number of children (including his own). This study has enabled Piaget to define what he regards as a series of sequential and well-defined stages through which a child's thought and language systems pass. These stages are quite well marked, and a child's progress through them can be mapped. What follows is a much abbreviated account of them, using Piaget's own terminology.[10] We return below to the question of the validity of Piaget's interpretations.

The first period is that of the development of sensori-motor thinking, which lasts from birth to about two years of age. It is common ground to all workers in this area that this period sees the extensive development of both the motor and sensory systems, so that while the fifteen-month-old infant can converge his eyes and focus his gaze on an object, he does not look at any one thing for any length of time and his attention is readily diverted. This is consistent with the fact that the part of the visual cortex which deals with objects in the center of the field of vision is less well developed than the part which deals with the edges of the field of vision. The child's ability to understand what he sees may therefore be limited. The structure of the auditory cortex suggests that at this point the sense of hearing is not even as well developed as the sense of vision. But by the end of the second year the structural development of the primary sensory area of the brain is already equal to that of the motor area. The visual association area is still in advance of the auditory association area, so there may still be more ability to discriminate and interpret what is seen than what is heard.

It is against this developmental background that Piaget analyzes the first two years of life as those in which a child develops from a baby with no awareness of the distinction between self and not-self to the state of regarding itself as an individual set into a differentiated environment. The experiences of touch, of different outcomes to reflex actions, of the development of vision, make possible simple discriminations—between the suckable and the nonsuckable for example. The child explores his universe and registers it primarily as a pattern of sensori-motor stimuli, of incoming data and responses to them, without being able to make significant intersensory analyses or matching.

Beyond the first two years, anatomy, biochemistry and physiology have little to say about changes in brain structure which may be related to performance, except perhaps for the observation that the continued laying down of myelin does seem, in general terms, to correlate with enhanced behavioral performance; those areas of the brain which are called into play in each developmental stage also obtain myelin sheaths to their axons at or around this stage. However, like virtually all relationships between brain and behavior, it remains an open question whether the information traffic along the nerve is the signal for the onset of myelination, or the onset of myelination makes possible the information traffic along the nerve. We are discussing here correlation across hierarchical levels of analysis, not necessarily causal relationships, and we will have occasion to make this point again several times in subsequent chapters.

Behaviorally, at the end of the first two years of age, the external existence of objects and their relationships are accepted and the next stage can be entered. This lasts from about two to about five years of age and is the period in which symbolic thought and PRECONCEPTUAL REPRESENTATION emerge. The child begins to use picture images as symbols to replace the real things—the objects which earlier filled his universe. In parallel to the use of images to replace objects, the use of language as a system of symbols for objects begins—a state about at a level at the beginning with its use by the chimpanzees Washoe and Sarah.

But while the images are internal symbols meaningful only to the child, language is the way to a measure of public communication. Language is nonrepresentative, unlike images. It is conceptual. Piaget identifies the emergence of "preconcepts" as intermediate between the image symbols and the concepts proper. They fluctuate between being symbols and concepts as the child learns what sort of power it can achieve over the real world merely by wishing: to pick up and assemble a toy, for example, which is an attainable objective; or that it will stop raining, which is not.

The next stage partially overlaps with the previous one: that described as "conditional representation". It runs from four to eight years of age, and forms the threshold of OPERATIONAL THINKING: the child begins to recognize that the universe does not revolve around him alone but that there are other viewpoints, other forces in the world; he begins to communicate coherently in language.

The next stage is "operational thinking" itself, which emerges from seven and runs to twelve years of age. The child begins to recognize relationships between objects, to operate with concepts such as more and less, longer and shorter, heavier and lighter, and also to use them in a commutative and conservative manner, so as to be able to perform simple operations which help relate weight, height and so forth in a logical manner. As the period progresses, the operations become more formalized so that these semiabstract concepts can be manipulated; experiments, in the genuine scientific sense of the word, can be made.

Finally, by a natural progression, from eleven onwards into adolescence the possibility of utilizing formal operations, which are completely abstract conceptual tools, emerges. The child has become an adult, although the biochemical maturity of the brain is not yet complete. Thus myelination continues throughout and beyond this period. One particular brain system, the reticular formation (chapter 11), goes on laying down myelin well into the individual's twenties. It has been claimed that the association areas of the cerebral cortex continue to increase their myelin content through maturity and into old age. Perhaps this continuous accretion of myelin may be related to the equally continuous development of those behavior patterns which only achieve significance in maturity. By contrast certain simple responses and those behavioral characteristics which develop early and remain unmodified throughout most of later life, in fact find their brain substrate also laid down at an early stage. The distinction may indeed lie between so-called "innate" behavioral patterns and those which are associated with social behavior, speech and higher conscious activities.

Piaget's developmental stages have not been received uncritically; there are not lacking those to point out that they have been derived from a very limited study of a few children in a particular environment. How absolute are the stages, how cross-cultural? Are they simply an analysis of the life style of the Swiss child at a particular point in social history? Anyone who is familiar with the critique which can be made of Freudian psychoanalysis will recognize that the same limitations may apply to the sort of work which Piaget has been doing. Other workers have not found the same constancy of stages as Piaget claims. For instance, there may be much more sensory and motor control in the weeks following birth than he implies; other variations seem to depend at least as much on the design of the questions being asked as on some fundamental age-linked difference. As to the question of how much is genetic, how much environmental, it will be argued in the next chapter that this is a meaningless question. These criticisms are however not relevant to the concerns of this chapter. It does not matter whether Piaget's stages are valid in all details. All that is necessary is the recognition that there *are* stages in intellectual and behavioral development which can be identified as part of the developmental progress of the child, and that the time span of these stages runs in parallel with the time span of the development of the adult brain.

Between birth and adolescence a series of stages in development clearly occurs in parallel with the final touches to the brain structure itself, its increase in mass, connectivity and so forth. Obviously one could not match each of these stages against a defined brain structural analog. The process is a gradual one, and a one-for-one matching of structure with behavioral observations is not necessary in order to make the general point that the growth of intellectual capacity in the human matches the anatomical and biochemical development of the brain when viewed ontogenetically, just as the growth of intellectual capacity matches that of brain complexity and, it was argued, neuronal connectivity, phylogenetically as well. This match has not been proved, of course. Nor could one at the current stage of the game. All that has been done is to note it as suggestive. But to take the argument further, it is necessary to consider not merely the specific developmental pattern of the normal brain, but the extent to which this development is genetically determined, or is plastic, modifiable in response to environmental influences. This is the task of the next chapter.

8 Specificity versus Plasticity

The Specificity of the System:
Nature over Nurture

How far are the ontogenetic pathways specific, how far modifiable by the environment of each individual? In chapter 6 it was
argued that certain specifically human brain functions–notably
language and consciousness–were "wired into" the brain
system; they were a specific property of the brain–or rather of
the organism possessing the brain. It was noted that at this point
the linguistic analysis of Chomsky and his followers reaches
down through the hierarchies of discourse to approach that of
the neurobiologist and his wiring diagram. Such an account is
appropriate equally for the Piagetian analysis. For not only is the
sequence of development from the neural tube to the cerebral
cortex wired in, and genetically specified in general terms at
least, but, Piaget would have us believe, so is the sequence of
behavioral events which begins with the baby's first smile and
ends with the development of logical and abstract concepts. The
growth of the ordering of human information about, analysis of,
and approach to the world, is itself genetically specified–so
Piaget claims. This is the core of his genetic epistemology.

Epistemology is the study of the way in which bodies of
knowledge grow and are organized; genetic epistemology
implies the extent to which the knowledge, observational and
analytical techniques at the disposal of the individual are themselves genetically programed. It should be pointed out, however, that what Piaget is describing is more properly referred to
as *developmental* epistemology, for he attempts to present no
evidence as to its *genetic* wiring-in. In this respect Chomsky
differs from Piaget, in that the former is apparently prepared to
grant relatively little importance to the developmental sequence
involved in the acquisition of language, for instance. To
exaggerate the difference, Chomsky seems to see the capacity
for language, with all that this entails, as not merely genetically
specified but as subsequently interacting with the environment
only to a small extent.[1] On the other hand, genetic epistemology
specifies a developmental approach which distinguishes between the developmental potential, which is genetically specified, and the actual results, which might be profoundly
modified. Such a rigidity of position puts Chomsky almost into

the idealist or Cartesian position of mind/body dualism. For Chomsky it appears practically to be the case that the mind is given, and specifies the brain that holds it, a viewpoint which also suffers from being ahistoric; it does not recognize the extent to which different historical periods, that is, different social environments, may produce different types of human.

It thus becomes important to understand what is meant by specificity in this respect; the developmental process which commences with the fertilization of egg by sperm is a pathway, the map for traversing which is contained in the genes, in the complement of DNA brought from each parent to the fertilized egg.[2] The journey from neural groove to the brain of the full-term human infant seems to proceed, in the account given in the previous chapter, as smoothly as if it were traced by a finger being run along that map. Yet such a sequence prompts the obvious questions: Just how specific is it? What mechanism controls it? How far is this mechanism inevitable and ineluctable? In terms of the brain: Is the pattern of every single nervous connection, every synaptic junction, genetically preordained, laid down in the DNA program? Where it has become clear that in its functioning the central nervous system is essentially an uncertain statistical structure, is it now necessary to concede that the uncertainty is itself genetically programed in all its details?

Regeneration and the Specificity of Visual Inputs

The incredibly complex pathways connecting the sense organs and the motor effector systems to the brain are laid down during embryonic and just-postnatal life. But what determines the functions of these systems? Do the nerves grow, and then, by virtue of their location at particular sites, make certain connections and fulfil certain functions? Or is it the reverse procedure? Do particular nerves grow into certain specifically laid down patterns, so that the pattern specifies the function rather than the function specifying the pattern?

A priori, perhaps, one might consider that the former is the more probable explanation. However, a series of quite dramatic experiments have demonstrated that this is not the case. Many of these experiments stretch back over a large number of years to the pioneering work in the 1930s and 1940s of Paul Weiss in New York and Roger Sperry in Stanford.[3] The approach used by Sperry and Weiss was not that of following normal mammalian development, but, instead, of experimentally manipulating the organism. The creatures they have used have been primarily amphibians such as frogs, toads, newts and sala-

manders. These organisms differ from the mammal in their
power of nervous-system REGENERATION. If the optic nerve of
a mammal is cut, the eye remains permanently blind. However,
in the case of an amphibian, the optic nerve will regenerate and
the eye will become sighted and functional once more.

The question that Sperry asked was: what determines the
pattern of regeneration of the optic nerve? Do the fibers grow
back along their old pathways or do they form new ones? He
first cut the optic nerve of an amphibian and showed that, as the
fiber regenerated and remade it connections with the optic
tectum, so normal sight, at least as judged by the behavioral
responses of the animal, developed as well. Next, he put an
obstacle in the way of the optic nerve, blocking part of the
nerve track. The regenerating nerve twisted around the obstacle,
regained its old pathways and once more made functional
connections with the tectum, so that the animal's sight was
normal again. Sometimes the path the optic nerve traversed in
surmounting the obstacle was tortuous, taking it far out of its
original route. None the less functional connections were made
eventually.

The third experiment was perhaps the most dramatic. Sperry
cut the optic nerve, removed the eye entirely from its socket,
rotated it through 180 degrees and replaced it in its socket
(figure 47). What would happen to the optic nerve now? In
this case the information received by the retina of the rotated
eye was precisely the reverse of the information it received
prior to the cutting of the nerve and its rotation. That is, information about the right hand side of the eye's visual field
arrived at the opposite side of the retina from that which it had
arrived at originally. How would the behavioral responses of
the animal match up when the nerve regenerated? Astonishingly
the behavioral response of the organism was inverted in exactly
the same way as the retina had been inverted. That is, the animal
behaved as if information which in reality arrived at the right-
hand side of the retinal field was instead arriving at the left-
hand side. If food was presented at the left, the animal would
misreact to it, aiming to the right to obtain it. The only way to
account for this was that the fibers had grown back, not to new
positions that would be appropriate to the new positions of the
neuronal cell bodies from which they had sprung in the rotated
visual field, but as if they had instead returned to their original
positions. That is, the axons had grown back to make the same
functional connections in the optic tectum that they had made
previously.

Several hundreds of thousands of nerve axons must have
crossed and recrossed one another in finding their way back to
make similar synaptic connections with the cells of the optic

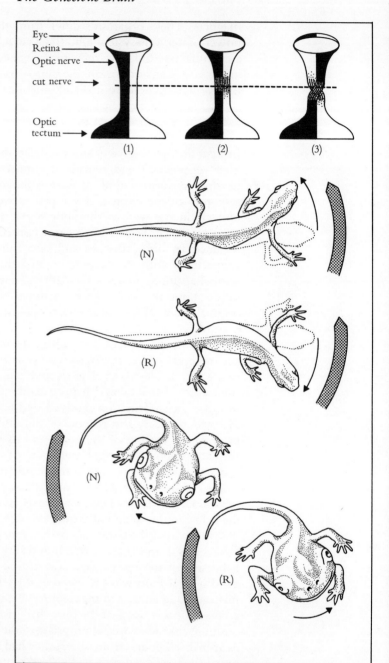

Eye
Retina
Optic nerve
cut nerve
Optic tectum
(1) (2) (3)

47 The Sperry experiment. *Top:* (1) Schematic diagram of connections between the amphibian eye and tectum. (2) Pattern of regeneration after the optic nerve has been cut. (3) Pattern of regeneration after the optic nerve has been cut and the eye rotated through 180°.

Bottom: Responses of salamanders with normal (N) and reversed (R) eyes to moving stimuli. (The long arrows indicate the direction of movement of the stimulus and the short arrows the direction of the salamander's responses).

tectum to those that they had originally made. It was as if the fibers "knew" which cells in the tectum they were "supposed" to synapse with–and in doing so, ensure that the animal makes a mistaken behavioral response! What is more, experience did not help these animals subsequently. Once the eye had been reversed the animal continued throughout its life to behave as if the eye was in its original position. The cells could not learn the necessary information to enable them to accommodate to the new situation. Food placed so that it could only be seen by such a rotated eye would always be missed by the animal attempting to strike at it and eat it. Indeed, Sperry explained that in order to keep such animals alive it was necessary to force-feed them, or feed them in the dark so that they were not dependent on visual information arriving from their eyes in order to reach the food.[4] Many other experiments of this sort have been made in which eyes, or portions of eyes, of such amphibia have been rotated, and always the results have come out comparably. The axons find their way back to the appropriate region of the optic tectum.

Chapter 4 discussed the functioning of the visual system. In the mammal, the cells from the retina project on to the lateral geniculate, the equivalent in the mammalian system of the optic tectum in amphibia or birds. Experiments of the type of Hubel and Wiesel, show that the lateral geniculate contains a map to which individual cells in the retina connect, so that a model of the retina appears in the cells of the geniculate, and subsequently, by way of the pathway from the geniculate into the visual cortex, in the cells of the visual cortex itself. Sperry's experiments tell us something further about this map of the retina in the tectum. They indicate that this map is not one born of practice, of the experience of a particular pattern arriving on cells of the tectum as a result of information arising from the retina, but that the map itself is inborn. It is as if–to use a now well-worn analogy–each of the neurons of the retina is "color-coded" so that its axon can make connections only with a specific region of the optic tectum and that this region is therefore genetically programed to match the appropriate region of the retina. This programming is invariant, and hence, when the fibers from the inverted eye regenerate, they grow back to the cells forming the original map, just as they would have done had the eye been in its natural position.

How universal is this remarkable observation, which might suggest that the whole of the brain and its connections is specified genetically and irreversibly? Other experiments have studied the regeneration of limbs or of skin regions following regrafting in the amphibian. None of the conclusions they come to is as unequivocal as that involving the optic system. None the less experiments in which, for example, an amphibian limb is grafted into an abnormal position and subsequently its nervous connections to the spinal cord allowed to regenerate, suggest that these too are genetically programed, so that in its abnormal position–provided it is not shifted too far, or else it fails to regenerate at all–the limb tends to make the same movements that it would have done had it been in its normal position. That is, movements which are behaviorally irrelevant to its new situation.[5]

Similarly, if a piece of skin is transplanted from the stomach of a salamander to its back, its nervous connections allowed to regrow, and the skin then stimulated with something mildly irritating–a dilute acid solution for example–the animal will tend to scratch the belly region from which the skin has been removed rather than the skin itself in its new position on the back. The animal is receiving, from its sensory input, information which is genetically specified to the extent that it gives the animal information concerning the position that the skin would have been in had it been where nature had put it, so to say. However, in some of these latter cases, there is evidence that, for example, continued utilization of a limb in its new position can result in some learning and therefore some modification of the response.

How far this type of specificity is confined to the amphibians, or is a universal property of the nervous system, is a question which cannot be approached directly experimentally, because in the case of the mammal the nervous system does not possess the powers of regeneration that would enable the experiment to be made. However, what evidence there is, based on indirect conclusions from other types of experiments, suggests that the situation in the mammal is not so very different–nor indeed is this surprising. For if this specificity is so fundamental a property of the system as the experiments of Sperry and others would suggest, then the likelihood that it would change during evolution between amphibia and mammals would seem low.

It is thus possible to answer the question concerning the specification of function by position or vice versa in a way in which at first sight seemed improbable. What is more, it would seem a reasonable postulate that many aspects of the coding for the wiring of the central nervous system operate in a similar way. They are genetically specified, so that certain connections are obligatory. This provides circumstantial evidence for the postulate that such functions as speech in the human nervous system are wired-in in the sense that Chomsky's theory would make necessary.

If this wiring-in is a fundamental property of the nervous system, it becomes crucial to try to explain what at first sight seems inexplicable. How can several million nerves "know" their way back to precisely the site that they should be located at–and indeed find their way back over a distance of millimeters or even centimeters? How to account for this degree of specificity is indeed one of the most intriguing puzzles of contemporary neurobiology. What is more it is obviously closely related to analogous problems in the fields of embryology and developmental biology, and it is not surprising to find that it has been the subject of intensive experimental exploration over the course of the last few years–although the answers are still distant.

One experimental approach has been to consider the problem at an even more fundamental level, that of the organization of the individual cells themselves. Cells from the central nervous system of young organisms can be maintained alive in isolation in tissue cultures for periods of many weeks and many cycles of cell division. In such cultures, neurons will put out processes and even make functional synaptic contacts with one another. The tissue culture therefore represents an even more simplified analog of the nervous system than the use of invertebrate preparations. Do neurons in tissue culture then show properties of organization and localization relative to one another?

In the last few years, experiments conducted by Michael Gaze in Edinburgh have suggested that this is indeed the case.[6] The cells Gaze used were from the amphibian retina. Retinae from young animals were broken up so as to leave their cells intact. The cells were mixed and grown up in tissue culture. After the initial shock of breakage was over, the cells began to aggregate in clumps once more, arranging themselves in characteristic alignment with respect to one another, so that any cell's relationship with its neighbors became defined. It turned out that certain cells were quite choosy as to which others they would locate themselves next to. They did not aggregate with merely any neighbor.

Retinal cells thus possess the capacity both to recognize one another and to accept or reject association with particular neighbors. Once again, it seems as if each of the cells of the retina is color-coded in some way. Thus the behavior of the regenerating optic nerve fibers in Sperry's experiments is mirrored at a more fundamental level by a property of the retinal cells themselves.

Indeed at this level it may be suggested that the phenomenon is precisely analogous to the other phenomena of developmental biology which ensure the organization of the cells of the liver or the kidney or the lung or the heart or any other tissue of the body. In these tissues as well, cells must locate themselves appropriately. There has to be a mechanism whereby the organ grows to a particular size, and then cell division slows down or stops. The entire embryonic development of the organism may be seen as specified in this sense. But nowhere is the problem so acute as in the central nervous system, for nowhere else is the organism faced with an issue where it is really critical which cell is associated with which neighbor. One liver cell is more or less like another and one muscle cell more or less like another; but, because of their connectivity, individual nerve cells are not. Although the cells may be identical, their addresses and their connections are far from being so. It is this which makes the question of their specificity that much more significant.

Models do exist to account in a relatively nonmysterious way for these strange recognition properties of the neurons. To describe them in detail, however, would go beyond the scope of this chapter. For the determined, an account of a simple gradient model for specificity is given in Appendix 4. The important thing is that, like all other biological phenomena, we have to understand the specificity of neuronal regeneration in a statistical sense. What seems an absolutely ordered process in macroscopic terms is less so in microscopic ones. All we really claim for specificity is that the optic nerves, for instance, can grow back to the "right" region of the optic tectum; but this "right" region may involve contacts with any one of many hundreds or thousands of cells. We are not dealing with an absolute phenomenon but a statistical one, in which the area of uncertainty extends to a number of cells which is only small when matched against the really astronomically large number present within the system as a whole.

The Plasticity of the Brain

If the specificity of the brain's growth and development, the precision with which its patterns are laid down, is difficult to explain, it is its plasticity which is in a sense more critical to the functioning of the brain, as opposed to the nervous system as a whole. It is the plasticity of the brain which enables learning and memory to occur, and which impresses upon each individual a set of unique and characteristic behaviors, thoughts and emotions. Specificity determines the characteristics of the species and the population; plasticity, the irreplaceability and inimitability of the individual, and the social evolutionary capacity of the human species, allowing essentially the same brain which once served the cavemen to enable today's men to operate in the vastly more complex environment that they have themselves created. Specificity may lay down the equivalence of identical twins, but plasticity distinguishes them, makes each the sum of his own unique experiences. If the brain were not plastic in this sense, individual humans would be almost totally and comprehensively programed, like ants or bees. Just as it has been argued that consciousness increases as we approach man, so too must plasticity. The uniqueness of the human is greater than the uniqueness of the dog or monkey precisely because of this enhanced plasticity.

At the behavioral level plasticity means the capacity of the individual to learn, to be modified, by experience. At the neuronal level we must expect to find the brain's modified experience expressed in terms of a modification of biochemistry, of cellular architecture and connectivity, of the electrical responses of the brain. So, in the investigation of plasticity of function, the relevant question concerns the effects of environmental alterations on brain structure and function and on behavior. Setting the question is relatively easy; providing experimental answers a good deal harder. For it should already be clear from what has previously been said, that however profound the environmental or behavioral changes that occur, the changes at the neuronal level are likely to be relatively small. Quite wide differences in behavior, intellectual capacity, social, political and moral views, are obviously coded in the brain in terms of rather small structural differences.

The vast majority of bodily and behavioral activities of the human are set within a very limited range. Humans are basically very similar. The numbers of those who are shorter than 4 foot or taller than 8 foot in height are limited. So are those with IQs (whatever that might mean) below 50 or higher than 180. The range of human capacity, in physical or mental terms, is actually not very large compared with the distance which separates man as a species from his fellow primates. So, although in our dealings with our fellow humans it is precisely the differences between them which loom so large, it should not be very surprising to find that the brain structures which code for them do not show such enormous differences.

The remainder of this chapter therefore considers the extent of the environmental influences on brain structure and performance during development, and sets some bounds on the possible modification of specificity by plasticity. This inevitably leads to a further consideration of the nature/nurture controversy, with which the chapter concludes, leaving the next chapter free to consider in more detail the fine mechanisms of plasticity – the changes that occur in the brain system during thought, learning and memory.

The relationship of human brain weight to body weight has already been mentioned. In general, although human brains vary considerably in size, when they are related to body weight then the range becomes much smaller. It is not clear whether the differences in weight reflect themselves simply in differences in cell number, but the probability is that, in general terms, cell number related to body weight is also fairly constant in adult humans. But, as we have already seen, brain development and body development follow different paths; at birth the brain is much more nearly fully developed than is the body. How far can environmental alterations during brain development affect its final structure and performance?

One of the severest environmental alterations which can be provided, short of actually physically damaging the brain, is to deprive the organism of food. When this is done in the adult the body weight declines sharply, but the brain weight is relatively unimpaired. The biochemical defense mechanisms of the body protect the brain against being used as a food reserve practically until death from starvation. The body sacrifices almost every other organ in preference to the brain.

But in infancy and during brain development the situation is different. Work on experimental animals has shown that if they are malnourished or undernourished for periods during or just following weaning, which are the times of rapid brain growth, then, although body weight will be more dramatically affected, brain growth itself will also be retarded. Even if the animal is subsequently fed freely, with as much food as it can eat, the brain growth may never catch up. John Dobbing's work suggests, too, that when growth is retarded by malnutrition in this way, not only is the subsequent brain development inadequate, it is also distorted compared with the normal pattern; the cerebellum, certain cortical neurons, and certain enzymes, seem to be disproportionately affected. During infancy, there are thus certain sensitive periods during which, if brain growth is impaired by malnourishment, the effect will last for the lifetime of the individual. In the case of the rat this malnourishment can be achieved by the relatively simple method of taking two litters of pups born the same day, mixing them and returning a few–three say–to one mother, and the rest–which may mean up to fifteen or twenty–to the other. The "large family" pups will have permanent deficits in brain weight which cannot be remedied after weaning, however good the diet they are fed.[7]

How far is this observation relevant to the human situation? Rats are different from humans not only in the obvious way, but also, as was suggested on page 154, in terms of the relationship of the development of the brain to its state at birth. So extrapolation from rats to humans is not necessarily very easy or very sensible. Nor would it be so important were it not for the fact that in many parts of the world, malnourishment to the point of starvation occurs on a massive scale. The key problem of this malnutrition is not one of general food deficiency but particularly of protein deficiency, critical for adequate growth. Protein deficiency is the most serious widespread malnutritional disease in the world, putting over half the world's children at risk–a risk especially sharp in the lower socioeconomic classes of the developing or stagnant countries. This is increasingly the case in countries such as many in Latin America, where the establishment of rudimentary health services has resulted in a drop in infant mortality, so that between 1956 and 1968 the average mortality in pediatric wards dropped from 30 percent to 5 percent. Yet the saved children are likely to remain grossly malnourished. By extrapolation from the animal experiments, we must assume that the damage done by childhood protein deprivation is largely irreversible, and that the apathy typical of chronic protein deficiency, and its related disease, kwashiorkor, which translates into a diminished learning potential, affects 350 million children–7 out of 10 children under the age of six in the whole world.[8]

Studies in Mexico and other parts of Latin America where the conditions are among the most desperate, show that children malnourished in early life, as well as many other signs of affected development, such as in height, body weight, and age of puberty, have a reduced head circumference (presumably a measure of brain size) when compared with children who have been well nourished–either rich children in the same country or those in the United States or Europe.[9] Gross malnutrition may also produce abnormal EEG patterns.

Studies over a period of many years on British children, where, although starvation of the desperate form experienced in Latin America or India is rare, malnutrition is not, have shown that small body size tends to be correlated with low socio-economic status and large family size–that is, a polite way of saying that the children come from a family with not much money to spend on food, if not actual poverty.[10] Nine babies in every hundred in Britain are of low weight when born –three of these because of some disorder in the last stage of pregnancy.

One may estimate that the sensitive period in human development, during which undernutrition is likely to have an effect on subsequent brain development, may last from birth to eighteen postnatal months. Over the next five or so years of childhood, if malnourishment over a prolonged period occurs, this too may be expected to produce effects on subsequent brain development and performance, although perhaps less severe ones. These studies suggest too that the nutritional state of the mother during pregnancy can also have a long-lasting effect on brain and body size.

Of course, the critical question is how far actual performance is affected by such treatments. While it becomes extremely difficult to sort out many of the other related variables in such studies, and while the question of how one measures performance remains subject to other sorts of criticism, none the less the longitudinal studies suggest that low IQ scores are associated with low socio-economic background of parents, large family size and poor state of health of the mother during pregnancy, in Britain as well as in poorer countries. In work with more severely malnourished children, in Mexico, J. Cravioto and his group have found that impairments even at the level of fairly straightforward sensori-motor skills occur.

Gross measurements of changes in brain weight or size or EEG pattern, while crude indicators, are good enough to make the *political* prescription that such malnourishment must be wiped out. This is obvious. But they tell us relatively little about what is actively changing in the brain in response to the environmental stress. Again animal experiments may be of help here, though the caution required for extrapolation remains. Some less extreme conditions have been studied in rats by Mark Rosenzweig, David Krech and Edward Bennett, at Berkeley, California.[11] They have reared litter-mate rats from birth in one of two types of conditions. The first group is raised in "environmentally impoverished" conditions, where, although they are fed enough, the animals are caged individually in conditions of low sensory stimulation either of light or sound, out of sight of their fellows, and their handling is reduced to a minimum or avoided altogether. The second group is reared in an "enriched" environment. The animals live in a communal cage and are handled often, have plenty of toys to play with and objects to explore. At the end of some weeks in either of these two conditions the animals are killed and certain characteristics of their brain chemistry examined. The environmentally enriched animals are found to have a thicker cerebral cortex than the impoverished group, and certain brain enzymes, including acetylcholinesterase, alter in concentration. As little as one hour a day of enriched experience is enough to cause measurable differences in these parameters.

In experiments I have made myself, examining other effects of deprivation during development, I have found that rats reared in the dark have altered (higher) concentrations of amino acids in their visual cortex. Other workers have found a diminished number of dendritic spines in Golgi-stained preparations of brain regions from functionally deprived animals. But the long-term consequences of such deprivation are not clear, because some of these changes, for instance those related to the amino acid levels, can be reversed by functional stimulation even after prolonged deprivation.[12]

Such anatomical and biochemical changes can be matched by performance changes as well. It is now very well known, following the classical experiments of Harry and Margaret Harlow in the United States, that rearing monkeys in isolation results in an apparently permanent incapacity to form normal social, sexual or parental relationships in later life.[13] Stress during infancy results in permanently enlarged adrenal glands, and altered responses to stressful situations in adulthood. But such research is only at a very early and primitive stage as yet. The extent to which brain structures can be modified, the subtleties of the environmental effects capable of causing measurable cellular change, and the exact correlation of these changes with performance deficits, is still almost completely unknown.

But there is one additional relationship which should be emphasized. The Harlows' work shows that social behavior in monkeys reared under abnormal conditions is itself abnormal. This abnormality reflects itself in the rearing of the animal's own infants. If a female monkey had itself been reared in isolation, then it was unable to make a normal maternal relationship with its own young. Thus the behavior of the second generation is affected by the childhood experiences of the previous one. In other words, the Harlows' monkeys are demonstrating the truth of the well-known observation that the sins of the parents are visited upon the children. Except that in this case – and maybe in most other cases as well – the parents themselves are more sinned against than sinners.

Condemning parents to live in poverty is a sure way of breeding starvation, large family size, and poor housing and education, and hence, because of the inadequacies of the social order of contemporary Britain and most other societies, more poverty, and potentially more ignorance. The impressive feature of all this is the human capacity to triumph in spite of adversity, to succeed, despite the odds. It is not that so much deprivation results in so much inadequacy, but that people reared under conditions which ought to defeat their creative capacity, none the less not only survive but transform their own situation. This is the uniquely human characteristic, a function, presumably, of the plasticity of the human brain, to which we return in the last chapter of this book.

All these effects are of the type we may describe as the transgenerational effects of environment on brain and behavior. They can be shown in other ways. There have been reports of experiments in which rats are environmentally stressed in infancy by malnourishment or the like. The effects of this stress manifest themselves in aspects both of brain structure and of behavioral performance, not merely during the rats' own lifetimes, but in that of their offspring, and their offsprings' offspring. Stephen Zamenhof and his colleagues, in Los Angeles, have recently shown that dietary protein restriction in maternal infancy may result in reduced DNA content and therefore probably a reduced cell number in the brain of second generation adults, even though the second generation had been fed well throughout their lives.[14] The development of the brain, such studies imply, is a delicately balanced affair; the brain is *state-dependent*. A variety of the most subtle changes in environment, especially during childhood, can produce long-lasting changes in its functioning. The fact that these effects prove to be transgenerational, even though they are environmental and not genetic, also makes a fair degree of nonsense of most claims to have isolated "inheritable" factors in intelligence, an issue to which we must now turn.

Plasticity versus Specificity:
The Inheritance of Intelligence

The interactions of plasticity and specificity are of a great deal more than just academic interest. If the brain were completely specified it would be determined by a set of genetic instructions carried in the DNA code inherited from the individual's parents; this specificity would then be expressed developmentally by the growth of the brain, more or less independently of interaction with the environment. The behavior of the individual and his performance would be precoded and predictable from birth – the most important thing about one's life would then be to have chosen the right parents, not just for social, but basic biological reasons.

developmental progress, the individual's flexibility is enhanced. It is obvious that there is a measure of genetic specification and a measure of environmental plasticity. Can one determine how much of each?

One may well ask why the question is important at all. One cannot yet, and probably never will be able in any meaningful way to interfere with heredity, but one *can* change environment. So we might expect that it would be important, in asking how far an individual's human potential can be expanded, to improve his environment so as to develop his genetic potential to the full. Or one can ask another sort of question: can one prove what a vocal group has maintained for many years, that one individual is genetically superior to another intellectually, so that little or nothing can be done environmentally to affect this distribution of brain power?

The tradition of attempting to answer Yes to this latter question goes back a long way. Many Victorians, philosophers, social and natural scientists alike, took it almost as axiomatic that certain groups were better endowed than others – middle- and upper-class white Englishmen for example, as compared with working-class Englishmen or "lesser breeds without the law". Such men as Francis Galton, a leading early geneticist, attempted to show that genius was hereditary, and advocated a policy of selective breeding to maintain the intellectual stock. During the 1930s some of the eugenicists who followed Galton's views argued for sterilization of workers on the dole—a cry which we may yet see repeated in the 1970s, if we are to take seriously some of the fashionable arguments of certain ecologists about population growth. This was a policy carried to its logical conclusion, of euthanasia and sterilization, by Hitler in Nazi Germany.[15]

In recent years this argument has been given new form by the writings of such psychologists as Hans Eysenck in Britain and Arthur Jensen in the United States.[16] Both have maintained a set of theses which may be stated as follows: Intelligence is largely inherited; the middle class is more intelligent than the working class; the working class has more children than the middle class; the national intelligence is therefore declining. In Jensen's case the proposition extends from the working class to the blacks in America and has therefore become the center of a substantial political controversy. Its conclusions have been made use of in the battle by white segregationists to maintain separate schools for whites and blacks in the south of the United States, for instance.[17]

The set of propositions that are advanced by Jensen and Eysenck begin from a prior one: that intelligence can be measured, and that its measure is reflected in the IQ score. Such a proposition may be challenged by an examination of the specific social assumptions made in the test itself for example, but it is not proposed to deal with this point, which is outside the compass of this chapter.*[18] More important for the present discussion is the genetic argument. The evidence on which this is based comes primarily from studies of the degree of similarity of IQ scores of related individuals. It is generally found that the more closely related genetically individuals are, the closer their IQ scores compare. Siblings in the same family are somewhat closer in scores than unrelated individuals, fraternal twins than sibs, and identical twins than fraternal twins. Even identical twins that have been reared apart are claimed to show a close matching of IQ scores. From all these comparisons the conclusion is drawn that, of the *variability* in IQ between individuals (not, note, the *"total"* IQ, but the *difference* between individuals)

*It is just worth pointing out, though, that in his recent book on the subject, Eysenck publishes a picture of what *he* calls a relatively "culture-fair" IQ test, which demands that the child tell the difference between a set of stylized faces wearing different sets of hats. All the faces are white and the hats typically those worn by middle-class figures!

some 80 percent is inherited, and only 20 percent is affected by environmental changes.

Eysenck and Jensen then go on to state what is undoubtedly the case, that the IQ scores for American blacks are, on average, lower than those of American whites, and the IQ scores for those in higher socio-economic groups are higher than those in lower socio-economic groups. These differences, they claim, are greater than can be accounted for by the "20 percent environmental" factor – that is they must be inherited.

The argument bears superficial conviction, but includes an incredibly simple genetic fallacy. In order to make the genetic comparisons leading to the 80/20 proportionality discussed above, it is necessary to restrict discussion to the genetics of a single population containing an essentially common pool of genes. But this only tells us about the genetic variation *within that population*. It says nothing about the genetic variation within another population with a different and not freely intermixing gene pool. In order to test the hypothesis with respect to the relative IQ of blacks and whites, it would for a start be necessary for them to form a totally freely interbreeding population. The more restrictions there are on this, the less meaningful can any genetic comparison be.[19]

While Jensen does not appear to appreciate this relatively elementary point, Eysenck at least does – but goes on notwithstanding to ignore it. Thus it is experimentally impossible to distinguish the relative contributions of environment and inheritance to the differences in IQ scores between blacks and whites, or middle and working class. On the other hand a very large number of factors are known, some of which have been listed already in this chapter, which can affect the brain performance of individuals due to environmental changes or stresses, both in the generation of the individual himself or in the generations of his parents or grandparents.[20]

All this, of course, is quite apart from the fact that the argument concerning the IQ score differences between populations is based on comparing the IQ scores of so-called "matched individuals", a white group and a black group, say, of approximately the same socio-economic background. It is argued that the environment of individuals in each of these two groups is likely to be sufficiently similar that if there are IQ differences between the groups they can only be accounted for on the basis of hereditary differences. The naïveté of an argument which suggests that the environment of the black in the United States at present is identical to that of the white is astonishing. The blacks's environment includes the experience of being black in a white culture – and has done from birth. So too does the environment of the "risen" working-class child include the experience of being an outsider in a predominantly middle-class culture. How can such effects not be taken into account in assessing the environmental contribution to differences in IQ scores?[21]

Indeed, it is known, such is the frailty of IQ measurements, that black children score better on an identical test when it is administered by a black tester than by a white one. Such scores themselves, and the whole IQ measure, must clearly in fact reflect not simply the score of an individual in isolation, but the score of an individual in an environment which includes his tester, and hence includes his tester's expectation of him. A neat example which demonstrates this can be provided by the class experiment, perhaps apocryphal, but now part of the folklore of research in this area, in which psychology students were shown two groups of litter-mate rats, and were told that one group was maze-bright (that is, were a strain which performs well on mazes) and the other group was maze-dull (that is, they were a strain which performed badly on mazes). Although the rats in fact were litter-mates, by the end of a few weeks in the hands of the students it was found that not only were the "maze-bright" rats *in reality* performing better on mazes than the "maze-dull" rats, but in addition had an enhanced body-weight and were generally in better condition. So much depends on the hidden and unstated assumptions and expectations of the individual performing such tests.

If the argument about genetic comparison between groups falls to the ground, it follows that the further conclusion drawn by both Jensen and Eysenck, that the national intelligence is declining (in the United States and Britain, respectively), must also fall as well. And indeed, what evidence there is points precisely in the opposite direction. Some of the best studies have been made of groups of eleven-year-old school children in Aberdeen over the period 1932–47. They have shown that there has been a consistent, if small, rise in the IQ scores of children over the period.[22] Thus the trend is in precisely the reverse direction to that predicted by Eysenck and Jensen. But it *is* the trend which would be predicted from the fact that there has been a steady improvement in the environment of these children in terms of dietary and health standards over the period during which the tests have been administered.

It is not relevant here to enter into a long analysis of the nonsense of what has become known as "Jensenism", or to point to the positive evidence of how far IQ scores could be boosted, by, for example, placing deprived individuals into enriched environments, impressive as much of this data is. One example only need be cited, the study of M. Skodak and H. M. Skeels, who followed the fates of one hundred foster children, aged around thirte, all of whom had been placed in foster homes before the age of six months. Sixty-three of the biological mothers had received IQ tests, and had an average score of 85·7. The sixty-three children had an average IQ of 106, and most of this difference could be attributed to the improved environment of the children. From what has already been said in this chapter, one would after all expect no more.[23] What must be pointed out is that the furore over this issue has been raised by the asking of questions which are scientifically speaking strictly both meaningless and unanswerable. To attempt to answer the question how far are racial or class differences in IQ genetically determined? is already in one sense to have prejudged the answer. Eysenck himself admits this candidly, when he comments that "any attempt to classify people into negroes and whites on the basis of IQ alone would be right only 5 percent more often than if we decided on the basis of tossing a coin." So what is the point of asking the question? It is not even a case of dangerous knowledge needing careful handling, but wrong and incorrect science being exploited for openly political ends.

Plasticity and Specificity: An Overview

Chapter 7 made the point that the development of structure in the brain, both pre- and postnatally, runs parallel with the development of function. But, by definition, function involves interaction with the environment and at this point in the argument plasticity becomes superimposed upon specificity. A variety of functions in the neonate, including muscular control and sensory processing, seem to develop at about the same time as the full development of cellular connectivity, in particular the myelination of the cells of the cortex associated with this control and analysis. The extent to which use determines this development or development determines use, is not clear, but in the early stages of postnatal development, a crude but reasonably convincing match of brain structure and performance may be observed. In the later stages of the developmental transitions in consciousness, skills and abilities, neurobiological data is too scanty and in all probability the changes involved too subtle to make any type of meaningful match, but the general postulate that changes in brain structure and properties must match these developmental changes in behavioral pattern, of genetic epistemology – or better, of developmental epistemology – is advanced.

This discussion led to an analysis of the conflict sometimes epitomized as nature/nurture. While it is argued that no parceling out of these two can be meaningfully attempted for behavior, a variety of environmental factors which directly affect performance are known. These include malnutrition during the period of rapid brain growth from conception to age about two years in humans and environmental impoverishment or rearing in environments of selected character in animals (in humans it is generally difficult to distinguish the two cases, as, in general, environmental and nutritional impoverishment occur together). The effects of nutrition and environment are directly measureable in terms of brain structure, biochemistry and performance. A further class of effects which are environmental in origin, yet strictly indistinguishable from genetic effects over a limited number of generations, are described as transgenerational. They include malnutrition in parental or grandparental infancy (which apparently directly affects cell number in the brain of the offspring) and, in the case of monkeys, social deprivation or isolation in infancy, which affects subsequent rearing patterns and the behavior of the isolate's own young. It is the existence of all these effects which leads me to take a stand against a neo-Cartesian position on the status of language as a wired-in property of the brain, and to a preference for the term developmental epistemology over the genetic epistemology which Piaget describes.

The existence of long-term environmental effects on brain structure and performance is an indication of the interaction of the two; a second is provided by the relatively recent recognition of the variety of short-term interrelations that occur. The extent to which brain structure and biochemistry is state-dependent, being continuously modified in response to changed environmental circumstances, is only now becoming apparent. "Pygmalion" effects on learning and performance as a consequence of the expectancy of the tester, both for humans and animals, are matched in animals by the occurrence of transient changes in such basic biochemical variables as protein synthesis and transmitter levels. These effects become even more marked when a further chemical variable, such as an administered drug, is added to the system. The state-dependence of brain biochemistry—to which we return in subsequent chapters—seems to be an example of cross-hierarchical interactions in a direction the reverse of that normally considered; it is, I suspect, of importance, but at this time of unknown significance. One important present implication which must be emphasized, however, is the impossibility of considering any aspect of brain function in isolation from its environment. Clearly it is always necessary to consider the brain as part of a system which includes all aspects of the environment of that brain.

In the face of the evidence of the state-dependence of the brain, the instability of the IQ score, depending as it does on so many factors, including the expectancy of the testers, the transgenerational environmental effects and the degree to which adult performance depends upon the proper development of the brain during its formative months and years, we can make only two responses. The first is a recognition of the wisdom of the old Jesuits, who used to claim that, if they were given a child for the first five years of its life, they were able to ensure that it would grow "straight" thereafter. The second is to ask the question which properly concludes this chapter, turning it into a prescription for social action: How can we improve the environment of *all* children so that their brains can develop to the maximum?

9 Memory – The Central Store

Individuality and Memory

Every human individual is unique. He is the product of his inheritance and his environment, and while two individuals may have an identical genetic inheritance, if they are identical twins, no two individuals can have developed in identical environments. Even for identical twins reared together, the environment and experience of each must differ in very many respects–more with every passing day. Of course, it is possible to talk meaningfully about the behavior of populations of individuals in statistical terms, and common environments are likely to produce broadly common ways of thinking, acting, being. One's mode of thought expresses the sum of the interactions of the environment upon one's genotype–a statement which is generally and more politically expressed in the form: "man's mode of thought is ideological"; it reflects the social structure in which he was reared.

But individuality remains and it is instructive to consider what it means. Where is my individuality, for example? If I consider this question, it is clear that individuality does not reside to any great extent in my limbs or internal organs, all or most of which can be replaced by prostheses or by transplants, or yet in my senses–if I were deaf or blind I would still be *me* in some sense. But suppose a brain transplant were possible? Transplant someone else's brain into "my" body, and "*I*" would not be "*me*". "I" would be the other person, whose brain now operates in "my" body–it would make more sense to talk about a body transplant! Where did my brain acquire this peculiar individuality which distinguishes it from all the other organs of the body? In a very real sense, it clearly did not have this individuality at birth–witness the earliest of Piaget's developmental stages in which the child learns to distinguish between self and non-self; individuation is itself a developmental process. Some have indeed argued that the newborn child is strictly speaking "mindless". But once individuality has developed it remains thereafter–with some exceptions which we will later come back to. This self must be defined as the sum of the experiences to date of the individual, and his internal reactions, conscious and unconscious, to these experiences stored within his brain, for within the limits laid down by the genetic specification of the system it is precisely these experiences which separate and distinguish one individual from another. If another individual had had precisely my experiences, stored precisely my memories, he would be me. If I lost the memory of my experiences I would not be me, but someone else, as indeed is the case of certain of the amnesias, an example of which is explored rather effectively in Doris Lessing's recent novel *Briefing for a Descent into Hell*.[1] A case may be made, therefore, that his memories are the most durable and vital characteristic of an individual. As he begins to lose them, through illness or old age, he descends from the status of the individual to that of the generalized state of second childhood.

Memories are the stored records of experience of the individual. They represent the plastic function of the brain, at its highest and most developed, and are central to our understanding of the brain, for they are one of the chief reasons for its existence. A wholly specific brain, as has been shown, would be an automaton. A wholly plastic one would be of little survival value, for prior experience would never modify subsequent behavior. Survival clearly depended, from an early point in the evolution of animals, on the capacity for such modifications to occur and then be stored. It has been argued that such storage of modifications has been found in organisms as primitive as the flatworm, or even the hydra. With slightly more advanced brains there is no doubt. Snails can learn not to advance their eyestalks, if they receive electric shocks whenever they do; octopus to distinguish black from white and squares from circles for food reward; fish to move to a different part of their tank when a light flashes or a buzzer sounds, to avoid an electric shock; rats to run mazes or to press levers for reward; pigeons to count; dogs to beg, round up sheep, attack or not attack humans; dolphins to talk, jump through hoops, and apparently to detect submarines; apes to count, generalize, form concepts, make tools and use primitive language—and humans to perform a vast range of skills and activities exceeding in scale by many orders of magnitude the capacities even of apes.

Memory is clearly thus a complex phenomenon. Indeed the word is a portmanteau within which is packed a whole set of processes. It is necessary to assume that to every memory must correspond a particular unique state of the brain—without saying at this stage exactly what such a "brain state" may be. When a new memory is fed into the brain system, the system must change in some way so as to accommodate it. This is axiomatic if there is to be a possible mechanism for memory at all. We can then distinguish a number of processes associated with this state. When a new memory is about to be stored in the brain, the brain is in one state. When storage has occurred it is in another. The change between these two states is called LEARNING and is a *process*. Subsequently a second event may occur. The memory is brought out of store to compare with some current event (Do I like that food? Have I seen that face before? How does that tune go? What did X say?). This comparison, or matching, is another process which may be described as *recall* or *remembering*. But to move from learning to recall must imply that something is physically present within the system which represents the memory once learned and before it is recalled. Various names have been proposed for this something–the memory trace, engram, the mnemon (or "unit memory"). Here, the term *memory trace* will be used. Note that, while learning and recall are processes, the trace is in some sense a permanent *thing*, a state of the brain which codes for the remembered event. We have then to do with two processes and a thing. And, in addition to this, it is necessary to consider a third process, which occurs if a trace cannot be recalled and which may be described as *forgetting*.[2] Also, it is not ruled out that the permanent trace may indeed itself be modified or distorted by subsequent experience.

The Nature of the Memory Store

One of the earliest successful attempts to experiment with the problem of the nature of learning and memory came with the work of Ivan Pavlov in what is now Leningrad, at the very beginning of this century. Pavlov's famous series of experiments began almost as an offshoot from some work with dogs on the physiology of digestion–for which he was to receive the Nobel Prize before ever his work on reflexes achieved much public acclaim. The dogs had had a minor operation to expose the salivary gland in their cheek so that the saliva was released to the outside instead of the inside of the mouth and its volume could then be measured. When the dogs were presented with food they salivated. In the course of these experiments it became the practice for a bell to be rung before the food was actually brought to the animals. Before long it was observed that the animals salivated when the bell was rung and before the food was brought in; the animals had come to anticipate food when the bell rang–and hence to salivate. What is more, they would now salivate when the bell sounded even if no food was subsequently brought.

Pavlov explained this phenomenon in terms of the spinal reflex model. Just as the knee jerk is a simple reflex involving spinal neurons, so salivation when food is presented is a central reflex which is wired-in. This natural stimulus is the unconditioned one and may involve a relatively simple neuronal pathway. The auditory stimulus of hearing the bell is the conditioning stimulus, arriving centrally at the brain by quite a separate pathway. But the continued presentation of bell followed by food eventually results in a new reflex being formed by the opening of a new pathway which connects bell-sound with salivation. This is the CONDITIONED REFLEX. The experiences are thus coded within the brain in terms of the formation of some new type of functional pathway.

Of course, it soon became clear that the analogy could not be pressed too far, for the events within the brain are far more complex than the spinal reflex even for the unconditioned stimulus, let alone the conditioned one. None the less Pavlov's approach made possible a whole new area of research on central learning systems which had hitherto been regarded as unapproachable by experimental psychology or neurophysiology—indeed he was much reviled in some quarters for daring to do research upon "the soul". These experiments were the forerunners of the mazes, the shuttleboxes, the Skinner boxes, in which animals have since been placed by generations of behaviorists and experimental psychologists, to learn to run complex pathways, jump barriers or press levers to obtain the rewards of food and drink, or to avoid unpleasant stimuli such as electric shock.

Pavlov's experiment may be said to relate only to one type of learning, which may be called associative conditioning, the process of acquiring the capacity to respond to a given stimulus with the reflex proper to another stimulus (the reinforcement) when the two stimuli are applied concurrently. A second type of learning is shown in experiments involving the Skinner boxes, where an organism establishes an association between a voluntary motor act and a subsequent reward. This is sometimes known as type II, operant or INSTRUMENTAL CONDITIONING. The boxes are named for one of the leading exponents of behaviorist psychology (see chapter 13), and the experiments they involve are generally of the lever-pressing type in which the animal is rewarded for pressing the correct lever, or pressing it in response to a particular stimulus, such as a light. There may be other types of learning as well; LATENT LEARNING, where stimuli are associated without obvious reward, and a type best summed up as "insight", where a response is the result of the understanding of new relationships. Negative learning (*not* to do something or punishment will result), sometimes known as avoidance conditioning, is yet another type. It is generally believed, though without proof, that the underlying neurobiological mechanisms are similar in all—and for that matter, between an animal learning to salivate and an English speaker learning Russian or a child learning to count. What distinguishes the memories is which cells in which parts of the brain are involved.

In all probability this assumption of uniform mechanism will turn out to be false, but it is convenient for the present in the absence of other information.

For all these types of learning then, the assumed mechanism is similar; essentially, that learning represents the opening of new functional pathways within the brain. It follows from this that the memory trace *is* the new pathway itself—each memory is coded for in some way by a unique pathway. What form could the opening of such a pathway take?

The most convincing model followed the development of the electroencephalogram. If the brain were in ceaseless electrical activity, could not this electrical activity be functioning as a memory store? Perhaps the memory trace took the form of a cir-

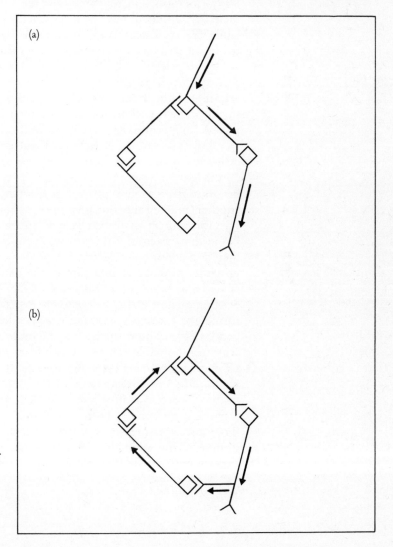

(a)

(b)

48 Reverberating circuit memory model. Firing of cells in (a) results in changed synaptic connectivity; a network is produced (b) round which current can flow continuously.

49 (*opposite*) Modifiable
synapse memory model.
(a) Synapse prior to
engram storage
(b) Synapse after storage
has occurred. Three
modifications are shown;
the synaptic ending is
larger; the thickening on
the post-synaptic side
greater; and the number
of synaptic vesicles has
increased. All changes are
speculative.

cuit of continuously self-exciting neurons, as in figure 48. As few
as two or three neurons could form a nerve net, and around this
net a continuously reverberating circuit of current could flow.
As each neuron could take part, by way of its synaptic connections, in many such nets, the coding potential of the 10^{10} neurons
of the cortex would be ample for the memories of a lifetime.

This model has the attraction of elegance and simplicity. It
was however not long before it was to be proved wrong. What
it proved unable to account for was the very durability of
memories. Memories are extremely difficult to erase once they
are established. We all retain memories of events which occurred
many years ago; a centenarian can remember his childhood.
Indeed a case can be made that, together with scar tissue on the
body, memories in the brain are the most durable environmentally imposed individual characteristic. But the EEG is
labile. Electrical activity of the brain can be reduced temporarily
to almost zero by a variety of drugs, or turned into frenetic over-
activity by electrical shock treatment. Drugs, body cooling and
concussion all temporarily abolish or distort the electrical
activity of the brain. Yet the organism, human or animal,
survives these treatments with his memories virtually unimpaired. So it cannot be merely an electrical phenomenon which
is coding for memory. A more profound structural change seems
called for, in the anatomical or chemical matrix of the brain.[3]

It might be proposed, for instance, that as the memory trace
becomes fixed, a new process grows out from one neuron to
another, making functional synaptic contacts with it and therefore forming an anatomically new pathway. The coding now
lies in the existence of the pathway, rather than in the fact that
there is a continuous electrical flow along it. While entire new
processes must be at best rare in the adult as opposed to the
developing brain, simply because of the density of packing of
existing ones, it would be relatively easy for new synapses to be
formed or existing ones modified in order to make such pathways viable. The doctrine that memory storage occurred by
way of modifiable synapses was advanced in the 1940s by the
psychologist Donald Hebb in Montreal (figure 49).[4] If synapses
are modified or activated during learning the implication must
be that the actual anatomy and biochemistry of a brain in which
a particular item has been stored must be different in some
(hopefully measurable) way from that of a brain prior to such
storage. This immediately opens the way to attempting
experiments actually to identify such changes as occurring.

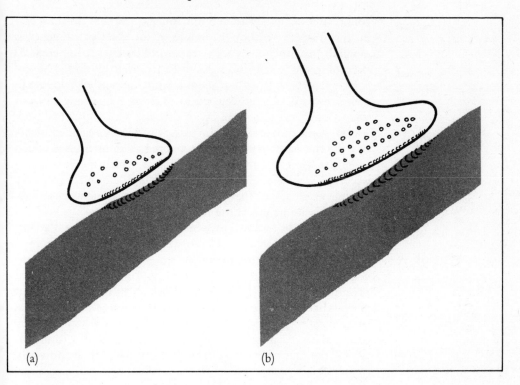

(a)   (b)

Long- and Short-term Memory

While it is not easy to devise an experiment in which one examines a brain before and after, the problem becomes simplified if rather than search for the trace as such one concentrates on the learning *process*, the period during which the memory is stored. It is almost always easier to obtain meaningful biological results in relation to a process than to a thing, and learning is no exception to this rule. The process of learning can be detected neurophysiologically, biochemically and anatomically.

The first important point to note is that learning is a temporal process. It takes time to occur. It takes time to learn a new trick, a word, a telephone number, or the way through a maze. It may make several trials to fix the information perfectly. A *cumulative* process is obviously involved, although there are certain sorts of learning called "one-trial" which generally involve unpleasant or aversive stimuli and which operate on the burnt-child-dreads-the-fire principle.

Even they however, take time to fix, as can be shown by a fairly common human experience, that of concussion. People recovering from a blow to the head which knocks them out, frequently show loss of memory for the events immediately preceding the blow. The classical hero of a gangster film coming round after being coshed and murmuring "Where am I?" is real in this respect. Although memory for long-past events is generally unimpaired by such treatments, the events immediately preceding the concussion seem to be irretrievably lost. The loss may extend back from half an hour to an hour, or even longer in some cases. W. Richie Russell in Oxford, examining cases of war casualties, found amnesias of this sort which stretched back several weeks but in which the patient generally regained memory for the past events as he recovered. The memories which were the most distant from the time at which the concussion occurred were gradually regained although complete recovery was never obtained; there was always a loss of memory at least for the few hours preceding the concussion.[5]

It is not only concussion which causes these effects. Patients undergoing electrical shock treatment in hospital generally show similar loss of memory for the events immediately preceding the shock. And rats taught to run a maze and then promptly vigorously electrically shocked, subsequently cannot recall what they have learnt. So we may assume that the process of fixation of permanent memory occurs over a period of the order of thirty minutes to three hours, and that within this period the memory is not stable but is in fact labile and easily obliterated.[6]

But there is also evidence that suggests that, over this period of instability, another type of memory process is also operating. Consider an experiment in which someone reads out a string of seven or eight random numbers at about one a second and then asks one to repeat them back. The chances are that one will be able to do so. If the experimenter asks again ten minutes later one just might be able to, depending on what one had been doing in the meantime? If the time is delayed to thirty minutes, though, the probability is that one will have forgotten. Clearly there was a time when the numbers are remembered and then one at which they are not. But there is nothing inevitable about this. Suppose the numbers had formed a telephone number which was important to recall. The odds are that half an hour later one would still remember the sequence. There are thus two classes of items, those remembered for a very short time and then forgotten, and those retained more permanently.[7]

There is obviously a strong relationship, at least in time, between the process of fixation of permanent memory and the two classes of memory shown in these experiments. From this has come the idea that there are two types of memory, long and short term. Short-term memory holds items for half an hour or so, over which period long-term memory is becoming fixed. This may mean that the short-term memory develops into long-term memory if the conditions are right (figure 50), or, more

50 Short and long term memory. In version (a), perceptual analysis is followed by short, followed by long-term memory, in linear array. In version (b), long-term memory is a separate process initiated at the same time as short-term memory, which decays over a period of minutes to hours. If the long-term trace has built up sufficiently by the time the short-term trace has decayed, permanent storage results. Observations on human patients with hippocampal lesions favor model (b) rather than model (a).

probably, that it represents a parallel holding procedure operating over the duration of the period during which long-term memory is being fixed. Either way, the lability of the short-term memory and its various other characteristics lead to the conclusion that it at least has some sort of electrical coding within the brain, perhaps by the reverberating circuit model discussed and discarded above for permanent memory.

There are other electrical models for short-term storage of memory. The attention of neurophysiologists has recently been drawn to the possibility of making an analog of short term memory which may be more accessible to analysis—habituation. This process has already been referred to, and is easy to illustrate by the example given in Chapter 4 of putting on clothes, when for the first few minutes one registers the feel of the fabric against the skin, and so forth. Gradually these sensations disappear. Yet the clothes are still there—indeed if they are taken off the sensations associated with them come flooding

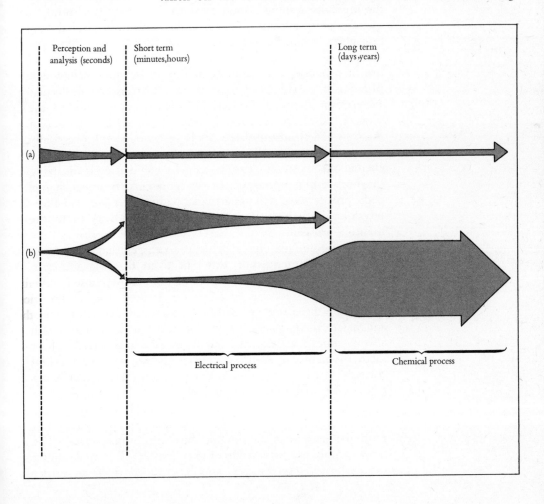

back. One has simply ceased to be aware of the messages arriving from a particular set of receptors. Similar phenomena occur in all organisms with nervous systems. Repeated presentation of a stimulus will eventually fail to elicit a response. It is then necessary to wait for a period before presenting the stimulus again if the organism is to respond. The interesting thing about the habituation process is that it is both a behavioral and a physiological phenomenon.[8] This has been most clearly shown in one of the simpler invertebrate preparations which have been very thoroughly investigated–the sea slug for example–where the individual cells involved in particular pathways are known. Eric Kandel in New York has been able to place microelectrodes in the cells of the pathway controlling a particular behavioral response, that of a swimming escape response, and show that, while the receptor cells continue to fire at an unchanged rate, so that the signal is still being fed into the system, the cells on which the receptors synapse, and which are responsible for coordinating the muscular response, soon cease to fire.[9] Nor is it simply a question of the exhaustion of available transmitter. The habituation phenomenon, in this case at least, thus involves the post-synaptic cells changing their properties–temporarily ceasing to fire in response to a stimulus in the pre-synaptic cell which previously would have fired them. What is the molecular mechanism involved? Presumably a change at, or close to, the synapse must have occurred. It must be a reversible change, for the cells, if left unstimulated for long enough, will eventually recover their response, and the withdrawal behavior will be elicited once more. It is easy to see why habituation is an analog for short-term memory, which also represents a transient change in the properties of cells or particular pathways. To many neurophysiologists habituation thus seems a good way in to the memory problem.

There is some anatomical evidence to suggest that the location of short-term memory is different from that of long-term memory. The issue of localization has not yet been raised in this chapter; it has rather been taken for granted that the site of memory is the cortex–probably the association cortex regions, and, in fact, this is generally agreed to be the case, although as will also become clear later, it is far from easy to define the exact locus of memory. And, of course, species without cerebral cortices–birds, for example–obviously must have other structures which serve the same function.

On the other hand, the events connected with short-term memory in the brain seem to be associated predominantly, not with the neocortex at all, but with the hippocampus. The hippocampus is a curved flap of gray matter which tucks under the cortical region proper, and is so-called from an earlier anatomical fancy that it resembled a seahorse. Evidence that it may be involved in the process of short-term memory includes the observation that patients whose hippocampus is damaged have difficulty with memorizing tasks, and that certain drugs which interfere with memory fixation apparently also cause electrical seizures in the hippocampus.

But the most striking indication of the rôle of the hippocampus comes from neurophysiological recordings of the behavior of cells within it. In a remarkable series of experiments E. N. Sokolov and Olga Vinogravoda in Moscow have found in the hippocampus classes of cells with very strange properties.[10] There are cells which, for example, can count and can remember – for instance a cell may be stimulated by a particular pattern of impulses, and may fire, say, five short bursts, and will proceed to repeat this pattern of just five bursts for some time subsequently. There are also "novelty-recording cells" which are normally silent, and fire only in response to a new stimulus, but if the same stimulus pattern is repeated again, will no longer fire. Clearly cells with such properties (and the discussion of neuronal pathways and coding properties of chapter 4 should make clear how, in general terms, circuitry to perform this type of function can be built up) could have an information-processing and short-term storage rôle.

Long-term Memory Mechanisms

But the permanent store must be something more substantial than this; by definition the synaptic change must be more durable. It is here that the biochemist comes in once more, for if there is to be a permanent synaptic change it must be reflected in a change in some biochemical property of the cells; some substance must change, in quantity or composition, in order to produce the relevant synaptic modification.

One of the most significant of biochemical generalizations is that all the molecules of the body are continuously being broken down and reformed, and the brain is no exception to this rule – indeed the average life of a small molecule in the brain may be a matter of minutes only, while 90 percent of the proteins of the brain are broken down and replaced by new, presumably identical, molecules within a period of no more than fourteen days or so.[11] None the less in this constant flux the structures which the individual molecules compose remain, though their components change. It is as though, in a brick house, individual bricks were continuously being taken out and replaced by other similar ones. The brick house remains a brick house although the bricks of which it is made are continuously changing. If a new brick addition to the house is built – a chimney added for instance–this is a permanent modification even though its bricks too are subject to the same law of replacement as the others. The difference between the normal replacement mechanism and that occurring during the building of the chimney is that, while normally the rates of addition and subtraction of bricks to the house exactly balance, during the period over which the chimney is being added, there is an excess rate of addition of bricks compared to the norm.

An exactly analogous situation may be presumed to be occurring during learning. If molecules like proteins or lipids are involved in some synaptic modification process, their rate of production during the learning process may be expected to show changes. The rate of synthesis of biological macromolecules can be followed fairly simply using radioactively labeled substances as precursors. Thus, if an organism is fed radioactively labeled amino acids, it will make radioactively labeled proteins. Measurement of the amount of radioactivity in the isolated proteins will then answer the question "How much synthesis has been occurring in a given time?"

Most of the relevant experiments have followed the rate of production, either of protein, or of the template on which the protein is made within the cell, RNA. In general it has been shown that the rate of production, of both RNA and protein, changes, generally increasing, during learning in many organisms and under many different conditions. It is always very difficult to eliminate the possibility that the changes are associated with behavioral events other than learning–changed amount of sensory input, motor activity, anxiety, attentiveness and so on could all affect the synthesis of protein, and not all of these can be easily controlled for. In one set of experiments, Edward Glassman and his group at Chapel Hill, North Carolina, taught mice to jump onto a shelf a little above the floor of their cage when a light flashed or a buzzer sounded in order to avoid electric shock.[12] The rate of RNA synthesis in their brains was compared to that in controls which also heard the noise, saw the light, and received the shock, but had no shelf to jump up to and therefore could not escape the shock. RNA synthesis in particular brain regions of the experimental animals increased compared to the controls. A perfect experiment at first sight, but wait: can one be sure the control animals have not learned *anything*?–for example they may have learned that buzzer, light, and shock are *not* associated–that there is *no* way of avoiding the pain of the electric shock. May they not therefore also have been more anxious than the lucky ones which knew they could escape, and perhaps anxiety reduces RNA synthesis? A variety of stressful treatments, such as forced exercise, are known to affect the rates of RNA and protein synthesis in particular brain regions. Of course, some of these factors can be controlled for, and it is probably true that Glassman's experiment proves what it seems at first sight to do, but there are certainly complications which should not be ignored.[13]

Some of my own experiments (with Patrick Bateson and Gabriel Horn in Cambridge) have followed the changes in protein and RNA synthesis during imprinting in the chick. Over the period during which the chick is exposed to an imprinting stimulus, a series of characteristic biochemical changes occurs in one particular brain region, the roof of the forebrain. In this brain region, shortly after exposure to the imprinting stimulus begins, there is an increase in the activity of the enzyme responsible for the manufacture of RNA—called RNA POLY-MERASE—in the cell nuclei. Within an hour of the onset of the stimulus, increases in the production of RNA can be detected, and within two hours, an increased production of protein. In an attempt to rule out non-specific effects, we have split the chicks' brains by cutting the pathways which transfer visual information between the two halves of the brain. If the chick is then offered the imprinting stimulus with one eye covered, the half of the brain connected with the covered eye does not learn the stimulus, while that connected to the other does. When we compared the rates of synthesis of RNA in the trained half of the brain with those in the untrained, we found substantial differences. So the effects seem to be fairly specific. But it is still true that not all the possible controls in this type of experiment have been made and the complications ruled out—for instance, the half of the brain connected with the exposed eye, as well as learning, also receives more sensory input than the other.[14]

The assumption that has been made is that learning produces a synaptic change. Neurophysiological studies show that, in the habituation model of learning, some changes in the electrical properties of the synapse do occur. Biochemical experiments suggest that, following the learning stimulus, more RNA is synthesized in the cell nucleus and acts as a template for the production of new protein in the cell body. How can these be related? The key question here is the function of this new protein. Is the increase generalized, or confined to particular types of protein with particular properties? Some ingenious experiments made in Göteborg, Sweden, by Holger Hydén, involving very complex micromethods, suggest that (during the learning process he has studied at any rate) rather special new types of protein are produced.[15] How can their function relate to the synapse? It may be no more than speculation, but it will be recalled that the rôle of the neuronal cell body is to synthesize substances which flow down the axon to the synapse, a region which cannot perform this type of synthesis itself. Perhaps the proteins made during learning travel down the axon to the synapse, and, arriving there, modify it so as to alter the efficiency and strength of its connections with the post-synaptic cell. Or of course, the proteins may flow to the dendrites and there alter the receptor sites so as to change the responsiveness of the cell to messages arriving at the site. In either way a permanent change in synaptic efficacy may have been achieved. A previously inactive synapse may be switched on, or a previously active one turned off; in terms of information theory the two processes are obviously functionally equivalent.

It is also possible to obtain direct anatomical evidence of changes in synapse structure. During experiments involving small changes in a few synapses this must be practically impossible. But big changes may occur if the learning process is massive; for instance the experiments in which animals are deprived of a particular sensory input for a long period and then stimulated.

Some such experiments were described in the last chapter, in which rats were reared in the dark for the first few weeks of their lives and then exposed to laboratory illumination for three hours before killing. Electron micrograph studies by Brian Cragg, in London, have shown that changes occur in both the sizes and numbers of synapses in the visual cortex, lateral geniculate, and retinae of these animals when they first see light—just those regions in which we have found changes in protein synthesis.[16] The Krech, Bennett and Rosenzweig group in Berkeley, California, have also found evidence suggesting that the size of the synaptic thickening (shown in figure 17) changes between their environmentally deprived and enriched animals.[17] This correlation of biochemistry and anatomy is really quite encouraging. However, it must always be remembered that showing that protein synthesis occurs when learning takes place is not the same as showing that it is a necessary and sufficient condition for such learning.

Drugs and Learning

There is another way of approaching the relationship of biochemical processes to learning mechanisms. If protein synthesis is necessary for learning to occur, then if one injects a drug that stops protein or RNA from being synthesized in an experimental animal just over the peiod of the learning experience, then the animal should be unable to remember. Several drugs do in fact function as inhibitors of protein synthesis, and the antibiotics acetoxycycloheximide and puromycin have been particularly popular among neurochemists. Injected into the brain in carefully controlled quantities they will prevent all protein synthesis from occurring for a period of several hours. They have been used by Louis Flexner, in Philadelphia, and Sam Barondes, in New York, with mice, and Bernard Agranoff in Ann Arbor, Michigan, with goldfish.[18]

In general the results of these experiments show that, if an inhibitor is injected into an animal either just before or just after the learning trials begin—for example before the first sets of correlations of flashing light with electric shock—then when the animals are tested a day or so later they do not remember the association, while animals which have received sham injections of saline but no inhibitor remember well. If the injection is made a few hours before or after the learning experience instead then failure to remember does not occur. The implication of such experiments is that protein synthesis is necessary for the fixation of short-term into long-term memory but that the temporary disruption of protein synthesis after fixation has occurred does not disrupt the memory.

The trouble with the inhibitor experiments is that, while they give clear information about the time course of the learning process, they can tell one rather little about its mechanisms. For the inhibitors have other effects than just on learning—they are also poisonous! Inhibition of protein synthesis is a rather drastic process during which lots of other things than simply loss of capacity to fix short-term memory may occur. This is scarcely surprising when it is recalled that protein synthesis is a continuous rapid process, not only in the brain but in every other tissue of the body. Not all these proteins are involved in learning, but the production of all of them, at least in the brain, is stopped by the inhibitor. So there are bound to be lots of other behavioral effects of the inhibitors, even at low doses, than just that on memory fixation. And equally, the processes inhibited by the drug may be other than those solely of protein synthesis; many drugs have secondary biochemical effects and it may be that it is one of these which is involved in the blocking of learning. Indeed, at the physiological level it has been shown that puromycin causes electrical seizures in the hippocampus which may well be associated with its effects on memory processes.[19]

So while these inhibitor experiments strengthen the hypothesis that protein synthesis is involved in the memorizing process, they cannot be conclusive. While they may show that protein synthesis is necessary for memory fixation to occur, they cannot show that it is a sufficient condition. It could merely be a precondition without which some other process which was more directly involved could not take place—and as almost no other biochemical systems have yet been examined with this hypothesis in mind, it is difficult to rule it out. Thus if synaptic efficacy is a membrane phenomenon, it would seem probable that lipids as well as proteins would be involved, for they are essential membrane constituents. It is indeed interesting to consider just why proteins have become the candidate molecules for experiments on the biochemical basis of memory, and I return to this point later.

However, it is worth emphasizing another side-result of these studies. If drugs which inhibit learning do so by blocking protein synthesis, could not drugs which speed up protein synthesis speed up learning? This question led to the search for agents which enhanced protein synthesis. For some years, one or two drugs have been known which speed learning. They include nicotine and strychnine, but both of these have other undesirable side-effects, such as being poisonous, and have no major effect on protein synthesis. The mid-1960s saw the report of the isolation of a new drug, magnesium pemoline, alleged to enhance the activity of the enzyme RNA polymerase, a key enzyme of protein synthesis. Pemoline was also alleged to speed learning in rats. A flurry of interest and attempts to replicate these experiments followed, and it was generally concluded that the initial claims were wrong on both counts.[20] Pemoline does seem to have some effect, however, not on memory as such, but on *attention*, functioning rather like amphetamine in this respect (see chapter 11). But the negative response did not prevent the drug company which had reported the initial observations, Abbott Laboratories, of Chicago, from patenting the drug and apparently embarking on large scale clinical trials with University of Chicago medical students as subjects. The effect on the students' examination results was supposedly beneficial, but it is difficult to be very impressed by the pemoline saga. There seems little likelihood of an effective drug which positively affects the learning process being developed in the near future, though this will doubtless not be for want of the drug companies trying to find one.

The Debate over Localizability, and Some Red Herrings

So far the picture I have painted, while lacking definition, has none the less been fairly self-consistent. It has, however, been so only as a result of deliberate selection from a mass of conflicting evidence in a bitterly contested field. Although the hypothesis proposed is the one which I personally favor, it is necessary to look at some of the contrary views.

In essence, the controversy springs from a difference of philosophy and hence of approach. The conflict bears a resemblance to the reductionist/holist dichotomy described in chapter 4. The memory model adopted here is reductionist, depending on specific circuitry. But a holistic model is also possible, in which memory is considered to be, not a property of individual circuitry, but a distributed function of the entire brain, or at least the entire cortex. At the psychological level the conceptual framework was set in the 1920s by the emergence of a distinct school of thought, the so-called GESTALT psychology. This school was concerned with the problem of perception, and it began by asking questions such as "What is it that determines the "A"-ness of an object?" As mentioned earlier, one perceives an "A" as an "A" whether it is upside down or sideways, large or small, left or right of one's field of vision; that is, whichever retinal regions and therefore lateral geniculate and visual cortex cells are involved. The brain has a mechanism for recognizing the whole "A" as an "A" rather than analyzing it into its separated sub-parts such as / and–and /. Because this analysis can clearly involve any of many different cortical cells, the property of recognizing "A"-ness must be distributive.

In chapter 4, the work of Hubel and Wiesel in analyzing the different types of simple, complex and hypercomplex cells of the visual cortex was described. Such cells can obviously classify visual inputs in increasingly specified ways. But are there also hyper-hypercomplex cells which respond to even fewer inputs, so that at the limit there is a simple neuron which recognizes an "A" and nothing else–what Sherrington, in one of his memorable if slightly florid phrases described as "a single pontifical neuron"?[21] The work of the Gestalt school, of ablation studies of the Lashley type and many other investigations of the perceptual process which do not directly concern us here, makes clear that such "pontifical" neurons do not occur; the property of analyzing an "A" as an "A" is in some sense distributed across the cortex. Hence there are no specific individual "pontifical" or hyper-hypercomplex neurons. And if there are not, the simple ideas of circuitry involved in memory-trace formation become less convincing.

Gestalt psychology achieved a considerable vogue, particularly in the 1930s, and its conclusions concerning brain mechanisms received a measure of support from the remarkable experiments of Karl Lashley, mentioned in chapter 4 in connection with ablation studies. Lashley was attempting to identify the locus of memory within the cortex, and, to do so, first trained rats to run mazes, and then removed various cortical regions. He allowed the animals to recover and tested the retention of the maze-running skills. To his surprise it was not possible to find a particular region corresponding to the ability to remember the way through a maze. Instead all the rats which had had cortex regions removed suffered some kind of impairment, and the extent of the impairment was roughly proportional to the amount of cortex taken off. Removing cortex damaged the motor and sensory capacities of the animals, and they would limp, hop, roll or stagger, but somehow they always managed to traverse the maze. So far as memory was concerned, the cortex appeared to be equipotential, that is, with all regions of equal possible utility. Indeed, Lashley concluded rather gloomily in his famous last paper "In Search of the Engram", which appeared in 1950, that the only conclusion was that memory was not possible at all.[22]

The extraordinary thing about Lashley's results was that at about the same time as he was obtaining such apparent evidence of nonlocalizability, the Canadian neurosurgeon, Wilder Penfield, and his team at Montreal, were obtaining precisely contrary results with human patients. Penfield's experiments were made on patients for whom neurological disorders made electrical probing of the brain necessary.* While performing the mapping by electrical stimulation, Penfield noted, as his electrode passed through a motor region of the cortex, that appropriate limb movements would occur without conscious volition on the part of the patient. When visual or auditory cortex was stimulated the patient saw light flashes or heard buzzing or musical tones. Stimulation of the various speech center regions (figure 30) produced either incomprehensible sounds, or, more frequently, the patient would temporarily be unable to speak or to name objects. And when some regions of the temporal cortex were stimulated, the patient recalled particular memory sequences—an evening at the concert, a childhood experience and so forth. Repeated stimulation of the same spot would evoke the same recollections each time.[23]

So there seems an incompatibility between Lashley's and Penfield's results. It is not easy to see how they can be reconciled. Perhaps because Penfield's work was with human patients and hence not "basic science", it tended to be underrated by the theorists in comparison with Lashley's, which for a long time has been held to be convincing evidence in favor of a distributed memory.

But how could such a distributed memory work if it did not depend on the integrity of functioning neuronal circuitry? No probable explanation emerged until the 1960s, when a new physical analogy was found, on which brain theorists seized with an almost audible sigh of relief. The analogy was a device

* This technique is used, for example, with epileptics for whom it is necessary (or at least could be regarded as medically justifiable) to stimulate various brain regions electrically under local anaesthesia in order to find the epileptic focus—the starting point from which the seizure spread—so as to be able to destroy it. During this procedure, the patients remain fully conscious.

invented by the engineer Dennis Gabor, in London, called a HOLOGRAM, for which he was awarded a Nobel Prize in 1971. A hologram is essentially a photographic plate on which information is stored in a dispersed manner; the daunting task of explaining how this is achieved will not be attempted here.[24] In principle it is made by photographing an object under slightly special conditions using a laser beam. The photographic plate does not show an image in the normal form of a photograph, but when a laser beam is in turn shone through the plate, a three-dimensional image of the original object is formed at the same distance from the plate that the original object was located. What is more, this image-forming property is dispersed through the plate. If a small chunk of it is broken off and the light beam shone through the broken piece the same image is formed, but, depending on the size of the piece used, it is more or less blurred.

Thus the hologram has many of the properties of the equipotential, distributive aspect of brain memory, and has received powerful advocacy as a model of the brain by the experimental psychologist Karl Pribram, at Stanford, California, and the theoretician Christopher Longuet-Higgins, at Edinburgh. But, attractive as the analogy is, it has always suffered from being only an analogy. No one has been able to show convincingly just what the physical structures in the brain must be if they are to possess the properties shown by a photographic plate illuminated by a laser beam. While analogs are often powerful tools of scientific method, they only can be so under conditions where the analogy suggests an experiment which can test it, and up till now the only experiment to offer a prediction concerning brain memory in which a hologram model would differ in its consequences from a nonhologram one has proved negative.[25] We may therefore tentatively regard this particular excursion into memory modeling as closed.

But Lashley's dilemma remains. And a spirited attempt to solve it was made in the 1960s by invoking biochemical rather than physical analogs. The analogy involved this time began almost as a pun, a play on the word memory.[26] For some years, geneticists had been in the rather slipshod habit of referring to the property of an organism in growing to resemble its parents as an example of genetic "memory"; in the same way, immunologists began to refer to the way in which antibodies recognized antigens in tissues as immunological "memory". In each case the analogy was derived from brain memory. But then a strange thing happened. A great deal became known about the mechanisms of genetic "memory" and immunological "memory". The one depends on the properties of the molecules DNA and RNA and the other on proteins; and DNA, RNA and protein became known collectively as "informational macromolecules", because the sequence of their subunits (nucleotide bases in the case of DNA and RNA and amino acids in the case of protein) can form a specific information-bearing code. The analogy became turned on its head. If genetic memory and immunological memory were like brain memory, and the two former depended on the existence of unique molecules of DNA, RNA and protein, perhaps brain memory too depended on the unique properties of the same classes of molecules. Perhaps, for example, a unique RNA or protein molecule (it couldn't be DNA, as DNA is the genetic material, and memory is certainly not inherited!) coded for each memory. Such an apparently unlikely idea was first put forward in the late 1950s by Hydén in Sweden. If it was true, then memory would be independent of neuronal networks, connectivity and the rest. It would perhaps be non-localizable, as Lashley had found.

Certainly, there is plenty of information-storage capacity along the amino acid chain of a protein or the nucleotide sequence of an RNA molecule–plenty enough to store the memories of a lifetime. And it is the case that, not only is protein synthesis rapid in the brain, but a greater percentage of the brain's DNA is "turned on" and involved in its synthesis than in any other tissue of the body. Thus, more different types of protein are being made in the brain than in other tissues.

The experiments showing changes in protein synthesis with learning and the effects of inhibitors of such synthesis on memory retention would certainly be compatible with such an hypothesis, although they are of course open to quite other interpretations. But could there be an unequivocal experiment which would validate the hypothesis? If unique molecules are made in order to store brain memories, then it ought to be possible, by extracting the brain of a trained animal, to collect some of these memory molecules. They then could perhaps be injected into another naïve animal and the learning transferred with the injected molecules.

Put like that it doesn't sound too sensible a way to spend a working day. None the less the experiment has indeed been done, not once, but many times in many different laboratories. The first of the experiments were done with flatworms, whose learning capacity is anyhow in dispute, as was mentioned in chapter 5. James McConnell, at Ann Arbor, Michigan, trained flatworms to respond to light as if it were an electric shock and then chopped them up, allowed naïve flatworms to cannibalize the debris of the trained ones and observed that the behavior was transferred along with the cellular debris. Food for thought perhaps?[27]

McConnell's results have come under severe methodological criticism from many other workers, and have fallen somewhat into disrepute, although they made popular headlines for quite a while. Fortunately it is not necessary to analyze them in detail, for practically all the salient features of the experiments have now been repeated, apparently with positive results, not in flatworms but in mammals.

Some of the first of these new experiments were done by Allan Jacobson, a pupil of McConnell's at Los Angeles, who announced in 1965 that, if he trained rats to approach the food dispenser of their cage when a light flashed or a clicking sound was made, then killed the animals, extracted the RNA from their brains and injected it into the gut cavity of untrained animals, the untrained animals now tended to approach the dispenser when the appropriate stimulus—light or click—was given, even though they received no food as a reward. Jacobson even managed to transfer the approach behavior from rats to hamsters in the same way.[28]

These results provoked a fierce controversy in the scientific literature; many laboratories attempted to replicate them. Some succeeded, but most failed. And later that year a joint report of "failure to replicate" was signed by twenty-three authors and published in the journal *Science*.[29] There the matter would perhaps have rested had it not been for the fact that it was noticed that the method that Jacobson had used for extracting his RNA also liberated a good deal of protein. Perhaps the active material was protein and not RNA? Many of these points were thrashed out in a series of conferences on the biochemistry of memory mechanisms that have been held over the years since 1966. By 1967 many labs were back in the memory-transfer business again, this time working not with pure RNA, but with various types of mush of whole brain. Quite a few found some sort of transfer appeared to occur, but the phenomenon seemed very fragile and hard to analyze, often disappearing if one went on trying long enough. Strange effects kept cropping up, like those obtained by the group which trained some rats to press levers for food with their left paw and some with their right paw, and found that while one behavior could be transferred the other could not. Or like the reports from several labs that if the material from one trained brain were injected into an untrained animal a positive transfer occurred, but if the material from two brains was injected the recipient animal scored below chance in its trials—an example of negative transfer!

In general, with a couple of notable exceptions, the anomalies have tended to drive memory transfer into disrepute. The major exception is Georges Ungar, in Houston, Texas, whose results seem to have gone steadily forward from positive instance to positive instance. Ungar now claims that the memory-transfer factor is not a protein but a shorter chain of the type classified as PEPTIDE, containing eight to fifteen amino acids. He has purified one such peptide, derived from the brains of rats trained to fear the dark by being presented with a choice between entry in a dark box and a lighted one, and then being shocked electrically as they try for the dark box. Mice presented with a similar choice would normally also try to enter the darkened box. If they have been injected with the peptide from the rats however, Ungar claims they choose the light area instead. Ungar calls his peptide "scotophobin", which is Greek for "fear of the dark", and claims to have synthesized it chemically and injected it into mice with the same effect as the natural substance.[30]

It would be wrong to assume that Ungar's results have been widely believed, although his experiments have not been refuted. Polite scepticism is at best the order of the day for experiments which, if verified, would certainly shake the traditional views of brain mechanisms. Although Ungar claims that his peptide works by passing through the blood-brain barrier into the cortex, where it is selectively absorbed on to particular synapses, rendering them specifically active and therefore coding for learning in something approximating the manner proposed in the conventional theories, such a model is beset with implausibilities. It is rather unlikely that molecules of this sort can actually pass in any number into the brain after injection into the gut cavity, and improbable that they could be selectively absorbed. Indeed, if peptides did code for memories one would expect to find that there were many more peptide molecules in the brain than is in fact the case. Indeed, if all memorizing peptides were present in the quantities of Ungar's scotophobin, then to code for the memories of a human lifetime would demand that the brain contained a mass of peptides weighing something of the order of 100 kilograms—rather more than the weight of a man!* But the other major objection to such memory models is that they seem simultaneously to impose huge strains on the biochemical mechanisms of the cell—after all the proteins of the cell have a lot of other jobs to do apart from coding for memories—while at the same time an intra-cellular coding molecule seems to make irrelevant or unnecessary the elaborate coding mechanisms of the synaptic/dendritic network that the previous chapters of this book have rather lovingly described.

After all, the brain is not the liver. The *relationships* between its cells seem, if only from the elaborate architecture of their

---

* This isn't quite a deathblow to the model, as perhaps the scotophobin is only made in such large quantities during the training period, and later is present in much smaller amounts.

structures, all-important. At their crudest, the models of memory mechanisms which depend on molecules rather than structures not only run counter to the conventional wisdom of neurobiology, but they are also unaesthetic, a matter of some significance for the acceptability of scientific theories.

It might well be thought that the memory molecule story was nothing but a red herring. But in a situation which is behaviorally so complex as learning, in which all sorts of features associated with attention, arousal, motivation, and sensitivity to the rewarding or aversive stimulus offered as learning incentive, may play a part in the phenomenon examined (just as much as does the central memory store itself) it may well be that the positive results recorded do indicate that some factor is transferable between animals which affects their capacity to learn, not specific items, but in a general way, by affecting one of these parameters. It may be this property which the transfer experiments are, somewhat inadequately, examining. But one should not always discard the implausible in favor of the plausible results, or too readily explain away data that do not fit one's preconceived framework of experimentation and theory, tempting as it is to discard such results as aberrations.

Meanwhile, of course, the results have had their impacts in other fields—quite apart from newspaper speculations concerning the prospect of feeding extracts of professorial brains to university students, or artificially synthesizing specific memories to be implanted later into unsuspecting individuals so as to give them new personalities under the control of Machiavellian or totalitarian plotters. Such schemata are fortunately far from realization, and even if Ungar were to prove to be correct so far as his animal experiments are concerned, they are never likely to be even theoretical, let alone practical possibilities for the transfer of the much more complex and specific memories which are significant for humans. Even he does not propose that there is a specific set of peptides coding for recognition of Beethoven's Fifth Symphony!

None the less, at least one Michigan clinical psychologist, Ewen Cameron, took the proposals concerning memory molecules seriously enough to test the effects of feeding massive doses of RNA to elderly patients with memory difficulties.[31] Cameron claimed that 100 grams of yeast RNA taken orally each day—a truly monumental quantity—did have significant effects on the patients' memory retention scores, though presumably even with these doses the yeast RNA did not cause them to remember their past experiences as yeast cells! More than likely, old people who are institutionalized and who formed the subjects of Cameron's studies, were simply only too pleased to be made a fuss of during an experiment of this sort and improved as a consequence of this. Perhaps the old people were just malnourished and responded to an improvement in their diet. In the absence of reliable control procedures, it is often difficult to tell whether such effects are real or not.

It may be felt that this excursion has raised more problems than it has solved. Can an explanation of the distributed nature of memory be found which does not involve memory molecules or holograms? In my view the answer is Yes. It is possible to reconcile Penfield's results with Lashley's without involving fundamentally new principles of brain function. The clue to this lies in the fact of the brain's redundancy. It has already been noted that the plasticity of the brain allows for one region to take over another's function at least partially even after lesioning, and the neat exposure of the fallacy of many ablation studies provided by Gregory's transistor analogy has also been discussed (page 94).

For almost all the mammalian brain systems examined, a common feature appears to be that of redundancy; the existence of very many duplicate pathways, routes by which instructions and information can pass from point a to point b. It has already been pointed out that, although each cell makes many synaptic contacts, a very large proportion of them may all be on the same post-synaptic cell. This is an example of synaptic redundancy. There are probably also present, within any part of the brain, many thousands or tens of thousands of cells with essentially identical tasks in relation to the system as a whole. Indeed, this must be the case, or the 10^4 or so neurons which supposedly die each day in the adult brain and are not replaced would result in a series of random performance gaps which in fact do not occur–detectably at least–until the individual is very old. Redundancy is clearly a condition of survival so far as brains are concerned. Indeed, one can prove this theoretically. Studies of model brain systems made by the mathematical biologist Jack Cowan, in Chicago, produced the conclusion that, if one wanted reliable performance from a machine with many parts, each of which could be faulty, the most effective way of achieving reliability was to connect the parts up randomly but with considerable redundancy in possible pathways.[32] That way, although it was extravagant of units (neurons in the case of the brain) it achieved high reliability of performance over long periods even with failures in individual parts.

Thus redundancy provides an answer to the Lashley puzzle. If the same memory is coded in many parts of the cortex; that is, if the state of threshold or synaptic efficacy of a large number of cells, not necessarily, indeed perhaps definitely not, all connected directly with one another, is altered during the learning process, then the memory may well be stored in many different

parts of the system. Particular sets of circuits and firing pa
may form the relevant code, but the memory will no
localized to a single network. Rather, it will be duplicated 1
both brain hemispheres and many times over. Thus cortical
ablation of a circumscribed region will not ablate particular
memories because duplicate copies are stored elsewhere. None
the less, stimulation of any of these particular regions will trigger
firing on at least one of the redundant coding networks. Thus
the memories invoked by stimulation in Penfield's experiments
become explicable. I do not think that there are any phenomena
of memory which cannot be explained by this redundant-
network/modifiable-synapse theory.

Recall: The Model in the Brain

The data and hypotheses I have discussed so far have all been
concerned with the mechanisms of learning, of the entry of
information into the store. I have supposed that the entry is
registered by some class of synaptic and/or biochemical changes
which are retained permanently thereafter. The changed state
is then in some way the memory-trace or engram. No mechanism has yet been proposed for the subsequent process, that of
"reading" of the information in the store and comparing of it
with some new situation; that is, the recall process. In fact very
little evidence concerning the nature of this process is available.
There is a variety of theories which provide more or less
plausible models. All of them assume that some such process as
has been described is operative during learning. The results of
such a learning process are that all organisms with memory
possess, in the form of a set of unique brain states, a model, in
the brain, of the outside world. Particular neuronal networks
or patterns of electrical activity diffused across the cortex, code
for particular memories. But how is a particular memory
invoked at a particular time? How is a particular brain state
recaptured?

A simple network comparator which can provide this recall
system has been proposed by J. Z. Young on the basis of experiments made with memory mechanisms in the octopus.[33] It
depends on modifiable synapses and point-for-point representations of particular behavioral patterns, and explains the
mechanism whereby an octopus may remember, when presented with a crab plus a black square, that to attack means to
receive an electric shock. Young's model is summarized in
figure 51.

But this phenomenon is relatively trivial to explain compared with the subtleties of memory as expressed in humans;
to take an at first sight obvious, but on reflection puzzling,

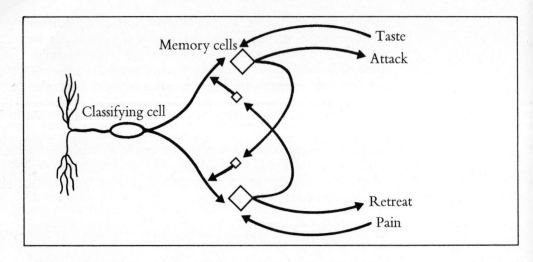

Memory cells

Taste

Attack

Classifying cell

Retreat

Pain

51 A model of a memory system in the octopus, due to J. Z. Young. The classifying interneuron responds to a particular type of event and has two outputs, which produce opposite motor effects–attack and retreat. Following one action, a signal that returns to the same unit can either reinforce or inhibit the action, with opposite effect on the antagonistic action. The small cells, which inhibit the unused pathway, have modifiable synapses.

phenomenon, why is it that it is easy to remember the alphabet in the "normal" order but hard to say it backward? easy to hum a tune but not to recognize it if played backward?–or indeed why does one remember any sequence of events as a temporally-ordered sequence at all? This must mean that in traversing a particular sequence of memory-traces, the brain proceeds from state to state along the different individual traces in an ordered manner. The phenomenon is analogous to synaptic conduction or axonal firing–all of these processes are undirectional. One state must "fire" another almost irreversibly. So the individual brain states associated with memories must presumably be linked by synaptic logic into a sequence in which one follows almost inevitably from another–try stopping a stream of memory in midflow and the difficulty will become apparent. It is as if the arrow of time is located at the synapse, at least so far as memories are concerned.

One interesting corollary of this might be that, if synaptic transmission were bidirectional, then memories might flow in either direction equally logically–and perhaps this may be the case for animals with nerve-nets and bidirectional synapses like the jelly-fish or sea anemone. Unfortunately, we shall never know!

This type of hypothesis can explain how a memory sequence, once initiated, proceeds. It does not explain the selection process whereby one can *choose* to recall a particular episode, tune or alphabet. How does a particular state get selected? If I say "I will now recall my fourth birthday party" I can indeed do so (although I do not seem to be able to recall my fifth). And sometimes the recollection will get plugged in apparently by accident, without apparent choice on my part; one of the keys to aspects of psychoanalysis is to induce just such free floating memories. Such chance plugging-in is not too hard to explain. Once the brain has "chanced upon" a particular state, perhaps as a result of random or spontaneous firing, as in dreaming, the ensuing states will follow almost by necessity. But what about the deliberate induction of the memory? The specific instruction must be to fire particular circuits, from which the rest will follow. Does the brain have as many knots in its handkerchief as there are patterns to choose from the store? The problem here is the same as that involved in the processing of visual information in the cortex, in relation to Hubel and Wiesel's simple, complex and hypercomplex cells. There is a danger of an infinite regress to that single pontifical neuron which decides—which *is* the "I" which chooses. The paradox is related to the problem of hierarchies of explanation, discussed in the Introduction, and to which we return in the final chapter.

The "I" that does the choosing of the memories and the synthesizing of the information provided by visual analyzer cells is not a little man in a control box, of the sort suggested by a telephone-exchange brain model, but instead the "I" itself is the *sum* of the activity of all these cells, the sum of all the memories in the store. The act of choosing is itself programed by the firing of particular cells; a "prestate" is necessary before the brain state relevant to a particular memory can be achieved, and this prestate is described at another level of the hierarchy of explanations as "me choosing to remember my fourth birthday party". And there are "pre-prestates" which can be described as "me deciding to write about choosing to remember about my fourth birthday party . . .", etc. The paradox only emerges if it is wrongly assumed that all these processes happen simultaneously rather than sequentially, and therefore that the "I" which perceives the infinite regress does so at the same time as the regress occurs, so that it must be different from ("above") the brain states involved in the regression.

The mathematician Christopher Zeeman, at Warwick University, has provided a mathematical model of the phenomenon of memory which takes these considerations into account.[34] He begins by regarding the brain as containing an n-dimensional "thought cube" where n is a number which is the total of all possible brain states. Then, pursuing a line of thought or memory is equivalent to running along the surface of this cube. Thought or memory associations occur if one comes to an edge and crosses over on to another face . . . but the verbal description in the previous paragraph is adequate to my purpose; the mathematics is ingenious but suffers from the disadvantage, for an experimentalist, that it doesn't seem to help obviously in designing experiments which distinguish between alternative theories.

Forgetting and the Capacity of the Store

Adding to the memory store, and recalling from it, thus fit into at least some sort of picture, although most of the canvas remains blank with just a few tentative guide lines sketched in, very likely to need redrawing in the light of new experiments and better paradigms within which to work. But there remains an important question which has not yet been answered. Recall does not *erase* memory from the store; indeed the more often a thing is remembered, the more fixed it seems to become. There appears to be no limit to the number of times an item can be retrieved and then replaced. But if it is never recalled, left instead to moulder unused in store, what happens? That is, does an unused item ultimately become erased?

It is obvious that there are items which are forgotten, which cannot be recalled. Does this mean they are irretrievably lost, or is it merely that they have been overlaid with other material and simply cannot be found, so that if one could only produce the key, the memory door would come unlocked and the memory come tumbling out? These questions take us deep into the realms of psychology – from the work of such experimental psychologists as Donald Broadbent, in Cambridge, through to the whole tradition of clinical psychology and psychoanalysis associated with the name of Sigmund Freud.

To simplify, there are two possibilities to account for the incapacity to recall an item. It could be either that it has indeed been lost from the store, erased irrevocably, or that it has become irretrievable because it has become overlaid with other traces and new information (perhaps because, as in the Freudian account, it has been suppressed as in some way prejudicial to the well-being of the organism). It is very difficult to design a critical experiment which will clearly distinguish between these alternatives, although some of Broadbent's work does go a long way toward this in examining the capacity of individuals to recall nonsense words and syllables, over varying periods of time and when subject to varying degrees of interference, such as by exposure to other nonsense syllables or words.[35]

It is common knowledge that memories that "one did not know one had" can be retrieved. The techniques of psychoanalysis and free association are designed to recover such memories; they clearly work. There are well-substantiated claims that hypnosis and so-called "truth drugs", like sodium pentothal, do the same. Presumably the analyst's explanation concerning "blocking" is a valid description, at one hierarchical level at least, of what happens; at the cellular level the description would be of restraints which act so as to prevent particular firing patterns appropriate to particular memories being achieved. Techniques, whether of drug therapy or hypnosis or analysis, which release these restraints, do so perhaps by lowering anxiety, a phenomenon reflected at the neurobiological level, as will become clear in the next chapter, by activity in particular regions of the hypothalamus and limbic system, of cells which are now known to have a substantial rôle in controlling such aspects of behaviour. If the controls imposed by the action of these cells can be removed, and the individual placed in a tranquil, relaxed state, where the pressure of immediate sensory information impinging on the brain system is reduced, then presumably the cells of the brain, triggered by relatively random firing as a result of their own uncertain synaptic mechanisms, will tend to "flip" into particular states which will then run their course, unrolling otherwise suppressed memory sequences as they proceed. Dreaming may be—and we return to this in chapter 11—an analogous procedure. Such a model is clearly comparable with the effects of cortical stimulation reported by Penfield, when the stimulating electrode triggered not just a single item but an organized fragment of memorized experience. The indication that so much is stored, even though it may normally be irretrievable, prompts questions about what is ever forgotten. Is there no limit to what the brain can store? This question is generally asked somewhat apprehensively, because to have a "good" memory is recognized as a desideratum, while to have a "bad" memory is a sign of human weakness. Yet the picture is perhaps more complex than this. A good deal of awe is often expressed for professional "memory" men, those characters who tour variety clubs or appear on the radio or television, able to recall the names of the Middlesex cricket team of 1896 and all the Cup Final or Grand National winners since 1900. Such feats of memory are well attested, and undoubtedly quite a number of people have this sort of capacity. There are indeed well-known "rules" for improving memory so as to make such recall possible, ranging from the secrets of ancient Greek and Roman orators (fascinatingly discussed by Frances Yates in a book called *The Art of Memory*[36]) through to contemporary advertisements in such magazines as *Reader's Digest* offering the recipe of "a well-known publisher" to do the same thing.

Basically these tricks seem to involve devices for "placing" particular objects whose recall is desired, in particular locations in a well-known street or geographical scene. They are then recalled sequentially as, in one's imagination, one "walks down the street". Yates quotes descriptions going back to Roman times for just such procedures. Those contemporary "memory" men who have described how they work generally provide similar explanations. There are obvious relationships between these procedures and another capacity sometimes described as a "photographic" memory. This is a term often ill-employed to imply simply a good retention capacity. But there are a small number of people at least who do have a memory which seems much more genuinely photographic; shown a page of print or a picture they really do seem subsequently to hold a picture of it in their brains. This can be tested by showing a picture with writing on it for a few minutes, and then, for example, asking them to spell a particular word out, perhaps backward. This phenomenon is known as EIDETIC IMAGERY and has only recently been studied in any detail. One of the most interesting features of such eidetic memory is the fact that it seems to be much more common in young children than in older children or adults. There are suggestions that as many as 50 percent of primary-school-age children may possess eidetic memory, although recent experiments put the figure rather lower. It is however relatively rare after puberty.[37]

Why should this be? Surely such a memory capacity would be extremely useful? The interesting thing is that this is perhaps not the case. A penetrating recognition of this comes in one of the most striking short stories of that astonishing Argentinian writer, Jorge Luis Borges. He entitles his story "Funes, the Memorious" and it is the tale of a young man who could literally remember everything by some sort of eidetic process.[38]

> We, in a glance perceive three wine glasses on the table; Funes saw all the shoots, clusters and grapes of the vine. He remembered the shapes of the clouds in the south at dawn on the 30th of April of 1882, and he could compare them in his recollection with the marbled grain in the design of a leather-bound book which he had seen only once, and with the lines in the spray which an oar raised in the Rio Negro on the eve of the battle of the Quebracho. . . . These recollections were not simple; each visual image was linked to muscular sensations, thermal sensations, etc. He could reconstruct all his dreams, all his fancies. Two or three times he had reconstructed an entire day. He told me: *I have more memories in myself alone than all men have had since the world was a world.* And again: *my dreams are like your vigils. . . my memory, sir, is like a garbage disposal. . . .*
>
> A circumference on a blackboard, a rectangular triangle, a rhomb, are forms which we can fully intuit; the same held true with [Funes] for the tempestuous mane of a stallion, a herd of cattle in a pass, the ever-changing flame or the innumerable ash, the many faces of a dead man during the course of a protracted wake. He could perceive I do not know how many stars in the sky. . . .

But the limitations imposed on Funes by this dreadful glut soon became apparent:

He had devised a new system of enumeration and . . . in a very few days he had gone beyond 24,000. He had not written it down, for what he once meditated would not be erased. The first stimulus to his work, I believe, had been his discontent with the fact that "33 Uruguayans" required two symbols and three words rather than a single word and a single symbol. Later he applied his extravagant principle to the other numbers. In place of seven thousand thirteen he would say (for example) *Máximo Perez*; in place of seven thousand fourteen *The Train*; . . . Each word had a particular sign, a species of mark; the last were very complicated. . . .

It is no accident that Funes dies young in the story—of an overdose of memory so to say.

Nor is Funes only a perceptive author's creation. For, quite independently of Borges, the Russian neurologist A. R. Luria followed the career of just such an individual as Funes for over thirty years in the Soviet Union, from the 1920s onwards. Luria has recounted the experiences of this protracted case in a book entitled *The Mind of a Mnemonist* which ought to be better known.[39] Luria's mnemonist was very like Borges' Funes: he suffered from being able to remember everything. Everything he saw he stored; conversations with him set up continuous trains of correspondence in his mind. Coming into Luria's room in the 1950s he reported accurately a description of a conversation held in the same room twenty years previously. Describing his techniques of memorizing, it became clear that the methods he used were exactly those eidetic techniques of the storage of images in particular places down a street and the other queer mnemonic tricks that the Greek and Roman orators had recommended, and Borges describes for Funes.

Luria provides the classic example. In 1934 his patient was asked to remember a nonsense formula:

$$N \cdot \sqrt{d^2 . x \frac{85}{vx}} \cdot \sqrt[3]{\frac{276^2 \cdot 86x}{n^2 v \cdot \pi 264}} n^2 b = sv \frac{1624}{32^2} \cdot r^2 s$$

Here, in his own words, is how he does it, after seven minutes' study.

Neiman (N) came out and jabbed at the ground with his cane (·). He looked up at a tall tree which resembled the square-root sign ($\sqrt{}$), and thought to himself: "No wonder the tree has withered and begun to expose its roots. After all, it was here when I built these two houses" (d^2). Once again he poked with his cane (·). Then he said: "The houses are old, I'll have to get rid of them ($\times$); the sale will bring in far more money." He had originally invested

85,000 in them (85). Then I see the roof of the house detached (——), while down below on the street I see a man playing the Termenvox (vx). He's standing near a mailbox, and on the corner there's a large stone ($\cdot$), which has been put there to keep carts from crashing up against the houses. Here, then, is the square, over there the large tree ($\sqrt{}$) with three jackdaws on it ($\sqrt[3]{}$). I simply put the figure 276 here, and a square box containing cigarettes in the "square" (^{2}). The number 86 is written on the box. (This number was also written on the other side of the box, but since I couldn't see it from where I stood I omitted it when I recalled the formula.) As for the x, this is a stranger in a black mantle. He is walking toward a fence beyond which is a women's gymnasium. He wants to find some way of getting over the fence (——); he has a rendezvous with one of the women students (n), an elegant young thing who's wearing a grey dress. He's talking as he tries to kick down the boards in the fence with one foot, while with the other (^{2})–oh, but the girl he runs into turns out to be a different one. She's ugly–phooey! (v) . . . At this point I'm carried back to Rezhitsa, to my classroom with the big blackboard. . . . I see a cord swinging back and forth there and I put a stop to that ($\cdot$). On the board I see the figure $\pi264$, and I write after it n^2b.

Here I'm back in school. My wife has given me a ruler ($=$). I myself, Solomon-Veniaminovich (sv), am sitting there in the class. I see that a friend of mine has written down the figure $\frac{1624}{32^2}$.

I'm trying to see what else he's written, but behind me are two students, girls (r^2), who are also copying and making noise so that he won't notice them. "Sh," I say. "Quiet!" (s).

Fifteen years later, in 1949, and with no advance warning, he could recall his "memory" and the formula–perfectly. But the fate of Luria's subject was no happier, though he lived longer, than that of Funes. He could not hold jobs down adequately because he found it difficult to understand what was being said to him, because of the recall chains that even a simple phrase conjured up. In the end, out of desperation, he became a professional theatrical memory man.

Such cases suggest that, in principle, the memory store must be very large indeed. If we assume that there is no basic difference in the memory system between Luria's patient and the rest of us, but that perhaps either the feed-in mechanism has failed to produce the forgetting aspect of short-term memory, or that his recall system was perfect, then one can calculate, as has been done by the mathematician John Griffith, that the capacity of the human memory store, assuming a lifetime of seventy years, must be of the order of 10^{11} bits,* or 10^{14} if redundancy is permitted; an enormously large but not impossible figure–

* A bit is a measure of information storage.

the whole of the Encyclopaedia Brittanica contains some 2×10^8 bits.[40]

There are two lessons to be drawn from this sort of calculation. The first relates to what happens to many as ageing continues. It is indeed a common experience that in very old people a relative incapacity to store new information is coupled with a considerable clarity of recall of older material (comparable difficulties sometimes occur in cases of specific brain damage). Individuals who cannot tell you what they did yesterday will remember very clearly episodes in their childhood. Perhaps the store is nearly full, so that it becomes increasingly difficult to find spare capacity, or likely neuronal nets to complete, or synapses to facilitate?

However, there are other possible reasons for difficulty in the storage of new information in old age; studies with patients with brain damage, or suffering from senility (which is actually a clinical syndrome whose effects can become apparent even in relatively young people) show that there are certain definite patterns of memory loss. There are cases of patients with selective losses of capacity either to hold information in short-term store, whilst the long-term store is unaffected, or the reverse, with satisfactory short-term memory but with deficits in the long-term store. These cases are often associated with hippocampal damage, and it may therefore not be a question of a "full store" in the case of elderly people with memory problems, but rather an impaired input mechanism.

The second point is that there are may be rather good reasons for not having an eidetic, Funes-type memory: that to *have* to store so much is not useful to the system; that to be able to forget is as important as to be able to store. It is clear that the brain has quite elaborate blockading devices to *prevent* new information arriving at the central store. Short-term memory is one, and there is another that even precedes it, the mechanism called perceptual filtering. Of all the information arriving at one's eyes at any given time, only a small proportion actually gets into even the short-term store. Sitting and writing this, I do not see the odd debris on my desk, the view from the window, or even my own hand as it moves with the pen across the paper. Yet the data concerning all these items is within my field of vision; I'm just not concentrating on it; it doesn't even get as far as my short-term store. An even better example of course, is the cocktail-party phenomenon, whereby in a room full of babel one can concentrate (more or less!) on the voice of the person who is talking to one, yet switch, almost completely at will, to listen in on other conversations going on around one. This is a remarkable phenomenon, the analysis of which is part of the study of the psychology of perception, which does not directly concern us here. Its relevance is simply to emphasize that there is good evidence that much filtering occurs in the sensory analytical system of the brain and sense organs rather than in the short-term store itself. Thus perceptual filtering and short-term memory are the two mechanisms whereby the brain selects the data to be placed into store, from the mass of redundant material around it. If this mechanism of forgetting did not occur, one's lives would become impossible – like those of Funes or Luria's patient.

It is now possible to propose one reason why eidetic imagery and this type of power of memory declines with age. If it did not, then the development of normal memory would be impossible. Perhaps all children have eidetic powers at a very early age, but the decline curves are widely varied. Anyhow, what must happen during development is that the selection mechanisms of the brain must develop so as to enable information to be classified, the relevant stored and the irrelevant discarded. Thus to begin with all information is of virtually equal value. Developmental processes single out what is appropriate to select and what not, which may be one reason why childhood memories are so very different from adult ones – often seemingly irrelevant to what an adult feels that he would remember himself under similar circumstances. What is singled out in this sort of way must differ according to the environmental circumstances of the individual during his development, which is why, for instance, what is noticed and stored by a country child is very different from what is noticed and stored by an urban child. Different types of filtering are needed to ensure survival in the different cases. In this process of selection, eidetic memory is replaced by normal "adult" memory, except in the case of rare individuals. And each individual's memory processes are thus unique, not merely in terms of content, but in terms of the selection of items to be put into store as well. Environmental influences determine the selection process.

If this description of the way in which the perceptual and short term filtering processes may become modified with development is at all correct, it is one more pointer towards human individuality, emphasizing yet again the way in which the entire nexus of an individual's environment, particularly during his early years, leaves its own unique impress on his brain processes and behavior, both then and during later years. Social scientists, who recognize that an individual's behaviour pattern and modes of thought are in a measure determined by his social and economic class position, have known this for a long time at their particular hierarchical level of explanation, and a recognition by neurobiologists of this individuality and social conditioning at the cellular and biochemical level is long overdue.

But perhaps the problem is that just the same developmental selection of what gets through the filters applies to scientists as well. Researchers in a particular area notice or select certain items that fit with their selection programmes, those that fit more or less preconceived theories (called paradigms) of what is worth doing and proper to study about a particular topic. The socialization process of the scientist, his apprentice period in which he comes to select "good" experiments from "bad" ones, "relevant" from irrelevant" information, is a long one, and as a novice one will notice quite different things from those one does as an experienced scientist.[41] An illustration of this is provided by the electron micrograph of figure 99. The novice will perhaps concentrate on strange artifacts in these pictures; are they real? The electron microscopist would certainly be trained to ignore them and to focus on what he regards, or his discipline regards, as the "real" and important regions of the picture. By the time the scientist is through his socialization process, it is very difficult for him to think, select and remember out of the experimental rut which the plasticity of his brain has dug during his training.

10 Emotion and Self-Regulation

Homeostasis, Hormones and the Pituitary

So far we have considered the action of the brain in its most computerlike rôle. Signals arrive from distant sense organs, are processed and analyzed, their significance considered by comparison with earlier information or in terms of genetically preordained instructions, and appropriate motor action undertaken. Such an account has been concerned primarily with the activity of cerebral cortex and cerebellum and, at a much lower level, with the spinal cord. Not only are there large areas of brain between, but also there are at least as substantial and important areas of human activity which the discussion has so far omitted.

These begin with what might seem relatively straightforward questions of bodily organisation; how does one know, for example, when to eat or drink? to sleep or wake? to be interested, angry, enthusiastic, sexually aroused? All these are descriptions of "states of mind" – and indeed of "states of body". As such they clearly must have brain representations, although as we shall see, it does not follow that they are *controlled* by the brain – indeed in considering these topics we shall find the reciprocal relationship between the rest of the body and the brain is extremely close.

The examination of these relationships begins with the concept of the body as a self-regulatory system. Single-celled organisms like bacteria, or the unicellular ancestors of all of today's living forms, live in a continuously changing environment; local concentrations of food molecules like glucose, or of harmful and irritating substances, may vary widely. The cell must, as we saw in chapter 5, be mobile enough to move toward one and avoid the other. The environment of the cell of a multicellular organism is very different. It is controlled within narrowly defined limits, represented in mammals by the circulating blood stream and extracellular fluid; the glucose, oxygen, carbon dioxide content, acidity and temperature of this circulating environment are closely regulated. Mammalian cells lack the resourcefulness and adaptability of paramoecium of bacteria; if the limits of composition of the bloodstream are much exceeded in any direction, they die. Survival of the organism then demands that the animal act upon its external environment so as to preserve the constancy of its internal environment—which forms the external environment of its cells. This constancy of the internal environment was remarked upon as early as the middle of the last century by the great French physiologist Claude Bernard, though the term by which it is now known, HOMEOSTASIS, was not invented until the 1920s.[1]

Homeostasis must be maintained, a continuous, second-by-second, balancing act performed by the organism. But also change must occur. In response to altered environmental circumstances, the entire internal program of the organism must change in order to preserve itself and the species. Salmon, for example, born in fresh water, live much of their lives in the sea and return to the rivers to spawn. The salt-water environment of the organism is quite different from the fresh-water environment. It is not merely a question of the salmon possessing the sensory or memory systems which enable it to find its way back to its home river, important as they are; a whole variety of physiological and biochemical systems must be adapted, switched from the salt- to the fresh-water situation. The "programs" for the control of the internal environment of the organism must be switched just as in humans the program must be switched to provide the internal pattern appropriate to the fact that there is a time to grow, a time to love, a time to fight, a time to sleep, and a time to die. A homeostatic mechanism which provided absolute internal stability would not allow for growth or change at all. Hence the need for a system which both provides internal stability at a certain wavelength and for the possibility of wavelength change in response to new situations.

A considerable part of this homeostatic regulation is conducted by the body's hormonal system. The levels of circulating glucose in the bloodstream are controlled by hormones such as insulin and glucagon secreted by the pancreas, the basic metabolic rate of the body by thyroxin, produced by the thyroid glands in the neck, the metabolism of calcium and phosphorus and part of the regulation of urinary excretion by the parathyroids, close to the thyroids. Homeostatic change is also, in part, hormonally controlled; the preparation of the body for "fight or flight" is partly achieved by the secretion of adrenalin by the adrenal glands near the kidney, which alters heart rate and blood circulation; the state of sexual preparedness by the sex hormones of the gonads, testosterone and œstrogen.

However, even here the nervous system plays a part. An excised heart with no nervous connections will go on beating for many hours provided it is kept warm and supplied with glucose and oxygen. But the *regulation* of heartbeat in the living organism, its speeding up or slowing down, is controlled both by the hormone adrenalin and the reciprocal action of the two parts of the autonomic nervous system, the sympathetic and the parasympathetic. Thus heart-rate is under a measure of dual control, and the closeness of the relationship between the two control mechanisms becomes more apparent when it is recalled that the transmitter substance of the sympathetic nerve, which speeds heart-rate, is related to adrenalin. Other homeostatic systems are under direct nervous control, though normally operating below the level of consciousness. Breathing is controlled by way of neuronal centers in the medulla which is capable of rapid transition between conscious (that is cortical), and unconscious (that is medullary) control.[2]

But the interaction between hormonal and nervous control becomes still more apparent when the question of what regulates the production of the hormones themselves is considered, for it is found that nearly all of them (insulin is the major exception) are in close reciprocal relationship with the pituitary, that tiny organ, pea-sized in humans, which hangs down from the base of the brain (seen in figure 53). The pituitary is itself a hormone-secreting organ; some of its hormones have a direct effect on a variety of the body's metabolic systems—growth hormone for instance, is particularly important during development. But at least five of the pituitary hormones are involved in the regulation of the *production* of other hormones. Thus the pituitary produces a thyroid stimulating hormone which regulates the amount of thyroxin produced by the thyroid gland. There is a neat negative feedback loop connecting thyroid and pituitary such that when the level of thyroxin in the blood stream falls, that of the pituitary's thyroid-stimulating hormone rises; as thyroxin level increases, the level of the thyroid-stimulating hormone falls (figure 52).

The relevance of these observations to the theme of this chapter is that the pituitary is anatomically part of the brain. And even more to the point, research over the last few years has shown that the action of the pituitary, far from being independent of the rest of the brain, is directly controlled by it. In particular it is connected in two ways to another brain region lying just above it, the HYPOTHALAMUS. Axons from the hypothalamic nuclei synapse in the pituitary, and, in addition, the organization of the blood circulatory system of the two organs is such that blood washing past the hypothalamus subsequently arrives at the pituitary. And with a consideration of the implication of the hypothalamic-pituitary relationships, we arrive at the core of the brain's control over the homeostatic functions of the body, one of the most intriguing areas of research and discovery of recent years.[3]

52 The feedback loops involved in the relationships of thyroid gland, pituitary and hypothalamus.

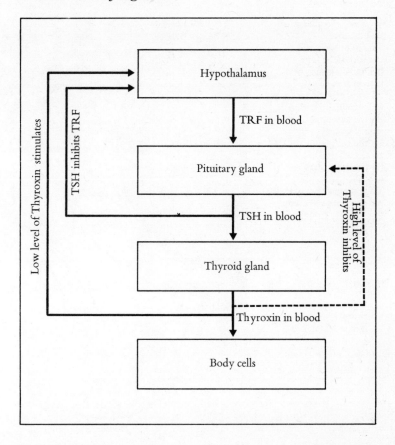

The Hypothalamus

The hypothalamus is a collection of several related groups of neurons lying just below the thalamus, at the base of the forebrain (figure 53). Its connections, other than with the pituitary and certain regions of the brain stem, are with a group of structures and regions of the forebrain, known collectively as the LIMBIC SYSTEM, which include the AMYGDALA, bedded deep in the temporal lobe, the HIPPOCAMPUS (whose rôle was discussed in the last chapter) and several other minor structures. It is the limbic system which is most extensively concerned both with homeostatic regulatory systems and with emotion and motivation. So intriguing are the rôles of this system that it is relevant to note the evolutionary changes which have occurred in it within the mammal. The proportion of the cerebrum occupied by the limbic system decreases in species evolutionarily close to man; a large proportion of the rabbit's cerebrum is occupied by the limbic system, relatively less of the cat's cerebrum, much less in the monkey and less still in man. In so far as the limbic system is concerned with the expression and

223

53 The hypothalamus
and pituitary.
The hypothalamus is
comprised of four
principal clusters of
neurons.
(1) the preoptic area
(telencephalic region);
(2) the supraoptic or
anterior area;
(3) the tuberal or middle
area, and
(4) the mamillary or
posterior area.
The connections with the
pituitary are apparent.

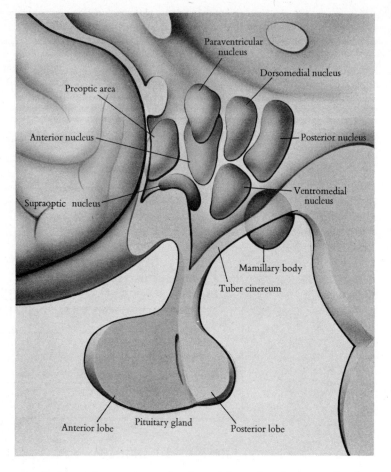

regulation of emotion, the increasing dominance of other
cortical regions in man and the primates gives greater weight
to other aspects of brain activity (cognition, for instance) and
allows for greater interaction with, and modification of, limbic
system activity.

The many functions of the various groups of neurons in the
hypothalamus have been approached by way of the pituitary
and the problem of homeostasis, and our discussion should
start with these systems. Neurons with their cell bodies in two
of the hypothalamic regions have axons which terminate in the
posterior region of the pituitary. These neurons manufacture
two substances which are closely related chemically to two
pituitary hormones: oxytocin, which causes uterine contractions and expulsion of milk from the breasts, and vasopressin
which controls water uptake into the body tissues and its
excretion from the kidneys. The evidence is very strong that the
hormones are fabricated in the hypothalamic neurons and are
transported down their axons, across the synaptic clefts and

into the pituitary. In the pituitary they are chemically modified and released into the blood stream. Lesions in these regions of the hypothalamus may cause a form of diabetes (known as diabetes insipidus) in which vast quantities of water are consumed and excreted as dilute urine.

In addition, other hypothalamic neurons synthesize substances which are released directly into the bloodstream which circulates through the front part of the pituitary. These chemicals stimulate the release of pituitary hormones such as the thyroid-stimulating hormone. They are known as releasing factors, and are in fact a class of hormones themselves; the cells which produce them are modified neurons known as neuro-secretory cells. The importance of this system in regulatory terms is obviously substantial. It adds, for example, an extra complexity to the feedback loop of pituitary-thyroid inter-relations described in figure 52. The two types of pituitary control between them bring a large area of the body's hormonal function under direct nervous control, and the potential evolutionary significance of these mechanisms of nervous-hormonal interactions in view of the model for the evolution of the nervous system advanced in chapter 5, is obvious.

Meanwhile there are other homeostatic control regions in the hypothalamus, which do not depend on hormonal mechanisms at all. It should be noted that many of the hypothalamic centers are rather precisely located, being groups of a few tens of thousands or hundreds of thousands of cells. Their detection has mainly depended on the techniques of precise localization by microelectrodes, followed by lesioning, electrical stimulation or iontophoresis of drugs or chemicals.[4] These hypothalamic centers are among the best examples of brain regions with precise and delimited functions—examples which should gladden the reductionist's heart. Yet even with such precise centers there is some evidence—such is the plasticity and redundancy of the brain—that following their removal, at least some re-learning and functional replacement by other regions can occur.

Temperature, Eating and Drinking

Temperature regulation is of major importance to the mammal, which becomes acutely ill if there is a fluctuation in its internal body temperature of more than a very few degrees. Yet the human can survive environmental temperature fluctuations over a range of 70°C—from 30° below to 40° above zero. The temperature regulatory mechanisms include sweating, panting, and increased blood flow to the skin, which all serve to lower temperature. Shivering and a diminished blood flow to the skin help raise body temperature. Both these sets of activity are controlled by the hypothalamus, but it appears that two separate groups of neurons are involved, a "heat center" and a "cold center". As long ago as 1939 it was shown that a lesion of one center, leaving the other intact, was possible. Animals so lesioned would lose the capacity to control either overheating or overcooling, depending on which center was destroyed. In the intact animal electrical stimulation of one of the centers would produce behavior appropriate either to overheating or overcooling.

How do the neurons of the hypothalamus "know" that the organism is too hot or too cold? Although some of the information concerning temperature arrives at the hypothalamus from sensory systems elsewhere in the body (skin receptors, for instance) the centers appear in addition to contain their own temperature receptor cells, neurons which can respond to very small changes in the temperature of the circulating bloodstream. If the neurons of the heat center are themselves directly heated (by way of a modified microelectrode, for example), the animal responds with the full range of "overheating" activities.[5]

Water balance is similarly regulated by a drinking center in the hypothalamus. Lesions or direct electrical stimulation of the intact animal can reduce or produce excessive drinking. In this case, the hypothalamic neurons concerned seem to have available receptor systems which respond to the salt concentration of the circulating bloodstream. Excessive drinking, for example, can be induced by injecting minute quantities of concentrated salt solution into the appropriate region of the hypothalamus, while temporary cessation of drinking, even in a rat deprived of water for many hours, can be induced by the injection of water in the immediate vicinity of the hypothalamic neurons concerned. As with the temperature regulating system, the degree of sensitivity of these receptors must be very high.

The control of feeding is rather more complex than that of drinking or temperature regulation.[6] Once again the basic observation, made with the rat in the 1930s, was that, if a particularly hypothalamic center was destroyed by lesioning in both halves of the brain, the animal tended to eat excessively, becoming markedly obese (a phenomenon called HYPER-PHAGIA). However, such a phenomenon could in principle be caused by a variety of factors. For example, there might be a change in the rate at which foodstuffs like glucose are metabolized by the animal, or in its sensitivity to taste or type of diet. These possible interpretations were extensively studied during the 1950s and early 1960s, particularly by Philip Teitelbaum, in Philadelphia.[7] Teitelbaum's experiments show that animals with lesions do not simply eat more because they "feel hungry", for if the foodstuff is bulked with cellulose, unlike normal rats,

which increase their food consumption to compensate for the
changed nature of the diet, the operated rats do not. They
therefore eat relatively less under these circumstances. Where
hungry normal rats will eat food dosed with the bitter-tasting
quinine, the operated ones will not.

These and other experiments have led to the suggestion that
the rats with lesions were more influenced by the taste of food
than the normals, and Teitelbaum's conclusion was that the
hypothalamic center is in fact a satiety center, which normally
acts to inhibit food intake beyond some sort of desirable
maximum. If the center is destroyed, other regulatory mechanisms come into play and a new maximum is set. Such a phenomenon has been described, in the language of those concerned
with the regulation of diet in humans, as an "appestat". In the
absence of the satiety center, the maximum can be very high
indeed. The obesity can become so great in operated animals
that they can scarcely move about their cages.

A satiety center probably functions by means of specific
sensory receptor neurons within it, rather as the temperature and
drinking regulatory centers do. The satiety-center receptor
cells seem to be sensitive to the concentration of glucose in the
bloodstream. They are known as GLUCORECEPTORS, and an
interesting example of their specificity is provided by the fact
that it is possible to identify them by means of a particular toxic
compound of glucose. If small quantities of the substance gold
thioglucose are injected into the circulation of an experimental
animal, it is taken up by the hypothalamic glucose receptor
cells which concentrate it until they die.[8] The animal then
becomes hyperphagig. Another indication of the rôle of the
receptor is provided by iontophoretic injection of an anaesthetic
like procaine, which blocks the center. Satiated animals then
begin eating once more. Electrical stimulation of the region,
or injection of glucose in minute amounts near the cells, even in
hungry animals, will tend to "switch off" eating.

To match the satiety center, Teitelbaum was able to show the
presence of a feeding center elsewhere in the hypothalamus.
Lesions in this center produce animals which will not eat or
drink (APHAGIA and ADIPSIA). Indeed an animal with a lesion
in this area will die if not force-fed. Although feeding behavior
will eventually recover if the animal survives, drinking behavior may never do so. Electrical stimulation and the injection
of certain transmitter substances into this center in intact
animals will induce eating, and an anaesthetic like procaine will
inhibit it. Thus the balance of food intake would seem to depend
on reciprocal action of two hypothalamic centers, although it
must be emphasized that this picture is probably something of
an over-simplification, particularly in light of the fact that some

recovery of the lost behavior can occur if enough time elapses after the lesion.

Nevertheless, from our point of view, the existence of a set of brain centers which operate so as to preserve homeostasis is of considerable interest. One of the most important aspects of the whole topic is that electrical stimulation of these regions does not simply activate *part* of a behavior pattern, in the same way as electrical stimulation of the nerve to a single muscle produces a twitch, or to the motor cortex produces a set of coordinated muscular movements. Instead, a complex and varied pattern of activity is set in train by electrical stimulation in the hypothalamus. A hungry rat will pace its cage, explore or learn a maze in search of food; when it is satiated, this type of behavior will diminish or cease. But if the feeding center of a satiated animal is stimulated, it will behave in the same way as if it is hungry: it will explore actively and learn a maze for instance, in search of food. On receipt of the food it will salivate, chew, lap and digest it. To the observer, such behavior is indistinguishable from that of an animal made "objectively" hungry by depriving it of food for several hours.

How relevant are these observations to the human situation? Extrapolation from animals to humans is always dangerous, but there is evidence that human patients with various forms of hypothalamic lesions may show hyperphagia, aphagia and other disorders which parallel the loss of homeostasis in the lesioned rat. The reciprocal of this, that all humans who show hyperphagia or aphagia have lesions in the satiety center of their hypothalamus, does not of course necessarily follow, although there is some evidence connecting hypothalamic disorders with the "noneating" disease, anorexia nervosa. Clearly the interactions involved in such behavior disorders may be a good deal more complex than this, but it would seem not unreasonable to expect that the properties of the cells in the hypothalamus of a hyperphagic human do differ from those of people with a normal degree of homeostatic control, perhaps in some subtle measure related to firing rate, quantity of transmitter or number of synapses. What would be wrong is to base upon this the statement that, in the case of the human the changes in the hypothalamus *cause* the abnormal behavior. It would be as legitimate to argue that changed behavior *causes* the hypothalamic changes. This is yet another example of the general statement that one cannot make causative statements meaningfully across several orders of a hierarchy, but only correlative ones.

There is another related point which may be drawn out here. Unlike many other homeostatic mechanisms, those of the control of feeding and drinking very certainly have conscious correlates. Feeling hungry or thirsty is something that all of us

know all about, at a very conscious cortical level. If one's hypothalamus is setting what the psychologists regard as a *drive*, that
of hunger, one's responses to it—going and buying food, or
cooking an egg, or opening the fridge to see if there is anything to
eat there—may be very varied; they demand quite different
patterns of sensory and motor activity, and certainly will require
cortical and conscious involvement. At the neuronal level, there
are pathways which connect a variety of cerebral cortical regions
with the hypothalamus, which make such varied responses to a
basic drive possible. At the level of the relationships between
mind and brain it is reasonable to posit that the statement 'I feel
hungry' has, as its correlate at the hierarchical level associated
with neuronal interactions, a changed pattern of activity in some
of the pathways linking the hypothalamus and the cortex.

Rage, Aggression and Fear

The point concerning the neural homologues of behavior has
been drawn in respect of such phenomena as hunger and thirst
because they are in a sense more neutral than the set of behaviors
which we must next consider. These are concerned not with
behavioral mechanisms related to the homeostatic regulation of
the body's internal environment, but with the reactions of the
organism to the external environment. In considering these
responses, the need to beware of extrapolation is perhaps even
more considerable than in the case of the mechanisms so far
considered. We are dealing with the areas broadly categorized
under the term, for humans, of "emotion"; physiological
psychology deals with them under the blanket of such rather
ill-defined terms as "drive" and "motivation".

One of the major problems in handling these concepts is that a
variety of behavioral responses may be possible as a result of the
same "motivational state". For example, in response to a "drive"
such as fear or a particular painful stimulus, such as an electric
shock, a rat may jump wildly about its cage or remain motion-
less, frozen; there will in either case also be changes in defecation,
urination, heart and respiratory rates. The same rat will generally,
but not always, behave in the same way on two identical trials.
Different rats, however, will tend to behave in characteristically
different ways, in response to the same stimulus. Indeed, it is
possible to breed strains of rats which behave characteristically
differently in response to similar stimuli—the animals of one
strain may tend to move restlessly about their cages, those of
another may tend to remain where they are but defecate more.
Strains of rats selected for such specific behavioral differences—
which generally require many generations of inbreeding—often
show very little difference on other types of behavioral measure.[9]

Obviously the interactions between internal "brain state" and externally observable behavior become very complex at this point; in all probability one is dealing with a situation of balance between the internal, genetically-programed state and external environmental interactions, as in the somewhat better-understood situations of memory and learning. As was shown in the last chapter, though, to agree that the interactions are complex does not mean that they are not in principle capable of being specified, or that they do not exist. What it does mean, however –a point expanded more fully in chapter 13–is that the specification has only probabilistic predictive value; the uncertainties allow one to apply the prediction to populations but not to individuals.

The earliest demonstration of the rôle of the hypothalamus in the regulation of emotion came in 1928 when P. Bard, in the United States, found that a fully developed "rage" could be shown by cats with the whole of the brain above the level of the hypothalamus removed, and W. R. Hess, in Zurich, showed that electrical stimulation of particular hypothalamic regions of the cat results in rage with all the characteristics of "real" anger–back arched, hair standing, tail lashing, snarling, spitting and a direct attack on the nearest potentially offensive object (often, one feels with a certain legitimacy, the experimenter himself; but any other appropriate object would also induce the response).[10] The moment the electrical stimulation is turned off, the cat's anger subsides as if itself turned off by a switch.

Anger is not the only response that can be evoked in this way; stimulation of other associated hypothalamic regions will evoke a reaction more akin to fear–clearly sufficiently unpleasant for the animal for it to be possible to train a cat to find its way through a maze to reach a spot at which the stimulus can be turned off. And just as with the reciprocal relationship of the feeding and the satiety centers, it seems as if there are reciprocal centers for rage and fear as well. In this case, however, the second group of centers lies, not in the hypothalamus, but in another part of the limbic system, the amygdala, which has connections both with the hypothalamus and the limbic region of the cerebral cortex.

Removal of the amygdala can result in a loss of fear and aggressiveness, resulting in tameness and placidity in a number of species, even notoriously savage ones like the wild rat. Thus the amygdala may act so as to suppress and moderate hypothalamic responses. But not all the experiments involving removal of the amygdala have had such unequivocal effects. There have also been reports that *increased* fear and aggressiveness occur following the removal of the amygdala; it may be that the phenomena associated with the centers in the amygdala are much more

complex, so that the anger or placidity may result as the in-
cidental consequence of the disturbance or destruction of some
other aspect of behavior. Karl Pribram, for example, has suggested that the damaged behavior relates to the animal's concept of territoriality; its recognition of some area as "home", in
which the animal will normally tend to attack outsiders, compared to other areas perceived as "foreign", in which it will
normally tend to retreat submissively when approached by the
owner of that territory. Other more complex effects, for example
the social relationships associated with dominance and submission, may also be involved in the response to lesions of the
amygdala.[11]

In a similar way to the situation with hyperphagia and aphagia,
hypothalamic and amygdala effects have been invoked to account
for certain aberrant human activities. Within their own terms,
such explanations may be of some value. But the extrapolations
need to be made with the utmost caution. The fact that at one
hierarchical level the activity of a group of cells in the hypothalamus or amygdala may "explain" an individual's rage or
aggressiveness, does not answer the question as to why that
particular individual has such an active hypothalamic center.
Such brain activity may well be a response to an environmental
situation in which aggressiveness, rage or fear are in fact homeostatic mechanisms, in that they serve to protect or ensure the
survival of the individual. In a threatening environment, an
enhanced activity of the brain's centers which respond to this
environment by generating aggressive or fearful behavior, will
quite probably be the most desirable response, the "correct" one,
from the point of view of the individual. And much of the
population of most countries does indeed live in just such a
threatening environment. Those who wish to invoke brain
structures to account for patterns of human behavior must
recognize not only that they are arguing across hierarchies,
which is under certain circumstances permissible, but that in
addition, the argument across hierarchies runs in two directions,
and not just in one; events in the environment affect brain
structures and activity.

But the matter does not end with a question of the philosophical significance of hypothalamic or amygdaloid stimulation.
Electrical stimulation of appropriate regions, will, as we have
seen, evoke specific behavioral responses. Such responses have
been demonstrated in an effective display of showmanship–it
cannot be described as an experiment–by José Delgado of Yale
University. Delgado has utilized a system in which stimulating
electrodes can be permanently implanted in the brain and can be
switched off and on by remote radio control. His demonstration
consisted of "taming" a bull by the use of the electrodes, and it

was carried out appropriately in a bullring, where, equipped with the traditional cape and less-traditional radio transmitter, Delgado was able to turn off the bull's attacking charges by "buzzing" the stimulator.[12] The significance of this impressive demonstration was doubtless not lost on those who give funds for research in this area. If ever there was an example of the potentiality, if not of thought control, then of mood control, this was clearly it. In the United States at least, where the ethical constraints on what doctors are allowed to do with their patients, particularly if they are in a mental hospital, are rather more lax than is the case in Britain, there have already begun to appear reports of experiments, by Delgado and others, of the use of permanently implanted, radio-controlled electrodes in the control of patients. The significance and consequences of these developments – at their mildest, disquieting, at their most sinister, obscene – will form the topic of further discussion in chapter 13.

Sex

The relationship of brain systems to sexual drives and behavior is even more complex than is the case for the types of behavior we have so far considered. Sexual activity is not dependent upon the brain; "spinal" male animals, whose nervous systems are severed below the base of the brain stem, can still respond to genital stimulation with erection and ejaculation. The entire sequence of sexual behavior from birth to puberty, and in the female through menstruation and menopause as well, is regulated by hormones. Such hormonal control, by way, for example, of the contraceptive pill, is very familiar. In addition, the level – and direction – of sexual interest in animals and humans can be modified by changed concentrations of oestrogens and androgens, or of the oestrogen- and androgen-controlling hormones secreted by the pituitary.

Yet it is obvious to the point of banality that nervous as well as hormonal effects are closely involved in sexual behavior. Sensory information is obviously crucial, and it has been clearly demonstrated that visual information alone – simply allowing individuals of the opposite sex to see one another – can cause significant changes in the level of the circulating sex hormones. As for so many of the other responses we have been considering, one major site for these brain/body behavioral interactions appears to be in the limbic system and particularly in the hypothalamus.

One mechanism for these interactions is provided by the hypothalamic-pituitary control system discussed earlier; the release of hormones from the pituitary is itself modulated by hypothalamic influences of the sort discussed on pages 222–4.

But this is far from being the only mechanism of control by the brain over sexual behavior. Lesions in particular hypothalamic centers will abolish sexual behavior in both male and female cats, rats or guinea pigs. The animals will not mate, even though the pituitary and gonads remain normal and there are no major changes in the levels of the circulating hormones. Even treatment of these animals with hormones will not restore mating behavior where the lesion is large.

If there is a hypothalamic "sex center" then electrical stimulation of it should produce enhanced sexual behavior, by analogy with responses of the other hypothalamic centers. Once again this is the case. In both male and female animals, electrical stimulation in the hypothalamus has been shown to induce sexual behavior. Male monkeys and rats maintain penile erections and frequent ejaculations while female cats become sexually receptive over extended periods of electrical stimulation. In addition, electrical recording from the hypothalamic sex center in the cat shows that changes in the firing pattern of the cells occurs during sexual activity.

As with the rage effects, the amygdala seems intimately involved in the regulation of sexual behavior, though the results obtained from experiments involving removal of the amygdala are once again ambiguous. Thus some reports—those that find the removal of the amygdala causes rage—also claim that removal results in a diminution of sexual behavior; others—those that find a loss of fear and aggressiveness following removal of the amygdala—claim that hypersexuality results. The explanation may lie in the amygdala being involved in more subtle behavioral effects, of which tameness, rage and sexual activity are only aspects.

Perhaps even more interesting is the mounting evidence of the direct interaction of the sex hormones with the hypothalamus. It is possible to make solid preparations of oestrogen which will dissolve slowly over a long period. These solid pellets can be implanted into an animal, either just beneath the skin, or directly into specified brain regions. Working with these pellets, Richard Michael, in London, has found that when oestrogen is implanted into particular regions of the hypothalamus of the female cat or monkey, the animal shows enhanced sexual behavior. A cat could be put into an oestrous state lasting as long as two months in this way, although the dose of oestrogen used was far too small to affect the uterus directly, and when implanted elsewhere in the brain was without effects on sexual behavior.[13]

These effects are far from straightforward. For example, while the male sex hormone testosterone will sometimes produce enhancement of male sexuality, there are also reports of it acting to produce femalelike sexual behavior in males. There is also evidence accumulating to suggest that the hypothalamic/ hormonal interactions may be even more critical in brain development than in the adult. In male rats for example, continued female sexual behavior in adult life can be induced by brief exposure of the hypothalamus to oestrogen in the very young animal–long before puberty and the time when the animal produces its own sex hormones in any quantity. There have been suggestions that homosexual behavior in adults may be connected with altered hypothalamic development during infancy, but they suffer from the same disadvantages as all such simplified explanations seeking to explain complex phenomena in terms of single all-embracing explanations.

Meanwhile, the apparent sensitivity of certain hypothalamic neurons to hormones may be the first direct demonstration of hormonal effects mediated by way of the brain, that is, the reciprocal of the effect of the hypothalamus in regulating the release of pituitary hormones. One may predict that specific receptor sites for oestrogen, analogous to glucoreceptors, will be found in particular hypothalamic neurons.

A study of these interactions may also cast light upon the ways in which hormonal levels appear to affect mood. While in all probability these effects occur in males as well as females, they are most strikingly observed in the rhythms of the menstrual cycle. As an oversimplification, the menstrual rhythm can be regarded as being controlled by the reciprocal levels of two hormones, oestrogen and PROGESTERONE. But associated with the rhythm are very clear mood changes as well. Premenstrual tension, a period lasting perhaps two or three days before the onset of menstrual bleeding, is experienced in some measure by a large proportion of women between puberty and menopause; it is associated with heightened levels of anxiety, sensations of stress and "emotionality".[14] The onset of bleeding, which is coupled with a sharp change in the relative levels of progesterone and oestrogen, very rapidly shifts this mood. The sex hormones are, in this sense, PSYCHOCHEMICALS, with mind-affecting qualities more usually associated, not with endogenously produced substances in the body, but with chemicals administered from outside (exogenous), like drugs. The relevance of this analogy with psychochemicals will become more apparent in chapter 12. However, it is at present only speculative that the hormones exert their mood-changing effects by interaction with the hypothalamus.

Pleasure and Self-stimulation

In 1954, James Olds and Brenda Milner, then working in Montreal, made the first of a series of extraordinary observations, more intriguing perhaps than any other aspect of the rôle of the hypothalamus with respect to motivation. They found that rats with stimulating electrodes implanted into particular hypothalamic regions would learn to press a lever to turn on the stimulus. The lever arrangement was such that, once the rat had delivered a shock to its own brain by depressing the lever, a pause of a few seconds was required before pressing the lever once again would administer another shock. Once they had learned this arrangement, rats would deliver themselves shocks at the rate of hundreds an hour with scarcely a pause, until they were exhausted. Even when starved and thirsty they would prefer stimulating themselves to taking food or water. They would learn a maze to arrive at the lever with which they could administer shock. They would cross a painful electrified grid in order to get to it. The stimulus was preferable to sex.

The discovery was of what has subsequently come to be called the "pleasure center" of the hypothalamus, although the actual region which will evoke self-stimulation is found to be considerably more diffuse than those involved in the other hypothalamic drive centers, and other regions of the limbic system can also yield "pleasure responses" when self-stimulation is used as a criterion of pleasure. Similar pleasure centers have been found to exist in a wide variety of species. Like the other hypothalamic centers, the pleasure center has its reciprocal, a region—or rather several different regions—which when stimulated are clearly not pleasurable but aversive; an animal implanted with electrodes in such regions will apparently actively avoid the possibility of stimulating itself.

What is the significance of such a "pleasure center"? Although described in these terms, because of the fact that the animal appears to enjoy stimulating itself in this way, the observed behavior of the animal does not correspond to any obvious and easily definable behavioral state as rage, or fear or sexual arousal, and the curiosity as to whether there is a human equivalent to the pleasure center of the rat has plainly been intense. However, one might have anticipated that it would be a curiosity incapable of satisfaction. This would indeed be the case were it not for the deplorable laxness, already mentioned, in the control over human experimentation in the United States. For over the last ten years, a number of reports have come from America of the implantation of electrodes into the "pleasure center" of the brains of humans—generally inmates of mental hospitals and particularly schizophrenics or people with low IQs. These individuals, it is claimed, find self-stimulation by way of the electrodes a pleasurable sensation, and are prepared to give themselves several hundred shocks an hour. Their statements about their subjective experiences when self-stimulated though, are vague in the extreme, involving such words as "feeling good". The experience does not seem to be sexual, but in some cases it is described as a feeling like that of orgasm or the relaxed sensation that follows orgasm.[15] It is hard to see how such "experiments" could in any sense be construed as "treatment", and their relationship to the so-called "experiments" of the Nazi concentration-camp doctors at Buchenwald and Auschwitz would merit closer attention.

The demonstration of the hypothalamic pleasure center has, more than the other behavior-controlling centers of the brain, raised questions of an ethical and "social control" type. The idea of implanting electrodes into an individual's brain and either stimulating him or arranging for him to stimulate himself, raises possibilities which are almost universally regarded as repugnant.[16] It is interesting to ask why, while the use of psychically active chemicals which directly affect quite a number of brain and mind phenomena is readily accepted both by the medical community and by very many people outside it. Is electrical stimulation something intrinsically different from the stimulation of another—or perhaps the same—brain region in a different way?

Clearly it is hard to maintain that it is so different. Yet the feeling of—at its mildest—distaste, persists and should be respected. Part of it is a response to the fact that in the human experiments the implanted individuals were under the control of, and manipulated by, the doctors and researchers concerned. This is a similar distaste that is aroused, quite properly in my view, by the Penfield experiments on memory stimulation. On the whole, it is desirable, in an absolute, ethical sense, that people should be able to keep their brains and what goes on in them private, except insofar as "what goes on" generates some form of communication with the outside world. If there is concern over the privacy of computer data banks, there should be even more concern over the privacy of the content of the individual human brain. In addition, a distinction may perhaps be drawn between self-medication and imposed medication. This is of course the nub of arguments concerning fluoridation, and clearly in some cases, medical decisions made by the community do have to be imposed upon the individual. None the less, there are limits. This is why addictive drugs, which eventually impose themselves necessarily on the individual, are hazardous assaults upon him; he who implants electrodes in another's brain is in the position of a drug pusher, able to give or withhold rewards, a position which is both ethically and socially undesirable.

These comments are a response to the ethical problems potentially raised for the individual by extrapolation from experiments of the stimulation type. Almost more significant, however, could be the potential social implications. Science-fiction stories of mood and thought control by electrodes and drugs, like those of memory control referred to in the last chapter, are common enough, and not too illegitimate an extrapolation from the present state of research. As will be argued in more detail in respect of psychochemicals though, this class of concern is probably both premature and unjustified. But, as the argument made there applies *a fortiori* to the case of electrical stimulation, a consideration of its significance will be postponed, for this survey of brain correlates of behavior is not yet complete.

11 Attending and Sleeping: The Experience of Time

Arousal and Attention

To complete the survey of brain correlates, it is necessary to turn from the limbic system to consider the properties of another set of diffusely located neurons with properties which seem to link their activity directly with phenomena ranging from attention, alertness and motivation to sleep and coma. The neural systems hitherto considered have been more or less discrete areas of the brain; conglomerations of neurons, either in the cortex or grouped into "centers". By contrast, the ASCENDING RETICULAR ACTIVATING SYSTEM, sometimes known as the RETICULAR FORMATION, is a mixed set of neurons and their connections, in some places arranged into small clusters, which runs as a sort of network through the brain stem up as far as the thalamus (figure 54).[1] The system is a difficult one to analyze, both because of its diffuseness and because the brain stem also contains a very large number of other pathways, both ascending and descending. In particular, the pathways from many of the reticular formation.

The role of the reticular formation has become a question which has raised even more dispute in physiological psychology than most others of recent years. Many of the experiments seem contradictory or inconclusive, and many of the relatively simple ideas which emerged following the initial work of F. Bremer, in Belgium in the 1930s, have become more clouded as time has gone on. In those early experiments, made in 1935. Bremer, using cats, made a series of lesions at various points along the brain stem. If the lesion is made in the midbrain (that is, above the brain stem), as well as cutting off the reticular formation, the remaining brain regions are deprived of virtually all sensory input, and most possibilities of motor putput. The animal goes into a state which closely resembles normal sleep, even in terms of the recorded EEG pattern and the behavior of the pupil of the eye. But it proves almost impossible to arouse these cats from their sleep; even strong stimuli produce only brief arousal and transient changes in EEG pattern. If the transection of the brain stem is made lower, at a point where the spinal cord enters the brain, then normal EEG patterns and sleep/wakefulness cycles are observed; the animal can be aroused from sleep almost as a normal one, despite the fact that, just as with the higher transection, all sensory input from the body (though not from the head) is eliminated by the cut.

The interpretation of these experiments is not conclusive. It was not until quite a few years later, in 1950, that a technique was developed in which *either* the sensory pathways traversing the brain stem *or* the reticular formation could be cut. In these experiments, made by H. W. Magoun and his group at North-Western University in the United States, animals deprived of sensory input into the brain but with intact reticular formations, showed normal sleep/wakefulness cycles and EEG activity; those with lesions confined to the reticular formation tended to be stuporous or comatose after a lesion and remained so until their death. It must however be emphasized that the interpretation of the effects of lesions in these experiments is not straightforward.[2]

Of more significance, perhaps, are studies involving electrical stimulation of the reticular formation. The key experiment was made by Giuseppe Moruzzi and Magoun, in 1949, when they

54 The reticular formation.
The reticular formation is the area stippled in this cross section of the brain. A sense organ (lower right) is connected to a sensory area in the brain (upper left) by a pathway extending up the spinal cord (heavy black arrows). This pathway branches into the reticular formation. When a stimulus travels along the pathway, the reticular formation may "awaken" the entire brain (dashed black arrows).

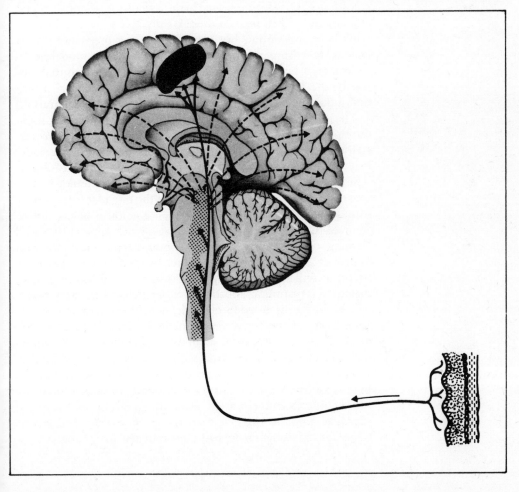

showed that electrical stimulation of the reticular formation of anaesthetized cats produces long-lasting signs of arousal in the EEG. Later experiments showed that, in unanaesthetized cats with electrodes implanted into the reticular formation stimulation produces behavioral signs of arousal, alertness and attention.

The model of activity that developed was one in which wakefulness and alertness are maintained by steady activity of its neurons sending inputs to the thalamus and cortex. The absence of these stimuli from the reticular formation results in sleep. Axons running from the sense organs to the cortex put out branching axons to the reticular formation, and hence sensory information transmitted to the cortex also triggers activity in the reticular formation itself. Presumably the reticular formation contains some mechanism which analyzes the sensory inputs, and, should they contain information which may be potentially worthy of consideration, its neurons fire. Signals from the reticular formation neurons thus arrive at the cortex concurrently with the incoming sensory information, alerting the cortex to "take note of" the sensory information. Studies with recording electrodes implanted in the reticular formation suggest that any individual neuron there is only able to respond to one type of sensory input, but some integrating mechanism must operate to ensure that information from many modalities is coordinated before the "arousal" message is transmitted upwards; the multiple synaptic pathways of the reticular formation would lend themselves to performing such an integration.

The effect of the enhanced attention paid to sensory input during stimulation of the reticular formation is well demonstrated by experiments in which monkeys with stimulating electrodes planted there are trained to discriminate between two objects which are only illuminated in brief flashes; the monkeys learn faster and respond more quickly when the reticular formation is stimulated than otherwise. This phenomenon is analogous to some of the effects produced by drugs which apparently speed learning, of the type discussed in chapter 9. If increased attention improves learning, then agents which have effects on arousal and attention will appear to have effects directly on learning. One such drug is pemoline, another, of more general interest perhaps, which will be discussed in more detail in chapter 12, is amphetamine, one of the active components of drugs sold as Benzedrine, Drinamyl, Dexadrine. In all probability, amphetamine exerts its effects in interaction with the reticular formation.[3]

This relatively straightforward picture of the mode of action of the reticular formation has been distinctly modified and made more complex in the last ten years. More careful studies of the effects of lesioning suggest that, under very controlled conditions, animals which have had their reticular formation cut can survive and show, if not normal behavior, then at least not total coma; the animals are merely sluggish. If they can be maintained alive for some period following the operations, more or less normal behavior patterns eventually reemerge. Although some deficiencies remain, once again the plasticity of the brain, its redundant capacity, seems to have been demonstrated. Most of the complexities of interpretation however, have come not here, but over the rôle of the reticular formation in the sleep/wakefulness cycle. The significance of this cycle for the brain needs to be considered further.

Circadian Rhythms

Sleep is a necessity, not merely for humans, but apparently for all mammals. Humans deprived of sleep for long periods become severely disturbed; animals will eventually die if sleep is prevented for long enough. The normal sleep/wakefulness cycle in mammals and humans is a twenty-four-hour one, with six to nine hours in most humans being the period spent asleep. But sleep is only the most conspicuous of many biological rhythms which have a more or less twenty-four hour cycle. Such cycles are known as CIRCADIAN RHYTHMS to distinguish them from the many other rhythms, the monthly one of the menstrual cycle, the yearly ones of activity and hibernation or migration and other more subtle cyclic changes that also occur in many species. To understand sleep, it is necessary to look more closely at these more subtle rhythms which have only just begun to be studied at the behavioral, physiological and biochemical levels. The more closely they are examined the more crucial does rhythmicity of behavior appear in life, from the rhythmically coordinated division of populations of bacteria, through the daily rhythm of the sea-shore organisms following the tide, to the sleep/wakefulness cycle itself.[4]

Any systems engineer will probably agree that, if one is setting out to design a stable system, it is easier to produce one which oscillates about a fixed point than one which is level throughout. Thus, in designing a thermostat to control water temperatures, one makes a device which shuts off the heater when the temperature rises above a certain point, and turns it on again when the temperature falls below another point. If the actual temperature of the water is plotted, it is found to go through a series of rhythmic oscillations with time. If the "switch on" and "switch off" temperature points are set too close together, the device is likely to fail through going into a frenzy of switching on and off.[5] Similar oscillatory feedback control mechanisms occur in biological systems as well: the mechanism which we discussed for regulating the level of thyroxin production by means of thyroid-stimulating hormone from the pituitary is one such (figure 52); the circulating thyroxin level will show just such rhythmic oscillations as the water temperature under the control of the thermostat. The regulation of the menstrual cycle by means of the rhythmic changes in the levels of estrogen and progesterone is another example. Within individual cells too, the maintenance of a steady state of production of proteins or other substances is in fact likely to mean that oscillations in the level of the product occur.

Thus in many dynamic biochemical and physiological systems, stability is achieved by some sort of oscillatory process in which the concentration of some substance, activity or process varies rhythmically round a mean. But what sets the period of rhythm? Twenty-four hour clocks provided by the day/night/day sequence would represent an obvious timing mechanism for living organisms to use, but there is a good deal of evidence— much of it obvious – that it is not the primary means of providing the timing. Thus volunteers who spend long periods down mines, or in caves in the absolute absence of time cues from the diurnal variation of light and dark, none the less manage to maintain their rhythms of eating, excreting, sleeping and wakefulness on a circadian base. Characteristically in these volunteers, the clock runs slightly slow, perhaps set to a cycle of twenty-five or twenty-six hours, so that when they finally surface again, they imagine that they have been cut off for shorter periods than is really the case.

At least in human adults, therefore, the circadian clock does not depend primarily on external cues for setting, although presumably when it shows signs of running fast or slow, its correction is based on these external cues. Under normal circumstances, the free-running circadian clock is continuously being adjusted to match the external twenty-four-hour day.

But such volunteers are adults who have lived their early years in a normal twenty-four-hour-day cycle. Perhaps the cycle has developed in some way as a result of environmental experiences? Experiments with animals reared in totally artificial environments in which the lengths of the "day" can be experimentally manipulated show this is only partly true. While laboratory animals can be adjusted to cycles which vary by as much as four or five hours either way from twenty-four hours, there are limits beyond which it is not possible to adjust the cycle by environmental manipulation, any more than an animal's hibernation cycle can be adjusted to fit the realities of experimentally manipulated "seasonal" changes.[6]

The clock then is predominantly an internal property of the

system, and we may expect to find that the behavioral manifestations of the rhythm are driven by internal biochemical or physiological events. A very clear demonstration of such internal rhythms is provided by some experiments with the sea hare, APLYSIA, performed by Felix Strumwasser, in San Diego, California.[7] Aplysia is one of those favorite organisms, the utility of whose giant and readily identifiable neurons was discussed in chapter 4. It is a tidal-living animal, and shows a rhythmicity of behavior related to this characteristic life style. In the laboratory the animals are readily entrained on a twelve-hour light, twelve-hour dark cycle of movement. Strumwasser placed a recording electrode into one of the giant neurons of the central ganglion, and found that at the end of each twelve-hour period and at the start of the next, that is both at the end of the light and beginning of the dark, and the end of the dark and the beginning of the light, the cell, which was normally quiet, showed a burst of firing. The intriguing follow-up of this observation came when the ganglion was dissected out of the organism and maintained alive, in a nutrient-containing solution, and in an environment of constant illumination.

Despite the removal of the environmental stimulus, the cell continued to fire at the beginning and end of each twelve-hour period. The cell itself thus had an internal circadian rhythm of firing which was apparently independent of environment. That this physiological rhythm may be dependent upon biochemical events was suggested by further experiments in which a drug which inhibits the synthesis of RNA on its DNA template was injected into the cell. Injected before the rhythmic burst of firing would normally have occurred, the drug abolished it. Thus as the basis of both physiological events and their consequent behavioral expression in the intact organism, it would appear that there is some oscillating biochemical system, perhaps associated with rhythmic changes in the levels or rates of production of particular types of protein.

The Sleep/Wakefulness Cycle

In laboratory mammals many biochemical processes in the brain are known to operate with a circadian rhythm. Thus the rates of synthesis of protein in several different brain regions of the rat oscillate according to the time of day, the lowest rate being at around midnight to 4.00 AM and the peak rate at around midday–4.00 PM (it should be recalled that rats are predominantly nocturnal creatures and are most active at night, being drowsy or sleeping by day).[8] The concentration of a number of transmitter substances in the brain, particularly serotonin, show wide circadian variations, and interestingly the variations are largest in the pineal gland, part of the thalamic system and, coincidentally no doubt, where Descartes located the seat of the soul. Rhythmic reciprocal changes of some enzymic levels in neurons and glia in particular brain regions of rabbits during sleep and wakefulness have also been claimed to occur. Can rhythmic change of this type account directly for sleep phenomena?

It would be an obvious suggestion that the sleep/wakefulness cycle was controlled by the build-up of some sleep-producing substance in the brain which was then gradually eliminated during the sleep period. Indeed, in the first years of this century experiments were made which purported to show that cerebrospinal fluid extracted from sleeping dogs and injected into waking ones caused the waking ones to sleep; however, the experiments were methodologically unsatisfactory and such "sleep toxins" have never been identified.

Despite intense and promising subsequent research on the biochemical correlates of sleep, the most positive results have come from the study of its physiological correlates. There is a characteristic EEG pattern associated with sleep, another with wakefulness and the simplest explanation of the cycle might be two reciprocal centers, one concerned with wakefulness, located in the reticular formation and which can be triggered by electrical stimulation, and the other a sleep center. Indeed a sleep center of this sort has in fact been located, not in the reticular formation but in the thalamus.

Rapid Eye Movement, Sleep and Dreaming

However, this relatively straightforward picture became a good deal more complex—and more interesting—when, in the late 1950s and early 1960s, it became clear experimentally, what had perhaps always been clear to anyone who had thought about his own sleep patterns, that "sleep" is not a homogeneous affair, that there are indeed different types of sleep. The EEG of a sleeping person, as well as showing the characteristic synchronized slow wave pattern, shows periods in which it becomes desynchronized, more erratic and more characteristic of the "waking" than the sleeping person—even though he is clearly asleep. Periods of "slow wave" and "desynchronized" sleep alternate. This new type of sleep has been termed PARADOXICAL and thanks largely to the work of Michel Jouvet, in Lyons, it has become clear that there are a very large number of other events associated with paradoxical sleep.[9] During paradoxical sleep the eyes show a rapid flickering movement, so that it has also become known as RAPID EYE MOVEMENT (REM) SLEEP. In addition, muscular relaxation, particularly of the neck muscles.

occurs, making it easy to observe when someone is in paradoxical sleep, particularly if they are asleep in a chair, as the head suddenly slumps forward, whereas in slow-wave sleep, it often rests lightly on the chair back. There is a decrease in heart-rate and blood pressure during paradoxical sleep. In males, even children, penile erection invariably occurs, in females vaginal moistening. It is harder to wake up a person in paradoxical sleep than in slow-wave sleep; he is in a sense deeper asleep. Dreaming is predominantly associated with paradoxical sleep, although some dreaming does occur in slow-wave sleep as well. It seems probable that there will be characteristic biochemical differences between the brain in paradoxical and in slow-wave sleep as well.

It has become abundantly clear that paradoxical sleep is a vital aspect of the activity of sleep, not only for the human but for other mammals as well. Sleep is itself essential, for, as has been said, sleep deprivation will eventually result in death. But slow-wave sleep without paradoxical sleep is inadequate. In a series of ingenious experiments, Jouvet was able to show this by placing cats onto small islands surrounded by water. The cats could stay awake or go into slow-wave sleep, but whenever the characteristic muscular relaxation of paradoxical sleep occurred, the animals would tend to slip off into the water and hence be woken up. Prolonged deprivation of paradoxical sleep resulted in aberrant behavior, including hypersexuality, and eventually in death. If humans or animals are deprived of paradoxical sleep for shorter periods, then allowed to sleep freely, then some "catch-up" of extra paradoxical sleep occurs. It is interesting that sleep induced by anaesthesia, such as barbiturates, is slow-wave sleep; lower concentrations of "sleeping pills" reduce but do not abolish paradoxical sleep.

It is also clear that paradoxical sleep is controlled by a different part of the reticular formation than is slow-wave sleep; according to Jouvet, it is a region in the area of the lower pons. Lesions of the pathway from this region to the cortex result in an abolition of paradoxical sleep, while electrical stimulation of the region during normal slow-wave sleep may induce it. There may also be another center which "turns off" paradoxical sleep and induces slow-wave sleep. However, all these experiments are complicated by the fact that precisely which effect is obtained may depend not only on the site of the stimulating electrodes but also on the rate at which stimulation is occurring. The same neuron may respond differently to stimuli of different frequency from the electrode. Jouvet's view of sleep and its mechanisms is reminiscent in some ways of the ideas of "sleep toxins" discussed earlier, involving a reciprocal interaction of two transmitter substances, serotonin, accumulated during slow-wave sleep, and noradrenalin, accumulated during paradoxical sleep, each transmitter being involved in activating a separate set of neuronal pathways. However, while a good deal – and increasingly more – is known of the psychological and biochemical correlates of both types of sleep, the question of the function of either type remains almost unresolved; it is a matter for speculation which is generally conceptually no more or less advanced than Macbeth's "sleep which knits up the ravell'd sleave of care. The death of each day's life, sore labour's bath. Balm of hurt minds, Great Nature's second course, Chief nourisher of life's feast." Today's analogies are different but perhaps not much better. Those who liken the brain to a computer, talk of the sleep period as one in which "the stores can be cleared", redundant information discarded and various program routines rehearsed and checked. How adequate such a description is in terms of the generation of experiments, however, yet remains to be seen.

What sleep is certainly *not* is a period in which the neurons of the brain are inactive; indeed many cells may be firing more frequently then than at any other time. While many body activities, such as heart-rate, are relatively slowed down, the activities of the brain are clearly not, although they are obviously redirected. It really is very remarkable that the cause of so universal a behavior characteristic of vertebrates is so little understood. One intriguing piece of information is that man appears to need *less* sleep than any other mammal which has been studied.

Dreaming is another function of sleep which is both widespread and obscure in rôle. The external signs of dreaming are as apparent in dogs as humans, although this does not necessarily mean of course that dogs are actually dreaming. Dreaming can be described – a description that would please the psychoanalysts as well as the neurobiologists – in terms of relatively random inputs triggering memory sequences at a time when the "waking" control mechanisms which keep fairly close direction over these sequences are reduced or absent. From the discussion of chapter 9 it should be clear that the memory-trace is a temporally ordered sequence. In dreaming, perhaps relatively irrelevant and random sensory inputs, which would normally be filtered out or ignored during waking, coupled with the random firing of cortical cells, can start one of these sequences running. The lack of filtering and control mechanisms then allows otherwise "forbidden" or "blocked" sequences to occur, and also allows sudden jumps from sequence to sequence to take place without apparent incongruity. But while the dreams themselves, because they are relatively "unguarded" sequences may, if properly interpreted, provide information about personality or the individual which is harder to obtain in other ways (though it is a common observation that the dreams of a patient under analysis vary with the analyst; the symbols the dreamer seems to choose frequently depend on whether the analyst is a Freudian or a Jungian) this still says little about the functional value of the dream to the individual himself. The functional value maybe more apparent if dreams are seen not so much as passive but as active, if cryptic, attempts to resolve conflicts within the system.[10] While we may discard primitive views as to the mystical significance of dreams in foretelling the future or communicating with the dead, there still remains the need for an acceptable neurobiological proposition which can integrate the rôle of sleep into the total description of the behavior of the organism and which goes further than the mere drawing of suggestive analogies.

Clocks and the Experience of Time

The sleep/wakefulness cycle is, we have suggested, but one example of an integrated series of behavioral, physiological and biochemical circadian rhythms. The maintenance of such rhythms can be seen to be an integral part of preserving the stability, the homeostasis, of the organism, even though the exact rôle that sleep plays within this set of mechanisms is uncertain. Intimately bound up with these rhythms must be in some way that strange human experience, so difficult to articulate, of the passage of time. What does the experience of time passing mean?[11] How do we know it has passed, and why does time seem under certain circumstances to "slow down" or to "speed up"? A good deal of philosophical, mystic and psychological ink has been expended on this topic, to which it is inappropriate to add much here. But insofar as the body must have a timekeeping device, this device is most likely to be a rhythmic oscillating one (as are the mechanisms of all man-made clocks). Insofar as it must involve the brain and hence be encompassed within neurobiology, the question is relevant, even though what can be said may be mainly negative.

The clock sense, at least of adults, is, like the sleep/wakefulness cycle, can endogenous function. Deprived of external cues, and relying only on their feelings for time, volunteers in caves or mines none the less manage to keep time with a surprising degree of accuracy. As we have seen, after several weeks they may be no more than 20 percent out. This clock is presumably kept primarily by way of the sleep/wakefulness cycle. But perhaps there are also internal biological mechanisms for the estimation of the duration of times smaller than twenty-four hours?

Such an idea has a respectable ancestry and is interestingly discussed in Robert Ornstein's little book *On the Experience of Time*.[12] One of the most appealing theories from our point of view is that derived from an observation of the biochemist Hudson Hoagland, made in the 1930s, that for an individual who was fevered time apparently speeded up. When asked to count in what she judged to be seconds, Hoagland's wife, while feverish, counted more rapidly than when she was recovered and at her normal body temperature. Hoagland's model for time duration was then some sort of biochemical clock process. All enzymic processes speed up substantially when the temperature is increased only a little from the normal 37°C of the human body. In a feverish person the enzymes may therefore be expected to be speeded up; all cellular processes would run faster, and the individual's subjective clock would also therefore be correspondingly speeded up. Unfortunately for this neat model, later experiments have not confirmed any systematic relationships between an individual's body temperature and his time perception.

Ornstein's model – more attractive to computer engineers than biochemists, perhaps – relates centrally to neurobiology. He proposes that the unit of time as perceived by the individual is computed in terms of a given amount of information processed by the nervous system. If the information input into the system is slowed down, then less will be processed per unit of clock time than normal; if information input is speeded up, more will be processed (up to a maximum defined by the limitations of the nervous system itself) per unit time. Periods when the input of sensory information is low, as during sleep, or for volunteers in mines or subject to sensory deprivation, will result in less information being processed per unit clock time; perceived time will be slow by comparison therefore. Where input of information is fast – and Ornstein has some interesting experiments in this regard – then perceived time runs fast by comparison with clock time.

In this model, rhythmic biochemical oscillators do not set the experience of the passage of time for the individual (except insofar as they may be involved in the rate of information processing). They may continue, however, to set the rhythm of a longer time scale, recording the passage of days in circadian rhythm and of months and years in the more complex hyperrhythms. But all such time models remain no more than tantalizing glimpses into the possible, domains for future exploration, with better conceptual tools than we have at present, dominated as we are in our analysis of time by particular, culture- and ideology-bound views of linearity and progression. It may be that time – perhaps also sleep and dreaming – cannot be meaningfully approached experimentally from within our present paradigms.

12 Where Brains Fail: Madness and Mysticism

All brain mechanisms, from genetic specificity and environmental plasticity through learning and drive, to sleep itself, may be summarized as systems functioning so as to maintain the organism in a state of continuous harmonic interaction with its environment, a dialectic in which the individual acts upon, and reacts to, changes in the environment. The life of the individual is a product of a continuous tension between these antitheses. But the implicit assumption in what has preceded is that, for the majority of individuals and under the majority of circumstances, the tension is a satisfactory one, so that action on, and reaction to, the environment are adequate.

This assumption is manifestly untrue. The official statistics state that nearly two hundred thousand patients are in hospitals for the psychiatrically ill in Britain today, about a third of them being classed as subnormal, the remainder as mentally ill in some measure. These figures mean that about 40 percent of the hospital beds of the country are occupied by these groups. The figures do, it is true, mask the fact that in the last decade there have been great changes in the hospitalized group. Many more patients are short-term now than ever before, while there is a continuing decline in long-term patients. Thus in the last ten years the number of in-patients per thousand of the population fell by 31 percent, although the number of admissions rose by 150 percent.[1] This change has largely come about as the result of the new methods of drug therapy which will be discussed below. But there are many others who are mentally ill but not in receipt of, or in need of, in-patient hospital care. There are those who are treated for illnesses in which the bodily symptoms may be responses to brain problems and others too who are classed as subnormal but are not in institutions or hospitals (about 8 per 1,000 of the population, it has been estimated). In addition, there are sufferers from what are classed as neurological rather than psychological disorders–central nervous system malfunctions, including multiple sclerosis, Parkinsonism, epilepsy and polio, affected nearly 500,000 people in Britain in 1971.[2]

Without prejudging the adequacy of the classifications upon which such statistics are based, it is clear that these figures represent but a small fraction of the "real" incidence of cases in which the dialectic of brain and environment is inadequate. It might reasonably be maintained that for all people at some time, and for many people most of the time, the system fails to accommodate adequately.

Note that this statement does not imply the failure of the brain but the failure of a system which includes both the brain and the environment. If an individual does not, or cannot, accommodate to an environment, it may well be that it is the environment that is at fault and that it is *that* which needs changing. When the majority of individuals in a particular class or social group fail in like manner to accommodate to their environment, then there is a high probability that it is the environment which is faulty, whether we are including for discussion poor nutrition or a class structure in which the individual is alienated from the products of his own creation. In making the statement that most individuals are not accommodating to their environment, we may indeed be stating, not that the individuals are sick, but that the environment to which they are forced to continue to attempt to accommodate is sick. The only way of "curing" the individuals then may well be to change society, either on the microscale of the particular circumstances of the individual, or on the macroscale of a total transformation of the whole of society. This revolutionary prescription, while advocated by some groups of psychiatrists, notably of the Ronald Laing/David Cooper school, would still be resisted by many.[3]

If this analysis is accepted, it may well be asked whether it is proper to discuss brain failure in a book about neurobiology at all. It may well be that the most meaningful hierarchical level of discourse at which the problems of "mental illness" should be discussed is that appertaining to society as a whole—that of sociology. Certainly it is arguable that cures for many forms of "mental illness" reside in sociological changes rather than at the level of manipulations of the brains of individuals, either surgically or by the use of chemicals. None the less, for any given individual diagnosed as "sick" a variety of surgical and chemical interferences with his brain, designed to improve its accommodation to the environment in which he operates, are both possible and widely adopted. An examination of the effects of these treatments is properly within the province of neurobiology irrespective of the nature of the "cures" produced. In so far as the treatments may involve the use of agents such as chemicals which profoundly affect the function of the brain not only in "sick" but in normal individuals as well, a study of the nature of "mental sickness" and of the effects in particular of drugs upon the brain, may very well be revealing, not only concerning the mode of action of the sick brain, but also the workings of the normal brain.

It is possible to recognize a gradation of malfunctioning of the brain, from those forms which clearly reflect internal brain failures to those which equally obviously indicate a failed environment. I do not intend to discuss neurological and psychological disorders in any depth (I am anyhow certainly not qualified to do so) but simply to indicate how they relate in principle to this schema.

Neurological Disorders

The most obvious brain malfunctions are those of a neurological nature, where there is specific damage to nervous tissue.[4] Lesions may sever tracts or disrupt pathways, as after accidents, resulting in the specific loss of particular motor outputs or sensory inputs. Greater or lesser areas of the brain itself, the cortex or lower centers, may be damaged or destroyed as a result of oxygen or glucose lack, produced for example by temporary stoppage of circulation by a blood clot–a cerebral thrombosis or stroke. Cancer of the brain–generally a massive proliferation of glial cells as a tumor, for the neurons do not divide–may create considerable pressure on other cells in the particular brain region, killing them or distorting their activity. Such tumors may be, often are, inoperable. Small scars in the midst of healthy tissue may act as the focus for epileptic attacks– massive electrical discharges which, starting at the focus, radiate out until a large portion of the brain is involved–there are said to be some three hundred thousand epileptics in Britain. There are genetic disorders in which particular enzymes or hormones fail to be produced and corresponding failures in brain development occur, like phenylketonuria, mongolism or pituitary cretinism, and a large number of much rarer types of genetic disorders which may affect only a few tens or hundreds of individuals in the country.[5] There are a variety of viral or bacterial diseases in which irreversible central- or peripheral-nervous-system damage may result: meningitis or polio for instance. Another example is syphilis, which, if untreated, eventually results in a condition classified by nineteenth-century physicians as "general paresis of the insane".

There are a variety of progressive and degenerative diseases which affect the central nervous system but which are still of unknown cause, perhaps partly genetic, partly environmental in origin. These diseases, over the course of the years, steadily impair an individual's capacity to act on his environment. Many of them are classed together as the "demyelinating diseases", as their symptoms take the form of progressive destruction of the myelin sheaths of the axons of the peripheral or the central nervous systems. Multiple sclerosis is perhaps the best known of this group. Finally, there are the degenerative diseases which are straightforwardly those of old age. Not only does cell death occur with ageing but in the living neurons particular structural and biochemical changes take place. The rate and efficiency of processes such as protein synthesis is lowered, individual cells may shrink in size and an actual reduction in brain weight occur, associated ultimately with the characteristic disorders of senility.[6]

Of course accidents and infections are part of an individual's environment as much as prenatal malnutrition is. One reason for classing these malfunctions together is that the symptoms shown by the afflicted individual are relatively clearly definable, and may be related to fairly readily detectable structural and/or biochemical changes within the brain. Once having occurred, despite the fact that they may initially have been caused by environmental effects, they are subsequently much more obviously malfunctions of the central nervous system than of the environment.

For some, but not all, there is hope of medical alleviation. Prostheses which replace or assist paralyzed limbs may aid motor functions by replacing the natural information transmission systems, in which axonal firing triggers synaptic transmission which in turn triggers muscular contraction. Devices which can replace or bypass any of these stages are in principle possible–some already exist and are in operation. Sensory prostheses, to correct for the malfunctioning of visual and auditory receptors, already exist, of course, in the form of spectacles and hearing aids, but such prostheses can do little to aid blindness or deafness caused by the destruction of the optic nerve from the retina or the auditory pathway. Some recent work of Giles Brindley, in London, has suggested that, once the coding mechanisms of the visual cortex are known, it may be possible to develop prosthetic devices which can be implanted directly into the brain, bypassing the optic nerve altogether. Light-sensitive devices coupled to implanted electrodes could stimulate the neurons of the visual cortex directly, though whether meaningful information could ever be conveyed to the individual, rather than mere disordered light flashes, is quite unknown and seems at present somewhat improbable.[7]

Some genetic disorders like PHENYLKETONURIA can be rectified by careful environmental control. In this case, the disease is caused by the absence of a particular enzyme, which in the normal individual metabolizes the amino acid phenylalanine. If the individual is placed on a special diet in which the phenylalanine is absent, the disorder can be regulated and brain development occurs normally. In the case of some hormonal disturbances, such as pituitary or thyroid malfunction, cures are possible by providing the missing hormone. At least one disorder of particular neural pathways concerned with the fine control of muscular movement, PARKINSONISM, can be treated by specific drug therapy using l-Dopa, one of the substances involved in the transmitter system of the pathways concerned.[8]

Virus- or bacteria-caused brain damage, once it has occurred, can only at present be treated in terms of the development of prostheses for the individual; prophylactic treatment for the population before the event, for example vaccination for polio, is of course possible. If the demyelinating diseases and cancer are shown to be at least in part caused by some sort of viral or related component, it may well also become possible to treat them in a similar way. Against ageing and senility there is at present no cure.[9]

Psychological Disorders

The diseases in which the interaction of brain and environment is much more continuous and subtle are those which are commonly classed as psychological rather than neurological. In general they are associated with no readily observable change in the brain at the level of its physiology or anatomy, while the biochemical changes that may occur are dubious in their interpretation. These illnesses are often listed as including NEUROSES, like anxiety, depression and hysteria, in which the individual relates to the same "real world" as does the "normal individual", but cannot act effectively upon it; and PSYCHOSES, of which schizophrenia is the outstanding example. In the psychoses, the individual's world ceases to be the "normal world" at all, at least for considerable portions of time. Instead it is replaced by one in which large elements seem to be of the sufferer's own making, composed of fragments of the "real world" seen through a many-faceted distorting mirror, appearing to the outside observer in the form of hallucinations or delusions.

The neurobiologist entering this murky territory is at a disadvantage. As with all other aspects of behavior, he is concerned to relate a "mental" condition to a particular brain state. Yet his weaponry for doing so is more limited than in almost any other aspect of his study. Experimental animals can show hunger or memory. They can sleep, be afraid; their genetics and environment can be partially controlled. Tumors, demyelinating diseases and lesions can all be examined in suitable non-human systems. Yet how can one study a neurotic or psychotic rat or monkey? Certainly some treatments of laboratory animals will lead to behavioral conditions which might in humans be regarded as neurotic; monkeys can be worried into ulcers for instance,[10] while some ethologically-minded workers might well argue that the conditions under which most laboratory animals are held is enough to make them neurotic! The effects of certain drugs on the behavior of dogs or monkeys might suggest that the animals were experiencing hallucinations. But the area of human mental disorder is incomparably richer than this, the province of the clinicians who are the stamp collectors of biology; they have to be, for we can offer them little better.

Partly because of these limitations, the neurobiological contribution has tended to be limited. Possible approaches include the examination of post-mortem preparations of brains of individuals diagnosed as suffering from particular disorders: biochemical analyses of their various accessible body fluids, from cerebrospinal fluid to blood and urine, in an attempt to check metabolic changes within them; examination of changes in EEG pattern and behavioral performance; study of the biochemical effects of drugs known to affect mental states in humans on nonhumans; and attempts to examine the genetic components, if any, of mental disorders. To these must be added the American experiments on direct electrical stimulation of particular brain regions in a variety of patients, on whose results and morality I commented earlier.

Most of these procedures are messy, complex, equivocal in interpretation and a vast waste of research money, manpower and ingenuity. Often their only justification may be that they are experiments performed by clinicians doing research as a sideline, and a clinician who does research as well as his doctoring may well be a better clinician as a result, irrespective of the quality of the research. It is "stamp collecting" research of this sort which has led in the last twenty years to the analysis of the urine or tissues derived from patients in mental hospitals for almost every fashionable biochemical enzyme and metabolite as the basic scientists' bandwagon rolls on. There have been innumerable false excursions and alarms; from the time when vast oral doses of glutamic acid, one of the amino acids present in the brain, were considered beneficial to mental performance; through a period when many abnormal metabolites were detected in schizophrenic urine only to be shown later to be breakdown products of the drugs that were being administered to the patients as part of a normal hospital regime; the period when "abnormal" EEG patterns were constantly being detected in mental defectives; the Cameron experiments where elderly patients were fed 100 grams a day of yeast RNA; right up to today's enthusiasms for "orthomolecular psychiatry".[11] After all this research it is possible to say, as a sweeping generalization which knowingly writes off tens of thousands of research papers, and many millions of pounds of research money, that to all intents and purposes, no meaningful abnormal pattern of brain anatomy, physiology or biochemistry has been detected in any "mental" patient, other than in the area of the rather specific neurological disorders of the type mentioned earlier.[12]

More profit might perhaps be expected to come of the genetic study of psychiatric illness. Here some positive results appear to have been obtained. Thus there does appear to be a genetic component in schizophrenia. In the general population some 1 percent is diagnosed as schizophrenic—there are said to be five hundred thousand schizophrenics in Britain. Among the brothers and sisters of a schizophrenic the figure is 14 percent, and with identical twins 90 percent if they have shared the same postnatal environment and 78 percent if they have been separated for five years or more. With one parent schizophrenic the chances of schizophrenia in the children are about 12 percent. The implication of these figures would seem to be straightforward.[13] Similar studies would suggest that in some sorts of depression, the so-called endogenous depressions, which are supposedly caused as a result of cyclical internal events rather than in response to obvious environmental factors (these latter are called reactive depressions) there is a genetic element as well. A genetic element implies that there is an altered biochemistry in the individual, determined by the abnormal genetic program. But such studies are open to all the criticisms made earlier in regard to the attempts to demonstrate a genetic element in intelligence; that is, the impossibility of distinguishing between some types of genetic and some types of environmental, particularly transgenerational environmental, effects.

And in addition there is another huge uncertainty, that of diagnosis. Schizophrenia is not the same as a cut on the foot; that is, unequivocal in interpretation. What one clinician may diagnose as schizophrenia, another might class as paranoia. One man's endogenous depression may be another's reactive depression. Nor is it necessarily the case that there is one "disease" called schizophrenia and another called "endogenous depression"; indeed there may well be groups of disturbances linked by certain common symptoms.

These negative results enhance the impression that the neurobiologist may have little to contribute to the understanding or analysis of these forms of "mental disorders". It may be that other types of analysis, at other hierarchical levels are more appropriate. Another hierarchical level is represented by considering the immediate social environment of the individual. Psychiatrists like Ronald Laing and David Cooper maintain that much mental illness, particularly schizophrenia, is related to the rôle of the individual within his family and class. It has been argued that mental illnesses are "family illnesses", so that if the ill member of the family is "cured", another falls ill. That is, the illness is a function of the relationship between the individuals within the family.

Another way of looking at the problem is to examine the class distribution of the illness. Just as some physical diseases (tuberculosis fifty years ago, coronary thrombosis or bronchitis today) show differential distribution across classes, so does schizophrenia. The incidence of schizophrenia in the British and American working classes is considerably higher than it is among the middle class.[14] One interpretation of this might be that there is something about a working-class environment which is more prone to produce schizophrenic effects than about the middle-class environment. Another may relate to differences in diagnosis, if only because consulting the doctor over "mental" rather than "physical" symptoms is not necessarily a practice equally distributed among the social classes. Such considerations might lead one to assume that the proper approaches to the problems of "mental disorders" are the techniques of individual psychology associated with psychoanalysis and psychotherapy, and social change, related to modifying the total environment in which the disorder is generated, rather than the manipulation offered by the applications of neurobiology.

Curing Disease by Kicking the Brain

There remains however one specifically neurobiological area which is an extremely important one, and which must be considered here. That is, examination of the effects on experimental animals of the physical and chemical treatments which are claimed to or designed to "cure" or "alleviate" certain specific mental disorders. The record of these treatments, largely developed in the twentieth century—indeed in terms of their effective utilization, within the last two decades—is admittedly not one of conspicuous success, although certainly drug therapy has revolutionized large areas of psychiatry.[15]

Early attempts to treat "mental disorders" by physical or chemical intervention involved such techniques as the induction of continuous unconsciousness or anaesthesia, induced for example by bromide and later by barbiturates such as phenobarbitone (Luminal). These substances may be presumed to interact with one of the centers controlling the sleep/wakefulness cycle of the reticular formation. Sleep therapy has not lost its attractiveness to some clinicians today. But as the rôle of sleep itself is obscure, as was indicated in the previous chapter, whatever their therapeutic properties, such treatments are unlikely to help in an understanding of the neurobiological basis of the illness concerned.

The treatment of schizophrenics, alcoholics and addicts by insulin shock, a mechanism of producing coma by glucose starvation, was introduced by Manfred Sakel, in Vienna in 1927. He believed that insulin affected the hypothalamus, which is dubious. What it certainly does do is to cause random cell death in the cerebral cortex. Mortality under insulin coma is high, and it is a reflection of despair that as recently as 1954 it was still quoted as a standard and effective treatment of schizophrenia in the textbooks. In fact, there is no evidence that it ever was more effective than barbiturates.

Equally discredited is the technique of severing the tracts linking the prefrontal lobes of the cerebrum with the rest of the brain or the removal of more extensive areas of the frontal cortex (LEUCOTOMY or LOBOTOMY). The technique of leucotomy was developed in Portugal in the 1930s by Egon Moniz and adopted in Britain and the United States through the 1940s and 1950s. In England and Wales, as many as twelve hundred patients were leucotomised in 1949, and by 1959 the figure was still running at an annual four hundred. The record of patients after such operations, according to one survey, quoted by Anthony Hordern, showed that 46 percent of patients suffering from schizophrenia improved, while 25 percent were unchanged and 4 percent died; but when in another survey, controls were made more carefully and followed up for several years, no significant improvements over nonleucotomised patients could be found. At the same time, the loss of so substantial a brain area tends to result in emotional and intellectual retardation, blunted creativity, selfishness, greediness and a whole spectrum of other poorly defined but undoubtedly deleterious consequences. Despite these negative conclusions, the number of such operations conducted in the United States has recently begun to rise again–and the technique is even being applied to young children–an extreme example of the manipulation of brains as a social control technique to which we return in the final chapter.

The use of the still popular ELECTROCONVULSIVE THERAPY treatment originated with Ladislas von Meduna in the 1930s in Budapest. He believed (erroneously) that schizophrenia and epilepsy were mutually exclusive diseases, and used first camphor and subsequently a drug called Metrazol to induce convulsions in schizophrenics. The treatment was soon superseded by the use of electroshock to induce convulsions instead, a technique developed by Ugo Cerletti, in Milan. The addition of anaesthetics or muscle relaxants prevented the wild convulsions with their attendant dangers of bone fractures, which were an undesirable side effect of the early treatments. The premises on which the convulsant treatments were initially developed were found to be false. No particular curative effect has been shown following the use of convulsion on schizophrenics, but, by the 1950s the convulsive treatment had also been tried on depressives as well, and here it was indeed claimed to have a positive effect.

Electroshock (ECT) remains a standard treatment for some forms of depression–particularly those such as postnatal or menopausal depression which do not readily respond to drug therapy. According to the standards used in the evaluation of any treatment for "mental disorders", it does often seem to work in such cases. Yet the neurobiological rationale is obscure, to say the least. Putting an electrical current through the head undoubtedly temporarily affects the electrical properties of most of the neurons; there are sharp biochemical changes in the level of glucose and its metabolites; oxygen consumption, protein synthesis and many other parameters are affected as well. Some, presumably random, cell death must occur. The treatment is analogous to attempting to mend a faulty radio by kicking it, or a broken computer by cutting out a few of its circuits. Even accepting the therapeutic value of electroshock, it is difficult to believe that so massive and crude a treatment will ever be able to tell us much about the neurobiological bases for the disturbances it claims to cure.

Drugs and the Brain

The possibility of achieving information about the bases of these disorders as well as therapy for them, seems to depend mainly upon the newer treatments, developed predominantly after the Second World War, which have transformed many mental hospitals and large areas of the cultural pattern of contemporary society; the use of psychoactive drugs. In evaluating their effects it is necessary to be conscious that pharmacology is a very empirical science–indeed it may even be too empirical to be a science at all. An unconscionable amount of pharmacological research is done, mostly by drug companies in synthesizing and screening possibly pharmacologically active substances, and by laboratory biochemists, all too often with less imagination than research budget, in observing their effects. Yet the biochemical site of action of very few of the drugs is known with certainty. It was only in 1971 that a possible mode of action for so universal and long-established a drug as aspirin was suggested,[16] and the problems of interpreting results with the psychochemicals, that is drugs specifically affecting mood and behavior, is even greater than with most other agents.

It is therefore necessary to be particularly cautious in assessing the effects of psychochemicals. All agents which interact with the brain are uncertain and probabilistic in their effects. "Mood" is itself a product of interaction between brain and environment; it is very changeable and hard to define. What appears to the outside observer as the same mood in two people, or the same person at two different times, may in fact be due to two very different underlying patterns of cellular activity. It is scarcely surprising that the interactions of the drugs compound uncertainty with uncertainty.

What will be described here are the "standard" effects of certain drugs, and in making the descriptions I have deliberately chosen to quote from standard textbooks of psychological medicine.[17] The "average" nature of the statements must clearly be understood. Not everyone is always sedated by barbiturates. It may be possible, by "trying", to stay awake despite doses which normally produce sleep. The effect of a drug varies enormously with the time, place and circumstances of taking. Thus the psychopharmacologist C. R. B. Joyce tells of the situation of two rooms of ten people. In one nine are given barbiturates and one amphetamine. In the second, the situation is reversed. In both rooms the "odd man out" behaves like his companions; the lone amphetamine taker behaves as if he has been sedated, while the lone barbiturate taker as if he has had sleep and fatigue abolished.[18] There is much evidence that the effects of drugs are "state dependent" in this way even with animals. Hannah Steinberg, in London, has made some particularly ingenious experiments using "open field" situations in which the exploratory behavior of rats in a large, relatively unstructured environment, with or without various drugs, is followed. The effects of the agents are markedly dependent upon the circumstances – of familiarity or unfamiliarity for instance – under which the test is made.[19]

What is more, tolerance to many drugs builds up quickly. The same dose of a given agent taken two or three days running will rapidly cease to be effective. This is the principle on which at least one ancient prince hoped to avoid death by poisoning; by regularly consuming small sublethal quantities of the most probable poisons he might be exposed to, he hoped to build up tolerance to the effects of larger quantities. It is the tolerance effect which makes it necessary for many drug users – whether the drug concerned is alcohol, nicotine, barbiturate or heroin – to increase steadily the amount taken to achieve the same effect that lower doses once produced.

All these considerations make the trial and evaluation of the effects of a particular drug on behavior an almost impossible task; the nearest one can get to such an evaluation is to be able to describe the properties of a *system*, which includes the drug, the doctor prescribing it, the individual taking it and his environment.[20] Chemicals do have effects on the brain, but so do all the other factors of the environment, and it may prove that the interactions are more interesting than the supposed "monolithic" effects of the agent. Such a view tends to be unpopular among doctors. For them it is easier to regard the patient as a relatively passive recipient of treatment, *to* whom drugs are given and *on* whom they act. To recognize the existence of interactions, which means taking into account the effect of the whole environment on the individual, and of the individual on the environment, would make prescribing virtually impossible. Indeed it would make much harder this entire approach to the manipulation of individuals, which is what much of medicine, as so much else of our contemporary society, is about. The successes claimed for drug therapy and the effects which the drugs are claimed to have, must all be seen in the light of these remarks.

Psychochemicals and their Effects

Drugs which come into the category of the psychochemicals and which we are considering here, may be broadly divided into SEDATIVES, TRANQUILIZERS, antidepressants and PSYCHO-TOMIMETICS.[21] We shall consider each of them in turn. Sedatives in large quantities are sleep inducers (hypnotics) and may be closely related to some substances also used as anaesthetics. In smaller doses, they are used for allaying agitation, restlessness and overexcitement. Apart from natural products like morphine and alcohol, which have been used for this purpose for centuries, the most widely used among the sedatives are the barbiturates, such as phenobarbitone (Luminal) or amylobarbitone (Amytal); others in the barbiturate group include Nembutal, Seconal and Pentothal.

The barbiturates are prescribed in vast quantities in Britain—there were 12·2 million prescriptions written for them in 1970[22] —and it is claimed that the "typical" barbiturate user is a middle-aged woman. With the barbiturates one enters the realm of drugs which can be physiologically addictive; that is, their use can alter the biochemistry of body and brain in such a way that the system becomes dependent upon the drug for its normal functioning. Absence of the drug can result not merely in a craving, as with nicotine for example, but a specific set of deleterious physiological symptoms. "Cooling out" addicts, whether addicted to barbiturates or heroin, is never an easy task. Yet the mode of action of the barbiturates at the biochemical level is quite unclear. It is known that they interact with a variety of systems, including the oxidative system which generates cellular energy, but such effects are not confined to

cells of the brain; a barbiturate-induced depression of metabolism is a very general cellular phenomena. Perhaps there are
specifically barbiturate-sensitive receptor cells in those parts
of the reticular formation involved in the sleep/wakefulness
cycle, for electrical activity of both the reticular formation and
cerebral cortex is certainly depressed during barbiturate sleep.
But considering the length of time for which drugs of the
barbiturate type have been available, the uncertainty as to their
mode of action is impressive.

The tranquilizers, unlike the sedatives, exert a calming effect,
allaying anxieties and tension without depressing the level of
consciousness or alertness–some indeed may increase alertness.
Like the barbiturates they are used in large quantities, some 16
million prescriptions being issued in 1970 in Britain.[23] They
can be separated for convenience into two groups: the minor
tranquilizers include meprobamate (Miltown, Librium, Valium)
and chlordiazepoxide; among the major tranquilizers are
reserpine (derived initially from a Himalayan shrub, tradition-
ally claimed to have semi-magical effects over a whole variety
of illnesses, *Rauwolfia*) and chlorpromazine (Largactil, Thora-
zine). The tranquilizers are without effect upon the electrical
activity of the reticular formation or the EEG; they do however
appear to suppress electrical activity in the hypothalamus and
limbic system. They exert a taming effect on experimental
animals such as monkeys–chlordiazepoxide is particularly
effective in this respect–and they may therefore operate by way
of the amygdala. Chlorpromazine is claimed to reduce synaptic
transmission in the autonomic nervous system, and as well as
having tranquilizing effects, it lowers body temperature. Biochemically the range of systems with which it has been shown
to interfere is large but inconclusive.

The introduction of the tranquilizers, and particularly
chlorpromazine, which was first used in Britain in 1952, is
claimed to have revolutionized psychiatry more than the use of
any other single class of agents.[24] Their major clinical use is in
the psychoses, where their effects are claimed, to quote a
standard textbook of psychological medicine,[25] to range from
the relief of endogenous depression through

> the allaying of the restlessness of senile dementia, the agitation of
> involutional melancholia, the excitement of hypomania or mania
> ... while they also help to control the impulsiveness and destruc-
> tive behaviour of schizophrenics. The patients develop a kind of
> detachment from their delusions and hallucinations ... especially
> striking is the effect on many cases with paranoid delusions, whose
> persecuted distress may be dissolved. ...

Within ten years of its introduction, chlorpromazine had been given, it has been estimated, to fifty million patients throughout the world. I shall return to the validity of these uses in the final chapter.

Among the antidepressants, the class which has most captured the popular imagination, is that related to amphetamine (Benzedrine, Dexedrine, Methedrine and, when mixed with the barbiturate Amytal, Drinamyl or "purple hearts"). An alternative is Preludin. In many respects amphetamine seems to act more as a psychomotor stimulant than an antidepressant; it generates feelings of alertness, counteracting fatigue and drowsiness while increasing confidence and decisiveness. Presumably the amphetamines affect the reticular formation, but they have in addition effects which mimic the action of the sympathetic nervous system, speeding heart-rate and producing sensations of nervousness. While the amphetamines have gained in popularity among the self-medicating public, as ideal for facing a bad day, taking examinations or going to an all-night party, so the medical profession seems to have cooled to their use as antidepressants. There is no doubt that much amphetamine abuse has occurred, largely due to overprescribing, and that amphetamine addiction can occur when it is used to excess. In 1964, it was claimed that traces of amphetamines were found in urine samples from 18 percent of the boys and 16 percent of the girls remanded in the London area. By 1969, however, the figures had fallen to 4·3 percent of the boys and 7·7 percent of the girls.[26] Perhaps amphetamine has gone out of fashion again (or perhaps more people were being arrested for other types of offences!) At any rate, the present alarm with respect to its consequences may be due more to the adverse publicity that amphetamine abuse has caused than to any more certain and rational reason.

Today's "medically approved" antidepressants include a group which may be seized upon with relief by the biochemist, as at least one class of chemicals with a more or less specific site of action. They act as inhibitors of the enzyme MONOAMINE OXIDASE (known familiarly and felicitiously as MAO). The importance of this inhibition is that the monoamines form one group of transmitters in the central nervous system, including serotonin, dopamine, noradrenalin, etc., and the oxidase is the enzyme which breaks them down subsequent to transmitter release. MAO then plays a similar rôle to that played by cholinesterase in the acetylcholine system (pp. 71–2). Thus the MAO inhibitors, by preventing the action of the enzyme, act in a parallel way to the cholinesterase inhibitors. MAO causes the systems operating by way of monoamine transmitters to become flooded with transmitter, and hence go into spasm. Because of the nervous systems involved, for the cholinesterase inhibitors the result is death, and the substances concerned include the nerve gases. The MAO pathways however are more subtle in their effects. The MAO inhibitors include derivatives of the substance iproniazid (Marsilid, Marplan and Nardil) and tranylcypromine (Parnate).

So far as behavioral effects are concerned, once again they are presumably related to interactions with the limbic system and reticular formation; the drugs are claimed to generate euphoria. One very specific effect of the MAO inhibitors is to block paradoxical sleep, which, as mentioned in the previous chapter, is known to be mediated by monoamine transmitters. In alcoholic terms, the drugs are the equivalent to being put several drinks ahead of the game. They and another set of substances of unknown biochemical consequence, derivatives of the substances imipramine and amytryptyline (Tofranil and Tryptazol), are freely prescribed both in and out of hospital, to deal with cases diagnosed as being either endogenous or reactive depression.

Hallucinogens

The last group of psychochemicals that must be considered are those classified as psychotomimetics, sometimes known as HALLUCINOGENS or PSYCHEDELICS.[27] These include the naturally occurring substances CANNABIS (known variously as MARIJUANA, hashish, pot, weed, shit or grass), cocaine, and mushroom derivatives like mescaline. In addition, there is an increasing group of synthetic substances of which the best known is LYSERGIC ACID DIETHYLAMIDE (LSD). To these may be added, if some of the more lurid claims are to be believed, such exotica as nutmeg, banana skins and the seeds of the Morning Glory flower. Hallucinogens are not generally advocated for use in therapy. Although there have been enthusiastic proponents of adopting them for this purpose, and LSD has been so used, in general the orthodox psychiatric community has remained sceptical. However, they have a proper place in this discussion for two reasons; first that, like other psychochemicals, though to an even greater extent, they affect mood; second, further than the other psychochemicals, they also affect perception, sometimes, although rarely, producing full-blown hallucinations. More frequently they result in distorted perceptions of existing objects. Third, there are proposals, which continue to carry a certain conviction, that the effect of the hallucinogens on the "normal" individual may be not dissimilar to the experience of schizophrenia.

The history of the hallucinogens is well known. For an indefinite time into the past, naturally-occurring substances like cocaine, cannabis and mescaline have been used in many parts of the world, either in the same way as alcohol has been used in Western cultures, or alternatively in solemn and deliberate religious techniques in which the experiences of the participants can only be expressed in terms such as ecstasy, or mystical sensations of a transcendental nature.

Over the past fifteen years, among certain groups in Western culture, the use of these agents, along with the new army of mood changers already discussed, has begun to replace the more traditional uses of alcohol and nicotine. The reasons for and consequences of this replacement must be of major sociological significance, but concern us only peripherally here. They may relate in part to the conscientious advocacy of other aspects of non-Western culture by a profoundly alienated youth. They were given intellectual respectability among older liberals by the enthusiastic advocacy of mescaline as representing an easy way to attain otherwise hidden truths by Aldous Huxley in his later years, and we shall shortly consider the validity of the suggestion that they do in fact provide an alternative way to truths more fundamental than those obtained in the nonmystic world.[28]

All these naturally-occurring agents were supplemented following the chemical synthesis of LSD in 1938 by A. Hofmann, in Basle from substances present in a fungus which affects rye, the organism *claviceps purpurea*. Five years later he accidentally ingested some while working in the laboratory, and experienced bizarre hallucinatory effects which he subsequently deliberately repeated by swallowing another sample of the material. The age of the synthetic "psychedelics" had arrived. Subsequent research was intense; in the next twenty years more than twelve hundred research papers on LSD appeared. The virtues of LSD compared with the natural hallucinogens include its effectiveness at much smaller doses (micrograms per kilogram body weight, as opposed to the milligrams per kilogram needed with mescaline); its relatively ready synthesis not merely in the laboratories of the drug companies but in the kitchens of amateur enthusiasts operating outside the law; and its seemingly more potent effects.

By the mid-1960s possession of LSD became illegal in many countries, including Britain, and the original manufacturer, Sandoz, had stopped distributing or manufacturing it. But the LSD cult was growing fast, with the advocacy of such figures as the ex-Harvard academic Timothy Leary, who for several years championed the establishment of a new religion based on the use of LSD to obtain transcendental experience. The cult was encapsulated in the phrase "turning on, tuning in and dropping out". At the time these words are written, however (that is in 1971), it would seem that the use of LSD, for these purposes at least, has begun to diminish, for Leary himself now advocates nonchemical ways of achieving mind expansion. None the less, tripping on LSD, while not yet as obligatory an experience for the inquisitive-minded as nicotine, alcohol or marijuana, has become common, well-established and unlikely to diminish.[29]

A neurobiological comment on the properties of the hallucinogens is likely to sound less exotic than Huxley's or Leary's enthusiasms. First, very little is known about the biochemical mode of action of any of the hallucinogens, despite intensive research. Mescaline and LSD may be regarded as substances which mimic the effects of the sympathetic system, and a common early hypothesis was that they exerted their effects by interfering in some way with the functioning of synapses where the transmitter was a monoamine, rather like, for example, the mode of action of the MAO inhibitors. There is still no real evidence on this point, although it is perhaps relevant that when radioactively labeled LSD is administered to experimental animals, what little activity enters the brain (most is to be found in the liver and other organs not normally associated with thought or transcendence) is concentrated in the pineal gland, also rich in the monoamine serotonin. A recent suggestion that LSD may affect protein and RNA synthesis seems to have little merit, though there is some not yet fully-convincing evidence that chromosomal breakage may be found in habitual LSD takers, potentially implying genetic hazards in its use.[30] Still less is known about the biochemical effects of cannabis, which does not mimic the sympathetic system, although it has been reported to be antagonistic to acetylcholine, serotonin and adrenalin, and to cause elevated serotonin levels in the rat brain.

Physiologically, cannabis lowers body temperature and increases appetite, despite also causing vomiting. It has a mild analgesic effect, and may abolish multisynaptic reflexes. LSD and mescaline stimulate the sympathetic system, increasing blood pressure, heart-rate and pupil dilation; the hair stands on end, body temperature rises, fatigue is reduced and sleep abolished, while the threshold for some simple reflexes like the knee jerk is lowered. The effect on the EEG is like that of non-hallucinogenic substances such as amphetamine; the slow alpha waves are suppressed and a typically "alert" pattern appears.[31]

None of these observations provides any rationale for the behavioral effects of the substances, which can be observed not merely in man but in experimental animals as well. After small doses of cannabis there is an initial increase in activity and sometimes in aggressiveness in rats. Maze-running performance improves (as it does with amphetamine as well); larger doses result in sedation and depression of aggressive behavior. Following large doses of cannabis dogs characteristically sway and are unsteady on their legs. The animal responses to LSD and mescaline are even less predictable. Depending on the agent, dose and species, there may be either depression or excitation of motor activity and aggressiveness. Pigeons have been claimed to show impairment of learning. There have been some reports of animals showing unusual responses to LSD, which may relate to its hallucinogenic effects in men; mice give characteristic head twitches, cats grope into the air with their paws, dogs growl at unseen objects in their cages and monkeys show excessive fear.

But it is of course with the effects on humans that most people are concerned. In many respects these are harder to quantify and describe than those of the drugs discussed hitherto. All drugs, including, as we have seen, psychochemicals, are uncertain in their effects. None are more uncertain than the hallucinogens. To give a personal example: the effects of cannabis are claimed to be the production of euphoria, with distortions of perception especially of vision, touch and taste. According to the psychopharmacologist Erik Jacobson, the taker of cannabis experiences a "cosmic" feeling characteristically accompanied by a tendency to discuss "high philosophical problems. In between, attacks of anxiety and fear may occur." I have smoked marijuana, both leaf and resin, on a number of occasions and have never observed any such effects, even in rooms in which other people were smoking the same material and claiming to be experiencing them. Indeed marijuana has never, in my case, given any other experience than that of an unusually pleasant smoke and rather lazy feeling of well-being. The effects of eating rather than inhaling it, are more considerable.

The effects of LSD for most people appear to be much more marked. Apart from an initial phase of conspicuous autonomic effects, including sensations of coldness and overheating, nausea, vomiting and dizziness, the experiences generally reported include distortion of sensations, primarily of the visual system, so that colors, shapes and distances become more intense or shift unpredictably. Light flashes and patterns, perhaps caused by firing of some of the visual cortex analyzer cells (as occurs in migraine), and in some cases full-blown visual hallucinations or dreamlike experiences, may occur.[32] Even when the drug is taken under controlled conditions, these experiences depend on the individual and the circumstances. They seem to be unpredictable. Particular effects may be more or less well marked and more or less pleasant depending on the individual and the circumstances. In some cases the experiences under LSD are claimed to produce mystical sensations of oneness with and understanding of the nature of the universe, which rarely last beyond the period of drug intoxication. At other times or in other individuals the experiences may be threatening or terrifying, resembling the nightmare world of the psychotic.

However, the controlled conditions of the laboratory or hospital are not those under which most LSD is consumed, and one would expect that, where effects are so unpredictable, whether it is used in the presence of a group, or at a party, or in a quiet room alone, may all affect the nature of the experience. And in recent years, since the legal use of LSD has virtually ceased, much amateurly synthesized material, possibly very impure and random in dose, has been in circulation. Under these circumstances the effects have been harder still to evaluate. It remains true however that there are well-authenticated cases of unstable individuals who, having used LSD have apparently been "pushed" into long-lasting and full-blown psychoses, suicide or acts which, undertaken while euphoria produces feelings of immortality, nevertheless result in death.

Madness and Mysticism

There are two questions of considerable significance that these effects raise. The first concerns the relationship between the hallucinogens and the psychoses. The similarity between the hallucinogenic effects of mescaline and LSD and those of the schizophrenias was first remarked upon by Humphrey Osmond twenty years ago.[33] Psychiatrists who have taken LSD certainly feel its use gives them some insight into the "mental state" of their patients. Of course there are differences. One of the most significant of these may be that the typical schizophrenic hallucination is an auditory one: like Joan of Arc, the schizophrenic hears voices in his head; the LSD-taker tends to see pictures instead. None the less the similarities are sufficiently striking for it to be proposed that LSD and mescaline might interfere with some biochemical process in the normal brain, which in the schizophrenic is continuously malfunctioning. Alternatively, perhaps the schizophrenic brain might synthesize particular substances which are biochemically analogous to LSD. Neither hypothesis, despite intense experimentation, has led to any particular identification of abnormalities in the metabolism of the schizophrenic brain. This does not mean that the hypotheses must be discarded, merely that it has not yet proved possible to test them adequately. The relationship between LSD and schizophrenia remains tantalizing, but it confronts us as the intriguing similarity of two unknowns.

The second question which the drug experiences raise is perhaps more profound, but not unrelated to the first. Mescaline and LSD in particular produce feelings which are described by their users as "mystic" or "transcendental". That is, their use is claimed to produce a knowledge and understanding of the world which far surpasses in significance and value the everyday understanding offered by science. Mystic experiences have apparently been actively sought–at least by a proportion of individuals–in most societies and at most times in history. The means used to induce the experiences have generally been arduous and prolonged, including extremes of physical discomfort and starvation–prophets in the wilderness tempted by devils, the physical activities of yoga, carbon-dioxide-induced trances, and the chewing of plants which contain mescaline or other related agents. In many societies the mystic experience has been regarded as akin to madness and prophet and schizophrenic have been bound in a queer relationship (like, of course, Joan of Arc herself).

It is difficult for those who have not had the "mystic" experience to be certain as to its validity, any more than those who have not been mad can comment in this sense on the terrors of being a schizophrenic. Unfortunately the experience of mysticism is clearly one which is hard to communicate. Huxley, Leary and their followers do somewhat better than the never-to-be-forgotten experience of Winston Churchill, who is claimed to have woken in the middle of the night in the belief that he had discovered the secret of the universe, and to have written it down, only to read the next morning the immortal words "the whole is pervaded by a strong smell of turpentine". None the less, reading the accounts of LSD-takers of their mystic experiences is uninformative to the uninitiated. If one has never had a mystical experience, the descriptions read rather like those strange, intense memories of early childhood and adolescence, when, lying in the summer grass, for instance, one may suddenly become obsessed with the shape of a leaf, or the movement of an insect, so that for a brief while it appears that one has never seen anything so beautiful and the world folds in upon the image and time stands still while one contemplates it.

One must not underrate the uniqueness and joy of such experiences for the individual. Like the joy of orgasm, it may be reasonable to assume that such experiences are, or can be, part of every human being's potential and that he should not be deprived of the choice of obtaining them, whether by the use of drugs, yoga or any other technique. It is just the same case as that people should not be deprived of the possibility of getting drunk or playing football or even stimulating their own pleasure centers. The question that we shall need to return to, however, is how far such mystic experiences for the few, in the present structure of society, are compatible with improving the opportunities for mind expansion, in the broadest sense, for all.

What must be disputed is the claim made in favor of such experiences that they have some transcendental significance, so that the knowledge vouchsafed during the experience has some special validity and importance. The obvious—almost cheap— comment is that, if it does have such significance, those who have experienced and understand it seem strangely incapable of describing the experience coherently to others. Even painting and music produced under the influence of LSD—to say nothing of scientific research—do not appear to show any significant improvement over the performer's usual standard when judged by outside critics, whatever he himself may feel.

The more important criticism is this however. The human brain is the product of more than three thousand million years of biological evolution, and its present performance the result of perhaps thirty to a hundred thousand years of human social evolution. It has proved the most exquisite instrument for interpreting and acting upon the surrounding world. Over the last three hundred years the most effective utilization of the human brain has been brought about by way of the organized activities of science, and the application of precisely those rational techniques of inquiry and observation concerning the universe which the "mystic experience" relegates to a secondary or inferior place. These "scientific" and cognitive functions are supremely the rôle of the cerebral cortex.

The techniques of obtaining a mystic experience are all, whether quick and chemical or long and physical, those of diminishing the effectiveness of the cortex, of temporarily blasting some of its circuits, by means of food or sleep deprivation, or by excessive sensory input, or by thrusting a biochemical spanner into the cerebral works. The impairments in the functioning of the cortex, in terms of the relationship of the individual with the objective world, are clear; the validity of the distorted and shadowy world which the drugs induce is minimal wherever it can be tested against the objective world of day-to-day experience—without explanatory or predictive value. In so far as the function of the brain is to enable the organism to exist in harmony with, survive in, operate upon, and understand the environment of its owner, the nonmystic brain manifestly functions better than the mystic one. The survival value of the mystic experience is low, and in evolutionary terms its potential or desirability is clearly equally low. Like poetry, music and art, its effects may be a moving and significant part of the experience of being human. But so for some may be the artificial induction of an epileptic fit by stroboscopic flashes.

It is highly probable that in due course it will be possible to explain the "mystic experience" in terms of neurobiology; it is highly improbable that neurobiology will ever be explained in terms of "the mystic experience". The dangers of the mystic experience may lie precisely in its intensity; that people come to live too much in search of it, just as they may come to live too much in search of the excitement of gambling, or alcohol – or science – withdrawn from the real world in which three thousand million or so of their fellow human beings live. Where so many of these human beings have not the opportunity even of mind expansion in the normal sense, because of the inadequacy of their diet or the cramping social environment in which they live, no higher order of argument than simple species loyalty must insist that there is no time for the exclusive pursuit of sensory or mental experience for the individual.

It may be argued that, if contemporary society consists of a world where a small proportion overeat while the huge majority starve, where men go to the moon but cannot educate their children, where weaponry to destroy all life a thousand times over is the end to which the majority of scientific spending and of much scientific skill is devoted, then it it better to be mad. Or if not mad, actively to induce madness. But if the situation is to be remedied for all, and not merely the individual acid-head or pot-head, often anyhow financially maintained by the continued exploitation of just this system, then the search for individual mind-expansion is inadequate. As well as merely experiencing the world mystically, or understanding it scientifically, the need to act upon it so as to change it remains, and in so far as the "drug culture" rejects this action, it is retrograde; like religion it becomes no more than the opium of the people.[34]

13 Have Brains a Future?

It is now possible to bring together the central arguments of this book, to attempt to state them as a set of reasonably concise propositions and to assess their significance both internally, in terms of future trends in neurobiology, and externally, in terms of their potential social and philosophical significance. I must apologize in advance to those who anticipate that this chapter will contain speculation–either optimistic or pessimistic–about the science-fiction futures open to neurobiology and its social applications. Unlike ancient maps marked "here be monsters", there will not be found here brains transplanted into bodies or bottles, thought, memory or mind control, telepathic communication or genetic engineering, artificial intelligence or robots. They are absent in some cases because I believe them impossible–or at least improbable; more importantly because scientific advance and its attendant technology only comes about in response to social constraints and social demands. Because there are at present no or few social demands in the direction of these lurid potential developments, they do not represent, in a world beset with crises and challenges to human survival, serious contenders for our concern. To argue otherwise, as some do, is at best irrelevant at worst a mystification tending to distract attention from more immediate issues. Instead, in this chapter, I attempt to evaluate what seems to me to be the real significance of contemporary neurobiology for man's image of himself and of his possible futures, and the real threats that the distorted views which neurobiology, conducted in the framework of our contemporary social order permits and encourages. This argument takes us back to the questions of the social and ideological determinants of research raised in chapter 1. This chapter then is concerned with neurobiology, epistemology and politics; but not with futuristic speculation.

It is relevant to begin by noting the relationship between the views advanced in this book and those expressed by others–in particular the three classes of interpretation of human brain and behavior referred to in chapter 1, and categorized there as chimpomorphic, machinomorphic and irrationalist. The epistemological framework of this book may be summarized in four major propositions.

1) In studying the human brain and its relationship to the

entity classified as "mind" and the activities classified as "behavior" there is now available a set of increasingly powerful techniques contributed by scientific disciplines ranging from the biophysical and the biochemical through the anatomical, physiological, behavioral and clinical. In addition, the conceptual apparatus provided by the language of mathematics, especially that of information and control theory, has proved fertile in terms of the generation of interpretations, albeit at present not so productive of experiments. These several disciplines and approaches, no one of which is adequate in its own right, are beginning to achieve a coherent semblance of unity in the form of a new scientific field, neurobiology.

2) Each technique or disciplinary approach reveals itself, by the experiments it produces and the questions it asks of its material, to be operating within a certain framework of belief about "the way the brain works". This framework of belief finds expression in the terminology and metaphor adopted to describe the brain–from the hydraulic and clockwork analogies of the seventeenth and eighteenth centuries to today's computer analogies. This framework of belief, which is the experimental paradigm in the Kuhnian sense,[1] is itself a complex product of the ideology of the individual researcher–and hence the society within which the work is being done–and the internal "state of the art"–the extent of the development of the research field and the predictive power of its theories.[2] Despite the delusions, distortions, false trails and erroneous interpretations which the framework imposes, scientific advance, in terms of better-fitting theories, more sophisticated experiments, and hence more useful results, is possible, and is proceeding rapidly in neurobiology.

3) The principle paradigmatic conflicts in contemporary neurobiology are two:

a) Between on the one hand *reductionists*, who maintain that it is possible, by a complete specification of the units of the brain, to achieve a specification of the functioning of the brain as a system, and on the other hand *holists*, who maintain that in some manner the brain is greater than, or different to, the sum of its components, so that there are expressed, within the brain as a system, emergent properties which are not predictable from the units of which it is composed.

b) Between on the one hand those who stress the extent to which the brain–and hence behavior–is genetically specified and as a result relatively unmodifiable by experience, so that a large part of human activity in general and of human

differences in particular are the product of evolutionary and
genetic forces over which the individual human has no
control—this group stresses most the behavioral significance
of *phylogeny*; and on the other hand those who emphasize
the flexibility and relatively general potential of human
brain and behavior, stressing the extent to which the
environmental factors which operate during *ontogeny* have a
profound influence on the shaping of human performance.
4) The position occupied by this book in relationship to the
conflict between the positions expressed in paragraph (3) is
as follows:

  a) A large portion of the reductionist/holist dichotomy is
  based on a semantic confusion as between, say, "mind" and
  "brain". The interpretation advanced here is a version of
  what the philosophers describe as the "identity hypothesis";
  that "mind" may be defined as the total of brain activity at
  any given time and "consciousness" as the summation of
  this total activity from some point (yet to be established)
  between conception and birth, and now. This definition,
  apart from anything else, avoids the danger of the infinite
  regress of an "I, thinking about myself, thinking about
  myself". . . .

  The semantic confusion which has led in part to the
reductionist/holist dichotomy is that which follows from
the interpretation that "explaining" is the same as
"explaining away"; that to say that the statement "He is in
love" is *the same as* a statement about the movement of
electrons, the turnover of molecules or the firing of cells, is
to reduce the statement "He is in love" to nothing but the
movement of electrons, etc. To avoid this semantic
confusion the concept of hierarchy has been introduced.
This concept orders statements concerning molecular,
cellular, physiological, behavioral and sociological events
into particular universes of discourse. It must of course be
understood that the concept of a "level" as introduced here
is an *operational* one. It is certainly not proposed that
absolute distinctions occur between events at one level and
those at another. Quite the reverse. But while it is possible
to translate statements in one universe of discourse into those
in another universe of discourse, because the statements in
each relate to those in the other as do points on parallel
lines, such translation has only limited, though definite,
value. Translation may often be illegitimate when
attempted between two adjacent levels of a hierarchy, and,
where an attempt is made to translate across more than two
adjacent levels, it is almost always illegitimate. This is
particularly the case with apparent causal statements, which

attempt to specify the causes of events at one hierarchical level–generally higher–in terms of events at another–generally lower. In broad terms it is usually adequate–and almost always safer–to specify only correlative relationships. No attempt has been made here–I suspect it is beyond me–to formulate more precisely the general specific rules of translation between hierarchical levels, or to specify more exactly when it is possible to use causal terminology. In addition, the possibility of crossing hierarchical levels in both directions must also always be considered.

Provided these limitations are understood, reductionist techniques have been the more fertile in the generation of interpretable experimental data, and have so far not faltered, either in neurobiology or in any other branch of biology, in providing theories with explanatory and predictive power as to the interpretation of phenomena. These theories are satisfying in that they link biological events to those of chemistry and physics. However, other theories, which do not cross hierarchical levels, such as psychological, sociological or evolutionary theories, have a utility and significance which reductionism cannot diminish.[3] However, biological holism, with its almost mystical insistence on the presence of emergent properties of mind and brain which the reductionist cannot explain in his own terms, has continuously failed to demonstrate what these are, to define systems which are unapproachable by the reductionist. Despite this failure, the concept of the value of the human being, which the protagonists of holism are trying to preserve against what they see as the attacks of the reductionists, must remain a central concern.

b) Concerning the second paradigmatic conflict, between the specific and plastic functions of the brain, a strong restatement of the importance of plasticity has been made. This restatement is considered crucial to the idea of man as "becoming" rather than "being", and of human society as dynamic rather than static. It has been argued that the question of partitioning aspects of brain performance and behavior between genetic and environmental influences is, in a strict scientific sense, meaningless, in that a test which distinguishes adequately between these two contributions for any individual cannot be devised. It is argued that the confusion on this issue arises precisely because of an error of the type considered in 4 (a) above; an attempt to produce a causal explanation across hierarchies from the lower level toward the higher without recognizing that interactions across hierarchies must be considered in both directions, not just in one. Thus the activity of the brain cannot be considered except as part of a system which includes the environment of that brain, anymore than the activity of a cell or of a macromolecule can be considered except in the context of a given environment.

These four statements, then, provide the framework within which the description, analysis and interpretation of brain function which I have attempted in this book are made; they provide, too, the framework within which my own research is conducted.

Essentially, what I am saying is that there are no properties of the brain which cannot be analyzed, defined, explained and interpreted in terms of the biological mechanisms which are known to operate in other systems. There are, to put it bluntly, *no mysteries*. There are puzzles and problems. There will surely be major surprises to come. There are vast murky areas where knowledge is at best sketchy. But it does not seem to me that there are insoluble paradoxes or major explanatory principles lacking in order to achieve the interpretation of brain and behavior, where we cannot now begin to provide the outline of a plausible mechanism. There is no point at which it is necessary for us to conclude, on the basis either of internal factors within our science, or within the structure of our own brain, that neurobiology can go only thus far and no further. What moulds the directions in which we go, therefore, depends not upon some internal gap, or incapacity in science, but the social structures in which we conduct our research. It may be that this is a statement full of a naïve hubris, but such has been the development of biology in the last decades that I make it with no apology, and with only faint doubts that I may be proved wrong.

It is undoubtedly the success of neurobiology however – at least its success in delineating where its breakthroughs are needed and of what type they must be – that has led, ideologically and socially, to the interlocking group of heresies to which I have periodically referred and with which it is now necessary to attempt to come to grips.

The Reductionist Heresies: Chimpomorphia and Nothing-But-ism

Although I have argued that reductionist approaches to the brain have offered great returns in experimental and explanatory terms, there has been a price to pay for these successes in terms of a number of interlocking, debased and crude versions of the "human situation" which reflect only too clearly the ideological positions of their proponents. These I classify as the "reductionist theories". There are really two related versions of the reductionist position, associated with the two principal modes of explanation in biology in general, which may be defined as (1) explanation of biological phenomena in terms of the chemical and physical properties of the system under study, in response to the question "What is this system made of?" and (2) explanation of biological phenomena in an evolutionary sense, in response to the question "How did this system arise?" The molecular biologist's reductionism is of the form (1) – that man is "nothing but" an assemblage of molecules, etc., while the chimpomorphs reductionism is of form (2) – that man is "nothing but" a naked ape, etc. The utility of biochemical explanations of brain phenomena, and of the techniques of experimental psychology and ethology, in describing and interpreting behavior, are unquestioned: It is the rigid philosophical stance adopted by the extreme proponents of each viewpoint which is scientifically and philosophically absurd.

The scientific limitations of these positions are that they blind their holders to the fact that a system of 10^{10} neurons is more complex in its potential interactions than either one of 10^4 neurons or one of 10^{10} bacteria, and that these interactions need consideration in any specification of the working of the system; part-specifications by themselves can only be of limited value and may be misleading. When the brain is specified it must be in terms of *all* of its components and their interactions, and not just a small proportion of them.

The philosophical limitations are however more serious. There really is a danger, represented by the exponents of these positions, of devaluing humans by denying the validity or reality of the higher order hierarchical explanations. To only examine the working of the brain at one hierarchical level is to run the risk of ignoring the others. To argue that, for instance, schizophrenia is exclusively a biochemical disorder, is to imply that it can be treated by purely biochemical means, leaving the environmental structure in which the sufferer is embedded untouched. From here to social control by the use of chemicals and to an argument that one must change humans to fit reality rather than change reality to fit people, is but a step – and one that is in the process of being made, as we shall see below. This is the danger of "orthomolecular psychiatry", the obverse of those slogans on the Oxford college wall, "Do not adjust your mind – there is a fault in reality". The related dangers associated with electrical stimulation of the brain have already been referred to; the issues are of course similar whether the instruments are chemical or electrical.

The related devaluation of humans offered by the chimpomorphs has so far received only passing mention. To assess it we must also recall that ethology itself arose in response to at least as serious a reductionist myth, the arid sterility of behaviorist psychology. A slight detour in the argument is needed in order to make this point clearer.

Behaviorist psychology itself emerged as a quite healthy reaction to the introspective psychology of the nineteenth century, which had viewed any attempt by anatomists or physiologists to define brain function in terms of hardware with great distaste. This distaste was part of the long-standing battle in which the phrenologist Gall had been an early participant. Freud and his school were perhaps the most significant of those who followed this introspective psychology into the twentieth century, and Freud's contributions, in terms of recognizing at least the complexity of a brain which consisted of many over-lapping parts, not all of which were always in open and un-hampered communication with the remainder–that is, his classification into the categories of ego, id and superego, and his demonstration of the extent to which information may be suppressed by the brain–will always remain a major achieve-ment. But despite the intellectual grandeur of the task Freud and the later psychoanalysts set themselves, and the potential significance of their methods for clinical use, they remained surprisingly uninterested in the hardware of the brain; how, at a nuts and bolts level, it actually worked–although in his youth Freud was responsible for a speculative account of a possible neuronal theory of mind.[4]

The morass into which this distaste led psychology was only traversed by the essentially physiological approach of Pavlov in the first two decades of this century–albeit Pavlov himself was subjected to much abuse for daring to approach the problem of central brain function in this way. This mechanistic approach was taken up and developed by a subsequent psychological school, the manifesto for which was produced in 1913 by the American psychologist James Watson: "The time has come when psychology must discard all reference to consciousness ... its sole task is the prediction and control of behavior; and intro-spection can play no part of its method."[5] With these words this school of psychology threw overboard all attempts to deal with such issues as consciousness, mind, free will, imagination and emotion, in the name of a rigidly interpreted scientific method-ology. This methodology, however, permitted them only limited use of the new precision of understanding provided by the physiologists; for all their determination to measure behavior only in the terms permitted by a scrupulous adherence to the description of activity, there remained a certain tendency to treat the brain as a sort of black box, the only permissible knowledge of which was to be found in a statement of input and output, and a series of quasi-mathematical statements about the intervening variables.

This particular philosophical approach found its apotheosis in two disciples of Watson-B. F. Skinner at Harvard and Clark Hull at Yale.[6] Skinner's contribution was the development of a new type of behavioral situation to replace Pavlovian conditioned learning. The language system of BEHAVIORISM was given its most rigorous form by Hull, in an attempt to interpret all brain events between two observed pieces of behavior on the part of the rat—for instance its being placed at the start of a maze and the drinking of water present as a reward at the far end in the "goal-box"—as a series of defined "stimulus-response" (S-R) relationships. He developed an elaborate nomenclature of semialgebraic form based on his S-R terminology, to account for this behavior as a series of links in an inevitable chain. The adherents to this school of psychology, which became known as behaviorism, thus put themselves into an exposed intellectual position not shared by other neurobiologists, who were happy to use their techniques without accepting their ideological puritanism of "reducing" man to nothing but a series of stimuli and responses in an operant situation. All other qualities were swept under the carpet by behaviorists as beneath consideration. To consider "mind" or any of its doings was spurious.

Now to some extent the adherents of behaviorism were well-motivated men. They became, in fact, extreme environmentalists, seeing the human brain as a tabula rasa written on by experience. Watson himself apparently inclined towards a neo-Lamarckianism, a belief in the inheritance of acquired characteristics.[7] Their reductionism was however in the interests of showing how humans could be better fitted to their environment, reared as independent geniuses or subservient slaves, depending upon their early experiences. It is this method of shaping humans to fit particular categories, be it alphas or epsilons, which is parodied so savagely in Aldous Huxley's *Brave New World*, where test-tube babies destined to be workers are given a lifelong distaste for books and flowers; they are electrically shocked as they crawl toward them.[8]

The parody of this version of chimpomorphia is not far from the real claims that were made by the 1930s behaviorists. But the limp radicalism of one generation became the high conservatism of the next. Thus the crucial flaw in the behaviorist's position, which revealed the essentially reactionary nature of its reductionism, is shown by the use of its key word in discussing behavioral motivation: "reward", conceived indeed in terms of a pre-Keynesian type of economic system, appropriate perhaps to the period of the flourishing of behaviorist thought, but scarcely relevant to subsequent developments. By interpreting all human activities in the S-R style of nomenclature, the behaviorists were compelled to search for a "reward" for each aspect of human behavior. Such a system of interpretation of human psychology was immediately sympathetic to high conservative exponents of market theory, but its rigidity went even beyond them, almost back to Adam Smith and the invisible hand of the market as controlling human action. It has not been surprising of late, during student activism in the American universities, to find the Skinnerians lined up uncompromisingly on the side of conservative orthodoxy against the liberalizing demands of the students. For Skinner, for instance, the design of an educational system should be one that provides appropriate stimuli, reinforcements and rewards for the students, in the form of a series of programed examination techniques, a view the reverse of that expressed in current student demands.[9]

Skinner's viewpoint is most coherently expressed, perhaps, in his latest book, *Beyond Freedom and Dignity*. In it, he adopts a rigid behaviorist line which reveals that, like the Bourbon kings of France, the experience of the last forty years has helped him neither to learn anything nor forget anything. Skinner still presents his interpretation of the human condition in terms of a set of "emitted" behaviors, occasioned as a result of prior contingencies of reinforcement, of association of either reinforcing (rewarding) or aversive (unpleasant, punishing) stimuli with that behavior in the past.

Many of the critiques of Skinner's approach have focused on the inadequacy or inutility of this sort of reductionism in describing the richness of the human experience. How valid is it to redefine for example, an individual's self-sacrifice in terms of his prior conditioning to regard praise by his colleagues as reinforcing or their displeasure as aversive? Others, such as Chomsky, have quarreled with Skinner's extreme environmentalism, which seems to deny any specificity to human behavior at all. In fact, neither of these seem to me to be the critical points, although I find Skinner's terminology at best arid and unhelpful. It is surely right to emphasize, as he does, that all techniques of control—even the extremely libertarian and ostensibly free ones— are in a sense conditioning procedures, which result in the individual to which they are being applied learning to do some things and not to do other things. It is important to understand this so as to avoid being mystified by spurious concepts, for example in comparing different child-rearing practices. And while Skinnerian environmentalism is phrased so apparently all-embracingly as to deny any wired-in behavior at all, a position obviously false at the physiological level, it seems to me a less dangerous aberration than the genetic determinism of chimpomorphia, which is one consequence of ethological extrapolation.

In a sense it is because Skinner is nearly right in some things that he is so fundamentally in error overall. He goes wrong first in his attempts to elide sociological into behavioral levels of explanation; a classical case of the illegitimate crossing of hierarchical boundaries which has concerned us so often in this book. Sociological events, he claims, are to be explained by individual behavioral ones; the alienation of youth in advanced industrial societies by the lack of an adequate reinforcing stimulus during their upbringing, and so on. This type of reductionism is at its worst when he then goes on to consider the relationship of "culture" to the individual, controlling and manipulating him. He cannot see that the contradictions between individuals are themselves a part of, contained within, the overall structure of society: that it is not culture as a reified abstract which controls individuals, but that culture is the product of competitive classes and groups within society. Parents and teachers manipulate and control children, as Skinner points out, but it is ignored that these parents and teachers have themselves in their turn been manipulated and controlled.

Because of this, despite Skinner's emphasis on the possibility of "designing a culture" there is a curious ahistorical, static quality about his concept of society. Nowhere does he present a vision of a future culture: instead, he emphasizes the "ethical neutrality" of his techniques, applicable, presumably, equally to fascism, liberal democracy or socialism. Simultaneously, he makes the strange error of claiming that "no theory changes what it is a theory about". Yet the remarkable thing about man and his societies is that they *are* changed by theories, precisely because theories modify consciousness. In fact, because Skinner's ahistorical concept carries conviction only within the atmosphere engendered by a society of the sort Marcuse has characterized as one of repressive tolerance, Skinner's position is irreconcilably conservative. Because he does not see himself, in Eldridge Cleaver's sense, as part of the *solution*, he is inevitably part of the *problem*.

But the response to the Skinnerians has been the emergence of an alternative form of chimpomorphia, albeit generated in revulsion from the rigid techniques of the behaviorists. An increasingly powerful voice in contemporary behavioral studies, it is one which was sanctioned by years of "Nature Study" in Victorian—and earlier—times, but which had been temporarily eclipsed by the rise of behaviorism and "laboratory-based" science. This approach argues that to place an animal in such unnatural surroundings as a Skinner box or a T-maze made of wood or perspex, can only tell us limited things about its capacities and behavior, and these may be false or misleading. The alternative should be the study of animals as far as possible unrestricted by laboratory conditions, in their natural environment and in communication with the rest of their natural community. Such an approach was pioneered with great devotion – and perhaps a considerable publicist sense – by the Austrian Konrad Lorenz, followed by William Thorpe, at Cambridge, and Niko Tinbergen, in Holland and later in Oxford. Many will be familiar with Lorenz' account of his relationships with the animals he studied, told in such books as *King Solomon's Ring*.[10] This is the approach which has become known as ethology, and it has extended to the point where almost all observations made on animals is confined conditions, particularly on their social relationships, are regarded as misleading, a point brought very clearly home by the conflict of early observations on the aggressive behavior of apes in the London Zoo by Solly Zuckerman and more recent studies "in the wild" by Jane Goodall and others, which suggest that in their normal habitat these animals are in fact rather social and unaggressive in their behavior towards one another.[11] This type of ethological approach to an understanding both of patterns of behavior and of relationships between individuals of a species has without doubt enriched our understanding of the complexities of social behavior and cast new light on the functioning of the nervous system.

My objection to it, and the hostility latent in my suggestion that there exists within it an aberration of "chimpomorphia" comparable to the Skinnerian one, is the extrapolations which have been based on ethological observations by Lorenz and his followers; to some, though a much lesser extent, by Thorpe, and most recently and sensationally by Robert Ardrey in his *Territorial Imperative*, by Desmond Morris in his *Naked Ape* and *Human Zoo* and by Claire and W. M. S. Russell in their *Violence, Monkeys and Man*. These latter books in particular seem to me to contain all the extravagances of really imaginative extrapolation.[12] Humans are, evolutionarily speaking, close to the apes; the human brain bears a close resemblance at the microstructural level, and a less close but still considerable resemblance at the macrostructural level, to that of the ape. Some patterns of social behavior in certain groups of apes bear a superficial resemblance to those found in some human societies, though often the societies predicated by the ethologist in his attempts to relate human to ape social behavior seem about as real as those found in the pages of *Woman's Own* or the Marquis de Sade. The comparison is at best superficial and naive, and at worst dishonest, when it attempts to prove the biological inevitability of the author's personal views concerning human social psychology or the future of the human species. No serious examination of either human history or of contemporary sociology could bear out the sort of sweeping generalizations about human aggressiveness, sexuality or the territorial imperative suggested by some of these chimpomorphic ethologists' wilder extrapolations. The parallels do not hold.

To argue in this way is not in the least to claim that man is anything other than "nothing but" the product of a particular series of physical and chemical systems organized in a particular way. Far from it. But it is to maintain that what man *is* nothing but, is certainly *not* an ape, either naked or hairy, and to use ape analogies to maintain that man is bound to destroy himself through "innate" aggressiveness is pernicious and pessimistic as well as being nonsense. This point has indeed been well made by Chomsky, for instance, in *Language and Mind*[13] in which he points out that the unique features of the human–the capacity to speak and to understand verbalized messages–are not shared to any measurable extent by any other species, even the apes. Yet it is just this feature which helps structure human society and which ensures that any chimpomorphic analogies are bound to be limited in their utility.

Yet there seems to be an enormous popular appeal to these extrapolations. Cocktail party speculation as to whether womens' breasts "really" derived from their buttocks as sex objects, which Morris maintains, are matched by such examples of pop-science as those of that man in a Clapham Rolls-Royce, the Duke of Edinburgh, who has used a classically chimpomorphic analogy when describing the ill-effects that might occur if human breeding were to go unchecked. Ignoring his own princely family size, the Duke argued on television that, because overcrowded rats showed social and sexual abnormalities, overcrowded humans would do the same!

This type of ethology thus leads to a view of human society as rigidly genetically determined. We are innately aggressive, acquisitive, nationalistic, capitalistic and destructive. The more well-meaning of the ethologists preach doom as a result of overcrowding or urge the space race as a way of channeling aggressiveness. Where the Skinnerian would modify humanity by environmental manipulation to fit the tidy science-fiction universe of *Walden 2* or *Brave New World*, the ethologist despairs in the genetic certainty that mankind cannot resolve its dilemmas, blandly ignoring the gigantic social transformations which have changed and continue to change both the world we live in and our relations with it. The tremendous importance of social evolution and of the continued development of Homo sapiens from his primeval "hairy ape" status is dismissed by these pseudo-prophets, although it is the single most significant fact about humans and their society. To draw analogies between human behavior at a cocktail party and the social dominance patterns adopted in monkey communities may be only funny. To claim parallels between the arduous but so often triumphant capacity of a human mother to rear her children in the slums and the behavior of rats overcrowded in a cage is not merely silly, it is disgusting.

This genetic chimpomorphia, with its insistence on order and static societies, finds itself naturally in alliance with conservative ideology of an almost feudal, precapitalistic sort, rather than the somewhat more progressive market conceptions of behaviorism, and it is in complete accord with the genetic views on racial superiority in brain and performance of the Jensen/Eysenck type. It is interesting to speculate as to why it has proved so popular in Britain. Perhaps this is because it is derived from a still popular tradition of nature study, perhaps because of the somewhat salacious pleasure of reading about the sexual habits of the apes, perhaps because of the comfort offered by believing that as fate lies in one's genes, one can do nothing about it anyhow. And above all perhaps, in the present atmosphere, the popular craze for accepting Jeremiad myths that preach inevitable doom, whether they be "ecocide", "population explosion" or "innate aggressiveness". For those on the verge of despair, inevitability provides its own wan comfort; of course we live in what is in many ways an intolerable society, where man's conduct towards man is often monstrous, where the social forms systematically deprive the vast majority of the population of achieving what most social theories would regard as their inalienable rights. But with ethology to help us, "That's life isn't it?"

A curious interactive process between scientific ideas and society occurs very frequently in biology, where each feeds upon and supports the other. The struggle for existence, the survival of the fittest and "Nature red in tooth and claw" as aspects of nineteenth century Darwinian evolution, both mirrored Darwin's own capitalist society and provided a biological justification for the continuation of just that capitalism. So with contemporary chimpomorphic ethology; a naïve view of human society is used to interpret the behavior of animal communities in an anthropomorphic way, and then projected back upon that human society once more in order to justify with its iron biological laws the inevitability of the grotesqueries and the injustices that occur. As Dennis Chitty has put it of an ethological conference "few people got beyond doing for mankind what Beatrix Potter has done for the Flopsy Bunnies and Jemima Puddleduck; that is, describing the behavior of one group of organisms in language appropriate to another. But whereas Miss Potter had an ear for language these [ethologists] did not."[14]

There is, as I have tried to make clear, a good deal of value to rescue from both ethology and behaviorism so far as the future of neurobiology is concerned. But such rescue is only possible on the clear understanding that our language system, when dealing with humans, must be that appropriate to humans and not to Flopsy Bunny, and that, in developing this language system, it must be one which is made responsive to the conception, not of man in a static and rigid society, but in a dynamic society which is being continuously transformed by man himself.

The Machinomorphs

We may now turn from chimpomorphia to the aberration which I have defined as *machinomorphia*. To recapitulate: machinomorphia has a long tradition, with deep historical roots. From biblical versions of God creating Adam, through the old cabbalistic "golems", or man-made men, and Frankenstein's monster, to the myth of the robot, the artificial creation which replaces man in contemporary science fiction, the line of thought is consecutive. Only in modern times, though, has it seemed close to realization. The coming of computers whose functioning seems in some respects to mirror that of the human brain, and the rapid development of ever larger and more sophisticated automatic devices in recent years, has suggested to many (a) that the human brain is "nothing but" a glorified computer and (b) that computers will shortly be built which will be so powerful and so intelligent that they will reduce humans to the status of servants to this class of machine. This "IBM-ism" suffers from the same problems as chimpomorphia. As with it, there is a grain of truth in the analogy – a sufficient one to make computer systems of a certain utility as brain models, as has been suggested in previous chapters. But as is the case with the chimpomorphs, the adherents of machinomorphia have become incapable of accepting that their model is *only* a model; the result is that wild things are said by some (Stuart Sutherland, at Sussex, and Donald Michie, in Edinburgh, are among the leading exponents in Britain of this tendency)[15] concerning the advantages of computer systems. Speculative comments as to the imminent replacement of man have become rife. One of the best discussions of this type of machinomorphia has been provided in his attempts to define the "laws of robotics" by the science-fiction writer Isaac Asimov.[16] Although his discussion is rational, none the less, in arguing as to how one should build and legislate for humanoid robots, it represents a considerable extrapolation from the present situation. The nearest we get today to such robots are the experimental teaching machines where pupil and teacher interact by way of an electronic device.

The case for artificial intelligence put by its protagonists is both confused and unconvincing. In the more extreme cases we are told that computers represent some sort of an evolutionary development of man; that it is man's "duty", in some obscure

Teilhardian view of the evolutionary imperative, to help to produce the devices which will one day replace him; that we may with perfect logic come to regard humans as merely "the computer's way of making another computer"–as existing in some symbiotic or parasitic relationship with these creations of his own society, until such a time as computers learn how to dispense with men altogether, and devise more effective means of reproducing. The computer here is seen as a sort of Nietzschean superman, with the exponents of artificial intelligence acting as midwives for the new world, currently being borne in the belly of the old.

But at a lower level the argument is that the computer and automation will be and must always be the servants of man and not his master; that their use will free man of endless routine drudgery, help rationalize his desires, make his life a better one, help us understand better the way the brain functions; and other justificatory but often ill-conceived arguments. At the lowest level of all, we are given another version of the old-fashioned technological imperative: that we must make bigger and better computers because we know how to do so. Man must do what man knows how to do–as Bertrand Russell once encapsulated it, "whatever folly man is capable of conceiving, man has always historically performed."

In order to examine the case for artificial intelligence, we can first consider the practicability of these predictions at a technological level before considering whether the machinomorph's computers can really be compared to brains. At a technological level none of the arguments quoted above seems valid. To take the last first, we must never forget that computers, like all technological innovations, arose out of particular and specific social needs–in this case the war-time need to devise better techniques for aiming and firing guns. Nor have computers been developed in social isolation, but for particular purposes–in general, to serve the needs of industry, the military and the bureaucracy. They will go on being developed for these needs and to serve particular purposes; therefore we may predict that the rôle they will continue to fill in society will be in a large measure set by the social pressures and demands of society itself. That is, if men serve computers rather than if computers serve men, it will be in some sense because our society has "chosen" (by which of course I do not mean the free collective choice of its individual members) this to be their rôle. The technological imperative is nothing other than a *social* imperative; to invest scientific funds and research efforts in particular directions. These directions can be changed, albeit it may require social revolution in order to change them.

But are computers really likely to be developed into super

intelligences? Obviously the things they can do at present, apart from performing routine and complex calculations at vast speed, are relatively trivial. Admittedly, they can be programed to do statistics, search the scientific literature for key words, play chess and perform mechanical translations from one language to another. With vast ingenuity robots can be built which will slowly and with difficulty clear a table, or pile sets of bricks on top of one another, or perform other simple mechanical operations. With very few exceptions involving special circumstances, such as operations at high temperature, in contaminated areas or on the surface of the moon, it seems doubtful whether mechanical men (robots, that is) will ever progress to a point where they have great utility, either to humans in general or to the industrial-military complex, which might commission their production, in particular. They are cumbersome, expensive and vulnerable. Microminiaturization may reduce dramatically their size, although scarcely their complexity, but the nature of the program that will have to be written if they are ever to perform more than simple operations will always be a daunting task. And if robots are really more vulnerable and in general perform worse than humans, while the technological imperative is no more than a spurious concept on the lips of publicity- or finance-seeking scientists short of a better argument, then why press forward with their production at all?

This leaves one with the possibility of computers without robots. Here, although the present performance of their pets may leave much to be desired, the machinomorphs are on better ground. We are at present in the third generation of computers since their serious introduction twenty-odd years ago, and each generation has surpassed its elders in terms of size, speed of operation and miniaturization of components. It seems likely that this rapid improvement will go on for at least another couple of generations before beginning to level out – and one must not forget that the time-scale of a computer generation is closer to that of dogs than humans. It therefore seems likely that rapid progress in computer technology and utilization will take place in the next couple of decades. The big computers of the present generation may have a storage capacity, including backup, of up to 10^{10} bits. It is far from inconceivable, therefore, that a storage capacity of 10^{14} bits – equivalent, as we saw earlier to the storage capacity of the human brain over a lifetime – could eventually be achieved in a computer no larger than, say, a fair-sized room. It would be, after all, equivalent to no more than ten thousand of today's largest computers.

But will such a computer show intelligence? Of course this depends upon what one means by intelligence. If chess-playing is an intelligent activity, a chess-playing computer is intelligent.

The conventional answer to this is that the intelligence of the machine is merely an expression of the intelligence of the programmer who instructs it. A computer can be programed, not merely to play chess, but to learn from its previous experience of playing chess, so as to play better. A computer can then learn to play chess well enough to beat its programmer, though not to beat a chess master. But perhaps it is not playing better than its programmer would if its programmer practiced? Two identical computers playing against each other are clearly "playing their programs" and, other things being equal, the machine with the better program should win (the same, of course, is true of man!).

Perhaps what is surprising is not that computers have done so well in only three generations, but that the have done so poorly, that despite intensive research efforts (and large defense research grants) machine translation is still so primitive and unsatisfactory; that machine literature-searching is of little value except to the most routine types of chemical and pharmacological research, and has scarcely any utility to the creative work of more serious sciences; that chess and draughts are the extent of a computer's capacity. It has not yet been suggested that a computer could learn to play adequate poker.

The fact is that, while as a calculating machine a computer is a very useful instrument, as a brain it isn't really above ground level. Even a computer with the storage capacity of the human brain wouldn't *be* a brain or replace a brain. The reasons for this are clear. Computers are far from perfect analogies for brains; only a little better than telephone exchanges. Computers consist of a set of individual units with a limited number of inputs and outputs; each unit can perform such functions as "yes/no" or "and/or". In response to determinate inputs a determinate output is generated. Depending on its program and its input the computer's output is absolutely predictable. Yet this is the reverse of the situation in the brain. The units of the brain are more than 10^{10} neurons, each connected by 10^4 to 10^5 synapses, with highly complex patterns of connectivity. Whether a neuron will fire or not depends on a vastly more complex set of variables than whether a particular circuit in a computer will do so.

This is not to say that the activity of the neuron cannot be mathematicized. Some early attempts were made by W. S. McCulloch and W. Pitts in the late 1950s and some more recent and much more complex mathematics has been attempted by Jack Cowan, in Chicago. This mathematics does enable a prediction to be made, for a simple neuron, of its response to particular patterns of input. But even when such predictions are perfected—and I have no doubt that in due course they will be—

the neurons of the brain are still not behaving like the units of the computer. They are far more subtle and complex.

And this says nothing yet about the program. In general, computers are doing one or a few specific jobs at any time, corresponding to individual programs fed into them. The brain, by contrast, is performing a vast number of separate tasks at any one time. As I write this my brain is not only concerned in the organization of the thoughts which will enable me to compose coherent grammatical sentences and a (hopefully!) powerful argument, and the direction of my hand, holding the pen, across the page, but also continuously monitoring random visual input, the noise of someone whistling elsewhere in the house and the pressure of the chair on my back, while my hypothalamus, limbic and reticular systems are regulating drives, homeostasis and attention .... A brain resembles a computer only in its most primitive, logical "computerlike" functions. Yet intelligence, if it is anything, must involve *all* the activities of the brain, not just the most computerlike.

To make computers which are like brains one would indeed have to make them of analogous units, connected in a similar way, capable of analogous plastic modifications and with analogous responses to incoming sensory data, both from outside the computer and from within its own works. No currently conceivable computer development will meet this specification. Indeed, it is difficult to see how a computer built of hardware components ever could.

It is possible to preserve isolated clumps of nervous tissue alive and functional in an appropriate medium, under slightly special conditions, for indefinite periods of time. Such isolated cells will make functional synaptic contacts, establish electrical connectivity and show resting and action potentials and signaling capacities. At present such cell populations can only be made on a very small scale—a few hundreds of thousands of cells. But if ways could be found of increasing the size of this complex, of tapping the inputs to, and outputs from, the system as a whole, one could presumably, in principle, build a biocomputer—a sort of brain in a bottle—which would have much more realistic brainlike qualities than equipment assembled from silicon-chip diodes.

This perhaps makes more legitimate a "thought-experiment" which we could conduct, in which we imagine that artificial brainlike computers, either of silicone chips or of neurons assembled in a bottle, had been built in reasonably compact form. Certain questions are then perhaps of speculative interest. Would such a computer resemble a brain? By definition, clearly yes. Would such a computer be conscious? According to the definition of consciousness advanced in this book, the answer again must be Yes. In fact, having built such a computer, one would really have created a golem; but in building it, one would have built a substitute human being, with similar powers, and, presumably, similar limitations, and would have to treat it as such. Faced with this possibility, one should perhaps ask, why bother? Such a task would be arduous, inordinately expensive, and not immensely rewarding. The traditional ways of making and programing human brains, which have been practiced with both delight and success since the beginning of the human species, seem adequate, to make no greater claim. Many indeed maintain that there are already too many real humans on earth, quite apart from artificial ones. What then is the case for attempting to make human brains another way?

The old argument that, if we could build a computer like a brain, we would learn more about the functioning of the brain, falls to the ground if we recognize that, in order to do the building, it is necessary *before* one starts, to know a great deal about the brain—enough to specify the computer. Models, including computers, are of course of value in testing predictions about how systems work, but it is likely to remain possible to test most such predictions about the brain more readily and more easily using an experimental animal, or tissue culture biocomputers of the sort mentioned above, than by turning to the computers the machinomorphs envisage. Thus the intellectual gains from the development of artificial intelligence are small, and it is difficult at this point to see the gains to society, either now or ever. We may take it then that neither the claims for support nor the predictions of the machinomorphs need be taken too seriously.

What is a good deal more interesting, perhaps, is to consider the significance and power of the computer analogy for brains in contemporary society. The argument was advanced in the first chapter that the analogies used to set the style of scientific explanation in any period reflect aspects of the social structure of that period; that is, they are ideological. We have so far considered how useful it is to think of computers as brains. But the reverse question is also clearly in order: why think of brains as computers? When the question is set this way a new scene appears to fall into place. To think of brains as computers is part of a process of thinking of men as machines, which can be controlled, programed and manipulated; into which goes input, and out of which comes output. Thinking of brains as computers— and persuading other people to think of their own brains as computers—is a powerful way of controlling and manipulating society for specified purposes, just as surely as computers can be used to program rockets to fire or warheads to explode. It is a parallel trap to the ethological one, which considers men as genetically programed apes. Lewis Mumford, as part of his continuing polemic against modern technology, has recently argued that what he calls "technics" converts men to machines; machine analogies are found for all aspects of human behavior from conception ("Mummy has a machine in her tummy which daddy starts with his starting handle") onwards.[17] Thinking of brains as computers is one part of this process, while projects such as the building of artificially intelligent machines are an example of doomed technological gigantism ("megatechnics") – part of what Mumford refers to as the "pentagon of power". It is for this reason that machinomorphia must be classed, along with chimpomorphia, as a dangerous delusion, derived, like the latter, from particular assumptions, both about brains and society, which must be clearly and decisively challenged.

The Irrationalists

Under the rubric of *irrationalists* I have categorized two rather diverse groups. The first group includes those who seek in mind the last refuge of emergent biological properties, of divine intervention in human affairs, and of a concept which appears to trouble some (though perhaps not most humans) – free will. With the arguments of the holists and their weaknesses I have already dealt at length. That aspect of mentalism and of the belief in divine intervention in human affairs which interests me here is the residual argument advanced by those small number of neurobiologists who continue to profess religious faith and who attempt articulately to reconcile this faith with their science. Several have done so; the neurosurgeon Russell Brain and the neurophysiologist E. D. Adrian for instance. Sherrington practices such a fluid prose style that is difficult to be quite sure, but lurking at the back of his views on mind and brain there seems to have been a "something of a something". The clearest recent exponent of these views, combining neurophysiology with Catholicism, is John Eccles.[18] For Eccles, god, mind and free will occur in the synaptic clefts. The fact that the synaptic/dendritic events are probabilistic, provides a chink in what Eccles sees as the rationalist armor of neurobiology. The brain, and the body it controls, are for him as much automata as they ever were for Descartes; but the world of the mental, coexisting in space with that of the physical, can exert sufficient pressure upon it to manipulate the uncertainty of the synapses by occasionally throwing the odd switch, thereby converting the human automaton into a sentient, purposeful being.

This argument is of course one which smacks of "saving the phenomenon" with a vengeance, for there is no *need* to postulate such a god of the gaps, any more than the uncertainty principle in relationship to the movement of electrons demands that it is necessary to claim divine intervention every time an electron moves from one quantum state to another. In any event, the version of the identity hypothesis adopted in this book, if accepted, makes Eccles' neo-Cartesian position quite unconvincing, even to his fellow-Christians. Thus Donald MacKay, in openly recognizing the inadequacy of Eccles' position, instead produces an argument concerning free will and the possibility of specifying the brain. He poses the question of the computer powerful enough to store all the information about an individual's brain state at any time.[19] Clearly, he argues, the computer can predict the subsequent state of the individual's brain. Hence the individual is determinate. Yet if the computer's prediction is made known to the individual, his brain state will cease to be that predicted by the computer, for the prediction did not take into account that the individual would have his brain state made known to him. Hence the individual has free will because his actions can only be predicted if he is not made aware of this prediction!

The paradox is apparently linguistically neat albeit somewhat trivial philosophically – as has been pointed out in a devastating attack by Tom Baldwin.[20] Essentially the point is that the "brain state" of the individual cannot exist in isolation from the environment, which *includes* the monitoring device and its predictions. That is, in order to produce his paradox, MacKay is committed to converting a system which is in reality open into one which he maintains is closed. Once it is recognized that the brain state of the individual must in fact relate to an open system then *by definition* it must include the possibilities of prediction of this brain state by the monitor. MacKay's paradox is in fact a classical case of confusion of categories. It is also somewhat irrelevant to our concerns. MacKay wants to use it to prove a particular point about the responsibility of an individual for his actions, which presumably is important to him from both the philosophical and the religious point of view.

But such responsibility is not at all incompatible with the argument advanced here, that it is possible, in a general sense, to produce a complete brain specification. The apparent paradox only emerges by virtue of the illegitimate elision of hierarchical boundaries. The concept of *responsibility* is one which is only meaningfully applicable at the level associated with social interactions. It is not one which is meaningfully associated with a discussion of the physiological properties of constellations of neurons or the synthesis of macromolecules. To talk about responsibility in association with a discussion on macromolecular turnover is as irrelevant as to discuss it in terms of the responsibility of individual hydrogen and oxygen molecules participating in the reaction which generates water. Thus this argument, as so many others, is seen to be a pseudo-argument.

MacKay's residual supposition, that it is *possible* to produce a computer which would contain a complete specification of the brain, is also one which, in its strictly determinist sense, is not accepted here. The position argued in this book is that, at any given hierarchical level, it is possible only to make probabilistic statements about either the present or future brain state of the individual brain under discussion. The probabilistic limitation does not diminish the *explanatory* power of neurobiology; it does limit its *predictive* power to statistical statements—and this for precisely analogous reasons to those involved in the situation in physics subsumed under the Heisenberg Uncertainty Principle; the act of measuring, whether it be of electrons or of brain states, itself affects the variable being measured in such a way as to limit the precision of any possible statement concerning the particular variable. In view of this uncertainty, which is built into the core of the preoccupations of neurobiology itself, the concern of MacKay with the "free-will paradox" seems a little redundant.

In short, the challenge advanced by those who wish to rescue mentalistic events from the clutches of neurobiology is weak in the extreme. Indeed, the more frank among the group recognize this. The Edinburgh philosopher John Beloff, for instance, concerned to rescue the mental, is forced back into a defense of so-called paranormal phenomena—extrasensory perception and so forth—which defy present physical explanation, as the only way of breaking the identity hypothesis.[21] As these phenomena also defy present adequate physical demonstration, one may doubt their existence at all, and Beloff's defense becomes a version of the blind defending the lame.

To face the real challenge to neurobiology one must look, not to these rescue parties sallying out to put up brave Cartesian pennants on outlying turrets, but instead to the direct conflict with the much more powerful and significant views of those who are now concerned to mount an attack, not merely against neurobiology but against the whole rational structure of science itself. It is this development, and not these minor skirmishes, which is of much more substantive contemporary significance.

For, at the same time as the old irrationality has declined and the advance of neurobiology has thrown up its own distortions, a counter-attack has occurred which has been of marked effectiveness in the last few years. In reasserting the value of the concept of mind and its essentially irreducible element, the attackers have mounted a substantive assault on the content of science in general. One element in the attack has been internal to science itself, following the shattering of the simpler post-Newtonian physical universe, to which I referred above when discussing brain models and analogies. This has resulted in a strange situation in which, as the explanatory power of biological theories has become steadily wider, deeper and more confident, physics, that former home of certainty, causality and rationality, has been seen increasingly to be faltering in all three respects. And insofar as physical rationality must in the long run, by definition, underlie biological rationality, the biologist, although confident of the extensions to the edifice he is creating, all the time has to build in doubt as to whether his physical foundations may not be in quagmire. This then is one reason for some loss of scientific confidence.

The second element does not relate so much to the internal philosophical problems of research but to the external logic of science; its relationship with society. There has been a loss of confidence in the capacity of science to contribute meaningfully either to the debate about what man is and what he should become, or to the discussion on the ways and means of achieving the objective of man becoming. This loss of confidence is associated with the seemingly inevitable involvement of science in the machinery of oppression rather than in the liberation of man; science as part of an industrial-military complex; as an agent of social control; as a way of preserving the oppressive status quo against those who wish to transform and humanize society. Chimpomorphia and machinomorphia are seen as examples, *intrinsic to the nature of science itself*, of this process by which man is dehumanized. Thus the loss of confidence in the goals of science has been extended to result in a loss of confidence also in its methods.

Neurobiology is then seen as a tool in the hands of those wishing to manipulate or reduce man. Neurochemistry is the producer of nerve gases and personality-changing drugs, neurophysiology of electrodes which control the mind, and mathematical biology is the progenitor of a nightmare world of the future dominated by computers. The effect has been a tendency among certain contemporary social philosophers with a wide following to reject science altogether in favor of a new irrationality. In a sense this is true of thinkers as disparate as anarchists like Lewis Mumford, prophets of student revolution like Herbert Marcuse,[22] the electronic purveyor of media as messages, Marshall McLuhan,[23] existentialist psychoanalysts like Ronald Laing and David Cooper,[24] religious obscurantists like Teilhard de Chardin[25] or Jacques Ellul,[26] bourgeois novelists like Aldous Huxley,[27] and conservative romantics like Arthur Koestler.[28] All these in their several ways argue that the aim of rationalist science is, having demystified the universe, now to demystify man as well, and, having demystified him render him amenable to manipulation.

It is this fear which is at the core of the legitimate concern of the holists with the intrinsic dangers of the application of purely reductionist techniques. It would be wrong to discount it, for the record of contemporary science in this regard is far from encouraging. I do not accept that the response offered by some of these philosophers to the challenge of an inhumane science–to stop doing science and to abandon the pursuit of rationality in favor of some variously conceived past golden age or future Utopia–is correct, although this is not the place to justify my assertion at length. Science, I believe, can and should be used in the service of the mass of the people. Its use *against* the masses is a reflection of its rôle within a particular social order. None the less, the present developments of neurobiology do carry within them a number of ominous potentialities, to which we must now turn.

The Social Control and Consequences of Neurobiology

The utility of certain modes of thought prevelant in contemporary neurobiology in devaluing and degrading the individual human or groups of humans, and human potential in general, has already been stressed. The use of certain types of ethological concepts, particularly evolutionarily deterministic views of human behavior, which argue the incapacity of humans to transcend the social mores of their apelike ancestors, in their turn suggest a set of techniques for the manipulation of human interactions. The use of ethological approaches to the study of human behavior, such as the examination of social interactions and communication patterns, is often explicitly geared to providing the reader of the research with a contemporary version of Carnegie's handbook on "How to win friends and influence people". By paying undue attention to the subverbal parts of the communication–who smiles first, who looks who in the eyes, the relative tone of voice in individual interactions, and so on–there is an implicit devaluation of the verbal content. Thus the substantive part of human communication is underweighted by comparison with the nonspoken part. It is almost as if such an approach were wilfully denying that human speech had significance at all, or that it is one of the major determining differences between human and nonhuman societies.

The use of ethology in this way, and the closely related use of genetic neurobiology to apparently demonstrate innate, unmodifiable behavioral patterns and limitations, serves to stress and encourage belief in the inevitability of certain static social orders, denying the manifest fact of change in society and in social relationships, which are in large part the results of the human social evolutionary process, with its changing modes of production within society. By contrast, the position adopted here is one which stresses not merely the *continuity* of evolution and the *specificity* of genetics but the *potential for change* within the brain, the way in which forms of human action are indeed responsive to environmental and plastic effects. In conformity with these paradigms, the ethological approach to human behavior might be seen as one which expressed major interest in the differences in behavior observable under different social situations, and in the rôle of specifically human attributes such as speech; it should be one which takes into account that human society is not an ape society.

Similarly, questions concerning the genetic aspects of intelligence and performance are, as has been emphasized, not only at best socially irrelevant, they are also scientifically spurious. A proper approach to a study of the factors operative in the shaping of adult intelligence and performance should take into account the implications of the individual's situation and interactions with his environment, the plasticity of the brain both to transient and to long term changes, and the transgenerational effects imposed by environmental alterations. A major shift of research interests towards the understanding of the mechanisms of developmental plasticity is also required. The mechanisms by which informational filtering systems develop with age and are themselves environmentally modified (so that in one study, for instance, it was found that in the United States, Southern white psychologists are *more* likely than average to believe in the genetic intellectual inferiority of the American negro, Northern and Jewish white psychologists *less* likely) are also topics which should concern a neurobiology seeking to aid in human transformation rather than manipulation.

Just as present day ethological and genetic paradigms may serve to devalue humanity, and provide a rationale for the maintenance of an unacceptable status quo, so too do the computer analogies which, by stressing the brain's machinelike functions, provide techniques and a rationale for regarding men as machines. This is not the place to analyze in depth the potential dangers and advantages to society of general developments in computer science, which are outside the scope of the present argument. The points to emphasize here are the limited applicability of computer models to a real simulation of brain properties, and the points of difference between brains and programable computers, and to insist that there is no technological imperative, in the absence of overriding social needs, toward the development of artificial intelligence or its substitutes. Such needs as can be identified in this area at present perhaps fall more obviously into the category of devices potentially of use in the oppression than in the liberation of mankind.

When we turn from ethology and artificial intelligence to

the domain of neurophysiology, neurochemistry and psychopharmacology, we move from the area in which social abuses are predominantly at the level of the setting of particular conceptual frameworks which permit of particular rationales of behavior (innate intellectual inferiority and therefore segregated schools for instance), to that of direct social impact. The dangers implicit in these areas are clearly those of the development of techniques of improved social control. The morality of implanting electrodes into the brains of individuals for research purposes is, I would argue, of the same order to that recently reported case in the United States in which terminal cancer patients were given fatal doses of radiation to test the radiation hazard to soldiers in the event of nuclear attack, or that in Britain in 1966 in which terminal leukaemia patients were infected with monkey encephalitis virus;[29] such episodes are consequences of a medical training in which human patients become regarded as objects rather than as individuals. But individual morality apart, the general question is whether the use of electrical brain stimulation portends general and more powerful techniques of social control. Has the refined experience of generations of torture chambers, culminating in the contemporary expertise ranging from South Africa to the United States in Vietnam, or the British in Northern Ireland, produced nothing better than electric shocks to the genitals? Is not the next step—and a much more humane one—electrodes to the brain?

This threat is, I believe, still in the realm of science fiction.[30] Granted that electrical control of mood *is* possible—and this does seem to be the case both in animals and humans—and also that radio-controlled implanted electrodes are already available—for such a technique to be applicable on any large scale would demand a degree of social acquiescence in being implanted which is hard to envisage, quite apart from demanding the production of doctors who would carry out the implantations and controllers who would presumably regulate a population's mood by the tuning of a radio dial. Traditional techniques of mass persuasion and mood change are likely to remain more practicable and more effective than this for the foreseeable future.

It is, interesting that this view is taken even by José Delgado himself, who is one of the most ardent exponents of the technique. In his book *Physical Control of the Mind*[31] Delgado discusses quite frankly his animal and human experiments. He is naïvely sanguine about the merits of this technique, nowhere discusses in any serious manner his right to manipulate patients in this way, and subscribes unhesitatingly to the myth of the technological imperative. His view of the right, in principal, of an informed, and of course humane, élite to control the remainder of the population is neatly encapsulated in his explanation of why electrical brain stimulation cannot be abused: "The procedure's complexity acts as a safeguard against the possible improper use of electrical brain stimulation by *untrained or unethical persons*" (my italics). The neat elision of training and ethics needs no comment. But even Delgado's rapturous view of the future (provided enough funds are granted to neurobiology) where he sees his science being placed at the service of the controllers of society, does not envisage radio stimulation techniques as being of major utility as social control devices, for much the same reasons as those I have suggested, though he does believe their use will tell us a great deal about how the brain works.

The potential hazards of psychopharmacology are undoubtedly much greater, for the uses of chemicals to relieve pain, induce sleep or euphoria or improve attention, are already widespread and generally accepted. When barbiturates and tranquilizers are prescribed in the quantities that they are in Britain, it is clear that this type of social control is already with us. What is needed is to distinguish between science fiction and reality. The science-fiction uses of drugs include the saboteur's drop of LSD in the drinking water, or the United States Army's publicity gimmick for the so-called psychochemical "BZ", which, when dropped on enemy troops, makes them so uninterested in fighting that they cease to resist, or the politician massively applying an aggression-inducing aid to his populus before declaring war ... all these are mere mystifications. They are mystifications because of the limitation on the predictability of the effect of drugs explained in chapter 12. The effect of any drug on any individual depends on his past history and present state; the effect of a given dose of a drug on two individuals is never identical. There is no dose of BZ which could be dropped on an enemy, or of an aggression-inducer to spray on one's own population, which would be sufficient to produce the desired effect on most of the population, without being at the same time at sufficiently high concentration to kill some, have unpredictable and possibly opposite effects on others, and leave yet others unaffected. What is more, because tolerance to the effects of many drugs builds up quickly, a second application would be likely to be even less effective than a first.

An obvious example of the ineffectiveness of this type of use of drugs is of course the use of marijuana in Vietnam. Despite the fact that marijuana is supposed to create a tranquil, peaceful, hedonistic and withdrawn state (see chapter 12), its massive use by United States troops has not notably succeeded in reducing the brutalities and the savagery of their conduct. The prospect of mass psychic medication for political ends is as artificial as the mass implantation of electrodes described earlier. On theoretical grounds, quite apart from practical ones, it is always likely to remain so.

Yet another science-fiction case is that of the erasing of old memories and the reequipping of an individual with new ones by the use of drugs or memory chemicals. The theoretical grounds on which this possibility was discarded were spelt out in chapter 9. All we are left with in this category are certain drugs which will enhance attention, and therefore potentially speed learning, like the amphetamines, and others, which, apparently by lowering "resistance" in the psychological sense, may permit the apparent retrieval of suppressed memories, like the so-called "truth drug" Pentothal. Kitting people out with new chemical memories just isn't on. There are other more certain techniques of "brain-washing"–for example those practiced by the British troops in Northern Ireland, apparently with official sanction until the public outcry in 1972. We need not see neurochemistry in this sense as advancing the horrific view of *1984*, when George Orwell's ultimate defeat of his hero Winston Smith comes, following a ferocious dose of brain-washing, classic style, when he traces in the dust on a table the last abnegation: "Two plus two equals five." Once again, despite the *schadenfreud*-filled prognostications of many science journalists on this score, the likelihood is that the potential of neurochemistry in this direction is another mystification.

The real threat of psychochemicals is a much more subtle one. After all, one may not require the spraying of chemicals from the air, or their dropping into the water supply, if the people can be sufficiently accustomed to regard the right response to any type of psychic distress as to obtain a prescription from a doctor for a chemical to put it right; if society is so conditioned that a substantial proportion of its members regard their sensations of pain in relation to that society, not as a sign of *society* being out of joint, but of *they themselves* being clinically ill. A vast amount of potential social unrest is thus avoided. This is a much more subtle form of social control through the use of chemicals than the rather crude fictional fantasies of the science journalists. With drugs to sleep and to wake, to sedate and alert, to ease pain and to generate joy, we have already arrived at one form of *Brave New World*, in which the medical profession, and in particular the psychiatrists, act as lieutenants in the campaign for the preservation of the status quo. The problem of the uneven effects of the mass use of drugs on a population does not arise when each individual will voluntarily experiment to arrive at that combination which suits him best.

In this analysis, the "drug cult" is in fact equally functional; by channeling potential social dissent into the search for individual experience, the social challenge to the established order is muted and diminished.

This is not to argue an "away with all drugs" position, which would be manifestly absurd. Although pain is functional to the organism in some senses, aspirin is good for toothaches—provided one also attempts to find and cure the cause of the pain as well as the symptoms. In any society, individuals are going to feel tortured by internal problems and contradictions, deriving from their own development and immediate situation. Coping with them is not made any easier for the individual by insomnia. Endogenous as well as exogenous factors can enhance anxiety and cause depression. Drugs which mitigate these symptoms are obviously beneficial to the individual. Thus the development and use of psychochemicals is a complex phenomenon in which many elements, of cure and of social control, are closely intertwined.

The strength of the social control element should not, however, be underrated. The most graphic account of the use of psychiatry and psychochemicals for this purpose in the Soviet Union has been provided by Zhores Medvedev in his book *A Question of Madness*.[32] Medvedev describes how, after a career of several years of more or less active dissent in the USSR, including the publication of two books in the West, on Lysenkoism and on censorship of literature, after both had been refused official publication in the Soviet Union, he was forcibly submitted to psychiatric examination. His persecutors claimed he was suffering from schizophrenia, in the guise of an interest in two disparate topics, biology and sociology—what one of his friends described as the Leonardo da Vinci syndrome! According to Medvedev, official Soviet psychology has defined a new clinical syndrome, "schizophrenia without symptoms". Once in hospital, he was repeatedly "threatened" with the use of drugs, in his case Tofranil, and that if he did not agree to take them orally, he would be given them by injection. He was eventually released following international protests, but other Soviet dissenters have not been so fortunate, and are still in either normal or prison hospitals. Allegations are made that they are treated with large doses of chlorpromazine and by physical methods such as being wrapped in wet blankets.

It is important to emphasize that these treatments are probably not seen directly as punishments. What is being meted out to dissenting intellectuals in the Soviet Union is part of the standard treatment for the medically ill there or elsewhere. In all probability, to the officials in charge of their case, they are genuinely ill. To dissent is obviously to be ill. But before the reaction to the Medvedev case is a pious lifting of Western hands in horror, let us recognize that specific uses of psychiatric techniques for social control purposes is frequent here too. Psychoanalysis, particularly in the United States, has a long history in this regard. The use of chemical psychiatry, however, is newer. There are allegations as to the deliberate use of psychiatric treatment as an alternative to prison for young dissenters, particularly hippies, in many states. The recently introduced practice in several American cities[33] of diagnosing children as "hyperkinetic" on the basis of their school reports and dosing them *en masse*, on a routine day-to-day basis, with amphetamines such as Ritalin, is a more flagrant example than most of this type of technique. Over 250,000 children in the United States are given Ritalin daily to reduce their so-called "hyperactivity". The possibility that the "hyperactivity" could be a response to undernutrition, poor environment or just plain boring teaching seems not to have been considered. And indeed there is an increasing tendency in the United States to seek, in any type of socially unacceptable behavior, an explanation in terms of brain mechanisms. One currently fashionable way to describe children who do not adjust to the system is that they are suffering from "minimal brain dysfunction"–a syndrome whose signs are precisely those of–not adjusting to the social order! A neat self-fulfilling prophecy; another example of how to define disease into existence.

Even more extreme and disturbing is the recent indication that the number of leucotomy-type operations being conducted, not just on adults but also on young children described as "unmanageable", for "personality disorders", after having been declining for many years, is now on the increase again in the United States, and are now being performed at the rate of four hundred to six hundred a year. Such episodes as the performance, in a Mississippi hospital, of six operations over a three-year period on a single child, starting at the age of nine, may not be isolated horrors. The practice, on the evidence, is as ineffective as it is obscene. Yet such is the urge to resolve the contradictions of societies such as that of the United States by manipulating, through drugs or surgery, the brains and minds of its citizens, that even this practice appears to have become medically tolerated.

In Britain the technique of pharmacological control seems to be applied, not so much against the articulate middle-class dissenters, or against children, but against the least articulate members of society–the unskilled working class and the unemployed. Among these groups the diagnosis of manic-depression or schizophrenia, hospitalization and drugged quiescence following massive application of chlorpromazine, is not unheard of. Certainly among people in these categories, the psychiatrists and the hospitals are seen as arms of the State, as part of the methodology of the denial of human rights. In the case of Medvedev, the mistake of the Soviet authorities was to do for the dissenting middle class what one suspects has gone on for a long time unchecked in many places as a standard way of dealing with the inarticulate working class. The worthy Western psychiatrists who have taken up the Medvedev case should bear the situation in their own hospitals also in mind.

The logic of such developments is impeccable. And after all, is it not so much more refined – the ultimate development in the society Marcuse has characterized as being one of repressive tolerance? If this is the result of neurobiology, or even a possible consequence of neurobiology, perhaps the irrationalists would be correct; better drop-out than be pushed? It should be clear from what has been said that, despite the real threats of the development of neurotoxic agents for chemical warfare purposes, the rôle of psychiatry, psychopharmacology and neurochemistry in assisting the generation of techniques of social control, is perhaps the most serious potential abuse that they present.

The other side of the balance sheet cannot of course be forgotten. Not only, as has been emphasized, are there major social *benefits* derived from the use of psychochemicals for the alleviation of the symptoms of psychiatric disorders, but neurochemistry also has a positive rôle to play in the development of agents which can cure or alleviate neurological disorders. The use of l-Dopa in the treatment of Parkinsonism has already been cited; the capacity to recognize and treat genetic neurological disorders, such as phenylketonuria, by special diets, has prevented and will continue to prevent irreversible brain damage to significant numbers of children; drugs have been developed to treat and diminish the symptoms of epilepsy; and there remains the potential of treatments for the degenerative diseases, such as multiple sclerosis. These are the positive fruits of even the lopsided development of neurochemistry which has occurred up until now.

Meanwhile, for psychiatry to release itself from the trap of monocausal or heavily reductionist views of mental illness demands a recognition of the interactions of brain and environment. While it may be that the Laing/Cooper school of psychiatry in Britain and analogous esoteric sects in America have overstated their case for the rôle of individual and social relations in respect of internal disorders, it is clear that the therapeutic communities into which their analyses have led them have had measurable success in the achievement of individual liberation. In this context, reports of the development of related psychiatric techniques adapted to the style and culture of the people of North Vietnam are of considerable interest.[34] Ultimately, what is needed is a recognition of the interactive nature of the "human situation" and hence of human brain states; both more profound research and inspired therapy will be required in an area where transient and state-dependent environmental interactions with brain biochemistry are only just beginning to be recognized as being of significance.

Just as in psychiatry a recognition of both the need for and dangers of hierarchical boundary-crossing is called for, so too is this necessary for neurochemistry and neurophysiology. The delicate and hazardous interfaces of these disciplines with behavior, the time-dependent changes in the brain's chemistry and physiology with development and in response to changed environments, are research areas of the profoundest social significance. They are also areas where the greatest advances of the next decades could, and should, be made.

Have Brains a future?

I do not argue that, if we can get our neurobiology right we shall automatically get our society right, nor that it is impossible –merely difficult–to do good neurobiology within an oppressive social order. But I do argue that we need good neurobiology and there now exist the tools and concepts to enable us to create it. A good neurobiology will reflect sound human values, emphasizing both the individual importance of the human and his social relations, together with the uniqueness of the human species and its relationship to humanity's fellow species on this planet. It will recognize and explain human capacities, but not devalue them. Equally, a good neurobiology will help build a good society, by providing the science required as weaponry in the battle against malnutrition, environmental and educational impoverishment, ignorance and disease. To reject this potential because neurobiology can be and is being used in support of oppressive social orders or for social control, is to reject the possibility of the creative transformation of our own society at all and under any circumstances, and to argue instead that the only solution for the individual lies in withdrawal.

But this is not all that a good neurobiology is concerned with. Francis Bacon's old dictum about science emphasizes that it represents both knowledge and power. An integral part of man's situation in a good society will be, must be, his understanding of and hence respect for himself, both as a product of past evolutionary development and as part of an ongoing sequence of historical and evolutionary change, and also as an individual whose brain, while similar to that of all other humans, is none the less unique in its own right. Such self-respect must be built on knowledge. It can never be built upon ignorance or blind support for irrational modes of thought.

In *Peer Gynt*, perhaps one of the theater's most searching analyses of the human condition, Ibsen portrays Gynt as an old man returning home after years of wandering over the face of the earth, still intent above all on analyzing his own character, stripping off onion-skin after onion-skin of personality, beneath which he eventually finds—nothing. His life has failed, because throughout it he has adopted the philosophy, not of men, but of the Trolls, those Scandinavian minor devils. For the Trolls the motto of life is "Troll, be to thyself enough"—seek self-sufficiency through one's own mind. The motto of true humans, however, according to Ibsen, should be instead "Man, be thyself"—to act fully as a human. To which one can add, as a scientist "Man, know thyself". This is the human path, and that of science.

This chapter is entitled: "Have brains a future?" Such a title has several implications. One of the most important is that of the survival of man himself. The evolution of man has followed a path of increasing brain size and complexity, of increasing consciousness. I have argued that this consciousness is an inevitable consequence of the existence of neuronal networks of particular size and complexity and hence of a particular evolutionary strategy. Clearly the emergence of consciousness has been successful in evolutionary terms, for in some if not in all respects, man dominates the planet. Yet for how long will this dominance last? So many and so intense have become the contradictions within society, which is the organized mode of man's existence on earth, that its total destruction, and with it man and possibly all life on earth, is the gravest threat we face. In terms of nuclear capacity, the stockpiles of weapons in the United States and USSR are enough to destroy the entire human population of the world many times over. The chances of humanity's survival into the twenty-first century are at best only middling. It may be argued that, if this is the consequence of consciousness, consciousness is an evolutionary dead end; that man will perish from excess of brain just as one of the many reasons claimed for the extinction of the dinosaurs was their lack of brain. If this were the case then truly brains would have no future; alternative life forms, perhaps without consciousness, might eventually inherit the scorched, polluted and impoverished earth.

But consciousness does not exist in isolation. Man's consciousness exists only in relation to his interactions with his environment, his existence as part of society. And that society can be, is being, daily transformed. For reasons of survival if no other, it is our responsibility to aid that transformation by means of our brains and consciousness. In society's transformation, our own consciousness will in its turn be transformed. If, and only if, we can achieve this, will brains have a future.

Appendix 1

The resting membrane potential

The maintenance of the cell's resting membrane potential depends on two things: The difference between the internal composition of the cell and the medium by which the cell is surrounded; and the properties of the cell membrane. As was pointed out in chapter 2, the cells of the body are bathed in a fluid whose composition resembles that of filtered blood, from which the red and white blood cells have been removed. This, in essentials, is a solution of common salt, sodium chloride; it contains predominantly the electrically charged ions of sodium (Na^+) and chloride (Cl^-). By contrast, the inside of the cell is relatively low in sodium – only one-tenth that of the extracellular fluid – but is relatively rich in the related substance potassium (K^+). The potassium concentration inside the cell may be up to thirty times that outside. The inside is also relatively low in chloride (one-fourteenth that of the extracellular fluid), and the negative ions that replace the chloride inside the cell include large molecules of protein in solution in the cell cytoplasm.

The difference between inside and outside would be interesting, but of only marginal significance, were it not for the particular properties of the cell membrane. If the membrane were to be replaced by a sausage skin or a cellophane bag, and liquid of the composition of the internal cell fluid were placed inside the bag, and of the external cell fluid outside, then eventually the composition inside and outside the bag would equalize. The cellophane membrane has microscopic pores in it which are big enough to allow the charged ions to pass through. Each ion will tend to move down a concentration gradient from a region in which it is highly concentrated to one which is less concentrated. (Another way of visualizing this is to imagine putting a drop of ink into a glass of water. The ink will gradually diffuse out until the entire glass is uniformly colored.) Thus in the case of the cellophane bag, the potassium ions will tend to pass out of the bag, and sodium ions in, until the concentration of both ions is uniform inside and outside, throughout the entire solution. If electrodes are placed, one into the bag and one into the surrounding solution, no potential could be measured.* If the cellophane bag were replaced by an impervious plastic or rubber one, no ions would pass through in either direction; each solution would remain unchanged indefinitely. Again no potential difference would be measured if one were to put electrodes into the two solutions.

However, if inside the cellophane bag we put, not just potassium ions, but a negatively charged large molecule, like a protein, which was too large to pass through the pores in the bag, the situation would change. Since the net ionic charges tend to balance out on both sides of the membrane, the small ions cannot be equally distributed; in order to maintain electrical balance inside the membrane, K^+ ions must be held back by the negative proteins. In such a system a balance is struck between the tendency of the ions to move down their con-

---

*For complex reasons which do not concern us here these statements are only nearly true, incidentally.

centration gradients and for the positive ions to be held back by the negatively charged large molecules which cannot so move. It is under these circumstances that a potential difference will now be registered between the inside and outside of the cellophane membrane.

What distinguishes the cell membrane from the cellophane bag or the impervious rubber balloon is that the cell membrane is selectively permeable; potassium and chloride can freely diffuse through the membrane while sodium cannot. Sodium and potassium ions are very similar chemically, and the reasons for the selective PERMEABILITY of the membrane lie in the intimate biochemical details of its structure. It has a characteristic appearance, under the electron microscope, of two dark-staining lines with a lighter interior, and it is probable that this membrane structure is achieved by an ordered array of complex molecules containing both fatty (lipid) and protein components. One molecular model for the cell membrane, due to the biophysicist James Danielli, is that it is a unit structure with its molecules arranged so that each of the faces of the membrane, external and internal, consist in part of protein; the spatial arrangement of the molecules helps give the membrane its characteristic properties.

Permeability of sodium or potassium is perhaps achieved because of the capacity of the membrane under certain circumstances to select between the ions, to bind one and not the other. Alternatively, it may be possible to conceive of the membrane as having "pores" in it—being punched through with holes through which one ion but not the other can pass. These several suggestions have all had their adherents, and the issue is far from resolved. Even the unit membrane structure is only a model and has had its critics. But the molecular details of the reasons for this particular membrane property do not concern us here.

The point which is of concern, is that the apparent impermeability of the membrane to sodium ions only operates because there is in fact a mechanism which in the living cell actively prevents the sodium ions from running down their concentration gradient. This mechanism may be regarded as a type of chemical pump, which operates so as to pull the sodium ions across the membrane on to the outside. This pump does indeed exist; its molecular mechanism depends on the special properties of the cell membrane, and like other mechanical pumps it depends on a fuel supply. In the case of the SODIUM ION PUMP, this is a continuous utilization of cellular energy, derived, as is the energy for all the biochemical and physiological functions of the cell, from the oxidization of glucose or other alternative foodstuffs.

Many of these mechanisms have been studied using red blood cells, which are easily obtainable and are readily capable of being subjected to experimental manipulation. With the red cells this energy dependence can be shown quite neatly, by adding a poison to the system, like fluoride, which prevents the metabolism of glucose. Sodium then rapidly leaks into the cell until the internal and external concentrations equalize. An even simpler way of preventing glucose oxidation is to put the cells in the cold, when all the enzymic reactions, on which the metabolism depends, are slowed down. Sodium then leaks into the cells. Warming the cells up to 37° (blood heat) once more results in glucose oxidation taking place; the pumping mechanism starts up, and sodium is pumped out of the cells once more.

This pumping operation is a practically universal property of cells; indeed they spend a considerable proportion of the energy available to them from glucose oxidation in achieving just the right balance of ions, in controlling their concentrations of internal and external potassium and sodium. Just why nearly all cells maintain these ionic differences is not certain. It is perhaps significant that the external cell fluid has a composition roughly that of sea water. If life arose in the sea, as most present-day evolutionary theories suggest, then cells would have evolved in an aqueous environment whose composition was remarkably similar to that bathing their present-day descendants. But why the difference in internal composition? What could have been the evolutionary advantage to the cell in differentiating itself in this way from its surroundings, particularly if to do so required the expenditure of large amounts of precious energy? The reasons remain obscure. It is known that some proteins and lipids within the cell possess the property of selectively trapping and binding potassium in preference to sodium, while some of the enzymes on whose functioning the cell depends for performing the myriad of complex chemical transformations in which it is continuously involved, work better in the presence of potassium than sodium. Could these have been compelling enough reasons for so universal a cell property, or is there some concept missing here, awaiting a crucial experiment or a particular imaginative leap to resolve? Despite the intense experimentation which the phenomenon of the cell's pumping mechanism has attracted, there remains a suspicion that there is something about the mechanism and its significance which currently evades research.

Figure 55 makes clear how it is that the ionic difference between the inside and the outside of the cell results in a potential difference across the cell membrane. Close to the inside surface of the membrane we can envisage a cluster of negatively charged protein molecules

55 Ionic differences across the cell membrane responsible for the resting membrane potential
Na$^+$ – sodium ions
K$^+$ – potassium ions
Cl – chloride ions
An – protein ions

attempting to move out of the cell down their concentration gradient, accompanied by K^+ ions which are in fact free to move out of the cell down their concentration gradient. This concentration of negative ions on the inside of the membrane attracts a matching concentration of positive sodium ions outside. The result is that there is a separation of plus and minus charges across the membrane – the resting membrane potential.

Appendix 2   The action potential

We have described the action potential and its significance at the physiological level. How far is it possible to provide a biochemical explanation for the events recorded electrically as a depolarization of the membrane followed by brief reversal of polarization? The model which follows has been derived primarily from work with the squid axon and analogous preparations, by the group led by Andrew Huxley and Alan Hodgkin, in London and Cambridge, in the 1940s and 1950s. These experiments proved immensely fertile of results, so much so that it is possible to regard the mechanism of axonal transmission as solved, at least at the physiological–though not yet the biochemical–level. Indeed Hodgkin and Huxley were able to derive mathematical equations which correctly describe axonal working–and few areas of physiology have yet proved amenable to treatment of this degree of precision.

The analysis begins with the model of the axon as a hollow tube, charged at − 70 millivolts to the interior as a result of the clustering of sodium ions along the external surface. When stimulation occurs, whether imposed experimentally by electrical or mechanical shock, or as a result of the normal course of events in the neuronal cell body, there is a temporary change in the structure of the cell membrane. The result of this change is to make the membrane permeable to sodium. Sodium ions therefore rush into the axon down their concentration gradient. As they pass in they lower the negative polarization of the inside of the membrane with respect to the outside. And the more this is lowered, the greater the change in permeability that occurs in the cell membrane. It is as if the cell membrane was kept in its sodium-impermeable form *because* of the electric charge across it. As this charge is diminished, so the sodium impermeability breaks down, and the more the sodium impermeability breaks down, the more sodium rushes into the cell, and the more the membrane becomes depolarized. This is a self-excitatory feedback system. It can be drawn as in figure 56. The result of this sequence is that even a small event, provided it is above a certain threshold, will act as a trigger and fire the response, because it will magnify itself to the right proportion.

The inrush of sodium continues until the membrane is not merely depolarized but the polarization is reversed; the membrane becomes positive to the inside until the figure of + 40 millivolts is reached. As this figure is approached the membrane conformation begins to change once more; it becomes decreasingly permeable, and finally impermeable to sodium. This sequence, which lasts some half-millisecond or so, accounts for the rising phase; the membrane, as it becomes impermeable to sodium, becomes permeable to potassium. The potassium accumulated inside the cell begins to pass out down *its* concentration gradient, until the membrane polarity not only reverses again but returns to the − 70 millivolts of the original. This is the decline phase of the action potential curve of figure 57. Indeed the potassium rushes out so fast that there is even a small overshoot which can be seen at the tail end of the curve. The time taken

crease in Na permeability

ane
isation   Na⁺ entry

56 Changes in Na⁺ permeability as a self-excitatory feedback loop during the passage of an action potential.

for the full sequence of the potential, including the overshoot (or *hyperpolarization*, i.e. increased polarization) is about a millisecond, the period which also constitutes the absolute refractory period of the axon.

This model explains how the action potential is formed at a point on the axon surface; it does not yet show how it is propagated from point to point along the surface. This becomes apparent if the axon is considered as a tube, at a point on whose surface a local disturbance results in a depolarization. Figure 57 shows the effect of this. The initial disturbance is at point A. The depolarization results in a mini-circuit being set up between the depolarized point on the surface and its neighboring regions, which are still negative to the inside. Current tends to flow along this circuit resulting in a further depolarization at (B). The depolarization at (B) results in an action potential there, and hence a minicircuit between (B) and (C); in the same way as before, the action potential then moves to (C) and so on along the axon. This "local circuit/depolarization" model can thus explain how the action potential is propagated as a wave along the axon.

It also explains an interesting additional property of myelinated axons. If a myelinated axon is dissected out along its length and

57 Propagation of the nerve impulse. Changes in the permeability of the membrane of the axon are correlated with the propagation of the action potential. As the impulse arrives at any point, Na$^+$ rushes into the axon, resulting in a locally positive region. In the wake of the impulse, Na$^+$ is prevented from passing into the axon, but K$^+$ rushes out of the axon into the extracellular fluid. The normal resting potential is now restored. At the site of the action potential (light region) the potential across the cell membrane is reversed (depolarized) until it approximates +40 millivolts. The length of the depolarized region on the nerve may extend over several centimeters. This type of impulse propagation is found in the squid axon and mammalian unmyelinated nerve fibers.

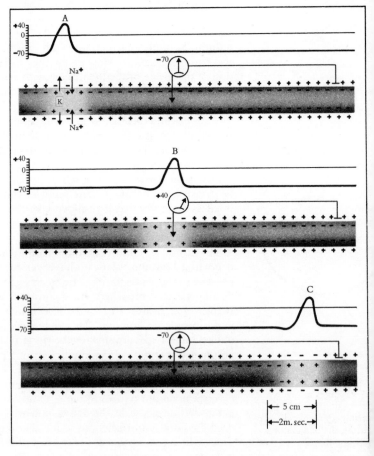

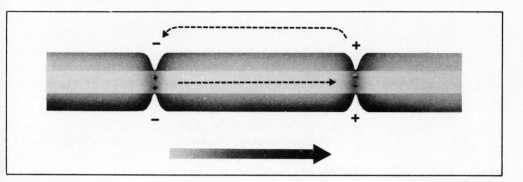

58 Saltatory conduction. The conduction of the nerve impulse in a myelinated nerve fiber occurs as a local circuit 'leaps' from one node of Ranvier to the next node of Ranvier. The excitation of the nerve fibers travels from node to node because effective contact of the axon with the extracellular fluid only occurs at the nodes.

examined, it is found that the myelin is not wrapped around the axon as a continuous unbroken sheath, but instead characteristic notches appear at regular points along the length of the myelin, exposing the naked axon (figure 58). These notches are known, for their discoverer, as "nodes of Ranvier". The myelin, it will be recalled, acts as an insulating sheath; ions cannot leak across it. Thus leakage can only occur at the nodes of Ranvier. This means that when a local circuit is set up during the passage of an action potential, it is not the minicircuit of the nonmyelinated axon, but must be larger; it must jump the gap between the nodes. The effect of the myelin sheath and its nodes is thus to speed up considerably the rate of propagation of the action potential down the nerve. Incidentally, the fact of the existence of the nodes of Ranvier and the ion leakage across them, is slightly to break down the insulation of each individual axon; some cross-talk thus occurs among the individual axons—a bit like a faint crossed wire on a telephone.

The passage of an action potential along the axon results in a change in the ion concentrations across it; there has been an entry of sodium, and an exit of potassium. If the true condition of the resting potential is to be reestablished, the sodium must be expelled once more and the potassium pulled in. This is the function of the ion pump, which must be set going in order to transfer the ions against their concentration gradients. It is this reestablishment of the ionic balance across the membrane which is so energy-consuming for the cell. In an actively transmitting axon or nerve cell it has been estimated that up to 40 percent of the total energy provided from glucose oxidation is used in this way, though the actual molecular coupling of the pump mechanism is still unkown. Nonetheless, the actual magnitude of the ion flow is very small. Even if the axon is poisoned so that no more energy from glucose oxidation is available for restoring the ion balance, some hundred thousand impulses will pass in an average-size axon before the ionic stores become exhausted.

Appendix 3   The cerebellum as a neuronal machine

The cerebellum is a highly convoluted mass of tissue, and was described in chapter 2 as a much folded cortical skin over a thin interior of white matter, lying at the back of the brain. In that chapter the rôle of the cerebellum in relation to the control of fine movement was suggested; indeed as long ago as 1917 it was recognized that cerebellar lesions resulted in phenomena such as dysmetria – the apparent inability to gauge distance. Movements in such patients were ill coordinated: reaching out to grasp something, the hand would overshoot or undershoot; instructed to flex one finger to bring it round to touch the thumb, the patient would flex all four; tremor and error replaced the supreme degree of coordination typical of normal human motor movements.

The actual direction of motor activity is the responsibility of the neurons of the motor region of the cerebral cortex – witness the motor homunculus of figure 29. Nor does electrical stimulation of the cerebellum elicit motor responses. How is it involved then? Even the superficial description of the cerebellar lesions of the last paragraph must suggest the involvement is at the level of control and coordination. Analogy with the effect of cortical influences on spinal reflexes (discussed on page 98) suggests that this control mainly takes the form of inhibition. The rôle of the cerebellum is to damp down cerebral overenthusiasm.

Analysis of the wiring diagram of the relationship of the cerebellum and the rest of the brain makes such a rôle clearer. The inputs and outputs of the cerebellum are severely limited and, despite the highly convoluted surface of the cerebellar gray matter, it actually consists of only a limited number of types of neurons, arranged in orderly repeated rows, and each with a well-defined relationship to the remainder. The largest and most obvious neurons of the cerebellum are the giant Purkinje cells (figure 59). The only efferent axons which leave the cerebellum come from these cells, which are

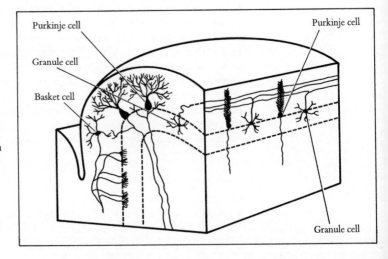

59 The organization of the cerebellum. The main types of neuron and their interconnections are shown. Purkinje cells, granule cells, and interneurons such as the basket cells are all related in a precise wiring diagram.

312

arranged in orderly lines parallel to the cortex surface. On the input side, leading into the cerebellum, are a set of smaller "granule neurons", while there are three different types of interneurons which can be distinguished from one another by their shape or location within the cerebellar cortex. The afferents to the cerebellum come from two groups of neurons, the *pontine nuclei* (located near the pons) and the *olivary nucleus,* and the external relations of the system can be summarized in the wiring diagram of figure 60.

The olivary and pontine neurons receive inputs from branches which spring from the main axon running down from the pyramidal cells of the motor cortex to the motor neurons of the spinal cord. From the olive the only output is to the cerebellum where the axons synapse on to the Purkinje cells. Under the light microscope the

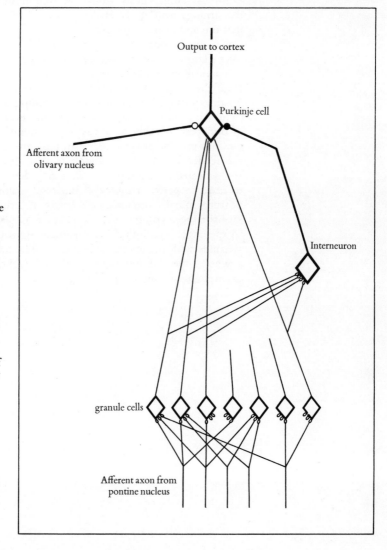

60 Wiring diagram of the cerebellum. The diagram selects the principal elements of the cerebellar cortex. There is one output system, the Purkinje cell axons, and two input systems:– fibers from the inferior olivary region, of which each Purkinje cell usually receives exactly one, and the 'mossy fibers' which come from many parts of the body and brain. They are imagined to convey information about the state of the animal. The mossy fiber input is translated by the granule cells, which synapse with a Purkinje cell. The inhibitory interneuron prevents the Purkinje cell from firing unless almost all its active afferent synapses have been facilitated.

Diagram labels: Output to cortex · Purkinje cell · Afferent axon from olivary nucleus · Interneuron · granule cells · Afferent axon from pontine nucleus axons from the olive can be seen to intertwine with the Purkinje cell processes, synapsing with them in vast numbers. From the pontine neurons synapses are made with the granule cells of the cerebellum, which in their turn again synapse with the Purkinje cells. There is also a pathway which connects the pontine neurons directly with the neurons of a staging point on the output side of the cerebellum, on which the Purkinje cell synapses en route back on to the pyramidal neurons of the cerebral cortex. This model is clearly reminiscent of many other types of feedback systems. Still more obvious does this become when it is added that direct cellular recording shows that the Purkinje cell output to the pyramidal cells is in fact inhibitory.

The advantage of the feedback system seems to be that there is not a one-for-one correspondence between the olivary and pontine neurons and the cerebellum; both of the former receive inputs from numbers of different pyramidal neurons in the cerebral cortex, while the arrangement of cerebellar granule cells and the other interneurons and axons in the cerebellum is such as to distribute information coming from any single neuron of the olivary or pontine nuclei over a large number of cerebellar Purkinje cells.

The elaborate rectilinear arrangement of the axons and synapses from the granule neurons and the other cerebellar interneurons in relation to the Purkinje cells are, according to David Marr's model (which is itself based on the data of John Eccles, Janos Szentàgothai, of Budapest, and others), a way of programing the Purkinje cell output, not only to provide the "damping effect" which is manifest in the feedback diagram of figure 60 but also to achieve the more sophisticated function of a memorizing device, enabling the system to learn to perform motor actions and maintain voluntary bodily postures initially organized elsewhere. It is this which makes necessary the sheer volume of the cerebellar cellular apparatus, indicated by the fact that each Purkinje cell makes some two hundred thousand synapses with the axons from the granule neurons alone. Taken as a whole, the elaborate system of the cerebellum is a remarkable example of precision engineering!

Appendix 4 A model for the brain's specificity

It is relatively easy to devise systems whereby one molecule can, so to speak, recognize another in the same way as an enzyme recognizes the substance on which it acts chemically. The trouble with such a recognition process is that it seems to demand a very high information content. If each of the individual cells of the central nervous system were color-coded with a specific chemical, a macromolecule like a protein for example, this would require the presence of no less than 10^{10} specific protein molecules simply to code for the neurons of the cortex alone. Not only would this produce a tremendous strain upon the protein synthetic mechanism of the organism, but it would also mean that an unacceptably large proportion of the total genetic information carried by the DNA of the egg and the sperm, which together grow into the future organism, would be taken up with simply carrying the information required for this particular specificity, without leaving adequate over for the other multifarious pieces of information which it is necessary that the DNA carries— like how to synthesize the specific proteins which form the enzymes which must be part of the complement of all the cells of the body. One gene for each cell is obviously an unacceptable number.

A more likely model perhaps might be one that is drawn from the recognition properties of the protein molecules of antibodies and antigens, which are critical to the body's immune response and have been very effectively studied in recent years. Without going at length into the details of such recognition molecules, essentially, although antibodies and antigens do have the sort of recognition capacity that an enzyme has for the molecule on which it acts, it is not necessary to have a specific gene for every single possible antibody that the organism can make. Instead there is a genetic potential which enables a very large number of rather random protein molecules to be made, each of which has the capacity for recognition of a particular antigen molecule, but the specific protein sequence of each of which is environmentally determined rather than specified genetically.

Such a recognition mechanism might indeed be a feasible one within the nervous system; but for it to function, it demands direct contact between molecules. Antibody-type molecules on the surface of one cell must come into direct physical contact with antigen-type molecules which can be recognized on the surface of another cell. This is a static model. But it is not what happens, at least in the regeneration experiments. In these experiments a dynamic recognition occurs in which the nerve fibers can grow over long distances in order to locate themselves in association with the specific cells.

All these considerations have led neurobiologists like Gaze, and developmental biologists concerned with similar problems, like Lewis Wolpert, in London, and Brian Goodwin, in Sussex, to suggest alternative models for these recognition properties. Such models propose that recognition is achieved by the establishment of a chemical gradient of a particular substance. To see how it might work, take the case of the alignment of the retinal cells as in the Gaze experiment.

It is possible to account for the specific alignment of the cells in one dimension in the following way. Consider a source producing a chemical which diffuses out from it at the left-hand edge of a field. As it diffuses, a gradient is established. Regions distant from the source have a lower concentration of the substance than regions close to it. Now assume that cells contain molecules on their membranes which can recognize the substance forming the gradient. Suppose that the recognition takes the form that the left-hand edge of the cell aligns itself with the higher concentration of the chemical. The cell will tend to move up the concentration gradient of the chemical until it arrives at the source, and then align itself with its left-hand edge closer to the source. The phenomenon would be analogous to that of the bacteria of chapter 5, which moved along a concentration gradient towards a region of high glucose concentration. Now consider a second cell. It is subject to the same forces as the first. It too will move along the gradient towards the source until its path is blocked by the first cell. It will then align itself with its left-hand edge along the right-hand edge of the first cell. Other cells arriving in their turn will align themselves likewise until a row of cells has been assembled, all in a specified relationship to each other and to the gradient (figure 61). The coordinates of each cell will be defined by a concentration (x) of the substance establishing the gradient.

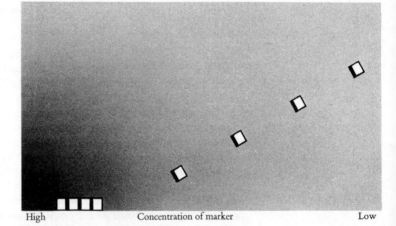

61 Cells aligning themselves in a linear gradient. The surface of the cells indicated ▣ has an affinity for the marker substance forming the gradient.

High   Concentration of marker   Low

This is a linear gradient. If a second chemical source is postulated, establishing a gradient at right angles to the first, then the position of any cell in a two-dimensional field can be established by means of two coordinates, the concentration (x) and that, (y), of the second chemical. The addition of a third chemical source diffusing in the third-dimension allows the coordinates in space of any cell to be established by means of three concentrations (x), (y) and (z). For tissues which have bilateral or radial symmetry, the number of such chemicals may be reduced to two. Thus, instead of as many recognition molecules being required as there are cells, the relationship of all of the cells in a homogenous tissue could in principle be specified by enzyme systems fabricating no more than three types of molecule for the gradients, and an appropriate recognition system of the sort already known to exist embedded in cell membranes. An alternative model favored by Goodwin, might have the gradient-forming chemical released in pulses so that it showed temporal as well as spatial variance. Such models obviously represent an enormous economy for the system, and could explain the aggregation properties of the retinal cells in experiments of the Gaze type.

Simple extension of this principle would allow the matching of retinal cells, lateral geniculate or optic tectal cells, for all that would be required would be the setting up of a gradient in the tectum which matched that of the retina; presumably a third matching gradient in the visual cortex would map the projections from the geniculate. When the optic nerve of the frog is cut it grows back along the pathway to the tectum by following the gradient; once in the tectal region its axons spread out across it and make synaptic contact, guided by the chemical coordinates of the concentration gradient. Such a system might not provide absolute specificity of recognition – but then the evidence of the Sperry experiments does not require that such absolute specificity occur. Although the behavioral response shows that the fibers grow back into *approximately* the right region of the map, a latitude of a few thousand cells in millions cannot be detected in this way.

Gradients can thus provide a mechanism whereby the brain's specific wiring system can be achieved. But in postulating them we have also made the concession—and an undoubtedly legitimate one— that even this phenomenon of specificity, striking though it is, is specificity only in a macroscopic sense; the area of uncertainty extends to a number of cells which is only small when matched against the really astronomically large number present within the system as a whole.

Glossary

A	Ablation	*Surgical destruction of part of the brain*
	Absolute refractory period	*The period after impulse propagation during which a nerve fiber is incapable of carrying a second impulse*
	Acetylcholine	*A transmitter substance liberated at synapses or neuromuscular junctions in the propagation of nerve impulses*
	Acetylcholinesterase	*Enzyme which breaks down acetylcholine at a post-synaptic membrane*
	Action potential	*Localized transient change in electrical potential across a neuronal membrane, which marks the passage of an impulse*
	Adipsia	*Cessation of drinking, e.g. following lesion of hypothalamic feeding center*
	Adrenalin	*Hormone secreted by the adrenal glands, and transmitter substance of the sympathetic nervous system*
	Afferent	*Conveying toward; e.g. of nerve impulses into the central nervous system*
	All-or-none law	*Signifies presence of threshold of reaction strength which must be exceeded before full response of invariant strength occurs; pertains to induction of the action potential in nerve cells*
	Alpha waves	EEG *pattern when the brain is "at rest" (i.e. not responding to sensory inputs), showing regular waves of large amplitude (see Electroencephalogram)*
	Amino acid	*Organic compound, twenty varieties of which constitute the primary components of proteins*
	Amphioxus	*Small chordate sea-animal; primitive ancestor of vertebrates*
	Amygdala	*Brain center, part of limbic system, thought to be associated with emotions of fear and aggressiveness*
	Aphagia	*Cessation of eating, e.g. following lesion of hypothalamic feeding center*
	Aphasia	*General name for psychological disorders of speech*
	Aplysia	*An invertebrate marine organism, sometimes known as "sea hare" or "sea slug"*
	Archicortex	*Phylogenetically older region of cerebral cortex which includes the limbic system*
	Ascending reticular activating system	*Diffuse net of cells in brain stem concerned with attention, sleep and wakefulness*
	Association areas	*Regions of the neocortex not concerned with primary sensory analysis, but having a secondary integrative rôle*
	Autonomic nervous system	*System of nerves running to smooth muscles or glands, controlling self-regulating activities like digestion and circulation. Divided into sympathetic and para-sympathetic systems*
	Axon	*The long process of a neuron which conducts impulses away from the cell body*
B	Behaviorist	*Adherent of the school of psychology known as Behaviorism, which, under a rigid methodology, considers only the measurable components of behavior, like stimulus and response (hence S-R theory) and treats concepts like consciousness, freewill, etc. as superfluous*
	Bilaterally symmetrical	*Consisting of two halves, each of which is the mirror-image of the other*
	Blood-brain barrier	*Diffusion barrier, of uncertain origin, between capillaries and brain cells, restricting uptake of substances from the blood stream*
	Brain stem	*Central core of brain or "stalk" to which other structures are attached; includes medulla and ascending reticular activating system*

C	Cannabis	*Hashish, marijuana, hemp, grass, shit, weed; a tropical plant smoked for its intoxicating effects*
	Central nervous system (CNS)	*Central aggregation of nerve tissue which in vertebrates forms the brain and spinal cord*
	Centrifugation	*High-speed rotation for the generation of strong centrifugal forces; used in the separation of subcellular components*
	Cerebellum	*Brain region originating as outgrowth of hindbrain; particularly concerned with coordination of motor activity*
	Cerebrospinal fluid	*Fluid derived from blood, filling the cavities of the brain and spinal cord and between the membranes (meninges) covering the brain*
	Cerebrum	*Brain region originating as bilateral swelling of forebrain and ultimately forming the cerebral hemispheres, the largest brain structures in mammals, concerned with association and coordination of nerve impulses and, in humans, thought and intelligence*
	Chemoreceptors	*Specialized nerve endings responsive to chemical stimuli; as in taste and smell*
	Chemotaxis	*Motility, especially in bacteria and protozoa, induced by a chemical gradient*
	Cholinesterase	*Members of class of enzymes which break down choline esters; e.g. acetylcholinesterase*
	Chordates	*Phylum of animals having a primitive dorsal nerve cord, or notochord*
	Circadian rhythm	*Endogenous rhythmic change in an organism occurring with an approximate periodicity of twenty-four hours*
	CNS	*See Central nervous system*
	Coelenterates	*Phylum of animals with simple saclike body; e.g. sponges, jelly-fish*
	Conditioned reflex	*Modified reflex in which the typical response is elicited by a new stimulus, usually as a result of experience*
	Cones	*Specialized, light-sensitive cells in the retina, having a cone-shaped outer segment*
	Corpus callosum	*Sheet of white matter between the cerebral hemispheres composed of myelinated fibers crossing from one side to the other*
	Cortex	*Superficial layer of tissue—usually pertaining to that part of the cerebrum which is rich in nerve-cell bodies and synapses*
	Curare	*Plant extract which antagonizes acetylcholine action by competitively binding to its membrane receptors; causes muscle paralysis*
	Cytoplasm	*Cell material, including membranes, organelles and fluid, but excluding the nucleus*
D	Delta waves	*See Electroencephalogram*
	Dendrites	*Branched processes of neurons which synapse with axons and receive impulses*
	Dendritic spines	*Subterminal projections on dendrite processes forming synapses with axon terminals*
	Depolarization	*Full or partial extinction of the resting electrical potential across a nerve cell membrane; if a certain threshold level is exceeded it will become propagated down the axon as a nerve impulse*
	Differentiation	*Process of change during the development of a cell*
	DNA	*Desoxyribonucleic acid, the genetic material of the cell, located in the nucleus*
	Dopamine	*Derivative of l-Dopa and putative synaptic transmitter*
E	ECT	*See Electroconvulsive therapy*
	EEG	*See Electroencephalogram*
	Efferent	*Proceeding away from; e.g. nerves carrying impulses from the central nervous system to effectors*

Eidetic imagery	*Process of memory showing an unusual capacity for assimilating perceived events with precision and detail ("photographic memory")*
Electro convulsive therapy (ECT)	*The application of a strong but brief electrical current across the brain, through electrodes applied at the sides of the skull; short convulsive muscular contractions accompany the process which is used to relieve some forms of depression*
Electrode–stimulating and recording	*Electrical conductor used to convey externally generated impulses to chosen brain areas, or, in an alternative form, for recording internal electrical changes, for example in response to stimulation in other regions*
Electroencephalogram (EEG)	*The recording of electrical brain patterns through electrodes placed on the skull; records include such characteristic waveforms as alpha, delta, etc*
Enzyme	*Member of a class of protein molecules which considerably accelerate the rates of biochemical reactions*
Epithelial cells	*Type of cell forming body surfaces; e.g. lining respiratory and other passages and forming the skin*
EPSP	*See Excitatory post-synaptic potential*
Ethology	*The study of animal behavior in its natural surroundings*
Euglena	*Microscopic single-celled organism, common in ponds and ditches*
Evoked potential	*Neural activity resulting from applied stimulation, e.g. by an implanted electrode*
Excitability	*General capacity of cells to respond to irritation; highly enhanced in neurons and receptors*
Excitatory post-synaptic potential (EPSP)	*Hyperpolarization of the post–synaptic membrane; the transient depolarization at a post–synaptic membrane which signifies the arrival there of a quantum of transmitter substance*
Excitatory transmitter	*Transmitter substance which, when liberated at a synapse, produces a depolarization at the post–synaptic membrane and which may result in a propagated impulse*
Exteroceptors	*Nerve endings specialized for the detection of stimuli impinging from outside the organism; e.g. light, sound*
Extracellular spaces	*Fluid-filled areas between neighboring cells*

F	Frequency	*Rate of passage of impulses per unit time*
	Frontal lobe	*Anterior region of cerebral hemispheres*

G	G Agents	*Nerve gases suspected of blocking synaptic transmission*
	GABA	*See Gamma-amino-butyric acid*
	Gamma-amino-butyric acid (GABA)	*An important brain metabolite and putative synaptic transmitter*
	Ganglion	*Small aggregation of nerve-cell bodies in the peripheral and autonomic nervous systems*
	Gestalt	*School of psychology chiefly concerned with perception and the organization of mental processes in relation to patterns of sensory stimuli*
	Glia	*Cell type constituting the supportive tissue of vertebrate central nervous systems*
	Glucoreceptors	*Hypothetical neurons in the hypothalamus specialized for detecting changes in glucose concentration in the circulating fluids*
	Glutamate	*Important metabolite of brain and putative synaptic transmitter*

H	Habituation	*Gradual adaptation to an irritation which, in nerve cells, is signaled by a cessation or reduction in the generation of nerve impulses*
	Hallucinogens	*Class of drugs which have the capacity for evoking hallucinations or related perceptual distortions; also called psychedelics*

	Hippocampus	Brain region situated in the temporal lobe of the cerebral hemispheres, having a prime, but unknown, rôle in memory formation
	Hologram	Stored image on a photographic plate in diffuse form, such that any portion of the plate can be used to reproduce the image, though diminishing size decreases the clarity of the image
	Homeostasis	General capacity of living organisms to adjust to a chemical or physical stress so as to preserve a stable activity and composition
	Hydra	Minute organism common in ponds and ditches, member of the phylum coelenterata
	Hyperphagia	Compulsive and continuous ingestion of food, e.g. following lesion of the hypothalamic satiety center
	Hyperpolarization	An increase in the resting electrical potential across a nerve-cell membrane
	Hypothalamus	Brain region, originating as an outgrowth from the floor and sides of the forebrain, known to contain centers regulating homeostatic mechanisms associated with heat, thirst, satiety, sex, pain and pleasure and emotions of rage and fear
I	Imprinting	Process in which newly hatched birds acquire a strong preference for a prominent moving object
	Inhibitory post-synaptic potential (IPSP)	An increase in the resting electrical potential across a post-synaptic membrane signifying the arrival of a quantum of inhibitory transmitter substance
	Inhibitory transmitter	Member of a class of transmitters which, when liberated at the synapse, increases the resting electrical potential of the post-synaptic membrane, rendering it less susceptible to a depolarization of threshold level
	Instrumental conditioning	A type of learning in which an animal acquires an association between a manipulation and some reward
	Interneurons	Small intercommunicating neurons connecting major pathways; particularly numerous in the cerebral cortex
	Ions	Charged particles generated from atoms or molecules by the loss or acquisition of electrons; important in neurons as a source of electrical potential
	Iontophoresis	Application of experimental solutions into tissues, driven by an electrical current
	IPSP	See Inhibitory post-synaptic potential
L	Latent learning	A type of learning in which passive association of stimuli occurs without the existence of any tangible reward
	Lateral geniculate body	Brain region of the ascending optic pathway located in the thalamus and receiving inputs from the optic nerve
	Learning	General term for a category of changes in an organism whereby behavior becomes modified, other than by drugs or fatigue
	Lesions	Tissue damage which may result from disease or trauma, or may be experimentally applied
	Leucotomy	Surgical severing of tracts of white matter in the brain
	Limbic system	An evolutionarily ancient part of the brain concerned with emotions and instinctive behavior
	Lysergic acid diethylamide (LSD)	A hallucinogenic drug
M	MAO	See Monoamine oxidase
	Marijuana	See Cannabis
	Medulla oblongata	A part of the brain stem; ending of the spinal cord
	Membrane	In neurobiology, two main types, those at cell boundaries and those within the cell, both very important in brain function

	Microelectrode	*A very fine glass capillary, filled with a conducting solution; can be inserted into cell bodies or axons*
	Mitochondria	*Organelles found in all animal cells, concerned with energy transformation*
Monoamine oxidase (MAO)		*An enzyme which breaks down transmitters such as noradrenalin*
	Motor cortex	*The part of the cerebrum concerned with movement and coordination*
	Myelin	*The fatty substance which surrounds axons and acts as an insulation*

N	Neocortex	*Cortical area responsible, in mammals, for coordination and for higher mental abilities*
	Nerve fibers	*See Axon*
	Nerve gas	*Chemical warfare agent which poisons by blocking synaptic transmission*
	Nerve net	*A primitive form of nervous system found especially in animals like hydra*
	Nerve tracts	*Concentrations of parallel nerve axons running through the body*
Neuromuscular junction		*The synapse where motor nerves contact a muscle fibril*
	Neuron	*A nerve cell*
	Neurosis	*Functional disorder of the nervous system apparently without organic disease*
	Noradrenaline	*A transmitter substance of the sympathetic nervous system*
	Notochord	*Cartilagenous rod that, in primitive chordates and in embryos, is the precursor of the spinal column*
Nucleus (of the cell)		*The central dark-staining organelle concerned with control of cell function; contains the genetic material*

O	Occipital cortex	*Posterior part of the cerebrum, contains area of brain concerned with vision*
	Occipital lobe	*Posterior lobe of cerebrum, merely an anatomical division and not a functionally discrete area*
	Olfactory bulbs	*Interior lobes of the brain concerned with sense of smell*
	Ontogeny	*Development of an individual, life history, as distinct from phylogeny – the evolutionary development of a species*
Operational thinking		*Hypothetical final stage in the development of thought; Piagetian concept*
	Optic nerve	*The long nerve leading from the rear of the eye to the brain*
	Optic tectum	*Roof of the posterior part of the cerebrum; concerned with visual processes, especially in lower chordates*

P	Palaeocortex	*An evolutionarily early region of the cortex*
	Paradoxical sleep	*Rapid eye movement sleep; a deep, dreaming stage of sleep*
	Paramœcium	*A unicellular freshwater animal, swims by beating of movable cilia*
	Paraplegia	*A bilateral paralysis of the body*
Parasympathetic nervous system		*One of the two parts of the autonomic nervous system*
	Parietal lobe	*Dorso-lateral area of the cerebrum*
	Parkinsonism	*Disease affecting certain nerve tracts in the brain producing a disabling tremor*
	Peptide	*Short chain of amino acids*
Peripheral nervous system		*All the nervous system not included in the brain or spinal cord*
	Permeability	*A measure of the porosity of a membrane to molecules*
	Phenylketonuria	*A genetically determined inability to metabolize the amino acid phenylalanine from the blood; results in severe mental retardation unless treated*
	Phototropism	*Moving either towards (positive) or away from (negative) the light, e.g. moths*

Phylogeny   *The evolutionary relationships of a particular species*

Pineal gland   *A dorsally located region of the midbrain of obscure function*

Pituitary   *A gland of great importance, in the base of the thalamus; secretes hormones which regulate the levels of many other hormones in the bloodstream*

Planaria   *Primitive flatworms having a simple ladder-shaped nervous system*

Plasticity   *The phenomenon of brain function and structure being changed by experience*

Polarization   *The phenomenon in which a net difference in electrical charge is generated across a membrane*

Pons   *Part of the hindbrain just ventral to the cerebellum*

Preconceptual representation   *A Piagetian term for a stage in cognitive development*

Progesterone   *Hormone concerned with pregnancy, produced by the corpora lutea of the ovary*

Proprioceptors   *Internal sense organs such as stretch receptors in the intestinal wall*

Protein   *Long molecules consisting of chains of amino acids joined by peptide linkages*

Psychedelics   *See Hallucinogens*

Psychochemical   *Class of substances which affect mental processes*

Psychosis   *A mental disorder, more severe than a neurosis, in which the sufferer "loses touch with" the real world*

Psychotomimetic   *Substance that has hallucinogenic effects*

Pyramidal cells   *Cortical cells involved in motor activity*

Q   Quantum (pl. quanta)   *In the neurabiological sense, the small unit quantity in which transmitter substance is released at the synapse. No smaller amount than a single quantum can be released; to fire the post-synaptic cell may require many thousands of quanta*

R   Rapid eye movement (REM) sleep   *See Paradoxical sleep*

Redundancy of function   *Many units which perform similar or closely related tasks, so that if one is destroyed, the task can still be performed by others*

Reflex arc   *The nerve pathway which passes from a sensory cell or organ, to the spinal cord and back, via a motor nerve to a muscle*

Refractory period   *The period necessary for the repolarization of the nerve-cell membrane before another impulse can pass*

Regeneration   *The ability of some animals to grow replacement organs for those lost by injuries, etc.*

Resting membrane potential   *The electrical imbalance that exists across a normal living cell membrane, -70 to $100\,mV$ negative to the interior*

Reticular formation   *See Ascending reticular activating system*

Retina   *The inner rear surface of the eye; consists of light-sensitive cells*

Ribonucleic acid (RNA)   *Intermediate macromolecule involved in transfer of information from DNA to protein*

Ribosomes   *Small organelles found on the endoplasmic reticulum, responsible for information transfer from RNA into protein*

RNA polymerase   *The enzyme necessary for the RNA molecule to be formed from precursors*

Rods   *White-light-sensitive cells in the retina*

S   Schizophrenia   *A "mental disease"; a form of psychosis*

Sedative   *Having the property of calming, soothing bodily or mental pain or excitement*

Semi-permeable membrane	*A membrane that is only permeable to certain small molecules*
Serotonin	*A transmitter substance found especially in the hypothalamus and midbrain*
Sodium pump	*The mechanism by which the cell maintains a membrane potential*
Specificity	*Used in this book to denote the "wired-in", unmodifiable aspects of brain activity*
Split brain	*A brain divided surgically into right and left halves so that each half can be trained and tested independently*
Summation	*The phenomenon where a number of small post-synaptic potentials add together to cause depolarization of the post-synaptic neuron*
Sympathetic nervous system	*A part of the autonomic nervous system*
Synapse	*The point where neurons communicate*
Synaptic vesicle	*The pre-synaptic membrane is backed by a capsule which contains sacs of transmitter substances; these sacs are the synaptic vesicles*

T	Telencephalon	*The forebrain; consists of olfactory bulbs and cerebrum*
	Temporal lobe, temporal cortex	*Part of the cerebrum, lateral and frontal regions*
	Thalamus	*Part of the brain below the cerebrum – a coordination area*
	Threshold	*The level at which a depolarization is of just-sufficient magnitude to cause an action potential in an axon*
	Thyroxin	*A hormone produced by the thyroid gland*
	Tranquilizer	*A drug which calms and quietens states of mental agitation*
	Transmitter substances	*Substances released into the synaptic cleft to inhibit or excite the post-synaptic membrane (see Ecitatory transmitter and Inhibitory transmitter)*

V	V Agents	*Class of nerve gases; among the most toxic chemicals known to man*
	Ventricles	*The hollow, fluid-filled spaces within the brain*
	Visual cortex	*The area at the back of the cerebrum responsible for interpretation of signals from the retinae*

References and Notes

1 The development of the brain sciences

1 Some of these points are discussed in the final chapter of ROSE, H. and ROSE, S., *Science and Society*, London : Allen Lane, 1969, and will be further amplified in a forthcoming work by the same authors, tentatively titled *Ideology and the Natural Sciences*.

2 For instance ECCLES, J. C., *The Neurophysiological Basis of Mind*, London : Clarendon Press, 1953, and *Facing Reality*, New York : Springer Verlag, 1970 ; KOESTLER, A. and SMYTHIES, J. R. (eds.), *Beyond Reductionism*, London : Hutchinson & Co. Ltd., 1969 ; A. ROSENBLUETH, *Mind and Brain*, Cambridge, Mass. : The M.I.T. Press, 1970.

3 The best-known exponent of this type of viewpoint is undoubtedly DESMOND MORRIS. See for instance, MORRIS, D., *The Naked Ape*, London : Jonathan Cape, Ltd., 1968, and *The Human Zoo*, London : Jonathan Cape, Ltd., 1970. But it is also expressed by other ethologists, e.g. LORENZ, K., *On Aggression*, London : Methuen & Co., Ltd., 1966 ; EIBL-EIBESFELT, I., *Ethology, the Study of Behaviour*, London : Holt, Reinhart & Winston Ltd., 1970 ; RUSSELL, C. and RUSSELL, W. M. S., *Violence, Monkey and Man*, London : Macmillan & Co. Ltd., 1968 ; and journalists, e.g. ARDREY, R., *The Social Contract*, London : William Collins Sons & Co. Ltd., 1970.

4 E.g. SUTHERLAND, N. S., "Machines like Men", *Science Journal*, 1968. For a somewhat less extreme position, see MICHIE, D., *Nature* 228 (1970) 717–22; and "Artificial Intelligence", *New Society*, 26 August 1971; WIENER, N., *The Human Use of Human Beings*, London : Sphere Books Ltd., 1968;

ASHBY, W. R., *Design for a Brain*, London : Chapman and Hall, Ltd., 1960; McCANN, G. D., *Science* 148 (1965) 1565–71; PASK, G. A., "A Cybernetic Model for Some Types of Learning and Mentation", London : *Systems Research* pamphlet, 1966.

5 BERKELEY, G., *Principles of Human Knowledge*, reprinted by Fontana, 1962.

6 This view of Lévi-Strauss's concerns derives not from a direct reading, which, I fear, has been beyond me, but from the account given by LEACH, E., *Lévi-Strauss*, London : Fontana, 1970.

7 CHOMSKY, N., *Language and Mind*, New York : Harcourt, Brace & World, 1968.

8 This view is prevalent in much of the writing of the underground press. *It, Oz* and *Frendz* magazines have all expressed it in their own particular styles. For a more coherent case, see MARCUSE, H., *One-Dimensional Man*, Routledge & Kegan Paul, Ltd., 1964; NUTTALL, J., *Bomb Culture*, London : Paladin, 1968; ROSZAK, T., *The Making of a Counter-Culture*, London : Faber & Faber Ltd., 1970.

9 These terms are used in the sense adopted by ARTHUR KOESTLER, for example in *The Ghost in the Machine*, London : Hutchinson & Co. Ltd., 1967, and *Beyond Reductionism*, op. cit. This is also the sense of LEWIS, J. and TOWERS, B., in *Naked Ape or Homo Sapiens*, London : Garnstone Press Ltd., 1969. The sense in which the term "reductionism" is used has changed slightly in recent years. It is only this recent usage which concerns me here. For a classic of modern reductionism see MONOD, J., *Le hasard et la nécessité*, Paris : Editions de Seuil, 1970; for a rather naïvely reductionist viewpoint on

brain mechanisms, TAYLOR,J.,
"The Shadow of the Mind",
New Scientist, 30 September 1971.
The classics of holism in biology
include SMUTS,J.C., Holism and
Evolution, London: Macmillan &
Co. Ltd., 1926; SCHRODINGER,E.,
What is Life?, Cambridge:
Cambridge University Press, 1944;
ELSASSER,W.M., Atom and
Organism: A New Approach to
Theoretical Biology, Princeton, New
Jersey: Princeton University Press,
1966. See also KREBS,H.A.,
Perspectives in Biology and Medicine
14 (1971) 448–57; OLBŤ,R.,
Journal of the History of Biology 4
(1971) 119–48.

10 See, for example, the collection
of papers edited by SMYTHIES,J.R.,
Brain and Mind, Routledge &
Kegan Paul, Ltd., 1965.

11 This point is made forcibly by
the authors of Naked Ape or Homo
Sapiens, op. cit.

12 This is a version of the "identity
hypothesis". See PLACE,U.T.,
"Is Consciousness a Brain Process?",
British Journal of Psychology 47
(1956), and, for a critique,
BELOFF,J., in Brain and Mind,
op. cit.

13 There was a very nice example
of this provided by a character in
PETER BROOKS' film Tell Me Lies
(a statement about the Vietnam
War). The character was shown
lying on a bed explaining the
virtues of television monitors, in
which one could "watch oneself
watching oneself watching
oneself . . ."

14 A good historical set of readings
on this topic is provided in
VESEY,G.N.A. (ed.), Body and
Mind, London: George Allen &
Unwin Ltd., 1964.

15 A history of the nineteenth-
century debates over brain
mechanisms and particularly
localization of functions is provided
in YOUNG,R.M., Mind, Brain and
Adaptation in the 19th Century,
Oxford: Clarendon Press, 1970.

16 For a discussion of some of the
implications of metaphor in biology
see ROSE,S. and ROSE,H.,
Impact of Science on Society 21
(1971) 137–149.

17 BURNS,B.D., The Uncertain
Nervous System, London:
Arnold, 1968.

2 The human brain

1 Some of the material in this
chapter has been used, in different
form, as part of the Open
University Teaching Course "The
Biological Bases of Behaviour",
Unit 1, and I am grateful to my
colleagues in the course team, and
to Professors P.D.WALL and
A.N.DAVISON of London, and
Dr.G.HORN of Cambridge, who,
as external assessors to the Unit,
have improved it (and indirectly
this text) by their critical comments.

2 There is a very good introduction
to this anatomy in NOBACK,C.R.,
The Human Nervous System,
Maidenhead, Berkshire: McGraw-
Hill Publishing Co., Ltd., 1967;
for an "idiot's guide" to the brain,
see BREWER,C.V., The
Organization of the Central Nervous
System, London: William
Heinemann Ltd., 1962.

3 SPERRY,R., "The Great
Cerebral Commissure", Scientific
American, January 1964, reprinted in
CHALMERS,N.R., CRAWLEY,R.,
and ROSE,S.P.R. (eds.), The
Biological Bases of Behaviour,
London: Harper and Row Ltd.,
1971.

4 See YOUNG,R.M., Mind, Brain
and Adaptation in the 19th Century,
Oxford: Clarendon Press, 1970, for
a discussion of this theme.

5 This number is one of the
folklore items of neurobiology.
It is variously quoted as referring
to the number of neurons in the
cortex, the brain and the central
nervous system, and it is uncertain
what it is based upon. For a
quantitative account of the brain,
see BLINKOV,S.M. and
GLEZER,I.I., The Human Brain in
Figures and Tables, New York:
Plenum Press, 1968. For a more
idiosyncratic account, BOK,S.T.,
Histonomy of the Cerebral Cortex,
Amsterdam: Elsevier, 1959.

6 A pioneer in the application of
biochemical techniques to the brain
is undoubtedly H.McILWAIN,
whose book, Biochemistry and the

Central Nervous System, London: J. & A. Churchill, Ltd., has run through several editions, the most recent being 1972. See also ELLIOTT, K. A. C., PAGE, I. M. and QUASTEL, J. H. (eds.), *Neurochemistry*, London: A. Thomas and Co., 1962; and the three volumes of LAJTHA, A. (ed.), *Handbook of Neurochemistry*, New York: Plenum Press, 1968–71.

7 For reviews of this technique see ROSE, S. P. R., in *Applied Neurochemistry*, DAVISON, A. N. and DOBBING, J. (eds.), London: Blackwell Scientific Publications Ltd., 1968, and *Handbook of Neurochemistry*, op. cit.

8 An account of this episode occurs in the autobiography: CAJAL, S. R. y, *Recollections of My Life*, Cambridge, Mass.: The M.I.T. Press, 1966. For Cajal's illustrative powers, see CAJAL, S. R. y, *Histologie du système nerveux de l'homme et des vertébrés*, Madrid: Consejo Superior de Investigaciones Cientificas, 1952–5.

9 CRAGG, B. G., in *Applied Neurochemistry*, DAVISON, A. N. and DOBBING, J. (eds.), op. cit.

10 For review see WHITTAKER, V., in *Handbook of Neurochemistry*, Vol. II, LAJTHA, A. (ed.), New York: Plenum Press, 1969.

11 For a comprehensive bibliography of the glia, see *Neurosciences Research Program Bulletin* 2 (6) (1964).

12 For review see DOBBING, J., "Brain Cell Microenvironment", *Neurosciences Research Program Bulletin* 7 (4) (1969).

3 The electrical maze

1 SHERRINGTON, C., *The Integrative Action of the Nervous System*, Cambridge: Cambridge University Press, 1906.

2 A basic account of nerve membrane phenomena may be found in THOMPSON, R. F., *Foundations of Physiological Psychology*, London: Harper and Row, 1967; WALSH, E. G., *Physiology of the Nervous System*, London: Longmans, 1964. See also KATZ, B., "The Axon", *Scientific American*, reprinted in *The Biological Bases of Behaviour*, CHALMERS, N. R., CRAWLEY, R. and ROSE, S. P. R. (eds.), London: Harper and Row, 1971.

3 BURNS, B. D., *The Uncertain Nervous System*, London: Arnold, 1968.

4 ECCLES, J. C., *The Physiology of Synapses*, New York: Springer Verlag, 1964.

5 KATZ, B., *Nerve, Muscle and Synapse*, New York: McGraw-Hill, 1966.

6 The technique is described in the books of chapter 3, reference 2, and also by ECCLES, J. C., in *Scientific American*, January 1965, reprinted in *The Biological Bases of Behaviour*, op. cit.

7 The diagrams in the ECCLES article of chapter 3, reference 6, make just this (probably erroneous) point.

8 MARCHBANKS, R. M. and WHITTAKER, V., in *The Future of the Brain Sciences*, BOGOSCH, S. (ed.), New York: Plenum Press, 1969; MARCHBANKS, R. M., in *Compartmentation of Metabolism in the Nervous System*, BALÁZS, R. and CREMER, J. (eds.), London: Macmillan, 1973.

9 MILEDI, R., MOLINOFF, P. and POTTER, L. T., *Nature* 229 (1971) 554–7; DE ROBERTIS, E., *Science*, 171 (1971) 963–71.

10 PERRY ROBINSON, J., in *Chemical and Biological Warfare*, ROSE, S. P. R. (ed.), London: George G. Harrap & Co., Ltd., 1968.

11 LOFROTH, G., *New Scientist*, 6 November 1969.

12 ROSE, S. P. R., in *Applied Neurochemistry*, DAVISON, A. N. and DOBBING, J. (eds.), London: Blackwell and Scientific Publications Ltd., 1968.

13 These synapses are mainly in the cerebellum. For a discussion of their possible functional significance see MARR, D. J., *Journal of Physiology* 702 (1969) 437–70.

14 GREY, E. G., "The Synapse", *Science Journal*, May 1967, reprinted in *The Human Brain*, London: Paladin, 1972.

15 E.g. McEwen,B.S. and Grafstein,B., *Journal of Cell Biology* 38 (1968) 494–508; Karlsson,J.O and Sjöstrand,J., *Journal of Neurobiology* 2 (1971) 135–143; Ochs,S., Sabri,M.I. and Johnson,J., *Science* 163 (1969) 686–7.

16 E.g. Lajtha,A. and Toth,J., *Biochemical and Biophysical Research Communications* 23 (1966) 294–330. Waelsch,H., in *Neurochemistry*, Elliott,K.A.C., Page,I.H. and Quastel,J.H. (eds.), London: A. Thomas and Co., 1962. Richter,D., in *Neurochemistry*, op. cit.

4 The brain as a system

1 Some of the material in this chapter has been used, in different form, as part of the Open University Teaching Course "The Biological Bases of Behaviour", Unit 2, and I am grateful to my colleagues in the course team, and to Professors P.D.Wall and A.N.Davison of London and Dr.G.Horn of Cambridge, who, as external assessors to the Unit, have improved it (and indirectly this text) by their critical comments.

2 Bullock,T.H. and Horridge,G.A., *Structure and Function in the Nervous System of Invertebrates*, London: W.H. Freeman & Co. Ltd., 1965.

3 Degeneration techniques are described in greater detail in Thompson,R.F., *Foundations of Physiological Psychology*, London: Harper and Row, 1967.

4 Penfield,W. and Roberts,L., *Speech and Brain Mechanisms*, Princeton, N.J.: Princeton University Press, 1959.

5 E.g. Wiersma,C.A.G., in *Short Term Changes in Neural Activity Behaviour*, Horn,G. and Hinde,R.A. (eds.), Cambridge: Cambridge University Press, 1970; Kandel,E.R., Castellucci,V., Pinsker,M. and Kuppermann,I., in *Short Term Changes in Neural Activity and Behaviour*, op. cit.; Eisenstein,E.H., in *The Neurosciences: A Study Program*, Quarton,G.C., Melnechuk,T., and Schmitt,F.C. (eds.), New York: The Rockefeller University Press, 1969; Kandel,E.R. and Spencer,W.A., *Physiological Reviews* 48 (1968) 65–134.

6 Actually the priority of EEG recording is a matter of some dispute. An English doctor, Caton, is claimed to have measured some brain electrical activity at the end of the nineteenth century. For an account of this history see Stevens,L.A., *Explorers of the Brain*, New York: Alfred A. Knopf, Inc., 1971.

7 The party-trick criticism of the meaning of alpha waves is due to Dr.C.Evans at a Brain Research Association meeting. A more academic account is that given by Lippold,O., *Nature* 226 (1970) 616–8, and *New Scientist*, 12 March 1970.

8 Walter,W.G., *The Living Brain*, London: Penguin Books Limited, 1961.

9 E.g. John,E.R., *Mechanisms of Memory*, London: Academic Press Inc., Ltd., 1967; "Slow Electrical Phenomena in the CNS", *Neurosciences Research Program Bulletin* 7 (2) (1969); "Evoked Brain Potentials as Indicators of Sensory Information Processing", *Neurosciences Research Program Bulletin* 7 (3) (1969).

10 Bliss,T.V.P., Burns,B.D. and Uttley,A.M., *Journal of Physiology* 195 (1968) 339–67.

11 McIlwain,H. and Bachelard,H., *Biochemistry and the Central Nervous System*, London: J. & A. Churchill Ltd., 1972.

12 Sherrington,C., *Man on His Nature*, Cambridge: Cambridge University Press, 1963.

13 For discussion see Young,R.M., *Mind, Brain and Adaptation in the 19th Century*; Oxford: Clarendon Press, 1970. *Explorers of the Brain*, op. cit.; Bruner,J.S., Goodnow,J.J. and Austin,G.A., *A Study of Thinking*, New York: John Wiley & Sons, Inc., 1956.

14 Lashley,K.S., *Brain Mechanisms and Intelligence*, New York: Dover Publications, Inc., 1963.

15 GREGORY, R. L., in *Current Problems in Animal Behaviour*, THORPE, W. H. and ZANGWILL, O. L. (eds.), Cambridge: Cambridge University Press, 1961.

16 In his comments on the substance of this part of this chapter, when it was presented as Open University teaching material, Dr. Gabriel Horn's view was that I had been too pessimistic about the meaningfulness of interpretations to be drawn from these types of study. Valid data can, I am sure, be obtained; the question of its interpretation however, as with all other areas of neurobiology, remains open to conflict. Horn also makes the point, with which I concur, that it is not possible to strait-jacket *all* possible approaches to functional neurophysiology and neuroanatomy into a holist/reductionist dichotomy; some defy such classification. This is obviously true, but I believe that the distinction drawn is useful methodologically and in terms of epistemology.

17 MOUNTCASTLE, V., in *The Neurosciences: A Study Program*, op. cit.

18 GREGORY, R. L., *The Intelligent Eye*, London: George Weidenfeld and Nicolson Limited, 1970.

19 This account is derived primarily from that given in HORRIDGE, A., *Interneurons*, London: W. H. Freeman & Co. Ltd., 1968. But see also MACNICHOL, E. F., "Three Pigment Colour Vision", *Scientific American*, December 1964, reprinted in *The Biological Bases of Behaviour*, CHALMERS, N. R., CRAWLEY, R. and ROSE, S. P. R. (eds.), London: Harper and Row Ltd., 1971.

20 HUBEL, D., "The Visual Cortex of the Brain", *Scientific American*, November 1963, reprinted in *Biological Bases of Behaviour*, op. cit.

21 ECCLES, J. C., ITOH, M. and SZENTÁGOTHAI, J., *The Cerebellum as a Neuronal Machine*, New York: Springer-Verlag, 1967.

22 MARR, D., *Journal of Physiology* 202 (1969) 437–70; BLOMFIELD, S. and MARR, D., *Nature* 227 (1970) 1224–28.

5 The origins of nervous systems

1 Part of the discussion in this chapter owes much to the account given by HORRIDGE, A., in *Interneurons*, London: W. H. Freeman & Co. Ltd., 1968.

2 This account of the origin of life is based on the Oparin-Haldane model. See OPARIN, A. I., *The Chemical Origin of Life on Earth*, London: A. Thomas and Co., 1964; OPARIN, A. I. (ed.), *The Origin of Life on the Earth*, Oxford: Pergamon Press Ltd., 1959. Other accounts occur in KENYON, D. H. and STEINMAN, G., *Biochemical Predestination*, New York: McGraw-Hill, 1969, and ROSE, S. P. R., *The Chemistry of Life*, Harmondsworth, Middlesex: Penguin Books Limited, 1966.

3 ADLER, J., *Science* 166 (1969) 1588–97.

4 This point is particularly emphasized in *Interneurons*, op. cit.

5 For a nice account of hydra, see BUCHSBAUM, R., *Animals Without Backbones*, Harmondsworth, Middlesex: Penguin Books Limited, 1966; an account of the evolution of invertebrate nervous systems and behavior is given in *Biological Bases of Behaviour, Unit 3*, Bletchley: Open University Press, 1971. For a more detailed and more controversial view of the evolution and significance of hydra's nervous system, see LENTZ, T. L., *Primitive Nervous Systems*, New Haven, Conn.: Yale University Press, 1968.

6 BULLOCK, T. H. and HORRIDGE, G. A., *Structure and Function in the Nervous System of Invertebrates*, London: W. H. Freeman & Co. Ltd., 1965. See also *Primitive Nervous Systems*, op. cit.; ELLIOTT, M. C., *The Shape of Intelligence*, George Allen & Unwin Ltd., 1970, gives a rather breathless account.

7 BEST, J. B., "Protopsychology", *Scientific American*, February 1963.

8 CORNING, W. C. and FREED, S., *Nature* 219 (1968) 1227–9.

9 WILSON, E. O., *The Insect Societies*, Cambridge, Mass.: Harvard University Press, 1971.

10 LINDAUER, M., *Communication Among Social Bees*, Cambridge, Mass.: Harvard University Press, 1961. For other aspects of insect neurobiology see ROEDER, K. D., *Nerve Cells and Insect Behaviour*, Cambridge, Mass.: Harvard University Press, 1963.

11 YOUNG, J. Z., *A Model of the Brain*, Oxford: Clarendon Press, 1964; WELLS, M., *Brain and Behaviour in Cephalopods*, London: William Heinemann Ltd., 1962.

6 The evolution of brains and consciousness

1 For a general account of the evolution of the CNS in vertebrates see ROMER, A. S., *The Vertebrate Body*, London: W. B. Saunders Co. Ltd., 1970. For a simple version, ELLIOTT, H. C., *The Shape of Intelligence*, London: George Allen & Unwin Ltd., 1970. See also *Biological Bases of Behaviour, Unit 4*, Bletchley: Open University Press, 1971.

2 This proposed evolutionary pathway is suggested by GREGORY, R., in *The Intelligent Eye*, London: George Weidenfeld & Nicolson Limited, 1970. It would not, however, command universal assent among evolutionary biologists.

3 This type of description finds expression in, for example, *The Shape of Intelligence*, op. cit.

4 JERISON, H. J., *Science* 170 (1970) 224–5. See also BITTERMAN, M. E., "The Evolution of Intelligence", *Scientific American*, January 1965.

5 DOBBING, J., in "The Human Brain", *Science Journal*, May 1967, reprinted London: Paladin, 1972.

6 LORENZ, K. Z., *King Solomon's Ring*, London: Methuen & Co. Ltd., 1952; THORPE, W. H., *Learning and Instinct in Animals*, London: Methuen & Co. Ltd., 1963; BATESON, P. P. G., *Biological Review* 41 (1966) 177–220;

HINDE, R. A., *Animal Behaviour*, London: McGraw-Hill Publishing Co. Ltd., 1966.

7 THORPE, W. H., *Learning and Instinct in Animals*, op. cit.

8 STEINER, G., ICA lectures: *The Limits of Human Nature* (1972). To be published.

9 CHOMSKY, N., *Syntactic Structures*, New York: Humanities Press, Inc., 1957; CHOMSKY, N., in *The Biological Foundations of Language*, LENNENBERG, E. H. (ed.), Cambridge, Mass.: The M.I.T. Press, 1967. See also LENNENBERG, E. H., *New Directions in the Study of Language*, Cambridge, Mass.: The M.I.T. Press, 1964.

10 Personal communication from Aaron Cicourel. See also papers in OLDFIELD, R. C and MARSHALL, J. C. (eds.), *Language*, Harmondsworth, Middlesex: Penguin Books Limited, 1968.

11 SPERRY, R. W., "The Great Cerebral Commissure", *Scientific American*, January 1964, reprinted in *The Biological Bases of Behaviour*, CHALMERS, N. R., CRAWLEY, R. and ROSE, S. P. R. (eds.), London: Harper and Row Ltd., 1971. See also GESCHWIND, N., *Science* 170 (1970) 940–44; BRAIN, R., *Brain* 84 (1961) 145–66.

12 GARDNER, A. R. and GARDNER, B. T., *Science* 165 (1969) 664–69; PREMACK, D., *Science* 172 (1971) 808–22; PREMACK, D., *New Society*, 29 October 1970.

13 E.g. ECCLES, J. C., *Facing Reality*, New York: Springer-Verlag, 1970.

14 ADRIAN, E. D., in *Brain and Conscious Experience*, ECCLES, J. C. (ed.), New York: Springer-Verlag, 1966; MACKAY, D. M., "The Bankruptcy of Determinism", *New Scientist*, 2 July 1970; QUINTON, A., in *Brain and Mind*, SMYTHIES, J. R. (ed.), London: Routledge & Kegan Paul, Ltd., 1965.

15 But see *The Evolution of Intelligence*, op. cit., and papers by Lennenberg, op. cit.

7 The child's brain, and the adult's

1 In fact, both Einstein's and Lenin's brains were studied after their deaths, to little avail.

2 The excellent little book by MARSHALL, W. A., *Development of the Brain*, Edinburgh: Oliver & Boyd Ltd., 1968, gives a useful account of brain development. See also: WOLSTENHOLME, G. E. W. and O'CONNOR, M. (eds.), *Growth of the Nervous System*, London: J. & A. Churchill, Ltd., 1968; and JÍLEK, L. and TROJAN, S., *Ontogenesis of the Brain*, Prague: Charles University Press, 1968.

3 The figures for the glial/neuronal ratio are very varied. See BLINKOV, S. M. and GLEZER, I. I., *The Human Brain in Figures and Tables*, New York: Plenum Press, 1968; also GLEES, P. in *Compartmentation of Metabolism in the Nervous System*, BALÁZS, R. and CREMER, J. (eds.), London: Macmillan & Co. Ltd., 1972.

4 DOBBING, J. and SANDS, J., *Nature* 226 (1970) 639–40.

5 WINDLE, W. F., *Biology of Neuroglia*, London: A. Thomas and Co., 1968.

6 This description of the developmental sequence is given in RANSON, S. W. and CLARK, S. L., *The Anatomy of the Nervous System*, London: W. B. Saunders Co. Ltd., 1959.

7 *The Development of the Brain*, op. cit.

8 ALTMAN, J. and DAS, G. D., *Nature* 204 (1964) 1161–3.

9 GEBER, M. and DEAN, R. F. A., *Courrier* 6 (3) (1956); COLLIS, W. R. F. and JAMES, M., in *Malnutrition, Learning and Behaviour*, SCRIMSHAW, N. S. and GORDON, J. E. (eds.), Cambridge, Mass.: The M.I.T. Press, 1968.

10 PIAGET, J., *Language and Thought of the Child*, London: Routledge & Kegan Paul, Ltd., 1959; PIAGET, J., *Genetic Epistemology*, New York: Columbia University Press, 1970; RICHMOND, P. G., *An Introduction to Piaget*, Routledge & Kegan Paul, Ltd., 1970.

8 Specificity versus plasticity

1 This interpretation of his position, which puts him in the Cartesian camp, derives, for instance, from CHOMSKY, N., *Language and Mind*, New York: Harcourt, Brace & World, 1968.

2 For a discussion of this type of developmental pathway see WADDINGTON, C. H., in *Towards a Theoretical Biology*, WADDINGTON, C. H. (ed.), Edinburgh: Edinburgh University Press, 1968.

3 SPERRY, R. W. and HIBBERD, E., in *Growth of the Nervous System*, WOLSTENHOLME, G. E. W. and O'CONNOR, M. (eds.), London: J. & A. Churchill, Ltd., 1968; HUGHES, A. F. W., *Aspects of Neural Ontogeny*, London: Academic Press Inc. Ltd., 1968; WEISS, P. A., *Neurosciences Research Program Bulletin* 3 (5) (1965).

4 SPERRY, R. W., in discussion of his paper in *Growth of the Nervous System*, op. cit.

5 SZÉKELY, G., in *Growth of the Nervous System*, op. cit.; *Aspects of Neural Ontogeny*, op. cit.; GUTH, L., *Neurosciences Research Program Bulletin* 7 (1) (1969).

6 FELDMAN, J., GAZE, R. M. and WILSON, M., *Journal of Physiology* 198 (1968) 65–6.

7 DOBBING, J., in *Malnutrition, Learning and Behaviour*, SCRIMSHAW, N. S. and GORDON, J. E. (eds.), Cambridge, Mass.: The M.I.T. Press, 1968; "The Human Brain", *Science Journal*, May 1967, reprinted London: Paladin, 1972.

8 These figures are quoted from KEPPEL, F., in *Malnutrition, Learning and Behaviour*, op. cit.

9 CRAVIOTO, J. and DE LICARDIE, E. R., in *Malnutrition, Learning and Behaviour*, op. cit. Also CRAVIOTO, J., in *IBRO-UNESCO Symposium on the Brain Sciences and Human Behaviour*, 1968.

10 TOWNSEND, P. (ed.), *The Concept of Poverty*, London: Heinemann, 1970.

11 KRECH, D., ROSENZWEIG, M. R. and BENNETT, E. L., *Journal*

of Comparative and Physiological Psychology 53 (1960) 509–119; *Physiology and Behaviour* 1 (1963) 99–108; *Journal of Comparative and Physiological Psychology* 57 (1964) 440–1; ROSENZWEIG, M.R., LOVE W. and BENNETT, E.L., *Physiology and Behaviour* 3 (1965) 819–25.

12 ROSE, S.P.R., *Brain Research* 38 (1972) 171–8.

13 HARLOW, H.F., ROWLAND, G.L. and GRIFFIN, G.A., *Psychiatry Research Reports* 19 (1964) 116–28; MITCHELL, G.D., RAYMOND, E.J., RUPPENTHAL, G.C. and HARLOW, H.F., *Psychology Reports* 18 (1966) 567–75; HARLOW, H.F. and SUOMI, S.J., *Proceedings of the National Academy of Sciences of the U.S.* 68 (1971) 1534–8.

14 ZAMENHOF, S., VAN MARTHENS, E. and GRAUEL, L. *Science* 172 (1971) 850–1. See also DENNENBERG, V.H. and ROSENBERG, K.M., *Nature* 216 (1967) 549–50. For review, see ROSE, S.P.R. in *Race Culture and Intelligence*, RICHARDSON, K., SPEARS, D. and RICHARDS, M. (eds.), Harmondsworth, Middlesex: Penguin Books Limited, 1972.

15 See HIRSCH, J., in *The Biological Bases of Behaviour*, CHALMERS, N.R., CRAWLEY, R. and ROSE, S.P.R. (eds.), London: Harper & Row Ltd., 1971; PICKENS, D.K., *Eugenics and The Progressives*, Nashville, Tenn.: Vanderbilt University Press, 1968; GASMAN, D., *The Scientific Origins of National Socialism*, London: Macdonald & Co. Ltd., 1971.

16 JENSEN, A.R., "Environment, Heredity and Intelligence", *Harvard Educational Review*, 1969; EYSENCK, H.J., *Race, Intelligence and Education*, London: Temple Smith, 1971.

17 Pointed out in discussion at meeting on Race, Intelligence and Education organized by the Brain Research Association and the Cambridge Society for Social Responsibility in Science. Reprinted in *The Biological Bases of Behaviour*, op. cit. See also "Science, Heredity and I.Q.", *Harvard Educational Review*, 1969. See also

FRIEDRICHS, R., *The Impact of Social and Democratic Factors upon Scientific Judgement: The "Jensen Thesis" as Appraised by Members of the APA*. In Preparation, 1971.

18 For a detailed discussion of these issues see *Race, Culture and Intelligence*, op. cit., and the Brain Research Association/Cambridge Society for Social Responsibility in Science discussion, op. cit.

19 BODMER, W.F. and CAVELLI SFORZA, L.L., *Scientific American* 223 (4) (1970); BODMER, W., in *Race, Culture and Intelligence*, op. cit.

20 ROSE, S.P.R., in *Race, Culture and Intelligence*, op. cit.

21 REX, J., in *Race, Culture and Intelligence*, op. cit.

22 Scottish Council for Research in Education, *The Trend of Scottish Intelligence*, London: London University Press, 1949; Scottish Council for Research in Education, *Social Implications of the 1947 Scottish Mental Survey*, London: London University Press, 1953.

23 SKODAK, M. and SKEELS, H.M., *Journal of Genetic Psychology* 75 (1949) 85–97; SKEELS, H.M., UPDEGRAFF, R., WELLMAN, B.L. and WILLIAMS, H.M., *University of Iowa Studies in Child Welfare* 15 (1938) 10–11.

9 Memory – the central store

1 LESSING, DORIS, *Briefing for a Descent into Hell*, London: Jonathan Cape Ltd., 1971, New York: Knopf, 1971.

2 HUNTER, I.M.L., *Memory*, Harmondsworth, Middlesex: Penguin Books Limited, 1957; ADAMS, J.A., *Human Memory*, Maidenhead, Berkshire: McGraw-Hill Publishing Co., Ltd., 1967; KIMBLE, D.P. (ed.), *The Anatomy of Memory*, Palo Alto, Calif.: Science & Behavior Books, Inc., 1964; JOHN, E.R., *Mechanisms of Memory*, London: Academic Press Inc. Ltd., 1967.

3 e.g. SCHMIII, F.P., *Macromolecular Specificity and Biological Memory*, Cambridge, Mass.:: The M.I.T. Press, 1962

4 HEBB, D.O., *The Organization of Behavior*, New York: John Wiley & Sons, Inc., 1949.

5 RITCHIE RUSSELL, W., *Brain, Memory and Learning*, Oxford: Clarendon Press, 1959 and *The Transient Amnesias*, Oxford: Clarendon Press, 1971.

6 BOOTH, D.A., *Psychological Bulletin* 68 (1967) 149–77.

7 McGAUGH, J.L., *Science* 153 (1966) 1351–8.

8 This point is made by several of the contributors to *Short Term Changes in Neural Activity and Behaviour*, HORN, G. and HINDE, R.A. (eds.), Cambridge: Cambridge University Press, 1970.

9 KANDEL, E.R., "Nerve Cells and Behaviour", *Scientific American*, July 1970.

10 VINOGRADOVA, O., in *Short Term Processes in Neural Activity and Behaviour*, op. cit.

11 LAJTHA, A. and TOTH, J., *Biochemical and Biophysical Research Communications* 23 (1966) 294–8.

12 ZEMP, J.W., WILSON, J.E. and GLASSMAN, E., *Proceedings of the National Academy of Sciences of the U.S.* 58 (1967) 1120–5; ZEMP, J.W., WILSON, J.E., SCHLESINGER, K., BOGGAN, W.O. and GLASSMAN, E., *Proceedings of the National Academy of Sciences of the U.S.* 55 (1966) 1423–31; GLASSMAN, E., in *Macromolecules and Behaviour*, ANSELL, G.B. and BRADLEY, P. (eds.), London: Macmillan & Co., Ltd., 1973.

13 BATESON, P.P.G., in *Short Term Processes in Neural Activity and Behaviour*, op. cit.

14 ROSE, S.P.R., BATESON, P.P.G. and HORN, G., in *Macromolecules and Behaviour*, op. cit.; BATESON, P.P.G., HORN, G. and ROSE, S.P.R., *Brain Research*. In Press (1972).

15 HYDÉN, H., in *Macromolecules and Behaviour*, op. cit.; YANAGIHARA, T. and HYDÉN, H., *Experimental Neurology* 31 (1971) 151–64; HYDÉN, H. and LANGE, P.W., *Science* 159 (1968) 1370–3; HYDÉN, H., in *The Neurosciences: A Study Program*, QUARTON, G.C., MELNECHUK, T. and SCHMITT, F.O. (eds.), New York: Rockefeller University Press, 1967.

16 CRAGG, B.G., *Nature* 215 (1967) 251–3; CRAGG, B.G., *Brain Research* 13 (1969) 53–67; ROSE, S.P.R., *Nature* 215 (1967) 253–5; RICHARDSON, K. and ROSE, S.P.R., *Brain Research*. In Press (1972).

17 BENNETT, E.L., ROSENZWEIG, M.R. and HEBERT, M., *Proceedings of the Third Meeting of the International Society for Neurochemistry*, Budapest, 1971.

18 AGRANOFF, B., in *The Neurosciences: A Study Program*, op. cit., and *Macromolecules and Behaviour*, op. cit.

19 COHEN, H.D., ERVIN, E. and BARONDES, S.H., *Science* 154 (1966) 1557–8.

20 GLASKY, A.J. and SIMON, L.N., *Science* 151 (1966) 702–3; BEACH, J. and KIMBLE, D.P., *Science* 155 (1967) 698–701; BURNS, J.T., HOUSE, R.F., FENSCH, F.C. and MILLER, T.G., *Science* 155 (1967) 849–51; FREY, P.W. and POLIDORA, V.J., *Science* 155 (1967) 1281–2.

21 SHERRINGTON, C.S., *The Integrative Action of the Nervous System*, Cambridge: Cambridge University Press, 1906.

22 LASHLEY, K.S., *Symposia of the Society for Experimental Biology* 4 (1950) 454–82; and LASHLEY, K.S., *Brain Mechanisms and Learning*, New York: Dover Publications, Inc., 1963.

23 PENFIELD, W. and ROBERTS, L., *Speech and Brain Mechanisms*, Princeton, N.J.: Princeton University Press, 1959.

24 METHERELL, A.F., "Acoustical Holography", *Scientific American*, April 1969.

25 VALENTINE, J.D., *Nature* 220 (1968) 474–5; CHOPPING, P.T., *Nature* 217 (1968) 781–2; LONGUET-HIGGINS, H.C., *Nature* 217 (1968) 104–6; GABOR, D., *Nature* 217 (1968) 584.

26 E.g. HYDÉN, H., in *The Cell*, Vol. IV, BRACHET, J. and MIRSKY, A. (eds.), London: Academic Press, Inc., 1960; *Macromolecular Specificity and Biological Memory*, op. cit.;

MEKLER, L.B., *Nature* 215 (1967) 481–4; for critical review, see ROSE, S.P.R., in *Short Term Processes in Neural Activity and Behaviour*, op. cit.

27 These experiments are reviewed, favorably, in CORNING, W.C. and RATNER, S.C. (eds.), *Chemistry of Learning*, New York: Plenum Press, 1967, and somewhat less favorably in BYRNE, W.C. (ed.), *Molecular Approaches to Learning and Memory*, London: Academic Press, Inc., 1970.

28 JACOBSON, A.L., BABICH, F.R., BUBASH, S. and JACOBSON, A., *Science* 150 (1965) 636–7.

29 BYRNE, W.L. and twenty-two others, *Science* 155 (1966) 849–51.

30 UNGAR, G., in *Macromolecules and Behaviour*, op. cit.; for critique see ROSE, S.P.R., in *Short Term Changes in Neural Activity and Behaviour*, op. cit.

31 CAMERON, D.E., SVED, S., SOLYOM, L., WAINRIB, B. and BARIK, H., *American Journal of Psychiatry* 120 (1963) 320–5.

32 COWAN, J., in *Nerve, Brain and Memory Models*, WIENER, N. and SCHADÉ, J.P. (eds.), Amsterdam: Elsevier Publishing Co., 1965.

33 YOUNG, J.Z., *A Model of the Brain*, Oxford: Clarendon Press, 1964.

34 ZEEMAN, C., at a London Brain Research Association meeting.

35 BROADBENT, D.E., *Behaviour*, London: Methuen & Co. Ltd., 1964; *Human Memory*, op. cit.

36 YATES, F.A., *The Art of Memory*, Harmondsworth, Middlesex: Penguin Books Limited, 1967.

37 HABER, R.N. and HABER, R.B., *Perceptual and Motor Skills* 19 (1964) 131–43; JAENSCH, E.R., *Eidetic Imagery and Typological Methods of Investigation*, New York: Harcourt, Brace, 1930.

38 BORGES, J.L., *Fictions*, London: Calder and Boyars Ltd., 1965.

39 LURIA, A.R., *The Mind of a Mnemonist*, London: Jonathan Cape, Ltd., 1969.

40 GRIFFITH, J.S., in *Short Term Changes in Neural Activity and Behaviour*, op. cit.

41 A rather good description of this period of scientific apprenticeship appears in RAVETZ, J.R., *Scientific Knowledge and its Social Problems*, Oxford: Clarendon Press, 1971.

10 Emotion and self-regulation

1 The term is due to W. CANNON.

2 PRIBAN, I.P. and FINCHAM, W.F., *Nature* 208 (1965) 339–43.

3 For an introductory account, see THOMPSON, R.F., *Foundations of Physiological Psychology*, New York: Harper & Row, 1967. A good account of his own research is to be found in HARRIS, G.W., *Neural Control of the Pituitary Gland*, London: Arnold, 1955, which, although now some years old, reads well. A more recent discussion will be found in WURTMAN, R.J., "Brain Monoamines and Endocrine Function", *Neurosciences Research Program Bulletin* 9 (2) (1971).

4 VALENSTEIN, E.S., "Biology of Drives", *Neurosciences Research Program Bulletin* 6 (1) (1968); OLDS, J., "Emotional Centres in the Brain", *Science Journal*, May 1967, reprinted in *The Biological Bases of Behaviour*, CHALMERS, N.R., CRAWLEY, R. and ROSE, S.P.R. (eds.), London: Harper & Row Ltd., 1971.

5 For a discussion of these experiments see *Foundations of Physiological Psychology*, op. cit.

6 Some of these complexities are described in *The Biological Bases of Behaviour, Units 9–10*, Bletchley: Open University Press, 1972.

7 TEITELBAUM, P., in *The Neurosciences: A Study Program*, QUARTON, G.C., MELNECHUK, T. and SCHMITT, F.O. (eds.), New York: Rockefeller University Press, 1967.

8 MEYER, J. and THOMAS, D.W., *Science* 156 (1967) 328–37.

9 TRYON, R.C., *National Society for the Study of Education* 39 (1940); 110–19; BOVET, D., BOVET-NITTI, F. and OLIVERIO, A., *Science* 163 (1969)

139–49; BOVET, D., BOVET-
NITTI, F. and OLIVERIO, A.,
Life Sciences 5 (1966) 415–23.

10 BARD, P., *American Journal of
Physiology* 84 (1928) 490–515;
BARD, P., in *Feelings and Emotions*,
REYNOLDS, M.L. (ed.), New
York: McGraw-Hill, 1950;
HESS, W.R., *Diencephalon:
Autonomic and Extrapyramidal
Functions*, Greene & Stratton, 1954;
AKERT, K., in *Electrical Stimulation
of the Brain*, Austin, Tex.:
University of Texas Press, 1961.
See also papers in PRIBRAM, K.H.
(ed.), *Mood States and Mind*,
Harmondsworth, Middlesex:
Penguin Books Limited, 1969.

11 PRIBRAM, K.H., in *Electrical
Stimulation of the Brain*, op. cit.;
PRIBRAM, K.H., in *Psychology:
A Study of a Science*, KOCH, S.
(ed.), New York: McGraw-Hill,
1962; for general discussion of these
problems see WEISKRANTZ, L.
(ed.), *Behavioral Change*, New
York: Harper & Row, 1968.

12 A description of this episode
occurs in STEVENS, L.A., *Explorers
of the Brain*, New York: Alfred A.
Knopf, Inc., 1971.

13 MICHAEL, R., *British Medical
Bulletin* 21 (1) (1965) 87–90.

14 This phenomenon is well
known, if not very fully referenced
in the scientific literature (as
opposed, perhaps, to the medical).
See for example, MICHAEL, R., in
BBC series on "Drugs and the
Mind" (1970); ROSE, S.P.R., in
Manipulation of Man, Gottlieb
Duttweiler Foundation Symposium
(1970).

15 OLDS, J., in *The Biological
Bases of Behaviour*, op. cit.;
OLDS, J., *Science* 127 (1958) 315–23;
OLDS, J., *Physiological Review* 42
(1962) 554–604.

16 HEATH, R.G. and
MICKLE, W.A.; and
SEM-JACOBSEN, C.W. and
TORKILDSEN, A., in *Electrical
Studies on the Unanaesthetized
Brain*, RAMEY, E.R. and
O'DOHERTY, D.S. (eds.), London:
Hoeber, 1960, quoted in
*Foundations of Physiological
Psychology*, op. cit.

17 I have, I must emphasize, no
written reference for this statement,

which is no more than an
impression. So far as I am aware,
discussion of these possibilities is
limited to a rather sensible comment
in COHEN, S., *Drugs of
Hallucination*, London: Paladin,
1970, and the speculation, more or
less alarmist, of science journalists,
e.g. RATTRAY-TAYLOR, G.,
The Biological Time Bomb, London:
Thames & Hudson, 1968.

11 Attending and sleeping: the experience of time

1 For an introductory account,
THOMPSON, R.F., *Foundations of
Physiological Psychology*, New York:
Harper & Row, 1967. See also
FRENCH, J.D., "The Reticular
Formation", *Scientific American*,
May 1957; LIVINGSTON, R.B.,
in *The Neurosciences: A Study
Program*, QUARTON, G.C.,
MELNECHUCK, T. and SCHMITT
(eds.), New York: Rockefeller
University Press, 1967;
SCHEIBEL, M.E. and
SCHEIBEL, A.B., ibid.;
ZANCHETTI, A., ibid.;
ADEY, W.R., ibid.

2 MAGOUN, H.W., in *Brain
Mechanisms and Consciousness*,
DELAFRESNAYE, J.F. (ed.),
London: Thomas, 1954;
MORUZZI, G. and MAGOUN, H.W.,
*Electroencephalography and Clinical
Neurophysiology* 1 (1949) 455–73.
For critique see *Foundations of
Physiological Psychology*, op. cit.

3 HORDERN, A., in
Psychopharmacology, JOYCE, C.R.B.
(ed.), London: Tavistock, 1968;
SMYTHIES, J.R., "The Mode of
Action of Psychotomimetic Drugs",
*Neurosciences Research Program
Bulletin* 8 (1) (1970);
SCHILDKRAUT, J.J. and KETY, S.S.,
Science 156 (1967) 21–30.

4 ASCHOFF, J. (ed.), *Biological
Clocks*, London: North-Holland,
1965; "Biological Clocks",
*Cold Spring Harbor Symposia on
Quantitative Biology* 25 (1960).

5 For a discussion of these models
in general see HARMON, L.D. and
LEWIS, E.R., *Physiological Reviews*
46 (1966) 519–30.

6 HARKER, J.E., *The Physiology of
Diurnal Rhythms*, Cambridge:

Cambridge University Press, 1964;
ASCHOFF, J. (ed.), *Circadian Clocks*,
North-Holland, 1965; BRADY, J.,
Nature 223 (1968) 781–4.

7 STRUMWASSER, F., in *The Neurosciences: A Study Program*, op. cit.

8 RICHARDSON, K. and
ROSE, S.P.R., *Nature New
Biology* 233 (1971) 182–3.

9 JOUVET, M., "The States of
Sleep", *Scientific American*,
February 1967, reprinted in
The Biological Bases of Behaviour,
CHALMERS, N.R., CRAWLEY, R.
and ROSE, S.P.R. (eds.), London:
Harper & Row, 1971; JOUVET, M.,
in *The Neurosciences: A Study
Program*, op. cit.; NAUTA, W.J.H.
and KUELLA, W.P., "Sleep,
Wakefulness, Dreams and
Memory", *Neurosciences Research
Program Bulletin* 4 (1) (1966);
OSWALD, I., *Nature* 223 (1969)
893–7.

10 FREUD, S., *The Interpretation of
Dreams*, London: Allen & Unwin,
1954; "Sleep, Wakefulness, Dreams
and Memory", *Neurosciences
Research Program Bulletins* op. cit.

11 There is a long, and not
necessarily very respectable, history
of attempts to answer this question.
See, e.g. DUNNE, J.W.,
An Experiment with Time, London:
Faber and Faber, 1927.

12 ORNSTEIN, R.E., *On the
Experience of Time*,
Harmondsworth, Middlesex:
Penguin Publications Limited, 1969.

12 Where brains fail: madness and mysticism

1 *Times* report (2 September 1971)
from *Psychiatric Hospitals and Units
in England and Wales*, London: Her
Majesty's Stationery. Office, 1971.

2 Department of Health and Social
Security Statistics.

3 e.g. LAING, R.D., *The Divided
Self*, Harmondsworth, Middlesex:
Penguin Books Limited, 1965;
LAING, R.D., *The Politics of
Experience and the Bird of Paradise*,
Harmondsworth, Middlesex:
Penguin Books Limited, 1967;
LAING, R.D. and ESTERSON, A.,
Sanity, Madness and the Family,

Harmondsworth, Middlesex:
Penguin Books Limited, 1970.
The total non-meeting of minds of
psychiatrists working within these
different paradigms was
demonstrated at a "debate" between
H.J. EYSENCK and D. COOPER,
organized by the British Society for
Social Responsibility in Science in
London in 1970, which rapidly
degenerated into incoherence. At
the conference on the Biochemistry
of Schizophrenia, organized by the
Schizophrenia Association in 1971,
remarks derogating psychoanalysts
of either the orthodox or the
Laing/Cooper school, by contrast
with "hard-nosed" scientists, were
greeted with great applause by the
audience.

4 BIEMOND, A., *Brain Diseases*,
Amsterdam: Elsevier, 1970.

5 SLATER, E. and COWIE, V.A.,
Genetics of Mental Disorders, London:
Oxford University Press, 1971.

6 COMFORT, A., *The Biology of
Senescence and Ageing*, London:
Routledge and Kegan Paul, Ltd.,
1964.

7 Some of these prostheses are
described in FISHLOCK, D., *Man
Modified*, London: Jonathan Cape,
Ltd., 1969.

8 CAINE, D.B., *Clinical
Pharmacology and Therapeutics* 11
(1970) 789–801.

9 The distinguished gerontologist
Alex Comfort believes otherwise.
In principle, he claims, there is no
reason why, in the near future,
methods of extending the human
life-span by 10 percent should not
become available.

10 BRADY, J.V., "Ulcers in
Executive Monkeys", *Scientific
American*, October 1958, reprinted
in *The Biological Bases of Behaviour*,
CHALMERS, N.R., CRAWLEY, R.
and ROSE, S.P.R. (eds.), London:
Harper & Row, 1971.

11 "Orthomolecular psychiatry" is
a term for which, I believe, the
chemist Linus Pauling is responsible.
The theory is that many "mental
illnesses" are related to the absence
of trace elements or vitamins in the
diet–a parallel to Pauling's
contention that massive doses of
vitamin C may help to cure colds.
The two theories have received

about the same amount of public acclaim and scientific contempt. But a recent conference (1971) of the Schizophrenia Association was heavily concerned with the topic, and its adherents included at least one psychiatrist who was prepared to go so far as to claim that 20 per-cent of the schizophrenics in the institution with which he was associated were suffering from glactosaemia – a deficiency of the minor sugar galactose. It is probably fair to say that most nutritional experts and epidemiologists would be very unhappy about attempts to show causal relationships between such deficiencies, if they indeed occur, and the illness, even though it is also far from improbable that individuals in institutions be they hospitals, prisons, the army or boarding schools, will show characteristic nutritional deficiencies.

12 On the paucity of present day biochemical knowledge in this area, see the Medical Research Council, Her Majesty's Stationery Office, 1970, *Biochemical Research in Psychiatry: Survey and Proposals*. Report by a Council Committee.

13 *Genetics of Mental Disorders*, op. cit.

14 JACKSON, D.D., "Schizophrenia", *Scientific American*, August 1962; ROMAN, P.H. and TRUE, H.M., *Schizophrenia and the Poor*, Cayuga Press, 1967.

15 HORDERN, A., in *Psychopharmacology*, JOYCE, C.R.B. (ed.), London: Tavistock, 1968; SARGENT, W., *The Unquiet Mind*, London: Heinemann, 1967.

16 COLLIER, H.O.T., "Prostaglandins and Aspirin", *Nature* 232 (1971) 17–19.

17 CURRAN, D. and PARTRIDGE, M., *Psychological Medicine*, (6th Edition), London: Livingstone, 1969.

18 JOYCE, C.R.B., at Bernal Library Conference on Chemical and Biological Warfare. Published as *Chemical and Biological Warfare*, ROSE, S.P.R. (ed.), London: Harrap, 1968.

19 RUSHTON, R., STEINBERG, H.

and TOMKIEWICZ, *Nature* 220 (1968) 885–90.

20 JOYCE, C.R.B., in *Psychopharmacology*, op. cit.

21 This classification is that used by HORDERN, in *Psychopharmacology*, op. cit., and in *Psychological Medicine*, op. cit.

22 Department of Health and Social Security Statistics.

23 Ibid.

24 SARGENT, W. and SLATER, E., *Introduction to Physical Methods of Treatment in Psychiatry*, Edinburgh: Livingstone, 1964.

25 *Psychological Medicine*, op. cit.

26 *The Times*, London: 21 August 1971.

27 JACOBSEN, E., in *Psychopharmacology*, op. cit.; COHEN, S., *Drugs of Hallucination*, London: Paladin, 1970.

28 HUXLEY, A., *The Doors of Perception* and *Heaven and Hell*, London: Chatto & Windus, 1968.

29 Leary is quoted in *Drugs of Hallucination*, op. cit. For the present-day popularity of LSD, I draw on a nonrandom sample of personal acquaintances.

30 SMYTHIES, J.R., "The Mode of Action of Psychotomimetic Drugs", *Neurosciences Research Program Bulletin* 8 (1) (1970).

31 JACOBSEN, E., in *Psychopharmacology*, op. cit.

32 *Drugs of Hallucination*, op. cit.

33 OSMOND, H. and SMYTHIES, J.R., *Journal of Mental Science* 98 (1952) 309–15; SMYTHIES, J.R., *Postgraduate Medical Journal* 39 (1963) 26–33; SMYTHIES, J.R., *Schizophrenia, Biochemistry, Metabolism and Treatment*, London: Thomas, 1963.

34 The references on this point may be culled from almost any issue of the underground Press in recent years, but are given analytical form in, for instance, NUTTALL, J., *Bomb Culture*, London: Paladin, 1968.

13 Have brains a future?

1 KUHN, T.S., *The Structure of Scientific Revolutions*, (2nd ed.),

Chicago: Chicago University Press, 1970; LAKATOS, I. and MUSGRAVE, A. (eds.), *Criticism and the Growth of Knowledge*, Cambridge: Cambridge University Press, 1970; ROSE, S. and ROSE, H., "The Myth of the Neutrality of Science", *Impact of Science on Society* 21 (1971) 137–49.

2 These points are expanded in the final chapter of ROSE, H. and ROSE, S., *Science and Society*, London: Allen Lane, Harmondsworth, Middlesex; Penguin Books Limited, 1969.

3 LEWONTIN, R. C., "The Bases of Conflict in Biological Explanation", *Journal of the History of Biology* 2 (1969) 35–47.

4 FREUD, S., *Project for a Scientific Psychology*, (1950 [1895]), Standard Edition Vol. I, pp. 281–397, London: Hogarth Press.

5 WATSON, J. B., *Psychological Review* 20 (1913) 158–67.

6 SKINNER, B. F., *Contingencies of Reinforcement*, New York: Appleton-Century Crofts, 1971; HULL, C. L., *Principles of Behavior*, New York: Appleton-Century Crofts, 1943.

7 WATSON., J. B., *Behaviourism*, London: Norton, 1924.

8 HUXLEY, A., *Brave New World*, London: Chatto & Windus, 1950.

9 This view was expressed, in a lecture on teaching methods, by Skinner at the Open University in 1970. See also SKINNER, B. F., *Beyond Freedom and Dignity*, London: Jonathan Cape Ltd., 1972.

10 LORENZ, K. Z., *King Solomon's Ring*, London: Methuen, 1952

11 ZUCKERMAN, S., *The Social Life of Monkeys and Apes*, London: Kegan Paul, 1932; LAWICK-GOODALL, J. van, *In The Shadow of Man*, London: Collins, 1971; RUSSELL, C. and RUSSELL, W. M. S., *Violence, Monkeys and Man*, London: Macmillan, 1968.

12 MORRIS, D., *The Naked Ape*, London: Jonathan Cape, Ltd., 1969; MORRIS, D., *The Human Zoo*, London: Jonathan Cape, Ltd., 1970; ARDREY, R., *The Territorial Imperative*, New York: Dell, 1971; ARDREY, R., *The Social Contract*, London: Collins, 1970.

13 CHOMSKY, N., *Language and Mind*, New York: Harcourt, Brace and World, 1968.

14 CHITTY, D., *Science* 173 (1971) 42–3.

15 SUTHERLAND, N. S., in *Explanation in the Behavioural Sciences*, BORGER, R. and CIOFFI, F. (eds.), Cambridge: Cambridge University Press, 1970; MICHIE, D., *Nature* 228 (1970) 717–22; "Artificial Intelligence", *New Society*, 26 August 1971.

16 ASIMOV, I., *I, Robot*, London: Dobson, 1967.

17 MUMFORD, L., *The Pentagon of Power*, London: Secker and Warburg, 1971.

18 ECCLES, J. C., *Facing Reality*, New York: Springer Verlag, 1970; ECCLES, J. C., *The Neurophysiological Basis of Mind*, Oxford: Clarendon Press, 1953.

19 MacKAY, D., "The Bankruptcy of Determinism", in *The Biological Bases of Behaviour*, CHALMERS, N. R., CRAWLEY, R. and ROSE, S. P. R. (eds.), London: Harper & Row, 1971.

20 BALDWIN, T., in *Forum*, O'REGAN, K. (ed.), Cavendish Laboratory, Cambridge, 1971.

21 BELOFF, J., in *Brain and Mind*, SMYTHIES, J. R. (ed.), London: Routledge and Kegan Paul, 1965.

22 MARCUSE, H., *One-Dimensional Man*, London: Routledge and Kegan Paul, Ltd., 1964.

23 McLUHAN, M. and FOORE, Q., *The Medium is the Message*, London: Allen Lane, The Penguin Press, 1967.

24 LAING, R. D., *The Politics of Experience and the Bird of Paradise*, Harmondsworth, Middlesex: Penguin Books Limited, 1967; COOPER, D., *The Death of the Family*, New York: Pantheon, 1971.

25 TEILHARD DE CHARDIN, P., *The Phenomenon of Man*, London: Collins, 1959.

26 ELLUL, JACQUES, *The Technological Society*, London: Jonathan Cape, Ltd., 1965, New York: Knopf, 1964.

27 HUXLEY, A., *Heaven and Hell and The Doors of Perception*, Collected Edition, London: Chatto & Windus, 1968.

28 KOESTLER, A., *The Ghost in the Machine*, London: Hutchinson, 1967.

29 *Red Mole*, 1 December 1971; WEBB, H. E., WETHERLEY-MEIN, G., GORDON SMITH, C. E. and McMAHON, D., *British Medical Journal* 1 (1966) 258–66.

30 For science fiction of this sort, see RATTRAY-TAYLOR, G., *The Biological Time-Bomb*, London: Thames and Hudson, 1968; some of the writings in CALDER, N. (ed.), *The World in 1984*,

Harmondsworth, Middlesex: Penguin Books Limited, 1965. See also LEACH, G., *The Biocrats*, London: Jonathan Cape, Ltd., 1970.

31 DELGADO, J. M. R., *Physical Control of the Mind*, London: Harper & Row, 1971.

32 MEDVEDEV, ZHORES and MEDVEDEV, ROY, *A Question of Madness*, London: Macmillan, 1971; New York: Knopf, 1971.

33 BAZELL, R. J., *Science* 172 (1971) 1223.

34 WULF, E., "Psychology in N. Vietnam", paper to the Conference on Medical Implications of the Indochina War; Paris, December 1971.

Name Index

Subject Index